Larisa Reisner: A Biography

Historical Materialism Book Series

The Historical Materialism Book Series is a major publishing initiative of the radical left. The capitalist crisis of the twenty-first century has been met by a resurgence of interest in critical Marxist theory. At the same time, the publishing institutions committed to Marxism have contracted markedly since the high point of the 1970s. The Historical Materialism Book Series is dedicated to addressing this situation by making available important works of Marxist theory. The aim of the series is to publish important theoretical contributions as the basis for vigorous intellectual debate and exchange on the left.

The peer-reviewed series publishes original monographs, translated texts, and reprints of classics across the bounds of academic disciplinary agendas and across the divisions of the left. The series is particularly concerned to encourage the internationalization of Marxist debate and aims to translate significant studies from beyond the English-speaking world.

For a full list of titles in the Historical Materialism Book Series available in paperback from Haymarket Books, visit: www.haymarketbooks.org/series_collections/1-historical-materialism.

Larisa Reisner: A Biography

Cathy Porter

Haymarket Books
Chicago, IL

First published in 2022 by Brill Academic Publishers, The Netherlands
© 2022 Koninklijke Brill NV, Leiden, The Netherlands

Published in paperback in 2023 by
Haymarket Books
P.O. Box 180165
Chicago, IL 60618
773-583-7884
www.haymarketbooks.org

ISBN: 978-1-64259-999-2

Distributed to the trade in the US through Consortium Book Sales and Distribution (www.cbsd.com) and internationally through Ingram Publisher Services International (www.ingramcontent.com).

This book was published with the generous support of Lannan Foundation, Wallace Action Fund, and the Marguerite Casey Foundation.

Special discounts are available for bulk purchases by organizations and institutions. Please call 773-583-7884 or email info@haymarketbooks.org for more information.

Cover art and design by David Mabb. Cover art is a detail from *Painting 14, Rhythm 69, (William Morris Block Printed Pattern Book, with Hans Richter Storyboard, developed from Richter's Rhythmus 25 and Kazimir Malevich's film script Artistic and Scientific Film – Painting and Architectural Concerns – Approaching the New Plastic Architectural System)*. Paint and wallpaper on canvas (2007).

Printed in the United States.

10 9 8 7 6 5 4 3 2 1

Library of Congress Cataloging-in-Publication data is available.

Larisa Reisner (1895–1926)

Contents

List of Figures IX
Timeline X

Introduction 1

1 Childhood and Exile 8

2 Student Life 37

3 Poets and War 55

4 In Petrograd 66

5 Red Kronstadt 80

6 Bolshevik Russia 90

7 'Unforgettable 1918' 97

8 Svyazhsk 116

9 Reds and Whites 129

10 From Moscow to the Caspian 140

11 *Rabfaks* and Commissars 161

12 Afghanistan 187

13 The New Culture 232

14 Berlin and Hamburg 249

15 Across Workers' Russia 276

16 Seifullina and Alyosha 303

17 Germany and China   317

18 'How Extraordinary to Be Alive'   333

19 Afterlife   344

   Appendix: Figures   365
   Bibliography   373
   Index   379

Figures

1. Aged six months with her parents in Lublin, 1895   365
2. With Igor and their father in Berlin, 1902   365
3. With Igor in Siberia, 1902   366
4. In Berlin, 1903   366
5. St Petersburg schoolgirl, 1910   367
6. Leonid Andreev (1871–1919)   367
7. Boris Pasternak (1890–1960)   368
8. Alexander Blok (1880–1921)   368
9. Nikolai Gumilyov (1886–1921)   369
10. Anna Akhmatova (1889–1966)   369
11. Fyodor Raskolnikov   370
12. Cavalry commander, 1919   370
13. Naval commissar, 1920. Watercolour portrait by Sergei Chekhonin, in Moscow's Tretyakov Gallery   371
14. Afghanistan, 1922   371
15. Karl Radek and his daughter Sonya   372
16. Igor Reisner in the 1930s   372

Timeline

1894	Tsar Nicholas I comes to the throne.
1895	2 May: Larisa Reisner born in Lublin, in tsarist Poland.
1896	Disastrous harvests and famines. Strikes in St Petersburg spread across Russia.
1898	Founding of the Marxist Social Democratic Workers' Party, headed by Lenin, affiliated to Socialist International. Larisa's father exiled to Siberia for his political activities. For the next five years the Reisners live in the city of Tomsk, where he lectures at the university.
1901–2	Terrorists in the new Socialist Revolutionary Party assassinate government officials. Workers strike, peasants loot and expropriate estates, students riot and occupy for reforms. Reisner supports their cause.
1903–7	The Reisners live in exile in Berlin.
1904	The Tsar's war with Japan triggers more strikes, riots and student demonstrations across Russia. Reisner joins the Bolsheviks, and successfully defends German socialists arrested for 'crimes against the Tsar'.
1905	9 January: 'Bloody Sunday' sets off Russia's first revolution.
1907	The revolution is defeated. Terrorists carry out over 2,000 attempted assassinations. The Tsar capitulates with an amnesty for political exiles. The Reisners return to Russia.
1908	The reaction is triumphant. Reisner is falsely accused of being a government spy.
1911	The Tsar's peasant 'holy man' Rasputin encourages him to embark on two disastrous wars in the Balkans. Unrest in the factories and universities gains new momentum, with more assassinations and peasant riots.
1912	Larisa leaves school with a gold medal and enters the university, writes poetry, and throws herself into St Petersburg's bohemian nightlife.
1913	Publishes her play 'Atlantis'.
1914	2 August: Russia declares war on Germany. St Petersburg renamed Petrograd.
1915	The tsarist army collapses, living costs soar, wages slump, and there is open talk of revolution. Larisa and her father publish their satirical anti-war literary magazine *Rudin*. That winter she embarks on a love affair with the poet Nikolai Gumilyov.
1916	*Rudin* closed by the censors. She writes for Maxim Gorky's socialist anti-war magazine *Chronicle*.

TIMELINE   XI

1917   March revolution topples the Tsar. She writes for Gorky's new socialist
        daily newspaper *New Life*, which publishes some of Russia's greatest
        writers, and joins the education programme of the Petrograd Soviet of
        Workers' and Soldiers' Deputies, teaching literacy and literature in the
        factories. Her teaching takes her to the Kronstadt naval base, where
        she starts an affair with the Bolshevik sailor Fyodor Raskolnikov, Chair
        of the Kronstadt Soviet.
        25 October: Bolsheviks take power at the 2nd All-Russian Congress of
        Soviets, and declare Russia's withdrawal from the war. She works for
        the new Commissariat of Education, preparing cheap editions of the
        Russian classics for mass publication, and cataloguing the tsars' art
        treasures in the Hermitage Gallery.

1918   April: moves to Moscow with her family when the capital is evacuated
        from Petrograd, in anticipation of the German invasion.
        Summer: Joins the Bolshevik Party and marries Raskolnikov, now
        Commander of the new Volga Naval Flotilla. Leaves with him for the
        Volga front to defend the Revolution, writing her 'Letters from the
        Front' for *Izvestiya*, the official paper of the Soviet.
        December: Elected first woman Political Commissar of Naval General
        Staff.

1919   Fights in the battles for the Volga city of Tsaritsyn. When it falls to the
        Whites, she leaves with the Flotilla for the port of Astrakhan, capital of
        Kazakhstan, to secure Bolsheviks' access to the Caspian Sea, patrolled
        by British ships.

1920   May: Joins campaign to drive British forces from the Persian port of
        Badar-e Anzali, Britain's main base on the Caspian.
        June: Returns to Petrograd. Speaks at writers' meetings, writes articles,
        teaches at Kronstadt and at the new workers' colleges, the *rabfaks*.

1921   April: Raskolnikov appointed Russia's first Ambassador to Afghani-
        stan. She works for Soviet diplomatic mission in Kabul, persuading
        women in the Emir's harem to support the Bolsheviks, writing articles
        for the Soviet press and reporting back to the Communist Interna-
        tional in Moscow, the Comintern.

1923   June: Returns to Moscow without Raskolnikov and divorces him.
        September–January: Works illegally in Berlin and Hamburg as a
        Comintern agent, writing articles and essays about the defeated Ham-
        burg uprising. Embarks on an affair with the Comintern Secretary,
        Karl Radek.

1924   January and May: Publication of her books *Hamburg at the Barricades*,
        Berlin, October 1923, and *The Front*.

	May–October: Travels to the Urals and Eastern Ukraine, reporting for *Izvestiya* on workers' lives in the mines and factories. Adopts fourteen-year-old Alyosha Makarov.
	December: Publication of her book about her travels, *Coal Iron and Living People*.
1925	May: Returns to Germany for medical treatment, then travels around mines and factories of the Ruhr Valley, writing the articles for *Izvestiya* that became her book *In Hindenburg's Country*.
	August: Publication of her book *Afghanistan*. Works on her essays on Russia's Decembrist uprising.
1926	early January: Publication of her first Decembrist essay and *In Hindenburg's Country*.
	9 February: She dies of typhoid fever in the Kremlin Hospital.

Introduction

To those who knew and loved her, Larisa Reisner embodied all the beauty and heroism of the 'new woman' of the Russian Revolution. She died in 1926, at the age of thirty, and she was mourned in hundreds of obituaries. Lev Trotsky called her the 'Revolutionary Pallas': 'She flashed across the sky like a blazing meteor, dazzling all in her path. With her appearance of an Olympian goddess, she combined a subtle and ironic mind with the courage of a warrior'. Poets remembered her poetic soul and her endless wanderings. Years later, the poet Boris Pasternak told a friend, 'I named the heroine of my novel *Doctor Zhivago* Lara in memory of Larisa Mikhailovna Reisner'.

Five thousand mourners followed her coffin through Moscow to her state funeral at the Vagankovo Cemetery, cemetery of writers, where Pasternak read his poem 'Memories of Reisner' at her grave:

> Larisa, how I regret I am not death,
> And am nothing beside it.
> I might have learnt how life's story
> Could hold together these scraps of days without their glue.
>
> Oh, I had the measure of my material!
> The winters slumped in heaps, the volleying rains,
> Blizzards wrapping the cities tightly in blankets,
> Like infants at the breast.
>
> People hurried through the cold streets,
> Trucks dragged round the bends.
> The years were up to their necks in water,
> Flooding the old fords with new streams.
>
> Life simmered fiercely in its still.
> New nests were built, new building sites,
> Ringed with streetlamps,
> Words, starlight, reason.
>
> Just look round – which of us wasn't made
> From a fog of snowflakes and half-truths,
> Raised on the beauty of ruins?
> Only you were above all praise.

> You alone, molded gloriously in battle,
> Burst through life with the arrows of your charm.
> You showed us what enchantment was –
> You hit it right on target.
>
> You blazed up like a tempest of the Graces,
> Lingering briefly in their flame.
> Mediocrity instantly fell from favour,
> Everything imperfect met with your rage.
>
> Walk in the depths of legend, heroine,
> Your path will not tire your feet.
> Soar into the heights, far above my thoughts,
> They are at home in your great shade.[1]

Pasternak beautifully captures her life, at the edge of the old and new worlds. Like Pasternak, she was born into Russia's cultured intellectual élite, and she had dreamed of being a poet before the Revolution. But unlike Pasternak, in October 1917 she immediately worked with the Bolshevik government, first at the Commissariat of Education, then at the Commissariat of Naval Affairs, as a Commissar of the General Staff in Trotsky's new Red Navy.

In the spring of 1918 she left for the front, to defend the Revolution against the invading armies of the West and their White Guard allies. For the next two years, she sailed on the River Volga on the great warships of the new Volga Naval Flotilla, as cavalry commander, reconnaissance officer and war correspondent, fighting with the sailors on the front line of the battles for Kazan, Svyazhsk and Tsaritsyn, driving British occupation forces from Astrakhan and Azerbaijan, and from their main naval base on the Caspian Sea in Persia.

Against unimaginable odds, the Revolution survived. The Whites were defeated and the invaders were thrown out of Russia, and she returned from the Persian front after the fighting ended.

Her next assignment after the Civil War was in Afghanistan, the key to Soviet Russia's complicated relations with British imperial power in Asia. Between 1921 and 1923, she was a member of the first Soviet diplomatic mission in Kabul, using the espionage skills she had learnt at the front to gather information about British activities, and gain access to the Emir's harem, encour-

---

[1] Boris Pasternak, 'Pamyati Reisner' (Memories of Reisner), published three weeks after her death in the paper *Evening Moscow*. Republished in vol. 1 of Pasternak's *Collected Works*, Moscow 1965.

aging his wife and mother and their entourages to trust the Bolsheviks' friendly intentions in Kabul.

In the autumn of 1923, the Soviet government sent its best intelligence officers to Germany, where mass strikes seemed to be taking the country close to revolution. She lived there illegally, with false papers, sharing the underground lives of workers in Berlin and Hamburg, reporting from the ruins of Hamburg's crushed communist-led uprising, as the party rallied its forces to fight the growing threat of Hitler's fascists.

A year later, she spent five months travelling around the industrial heartlands of the Soviet Union, in the Urals and Eastern Ukraine, living with workers' families as she had in Germany, joining them on their shifts in the mines and factories, reporting on their heroic achievements and sacrifices and suffering, dragging Russia out of poverty to build the foundations of the new Soviet economy.

She returned to Germany as a journalist in 1925, travelling across the country reporting on workers' lives under the new President, Field Marshal von Hindenburg, former Chief of the German Imperial High Command, witnessing the government's drastic shift to the right and its drive to rearm for a new war, and the Nazis' first armed SS units on the streets.

All this was material for countless articles and essays, and six powerful beautiful books, to be published for the first time together in translation with this biography – *The Front*, *Afghanistan*, *Berlin, October 1923*, *Hamburg at the Barricades*, *Coal Iron and Living People*, and *In Hindenburg's Country*.

Brought out in huge print-runs, they were read by a new mass audience of workers, intellectuals and the newly literate – filled with sharp observations and big ideas, tender, funny, satirical, deeply political, each with a vast cast of characters, all of them unforgettable. Of her last book, *In Hindenburg's Country*, the poet Vera Inber wrote: 'People, places and ideas are described by a writer who has achieved new brilliance. The characteristic beauty and refinement of her prose is transformed by a mature pen, unafraid to write well today, knowing it will be even better tomorrow'. The young journalist Lev Sosnovsky wrote: 'There was simply no better writer amongst us. Had each of our underground organisations that had undergone their great revolutionary experiences possessed her sharp eye and sense of colour, we could have achieved a hundred times more. If added to our Bolshevik temperament were her education and her European experience – which didn't pass without trace – we could have produced miracles'.

She also had her vocal critics in Russia. Hardline defenders of proletarian purity attacked her writing as 'feminine' and self-indulgent, and claimed her class excluded her from reporting on the Revolution from the proper political perspective. Writers hostile to the Revolution called her a Party hack. She was inspired throughout her life by the great poet Anna Akhmatova, but her feelings for her were never reciprocated. 'Poor thing, people will speak badly of her abroad for having been so quick to support Soviet power', Akhmatova said after she died. And she was right, writers in the West have not been kind to her.

British historian Robert Service fantasises luridly in his biography of Trotsky about her sex life with the Party leaders – 'flitting from lover to lover in the manner of Alexandra Kollontai's worker bees'. Oxford professor Catriona Kelly dismisses her enigmatically in her book on Russian women writers as 'a not terribly successful practitioner of "committed Symbolism"', and clearly hasn't read her. In a long venomous piece by US 'independent scholar' Alla Zeide, she is a cold war cartoon Bolshevik, ruthless, greedy for power and barely human, with 'a superficial, abstract interest in politics', who 'signed up to the October *coup*' to 'fill the emptiness', did a bit of writing – 'a variant of Soviet poster propaganda art, glorifying the revolution and compliant with the regime' – and was 'finished' by the age of twenty-two.

And she was anti-Semitic of course. The Jewish Pasternak had clearly not seen this in all the years of their friendship. His poem to her should be read not as a love poem, but for his 'complete failure to understand her', and its 'sinister overtones'.[2]

Larisa would have had great fun with all this. She was a brilliant satirist and exposer of lies and lazy writing, and she was remembered truthfully and intelligently after her death by some of Russia's greatest poets, novelists and journalists.

She began writing as a schoolgirl and a student before the Revolution, pouring out a mass of poetry on grand historical political themes, much of it published and quoted in the first chapters of this biography. 'Her poems were totally worthless, thank goodness she had the sense to stop', Akhmatova said of her early teenage efforts.

It was in the Revolution that she found her voice as a writer, and she put all her poetry into her journalism for the new Bolshevik press. She wrote of the drama and beauty of the Revolution, and she told the stories of its heroes and heroines. She wrote of workers' epic struggles to make a new Russia free of capitalism that would inspire the world, their miracles of courage and endurance, their hopes and dreams, their conflicts and inner struggles. She believed journ-

---

2   Service, *Trotsky. A Biography*, 2009, pp. 341–2; Kelly, *A History of Women's Writing, 1890–1992*, 1994, p. 234; Zeide, 'Larisa Reisner. Myth as Justification for Life,' *Russian Review*, January 1992, pp. 172–87.

alists should report on their lives in the Revolution without moralising political commentary or 'varnish and adornment', and that 'workers' labours and sacrifices give them the right to make the widest criticisms. And the sharper these are, the closer to production and its needs, the more clearly we will see the face of the new post-revolutionary Russia'.

She was writing this in 1924, in her book *Coal Iron and Living People*, at the start of the Stalin personality cult, before the purges and show trials and the stifling of political and literary dissent, when writers were arrested for failing to serve the ideological goals of the state. She was surely too critical a writer not to have shared the same fate, and her close friendship with Trotsky made this inevitable. 'Larisa died just in time', the poet Osip Mandelstam said.

In 1928, two years after her death, her two-volume *Collected Works* were published, with a preface by her lover Karl Radek – interestingly, as Radek had been expelled from the Party by then with Trotsky. Trotsky's name was missing from her works, as were those of dozens of her comrades who later perished in the purges. Her writings were then unpublished for thirty years, and she became a 'non-person' by association.

She began to be rediscovered in the de-Stalinisation of Soviet life and culture after his death, with the publication in 1958 and 1965 of two carefully edited and annotated editions of her *Selected Works*, with warmly sympathetic introductions, and all references to Trotsky and other purged revolutionary leaders removed. There are less obvious gaps in *Larisa Reisner Remembered by her Contemporaries*, published in 1969, a wonderfully vivid collection of essays, poems and stories by those who had known her at different times in her life, in Russia, Germany and Afghanistan – her student friends, her comrades at the front and fellow writers. Another rich source of information about her is Eleonora Solovei's brief *Larisa Reisner. A Sketch of her Life and Work*, published in 1985, a discreet but touching and affectionate account of her family life and friends, her writings and her travels.

She lived for long periods in Germany, and her books and articles were published in German. But she never visited England, and readers here first discovered her works with Richard Chappell's 1977 translations of her German writings, published with our collected translations of her six books. In her lifetime, communists in England knew of her from her friend the late Andrew Rothstein, who generously shared with me his memories of her in Russia for the first 1988 edition of this biography. He remembered her with huge respect and affection, but was never over-worshipful, and he made her warm, funny, sometimes maddening, and endlessly fascinating. I learnt so much from him about her politics, her language, and her extraordinary personality, and couldn't have written the book without his help and encouragement.

Three years after it was published, the Soviet Union collapsed, and it was a new capitalist Russia when I started work on this second edition almost thirty years later. A wealth of new material about her life has now been released from the Russian archives, and her works are appearing online and are being seriously discussed. She is also mocked, slandered and pornographised. She has always been a favourite target for the Revolution's enemies, with their hatred of the women who fought for it, and there are plenty of unsourced stories on the internet about her wickedness and depravity – parading before the starving Russian people in the furs and jewels of the murdered royal family, playing sex games with her White Guard victims before she had them tortured to death.

Galina Przhiborovskaya's finely balanced and extensively researched first full-length Russian biography, published in 2008, does not share her revolutionary politics, but is wonderfully attuned to her poetic spirit, particularly before the Revolution. Most valuable are Przhiborovskaya's interviews in the 1960s and 70s with several of Larisa's surviving friends and family members, and this second edition of mine owes a huge debt to her.

My main sources though for her life were her own writings, her letters and conversations, and the memories of those who had been close to her. I was guided throughout by Radek's obituary of her, later the Preface to her 1928 *Collected Works*, his long love letter to her memory:

> She was a legendary Amazon, with her nimble self-confident figure, and her halo of chestnut hair, seen in armoured cars, on our Red warships, among the rank and file soldiers ... She hated everyday philistinism, she wasn't interested in accumulating things or settling down, she didn't want to sink into dull routine. As an artist and fighter for the Revolution, she could always find in life's prose the lofty, the gripping, the substantive, the great. At the same time she knew the bourgeois element was a swamp that could devour the strongest, and she could see the path of struggle that must be taken against the dangers threatening the workers' republic, the dams the Communist Party must build to defend itself.[3]

A century later, the Russia she had dreamed of and fought for is gone, but the capitalist propaganda machine is still frenziedly putting out its lies about the

---

3 Radek's Preface was originally published in 1927 in the literary journal *Novy Mir* (New World), and in 'Deyateli SSSR i Oktyabrskoi revolyutsii' (Activists of the USSR and the October Revolution), in the *Encyclopaedia of the Granat Russian Bibliographical Institute*, 7th edn., Moscow, 1927–9. The Preface is quoted extensively in the book, and is not footnoted from now on. (The *Encyclopaedia* also includes a biography of Radek).

Revolution and those who fought for it so they don't give us ideas. Millions across the world are crying out against the misery of austerity, the racism and police brutality, the mass surveillance and endless media lies, the criminal lunatics and state terrorists destroying our planet, killing millions of the earth's poorest people in their illegal imperialist wars, jailing and torturing journalists who expose the truth of their crimes. She tells us how people made the first revolution in the world to overthrow capitalism, and how the Revolution made them. She shows us the deadly forces they were up against, and she shows us their mighty struggles and victories – 'when everything that was alive was fighting for the Revolution, bound by voluntary ties of discipline in a struggle that had seemed so hopeless at the outset'. I wrote this new edition of her biography to inspire new struggles with her message of hope, solidarity and resistance.

Thanks to Sebastian Budgen at Historical Materialism for his enthusiasm for the first edition, and inviting me to write about her again all these years later, to the Amiel-Melburn Trust, for generously making the work possible, to Bart Nijsten and the production team at Brill, for their scrupulous attention to detail with the manuscript, and to Danny Hayward at HM, whose encouragement and patient careful constructive editing helped in so many ways to make it better.

Cathy Porter
2019

CHAPTER 1

Childhood and Exile

Russia entered the late nineteenth century poor and illiterate, populated mainly by peasants recently emancipated from serfdom, ruled by an outdated autocracy and the Orthodox Church, from which the tsars derived their divine authority to rule. A succession of laws and religious edicts under a succession of tsars banned dissent, reduced women to the status of chattels, and sanctified the exclusion and persecution of Russia's religious and ethnic minorities. Russia's fifteen million Muslims, living mainly in Central Asia and the Caucasus, the Urals and Siberia, were periodically rounded up into the army, or shipped off on boats to Persia or Turkey. Jews were driven into the 'residential provinces' of the Pale of Settlement, established in the eighteenth century by Catherine the Great in Russia's western areas and Poland, which already covered over a million square kilometres of the Russian Empire, from the Baltic to the Black Sea. Special police permission was needed to settle in towns and cities outside the Pale, forcing thousands to live there illegally, and a punishing quota system restricted their access to education and the professions. Jews were sent to the most dangerous fronts in the tsars' wars, then were attacked for their cowardice and treachery, and the Church resurrected the 'blood libel' cases of the Middle Ages, which accused them of killing Christian children to use their blood for their religious rituals – later a staple of Nazi propaganda.

Critics of the regime were arrested and jailed by the state's vast draconian police and censorship apparatus, directly controlled by the tsars and the Church, and women were associated by the Church with every conceivable vice and sin. The patriarchal virtues of female fear and submission were to be enforced with the rod, which must hang over the marriage bed. Peasant women were seen as barely human, with no voice in family or village affairs, and even many noblewomen lived lives of constant childbearing, drunken husbands and domestic abuse. Divorce was virtually unheard of, and was beyond the means of all but the wealthiest, involving gross intrusion by the religious authorities into people's personal lives, with women forced to confess their sins before members of the Holy Synod.

Under Tsar Alexander II's emancipation of the serfs in 1861, Russia's twenty-three million peasants, eighty percent of the population, eighty percent of them illiterate, paid a high price for their freedom. The land was re-divided to give two-thirds to the royal family, the wealthiest landowners and the Church, leaving them with the rest, the miniscule unproductive plots known as the 'paupers' allotments', for which they paid the landowners crippling taxes.

Under the next Tsar, Aexander III, entire villages were wiped out in the catastrophic famine that hit the Volga region and Russia's southern Black Earth provinces between the autumn of 1891 and the summer of 1892, leaving over two million peasants dead. Food aid poured into Russia to the starving villages from Europe and America, but government food supplies were sabotaged by wealthy landowners, mired in embezzlement and corruption, and famine relief work was organised mainly by volunteers, led by the writer Lev Tolstoy.

Two years later, Alexander's son Tsar Nicholas II came to the throne, a convinced autocrat and rabid anti-Semite like his father. His first laws forbade peasants to leave the land, and further restricted Jews' right to live in the cities, and he personally sponsored the Black Hundreds gangs – prototypes for Hitler's Brownshirts – to conduct pogroms in areas of the Pale, killing Jews and burning homes, shops and synagogues in orgies of public violence, often led by bishops and priests, shouting 'Kill the Jews!'

Thousands of peasants were forced by poverty, debts and famine to defy the Tsar's new laws and leave the villages for the cities, where they worked in atrocious conditions in domestic service, or in the new factories. The 1890s saw a spectacular growth in industry in Russia, and the birth of its small new merchant capitalist class. But over three-quarters of the new factories, mines and railways were owned by British, French, Belgian and German companies, attracted by Russia's vast natural resources and cheap peasant labour. Yet despite all the foreign technology and improved communications, peasants continued to live in poverty, and workers still lacked the most basic political rights, including the right to vote. Those years saw an explosion of industrial unrest across Russia, angry and unfocused, but potentially revolutionary. Women were slower than men to leave the villages to work in the cities. Exhausted by endless toil and pregnancies, sexually abused by their employers, their energy drained by the double burden of paid work and caring for their children, they were also slower than men to protest. But once their anger was roused, they did so with extraordinary courage and violence, and some of the largest strikes in Russia's history were in the capital's tobacco-pressing factories, and in the textile towns around Moscow, where women made up almost half the workforce. In St Petersburg's 'cigarette girls' strike in 1895, thirteen hundred workers at the Laferme tobacco factory stormed through the building protesting against the new sackings and pay cuts, smashing machines, attacking scabs and managers. For the revolutionary Alexandra Kollontai, who had been struggling to find her place in the political underground, these women were her inspiration to work with men to give practical support to the strike movement.

Students were rioting for reforms and occupying the universities, and it seemed to many in Russia that the autocracy's days were numbered. And in underground discussion groups, socialists were discovering a new philosophy and strategy of revolution in the works of Karl Marx.

In the *Communist Manifesto,* Marx wrote of the historical limits of capitalism, and of the inevitable breakdown of the capitalist order, and he identified class struggle as the engine of history. Revolutions would begin as bourgeois ones in their immediate goals, he wrote, but the ruling class would soon reveal its contradictions, allowing the new revolutionary class, the industrial proletariat, 'to rise up against its exploitation, and put an end to hired labour. Then will begin the kingdom of socialism, the kingdom of peace, the kingdom of the toilers'.

Capitalism had been barely developed in Russia when the first translation of *Capital* was published in 1872. Socialism had been defined then by the Populists, who saw the peasants as the agents of revolutionary change. Marx had seen Russia's proletariat of three million, three percent of the population, as still too small to fulfil its historic role, and like the Populists, he imagined a peasant-led revolution in Russia which skipped the capitalist stage – 'sending the signal for proletarian revolutions in the countries of the West'.

But the industrial turmoil of the 1890s seemed to be proving him wrong. And it was then that factory workers began to look to the new underground Marxist groups in the cities to support them in their struggles.

In 1895, convinced by Marx's compelling class analysis of history and economics, revolutionaries in St Petersburg united around Vladimir Lenin in the League of Struggle for the Emancipation of the Working Class, the first political organisation in Russia to recruit mass support from factory workers, and offer tactical support to the strike movement. Organisers risked arrest to meet workers and plan strike action, and the summer of 1896 saw a new wave of economic strikes for better pay and conditions, which increasingly turned into political strikes against the autocracy itself, spreading across the country to the Baltic provinces and the Kingdom of Poland.

The greater part of Poland, through repeated partitions by Imperial Russia and Habsburg Austria, was under tsarist rule, and was one of the most prosperous parts of the Empire, known by the Russian officials drafted in to run it as 'Vistulaland'. Polish culture and language and other 'local dialects', specifically Yiddish (the language spoken by over ninety percent of Russia's Jews), were more ruthlessly suppressed in the Russian than in the Austrian sector. Russian was the official language, taught in all schools and universities. Banks and businesses were russified, and Poland's old landowners, driven off the land by debts and famine, were replaced by autocratic Russian administrators, for whom they worked in menial government jobs. A mass of new Polish political groups sprang up in the 1890s, all with their roots in the struggle for national independence. Striking factory workers poured onto the streets in riots against Poland's Russian administrators, were arrested by Russian troops, and sentenced to long jail terms in St Petersburg's brutal Schlusselberg Fortress.

Close to the border with Ukraine, in an unspoilt area of forests and rolling hills, lay Western Galicia, the poorest and least industrially developed part of Poland's Russian sector. Rosa Luxemburg, founder in 1893 of Poland's Marxist Social Democratic Party, grew up in the town of Zamość, in Lublin province, in the Jewish Pale of Settlement. Lublin itself, fifty miles north, was also in the Pale, at the centre of two major trade routes connecting Ukraine to the Baltic, and Lithuania to Kraków, the Czech lands and Austria, a vibrant multi-ethnic town of Poles, Russians, Ukrainians, Belorussians and Jews, who made up over half the population. Jews enjoyed more cultural and religious tolerance in Lublin than elsewhere in the Pale. Birthplace in the eighteenth century of the Hasidic movement, the town was now an international centre of Jewish scholarship, known as the 'Jewish Oxford'. Mingling with its fourteen Russian Orthodox and Catholic churches and cathedrals were two synagogues, and dozens of cheders and yeshivas, and Jews flocked there from all over the world to pray and study with its rabbis.

The noblest and most cultured of Lublin's Russian families were the Pakhomovs, Alexander Pakhomov and his wife, Anna Khrapovitskaya. Both were descended from generations of aristocrats and intellectuals close to the court. She was the great-granddaughter of the poet Alexander Khrapovitsky, diarist and editor of Catherine the Great, whose library she had inherited. Both families had lost most of their lands in the Emancipation, and they raised their three daughters to be cultured and accomplished, with the qualifications to support themselves if necessary in the new Russia.

The end of serfdom had been the signal for women too to fight for their liberation. Women from the poorer landowning families bankrupted by the Emancipation were forced to find work as teachers, governesses and secretaries in the cities, where groups of aristocratic feminists were energetically petitioning the Tsar for their access to education and the professions. Russia's first girls' secondary schools opened in the 1870s, but women, like Jews, were still excluded from higher education, and the better-off left Russia to study at universities abroad, returning as doctors, teachers and lawyers. Many returned as socialists, and joined the new Populist groups in the cities, which put complete sexual equality at the top of their programme. Women became leading organisers, travelling with men 'to the people', working in the villages as doctors and teachers, preaching peasant revolution. They were arrested with the men, and were sentenced to long terms in Siberia, and revolutionaries still at liberty formed the new underground People's Will Party, committed to killing Tsar Alexander II. Two of the five main organisers of the Tsar's assassination in 1881 were women. One was pregnant, and was sentenced to hard labour for life. The other was driven with the men through the streets of St Petersburg to the gallows.

The new girls' schools were widely seen as hotbeds of 'dangerous ideas', and like most girls of the aristocracy, the Pakhomov sisters were educated at home by governesses, and all passed the boys' school examinations at the age of seventeen. The town was full of governesses, and they were cheap. Many were also members of socialist groups who taught in the factories, and were in contact with the strike movement and the revolutionary underground, and they educated their private pupils about social justice and women's liberation.

The youngest of the sisters, Ekaterina Alexandrovna, was seventeen and had passed her exams when she began defying her parents to go to socialist meetings in town. And it was at a student meeting at Lublin University that she fell in love with the speaker, the young law lecturer Mikhail Andreevich Reisner, recently arrived from St Petersburg.[1]

Reisner was from an equally cultured and impoverished aristocratic family of Baltic German barons and landowners, descended on his father's side from the sixteenth-century authority on Roman Law Nicolas von Reusner, an associate of the philosopher Erasmus of Rotterdam.

He had grown up on the family estate near the Lithuanian capital, Vilna (now Vilnius). The city was mainly Polish, with a small number of Lithuanians and Germans, like the Reisners, and almost half the population were Jews. In the seventeenth century, Vilna had been known as the 'Jerusalem of Lithuania', with its three synagogues, over a hundred prayer schools, and flourishing Hebrew and Yiddish press. A century later, the greater part of Lithuania came under Russian rule, and Vilna became a provincial capital of tsarist Poland, like Lublin, and was added with Lublin to the Pale. Jews, Catholics and Lutherans like the Reisners were forced to convert to the Orthodox Church, Russian was imposed as the official language, and the Reisners and other German landowning families were stripped of their lands.

Banned by Tsar Nicholas from settling in the villages, Jews poured into the city looking for work and a better life, and they were attacked on the streets, in the press and in church services, accused of stealing gentiles' jobs and homes.

---

1 Details of Ekaterina Alexandrovna's life from the Russian online *Encyclopaedia of St Petersburg Writers of the 20th Century*, 2005.

Thousands emigrated to America, the 'Golden Land', or became Zionists and 'swam to Palestine'. Others stayed to set up self-defence groups, and joined the revolutionary underground. In 1897, the Union of Lithuanian, Polish and Russian Jewish workers, the Bund, held its illegal founding conference in Vilna. A year later, three of the nine delegates at the founding conference of Russia's new Marxist Social Democratic Workers' Party were Bundists.

Russia's revolutionary movement had deep roots in the Pale. The socialism of the Pale was both visionary and highly organised, and internationalism was part of its being, rejecting national differences, fighting for a world without borders or nations. Rosa Luxemburg and many of the Bolsheviks' future leaders, Lev Trotsky, Radek, Grigory Zinoviev and others, were Jews from these border regions of the Russian Empire, with their large Jewish populations and rich mixtures of languages, cultures and religions, ruled for a thousand years by the Moguls, the Cossacks and the Varangians, the Grand Duchy of Lithuania, Habsburg Austria, the Kingdom of Poland and the Tsarist Empire, later in the Soviet Union or one of its satellites, now in independent Poland, Belarus and Ukraine.

Reisner's family had suffered under a succession of brutal Russian military dictators, who murdered Lutheran priests and burned their churches and villages. He discovered socialism as a boy, through reading Tolstoy's writings on the Church's persecution of minority religions, and his call for non-violent resistance to tsarist brutality. His hero was his grandfather, a Lutheran pastor, who had put Tolstoy's ideas into practice by leading his parishioners in a peaceful mass protest to defend their church, and he had dreamed of being a pastor too.

After boarding-school in St Petersburg, he studied law at the Universities of Warsaw and Kiev, then returned to enrol for a doctorate at St Petersburg University, on the constitutional relationship between the state and the Orthodox Church. In the capital he went to socialist meetings and joined an illegal Marxist study group, and inspired by Marx's vision of a classless society based on social justice, he became a Marxist and atheist. His doctoral thesis, now titled 'Monarchical Authority as a Substitute for the Divine', turned into a fierce indictment of the autocracy's criminal alliance with the Church in suppressing non-Orthodox faiths, and he was already of interest to the police when he arrived in Lublin in 1893, to lecture at the University and work on his thesis.[2]

When he and Ekaterina Alexandrovna married the following year, it was without the blessing of either of their families. Her parents worried that he was more interested in politics than in his career, and that they were both far too

---

2 Details of Reisner's life from *Vestnik kommunisticheskoi akademii* (Chronicle of the Communist Academy), 1928, and from the 1927–1929 *Granat Encyclopaedia*.

young – she was only nineteen, he was just five years older, on the basic Ministry of Education lecturer's salary of a thousand roubles a year. His two elder sisters in Vilna, both widows, struggling to support themselves and their children as schoolteachers, had also hoped he would marry someone with money, and apart from his younger sister there, and Ekaterina Alexandrovna's eldest sister in Lublin, they seem to have had little contact with their families from then on. There was certainly no family money coming in, and when their daughter Larisa was born, a year after they married, he struggled to support them on his salary. 'I married very young to a penniless girl, and our material situation was very hard', he wrote later.

Larisa's new Russian biographer, Galina Przhiborovskaya, stirs an intriguing brew of myths around her birthday, 2 May 1895, involving the ancient pagan rituals of Mayday, and her star-sign, Taurus – creative, stubborn, industrious, etcetera.[3] In a studio portrait of her as a six-month-old baby with her parents in Lublin, she is proudly centre stage, glaring at the camera in her starched white baby dress and fantastic lacy bonnet, propped up by their linked arms, her mother laughing, eager and indomitable, her father with his gentle slightly awkward smile.

Vadim Andreev, the son of the Reisners' friend the writer Leonid Andreev, who later lived with the family for two years as a child, remembered Mikhail Andreevich as 'a large peaceful man, with a surprisingly sweet voice', 'one of those rare people who from childhood have followed a life of travel and study'.[4] He was remembered by his students at the University as a popular supporter of student causes, and an inspiring and exacting teacher, intolerant of carelessness and laziness, who to the end of his life would brace himself for work every morning with exercises and cold baths.

His Soviet biographer in the 1920s wrote of his 'broad historical socialist view', and 'the tireless pulsing of his thoughts'. He was also a published poet, 'impetuous, and prone to be lost in waves of contemplation'. His early poetry had been inspired by Tolstoy and the social critics of the 1860s, Nikolai Chernyshevsky, Vissarion Belinsky and Alexander Herzen, who believed writers must shine a light on the evils of tsarism. The strike movement of the 1890s produced a completely new kind of political literature, with pamphlets and leaflets by Lenin and others flooding into the factories from the revolutionary underground. Far from the political struggle, Reisner's published poems then were written in the style of the new Symbolist poets, Konstantin Balmont, Valery Bryusov and Andrei Bely, who expressed the changes in the air with their mys-

---

3   Galina Przhiborovskaya, *Larisa Reisner*, Moscow, 2008, pp. 71–77.
4   Vadim Andreev, *Detsvo* (Childhood), Moscow, 1966, pp. 71–7.

tical 'correspondences' and connections, and images from Greek antiquity. His lifelong inspiration would be the greatest Symbolist of them all, Alexander Blok, the son of his old supervisor at Warsaw University. Blok was still in his teens then, and would publish his first poems in the new century, romantic, tender and prophetic, vitally connected to the upheavals in Russia, filled with the miraculous and transcendental.

Vadim Andreev saw the Reisners as perfectly matched. Ekaterina Alexandrovna was a free spirit, he wrote, funny, freckled and clever, 'with a small body filled with willpower, a fantastic poetic imagination, and the mind of a mathematician, constantly excited about something, proving something, making some point'. She had learnt to speak up for herself at political meetings, and she had a quick ear, a passion for literature, and a gift for story-telling, and her family and friends were always urging her to write. She was in charge at home, Vadim wrote – 'and woe to anyone who defied her'.

Another valuable, more critical, source of information about the family is Reisner's niece, the actress and writer Ekaterina Sheremeteva, the daughter of his estranged elder sister in Vilna, who spoke to Przhiborovskaya in the 1960s. According to Sheremeteva, neither of the sisters liked Ekaterina Alexandrovna. They saw her as a snob, despite her socialism, obsessed with birth and breeding and his academic career, who had even campaigned unsuccessfully after they married for the 'von' to be restored to the Reisner name, claiming the title would make life easier for their children. They remembered her fussing endlessly over Larisa as a baby, worrying she wasn't pretty enough, rubbing castor-oil on her eyebrows to make them grow.[5] Years later, she could laugh at herself. 'Kant's *Critique of Pure Reason* lay on Papa's desk when you were born, and mocked me for fussing over my ugly daughter!' she wrote to her on her twentieth birthday.[6]

The Reisners were adoring, demanding parents to 'Lara', or 'Lyalya'. 'There was never conceivably any talk of punishment. One word from Ekaterina Alexandrovna made it a pleasure to do what she wanted', Vadim wrote. And like Vadim, others close to them over the years saw their marriage as an exceptionally happy one, based on their shared politics and values. As socialists, they hated the tyranny and privilege of their class. They also believed deeply in the aristocratic virtues of decorum and civilised conversation. Both were proud of their ancestry, and had an aristocratic disdain for philistines and reactionaries. 'This pride, their response to the prevailing vulgarity and reaction in Russia,

---

5   Przhiborovskaya 2008, p. 21.
6   Her letter in Sofia Zhitomirskaya, 'Muzyka revolyutsii. Po stranisam rukopisei Larisy Reisner' (The Music of the Revolution. Pages from Larisa Reisner's Manuscripts), *Literaturnaya Gazeta* (Literary Paper), 21 May 1975.

went with them like the sword and dagger of the Three Musqueteers', Vadim wrote, 'along with their deep faith in socialism, which they preached like a religion'.

Being a socialist in Russia meant never knowing who might be an informer, and outsiders often found them prickly and standoffish. But with their circle of trusted friends they were warm and hospitable, prone like all families of the Russian intelligentsia to long political discussions around the samovar. And throughout Larisa's earliest years, the upheavals in Russia were driving them further to the left and away from their pasts.

Her father was first interrogated by the police in Lublin a month after she was born, after he spoke at a meeting at the University in solidarity with students in St Petersburg, Moscow and Kiev, jailed for refusing to swear the oath of allegiance to the new Tsar Nicholas. The following May, three days after Nicholas was crowned Emperor of Russia, King of Poland and Grand Duke of Finland, over a thousand of his citizens were trampled to death on Moscow's Khodynka Field, where they had come to receive their promised coronation gifts. A month later, when Reisner returned to St Petersburg to defend his thesis at the University, workers were retaliating with mass illegal strikes and demonstrations. The strikes spread across Russia, and thousands of strikers were arrested and jailed. Socialists at the universities were sacked or sent abroad, and in the summer of 1897, the Ministry of Education ordered Reisner out of Lublin, with his police files and his family, for an eighteen-month sabbatical in Germany, teaching law at the University of Heidelberg.

The family's flat became a popular meeting place for Heidelberg's large community of Russian exiles, and Reisner published articles in the student press denouncing the Tsar and the Orthodox Church – his 'spiritual police-force'. 'Law and religion in Russia are dictated by the requirements of the tsarist police state, whose unaccountable rulers have authority over every aspect of citizens' lives', he wrote. A month after arriving in Heidelberg, he was threatened with the sack, for refusing to condemn a series of student occupations at the University. But he was kept on, with his growing police files, supporting his wife and daughter with difficulty on his reduced salary.

The summer of 1898 brought more disastrous harvests in Russia, and another famine, and a mass strike at Moscow's giant Gubner cotton mill, with its mainly female workforce. Strikes spread to over three hundred factories across the country, and workers, Jews and students were jailed and sent to Siberia, or fled abroad. Reisner's Russian friends in Heidelberg put him in touch with underground political groups in St Petersburg, and he began to apply his studies under the tsarist legal system to a more systematic support for the strike movement in Russia. All this was reported back to the Ministry of Education, and in

September he was ordered out of Heidelberg, and banished into semi-exile in Tomsk, the ancient capital of Siberia, to teach jurisprudence and comparative religion at the University's new law faculty.

The University of Tomsk had been established twenty years earlier, the first of over a dozen new universities to open in distant parts of the Empire and Asiatic Russia. In 1891, work had started on the construction of the new Trans-Siberian Railway, connecting Moscow to the eastern port of Vladivostok, and the Siberian Rail Company had been encouraging the adventurous to emigrate east and populate Siberia's barren wastes. In 1893, a new branch-line had opened Tomsk to visitors, and the city was now a thriving cultural and economic centre, employing mainly print and railworkers. But it was better known as a historic dumping ground for socialists and revolutionaries.

Larisa was three, and Ekaterina Alexandrovna was seven months pregnant with their second child, when the Reisners set off on the two thousand mile journey east on the Trans-Siberian line to their new home in Western Siberia.

On a return visit to Tomsk, two years after the Revolution, Reisner wrote ecstatically to a friend:

> The bright Siberian winter, the sweet frozen air, the transparent green of the rushing Angara River, the black depths of mighty Lake Baikal, the azure Manchurian nights. And the people! The flea-ridden aristocrat, the Chinese with the torso of Apollo and the little hands of a marquis. Buryat fur-trappers with red tassels on their knees, colourful Mongolians in their sheepskins, American gold traders, Siberians with a few crimes on their conscience – my god, we're in a Jack London novel![7]

In 1898, he was there at the mercy of the University authorities. The Rector, Professor Rudakov, encouraged lecturers to spy on each other and report back to the police, and academic standards were not high. Seven years earlier, the great physiologist Professor Pavlov had had his application to teach there turned down, for fear that as the first scholar in Russia to open his laboratories to Jews and women, he would enflame the minds of the University's already riot-prone students.

Two months after the family arrived, on 28 December, Larisa's brother Igor ('Goga') was born, and was baptised in Tomsk's Russian Orthodox Cathedral of the Resurrection – for pragmatic reasons presumably, since as an open atheist Reisner would have lost his job. He first clashed with Rudakov a month later,

---

7 Reisner's letter quoted in his biography in the *Granat Encyclopaedia*.

when a distant relative of his living in the city was jailed as a socialist. He campaigned for his release, and defended him successfully at his trial, hiring his daughter as a governess for Larisa, and paying for medical treatment for his son, who had tuberculosis. The harassment he suffered for this from the University authorities drew him closer to his radical students, and his lectures were increasingly disrupted by sit-ins and occupations. 'There is no law in Russia. Laws are dictated by the openly political nature of the tsarist state!' he told them.

As the new century opened, the new Socialist Revolutionary Party launched its assassination campaign against hated government officials and members of the royal family. Peasants burned and ransacked estates, and villages and Jewish communities were massacred in retaliation. Strikes and student riots spread across Russia to Latvia, Poland and Siberia, and in February 1901, Tomsk's railworkers led a general strike in the city. The University was in turmoil, and dozens of Reisner's students were jailed or drafted into the army. He campaigned for their release, and began attending underground meetings of the Siberian branch of the Russian Social Democratic Party, led by Tomsk's political exiles, and he joined an illegal strike support group in the city, where he was known as 'Barin' (the 'Gentleman'), for his aristocratic ways.

That spring, as the riots and pogroms reached their height in Russia, he defied the police ban on student meetings to speak at another occupation of the Law Faculty, and Rudakov called on the Ministry of Education to sack 'this arrogant liberal', for 'playing with the anarchistically inclined section of his students'. Instead, he was sent on another long sabbatical to Germany, not on his professor's salary this time, but on a small research grant of sixty roubles a month.

Between May 1901 and the following autumn, the family lived in Berlin and Heidelberg, where they already had friends, and he struggled to support the four of them on his grant. But the children were taught the importance of keeping up appearances, and darned clothes were always spotless. In a studio portrait of them with their father in Berlin, they are immaculately dressed, in matching stiffly starched white suits, slightly too large, so they can grow into them, and enormous white hats like bakers' hats. Reisner is leaning protectively over three-year-old Igor, who has a toy train on his lap. Larisa stares solemnly at the camera, wearing a boy's tie and holding a doll, which looks borrowed for the occasion.

The campaign against Reisner continued when the family returned to Tomsk, in the autumn of 1902. Surrounded by spies and informers, they closed in on themselves and against the outside world. In another portrait of the children that winter, they are half-turned to the camera, bundled up in their thick school uniforms against the Siberian cold, with eight-year-old Larisa standing in front of her little brother, as if ready to defend him.

The following April, Reisner was summoned to the Ministry of Education in St Petersburg, where he was presented with Rudakov's files, and was interrogated for four days by the police. 'Has politics consumed every aspect of scientific thought, to the extent that there is no room in Russia's vast organism for a modest scholar seeking only the truth?' he pleaded in his defence. But a month later he was sacked from the University, for 'abusing his chair to make speeches promoting enmity and disrespect for law and order in Russia', and his students occupied the Law Faculty, and sent Rudakov a telegram calling him a 'victim of political oppression'.

The family fled Russia for Germany, and for the next four years they lived as political exiles in Berlin, under constant surveillance by the German police, surviving on whatever teaching, writing and translation jobs Reisner could get. They rented a small flat in the working-class Zehlendorf district, where the schools were cheaper, and the environment in which Larisa had grown up changed sharply. Food was often short, and there were few new clothes, and she would suffer lasting damage to her feet from having to share Igor's boots. But those years in Berlin would be the start of her lifelong love of Germany.

As the children of exiles, she and Igor were expected to be fluent from an early age in several languages, and there were English and French lessons, and Russian and German were spoken at home. But German became her first language, and she made close friends with the children at her primary school. Her experiences in exile would be formative for her, and exile would be a central theme of the unfinished autobiographical novel she wrote later, *Requiem*, about her life before the Revolution:

> Two children, born into great danger, raised on the easy genius of analysis, learnt to predict each new hurricane as it threw their shaky nest from place to place, and to see their father and mother as their eternal defence against an implacable hostile world.[8]

In Berlin, her father 'breathed the pure air of Marxism', she wrote. Home of the mighty German Social Democratic Party, the largest socialist party in the world, leader of the Socialist International, the city was at the centre of a great cross

---

8 *Requiem* was never finished. The novel's surviving three chapters, some fifty pages, were published in 1983 under its new title, *Rudin*, in the journal *Literaturnoe nasledstvo* (Literary Heritage), vol. 93, pp. 209–32. As *Rudin* was also the title of a magazine she brought out later, the original title *Requiem* is given in the text to avoid confusion. Excerpts from the work aren't footnoted from now on.

current of exiled Russian revolutionaries across Europe. Alexandra Kollontai was part of its large settled community of exiles. Trotsky, Radek and Nikolai Bukharin visited from Vienna, Warsaw and Paris to speak at meetings, and hundreds were living there illegally, without work or money. The Reisners kept open house for them in their flat, sheltering them from the police and finding them jobs, and Larisa recalled an endless series of Russians arriving and leaving with mysterious haste.

Reisner joined the German party, and allied himself with its left revolutionary wing, led by Rosa Luxemburg and the lawyer Karl Liebknecht. Both saw capitalism's insatiable greed for markets leading inexorably to world war, and both were fiercely critical of the party's growing conservatism, bureaucracy and chauvinism. Luxemburg travelled the country speaking at factories, calling on workers to organise mass strikes against the Kaiser's rocketing arms programme. Liebknecht spoke at anti-war meetings in schools and colleges, building a new youth movement to fight conscription, and he enlisted Reisner to write articles on Russia's strike movement for the party paper *Vorwärts*.

Liebknecht and his Russian wife, the artist Sophie Borisovna, became the family's closest friends in Berlin. In *Requiem* Larisa described the lively international crowd of socialists and revolutionaries who gathered for parties at 'Comrade Karl's', where 'Aunt Sophie' would give her and Igor milk and shortbread. Another of their 'party aunts' was 'Aunt Julie', wife of August Bebel, the party's chief spokesman in the Reichstag, and an ardent campaigner for women's rights, whose book *Woman and Socialism* Kollontai called 'Women's Bible'.

The Reisners' flat was small and shabby, but Larisa described her mother working her magic to make it warm and welcoming, and a safe home for the family. Her only concession to luxury was the magnificent green fringed tablecloth she bought at a department store, to cover the rough wooden table where they ate and Reisner worked on his writing, and to hide the piles of books and toys underneath, where the children would play.

In a 1903 studio portrait of Larisa in Berlin, the solemn schoolgirl is gone, and she is a fairy, in a frilly white dress with winged sleeves, with a knowing amused expression on her face, and a birch switch in her hand for a wand. At the age of eight, she was encouraged to explore Berlin on her own, and she quickly learnt her way around. Some Russian friends of the family visiting them then remembered 'the bold, lively little girl who took us and our son around the city on the buses and trams, looking after us and crossing us over the roads. It amazed us that this child had been given so much responsibility'.[9]

---

9 Quoted in Przhiborovskaya 2008, p. 31.

In exile she was learning the disguises and survival skills she would need later as a revolutionary. Revolutionary vigilance came naturally to her. She had learnt very young to be wary of careless words and false friends, and this guardedness would be a feature of her character as an adult, noted by those close to her – even at the height of Revolution, when she was much written about and constantly in the public eye.

The first sparks of revolution in Russia were lit in the summer of 1903, by the economic slump that hit the industrial south. Workers suffered wage cuts, layoffs and deteriorating conditions, and mass strikes across a vast area, from Ukraine to the Caucasus, brought factories, railways, mines and oil wells to a halt. Local revolutionaries organised strike support groups, and demonstrated with banners saying 'Down with the Autocracy!' and 'Long live the Democratic Republic!', and the army put down the unrest with mass arrests.

In August, Marxists from Russia and exile met in Brussels (before reconvening in London), to discuss their tactics in the struggle, and split on how they saw the party needed to lead it. The Mensheviks wanted a large party, modelled on those in Germany and Britain, open to revolutionaries and non-revolutionaries alike, to campaign with the trade unions for social reforms. The Bolsheviks, led by Lenin, argued that legal work was impossible in autocratic Russia, and that without a tightly organised and largely underground party to coordinate and politicise the fight, the workers' movement would be smashed.

In January 1904, Tsar Nicholas used the time-honoured tactic of liquidating dissent by mobilising men into the army, to fight in Russia's war with Japan – 'a small victorious war', for the Japanese protectorates of Manchuria and the Korean peninsula. Six months later, most of the Russian fleet was at the bottom of the Tsushima Straits, and the Tsar's imperial ambitions in Asia were in ruins.

Living costs rose so quickly that real wages fell by twenty percent, and the country was convulsed with more strikes. Students rioted and occupied the universities, and the war produced a surge of support for the Bolsheviks and the terror tactics of the Socialist Revolutionaries. That summer, the brutal Governor-General of Finland was assassinated in the Finnish capital Helsingfors (now Helsinki), and Socialist Revolutionaries in St Petersburg blew up the carriage of the Minister of the Interior and Chief of the Imperial Police, von Plehve, famous for his role in crushing the Populists in the 1880s.

Terrorists and suspected terrorists were tried in special courts and hanged, and revolutionaries fled into exile. Russians in Germany came under increased police surveillance, and dozens in Berlin were arrested. Reisner widened his legal expertise to construct defences for them at their trials, and in November, he accepted Liebknecht's invitation to defend a group of German socialists in the town of Königsberg, close to the Russian border (now Kaliningrad in Russia), jailed for 'crimes against the Tsar', and he secured their release.[10]

On 9 January 1905, twenty thousand workers in St Petersburg marched with their families to the Winter Palace, to present the Tsar with their petition for some improvements in their wretched lives. Over two thousand men, women and children were gunned down by the Tsar's troops that day, and the 'Bloody Sunday' massacre was the signal for Russia's first revolution. Month after month, as the war with Japan brought fresh agonies of defeat and suffering, the countryside blazed with riots, factories were paralysed by strikes, and Black Hundreds gangs roamed the cities, killing workers, students and Jews.

120,000 workers in the capital came out on strike that year. Children as young as twelve were organising revolutionary 'cells' in their schools, marching in demonstrations and throwing stones at the police, and a survey after the Revolution revealed that over a third of the Party Central Committee had joined the Bolsheviks in 1905 as teenagers. Women too were joining the strike movement in their thousands, often outdoing men in militancy. Many women of Kollontai's generation who had joined the revolutionary underground in the 1890s had put aside the fight for their equality in the interests of the wider class struggle. Kollontai herself always campaigned for a synthesis of the two, calling on women toiling in the factories to do battle with the old patriarchal values, demanding that the Social Democrats pay serious attention to their needs. And now the downtrodden slaves were fighting on the streets, finding their voices as organisers and public speakers, giving the strikes unprecedented strength.

The Socialist Revolutionaries' next major target, assassinated in February 1905, was the vicious anti-Semitic Governor-General of Moscow, the Tsar's uncle the Grand Duke Sergei, who a decade earlier had ordered the expulsion of Moscow's twenty thousand Jews from the city, issuing his decree during Passover, allowing Jewish women to stay only if they registered as prostitutes.

Terrorists were rounded up and executed, and universities across the country were closed. In May, workers began a general strike in the Ukrainian Black Sea port of Odessa, the fourth largest city in Imperial Russia, supported by the sailors' mutiny on the Battleship *Potemkin*, and workers in Moscow downed tools for a month in solidarity with them.

Thousands of strikers had been jailed at the height of the industrial unrest a decade earlier, and workers had seen virtually no improvements to their inhuman conditions. Now there was an angry new young workforce in the capital's

---

10   Reisner reported on the trial in his pamphlet *Sudebnyi protses Karl Liebknechta protiv russkogo tsara* (Karl Liebknecht's Case Against the Russian Tsar), published in Russia in 1905, and republished twenty years later.

vast engineering and munitions plants and shipyards, who were reading Lenin's strike leaflets, and setting up workers' councils, soviets, to keep them in touch with the revolutionary underground.

In the summer of 1905, Lev Trotsky had escaped from Siberia to live illegally in St Petersburg and work underground with the soviets, which he saw as the models for a completely new kind of workers' government, with the potential to lead a proletarian revolution in predominantly peasant Russia. Trotsky was a Menshevik, and would join the Bolshevik Party only three months before the Revolution. But like Lenin and the Bolsheviks, he believed workers could not wait for the first bourgeois stage of the revolution envisaged by Marx, and that instead of begging for concessions from capitalism, they must seize power directly from the state.

In his essay *Results and Prospects*, he analysed the soviets' role in the revolution in terms of Marx's theory of 'permanent revolution'. Marx wrote of the process whereby the old social formations created the conditions for the new ones. Just as the bourgeois class had overthrown feudalism, capitalism would be swept away by the revolution to socialise production – 'making revolutions "permanent" until all the more or less propertied classes have been driven from their ruling positions'. According to Marx, the contradictions of world capital necessarily made revolutions international, and he had seen these starting in the industrially developed West, not in backward impoverished Russia, isolated in hostile capitalist Europe. Trotsky argued that capitalism's uneven development throughout the world made it quite possible for the new socialist order to be built in Russia, through an elected workers' government of soviets. Russia would go through the first bourgeois stage of the revolution, he wrote, but its small weak bourgeoisie would almost immediately be forced to surrender to the proletariat, the only class capable of taking power. Revolutions would then spread to the more advanced capitalist countries, which would share their wealth and resources with Russia, and nation states would disappear in one socialist world: 'The International Revolution will attain completion with the final victory of the new society across the entire planet'.

Soviets quickly spread to factories and military garrisons across Russia, and to the fortified island of Kronstadt, Russia's largest naval base, twenty miles from the capital. On 10 October, thirteen thousand Kronstadt sailors came out in a mass armed mutiny against their officers. Three days later, Trotsky chaired the first session of the St Petersburg Soviet of Workers' Deputies – a Jew in anti-Semitic Russia at the head of the world's first workers' government in waiting.

On the 17th, the Tsar capitulated, rallying his citizens to the throne with his 'Manifesto', promising universal male suffrage in elections to Russia's first parliament, his new 'consultative' State Duma, and an amnesty for political exiles. In the 'days of freedom' that followed, new soviets and workers' clubs sprang up across Russia, and revolutionaries emerged from the underground and returned from exile.

Since the Reisners did not hurry back to Russia in October, they clearly had little faith in the promised amnesty. And that month Reisner joined the Bolsheviks. He corresponded with Lenin, travelling twice to Switzerland to meet him, attending the party's first All-Russian Conference in Finland as a delegate, where he met him again with most of the Bolsheviks' future leaders, and writing articles for the new party paper *Proletarian*, which published his pamphlet *The Struggle for Rights and Freedom in Russia*.[11]

1905 changed the face of Russian literature. Revolutionary leaflets poured into the factories, writers became revolutionaries, and workers and peasants became writers. The writer Maxim Gorky, jailed for six months for putting out a leaflet calling for 'a united fight against the Autocracy', gave literature classes in the factories on his release, and encouraged workers to publish their songs, poems and stories in the Bolshevik press. *Proletarian* published the works of the peasant and factory poets Sergei Esenin, Nikolai Klyuev and Demyan Bedny (the 'Poor'), and the new Russian version of the *Internationale*, by the miner Arkady Kotz, was sung at demonstrations. Blok marched on the streets with a red flag and visited arrested strikers in jail, and even the Symbolist poet Konstantin Balmont called for the Tsar's assassination.

Strikes and riots continued until the end of 1905, but with less intensity than before. Strikers were arrested, and revolutionaries were forced back into the underground or fled abroad. In December, Trotsky and the other leaders of the St Petersburg Soviet were jailed for conspiring to organise a revolution. The Moscow Soviet led workers in a mass armed solidarity uprising, and the army was sent in to crush them, leaving three hundred dead. In April 1906, the Tsar dissolved his Duma, with all its proposed reforms rejected, and dozens of deputies arrested. The 'days of freedom' were over.

People suffered in many terrible ways in the years of reaction that followed. The Tsar and his hysterical wife, the Empress Alexandra, locked themselves in the Winter Palace with endless charlatans peddling magic cures. There was an epidemic of murders and suicides, child prostitution flourished, and a mass of cheap pornography flooded the market. Workers' organisations were smashed, and the strike movement slumped. Socialists were jailed or escaped into exile, and the Socialist Revolutionaries gained new mass support. By 1907, assassinations and attempted assassinations of government officials had leapt to a stag-

---

11 Lenin's letter to Reisner on 4 October 1905 is in vol. 36 of his *Complete Collected Works*, 4th edn., Moscow, 1957.

gering 2,500, and the party became riddled with police agents. The Bolsheviks opposed the tactics of terror with their programme of workers' class war against capitalism. But they were operating deep in the underground, and it was a fight to the death to smuggle their message into the factories.

In February 1906, Reisner was invited by his colleague the Marxist law professor Maxim Kovalevsky to teach at his International Socialist University in Paris for exiled workers, and the family lived there for a month, while he gave his lectures, spoke at political meetings, and wrote articles in the French socialist press about the criminal tsarist state. He took a more conciliatory tone in the articles he was publishing in Russia then, in the moderate socialist journal *Russian Wealth*, which called for gradual political reforms, rather than revolution. And on their return to Berlin, he applied to the Russian government for permission to return to St Petersburg.

His politics had condemned his family to years of hardship and exile, and the children's education had suffered from having to 'jump from desk to desk', he told a friend. He would always call himself a Marxist. Marx's 'social existence determines consciousness', which saw people as capable in the right environment of revealing unlimited potential, was the guiding principle of all his work as a teacher and writer. But with reaction once more triumphant, Marxism in Russia, and its party, the Bolsheviks, were in crisis.

For Reisner, only the Bolsheviks had seemed capable of leading the revolution against the autocracy, and he was one of hundreds who left the party that spring, sickened by the chaos and violence of the revolution, alienated by the Bolsheviks' new hardline underground politics, which saw any discussion of the great changes people experienced in their personal lives in the revolution as a distraction from the class struggle.

Many socialists abandoned socialism for the parties of bourgeois liberalism, which they saw as the only alternative to tsarism. Reisner was never remotely tempted by the liberal argument that capitalism could be reformed to serve workers' interests. Instead, he was drawn to the new school of 'seeking Marxists', who were discovering revolutionary new insights into human behaviour in the works of Sigmund Freud.

Psychoanalysis was studied seriously in Russia long before it became popular in the West. The concept of the Unconscious had been investigated by Russia's religious philosophers of the nineteenth century, and Freud saw Russians as closer to his ideas than people elsewhere in Europe. Russians travelled to Vienna to meet him and train as analysts, and by 1912 more copies of his works were being sold in Russia than anywhere else in the world. 'There seems to be a epidemic of psychoanalysis in Russia', he wrote to his colleague Carl Jung that year.

For the 'seeking Marxists', Freudian theories of repression and sublimation were the key to a new understanding of social relations and the family in bourgeois society, and people's feelings about love and sex. Reisner saw his teachings as the starting-point for a new 'psychoanalytic, intuitive' approach to the law, based on Marxist principles of social justice and class struggle, and he explored these connections in his book *Russian Absolutism and European Reaction*, published in St Petersburg in 1907.

Hundreds of Russia's writers and intellectuals after 1905 became devotees of Madame Blavatsky and her disciple Rudolf Steiner, and their new-age religions of Theosophy and Anthroposophy; the Symbolist poet Andrei Bely was a close friend of Steiner's, and lived with him for three years at his Anthroposophy commune in Switzerland. Others joined anarchist circles. The romantic and visionary in Reisner was attracted to a group of poets and utopian socialists close to Blok, who called themselves 'mystical anarchists'. Like Tolstoy and Thoreau before them, and the political anarchists Bakunin and Kropotkin, the 'mystical anarchists' rejected the institutions of private property and the state, but believed there could be no social programme for the revolution in Russia. It would be a bloodless revolution, their manifesto declared, achieved not through violence, but through love. Revolution meant 'a revolt against all external conditions towards complete freedom of the spirit, in the name of the free union of people, based on the principles of the anarchist union of love. We are there where there is revolution. But we do not only destroy, we create. And our creativity is the creativity of love'.[12]

In the spring of 1907, Karl Liebknecht was arrested for high treason for publishing his anti-war masterpiece *Militarism and Anti-Militarism*, and was sentenced to eighteen months' hard labour in jail. Most of his former comrades abandoned him, and denounced him as a madman and a traitor. Reisner joined his supporters in Germany and abroad in the fight for his release, and threw his legal expertise into the successful campaign for him to be elected in jail to the Reichstag.

The Russian government was clearly taking a big risk with him, but that May, under the Tsar's new amnesty to celebrate the opening of his Second Duma, he was one of over two hundred political exiles allowed back to Russia, as associate professor of Constitutional Law at St Petersburg University.

The family packed up their life in Berlin, and while they looked for a new home in the capital, they rented a dacha in the Finnish village of Vammelsuu, five miles from the Russian border, close to the home of their friend the writer Leonid Andreev.

---

12   Quoted in Christopher Read, *Religion, Revolution and the Russian Intelligentsia, 1900–12*, 1979, p. 27.

In 1939, in the build up to the Nazi invasion of the Soviet Union, Soviet troops would occupy these border areas of Finland, vital to the defence of Leningrad. In the brutal Winter War that followed, Russia gained dozens of towns and villages on the Finnish side, and Vammelsuu is now part of the St Petersburg district, and is named Serovo, after the Russian artist Valentin Serov, who had lived and painted there.

In the early years of the century, Vammelsuu was still wild Finnish countryside, a retreat from the capital and its politics, and a place of spectacular beauty, with its sandy beaches and forested slopes and distant views of the city's domes and spires. The poet Osip Mandelstam stayed there later to write, and many of St Petersburg's artists, writers and intellectuals had dachas overlooking the coast – Serov, the painters Alexander Benois and Nikolai Roerich, and the eminent neuroscientist Vladimir Bekhterev, who became a close family friend and colleague of Reisner's.

Another new friend of the Reisners' in Vammelsuu, also returning to St Petersburg under the Amnesty after many years in exile, was the highly respected socialist historian and journalist Vladimir Burtsev, known as the 'Sherlock Holmes of the revolution', for his work exposing police spies and *agents provocateurs* in the Socialist Revolutionary Party.

Looming over them all was Andreev, in the enormous wooden 'Norwegian castle' he had had built after the death of his beloved first wife in childbirth. He had given away the baby, Daniil, to be raised by her sister, and the Reisners had first met him when he was visiting Berlin with his second wife and Vadim, his older son from his first marriage, who later lived with them in St Petersburg.

Like Gorky, Andreev was a deeply romantic figure, much painted, photographed and interviewed. Both writers were preoccupied like Tolstoy with the elemental realities of sex and death, and both were spoken of then as Tolstoy's successors. Gorky's works were more popular with workers, but Andreev's disgust at the insanity and sadism of tsarism struck a responsive chord in intellectuals like Reisner and his hero Blok.

His plays, novels and stories mixed symbolism, realism, eroticism, gothic horror and spiritualism with political radicalism. In his best-selling novel *Red Laughter*, published in 1904, he mined the depths of the horrors of the war with Japan, through excerpts from the diaries of a Russian soldier who had fought in Manchuria. The following spring, he was arrested and jailed for two months in St Petersburg's Taganka Prison, for allowing a Bolshevik meeting to be held in his flat, and on his release, he fled Russia for exile in Finland.

Like Gorky, he had become very wealthy from his writing, and both used their money to support impoverished exiles and writers, and fund political causes and publishing ventures. In the summer of 1906, he financed a sailors' mutiny at the Finnish garrison of Sveaborg, and that year he became chief financial backer and editor of the new St Petersburg literary journal *Wild Rose*.

Wild Rose had been dreamed up in 1905's 'days of freedom', to keep great literature alive in the revolution, and was the brainchild of the artist and cartoonist Zinovy Grzhebin and the poet and violinist Solomon Kopelman, who had both worked on the satirical political magazines of the revolution, and had spent time in jail. Edited by Andreev and Kopelman, beautifully designed and illustrated by Grzhebin, *Wild Rose* soon became Russia's leading literary publication, publisher of some of the country's greatest poets, novelists and playwrights, old and new, with translations of foreign works, and a long political section, with works by Marx and Engels.

But for all Andreev's successes as a writer and publisher, the collapse of the revolution and his wretchedly unhappy second marriage had turned him to drink. His daughter Vera, the second of his three children with his second wife, recalled him filling the house with his sadness – 'pacing at night with a candle, swathed in the grey folds of his robe, his stony face and staring eyes seeking the ghost of his dead wife'.[13]

Five-year-old Vadim had little to do with the adult world, and was left to his own devices. He remembered the freedom of that summer with Larisa and Igor, playing for hours with them on the beach, swimming in the rough sea, climbing trees, making bonfires on the sand. Sixteen years later, Larisa wrote of those months in Finland in her unfinished autobiographical essay 'A Mother Sings:'

> Perhaps all of us, as we leave babyhood behind, experience moments when we glimpse all the joy and suffering of our future lives. These sudden illuminations, inexpressible in words, leave their trace, like the rainbow at the edge of the grey harbour on a gusty evening, and the pink clouds racing across the damp mossy slopes and the sands, glowing amber in the sunset ...[14]

At the end of August, a month before the start of the University year, the Reisners left Vammelsuu for their new home in St Petersburg, the famous Leuchtenberg Building, on 28 Bolshaya Zelenina, Great Gunpowder Street, named after the powder works and explosive factories built there during the reign of Peter the Great.

The building was one of many new apartment blocks going up on the St Petersburg Side, one of the poorest districts in the capital, which was rapidly

---

13 Vera Andreeva, *Dom na chernoi rechke* (House on the Black River), Moscow, 1974, p. 49.
14 Przhiborovskaya 2008, p. 32.

being gentrified. Most of its population were poor workers' families, paying a hundred roubles a month to live up to fifteen to a room in its slums and tenements. Running off Great Gunpowder Street were unlit alleys lined with workers' barracks without electricity or running water, standing in cesspools of sewage, where tuberculosis and typhus were rampant, and thousands would die in the cholera epidemic that swept the capital a year later.

Many of the new mansions appearing among the slums of the St Petersburg Side were like castles, with ostentatious domes, wings and turrets, huge courtyards and extensive gardens, with statues and fountains. The owner of the Leuchtenberg Building, Duke Alexander Leuchtenberg, a great-grandson of Tsar Paul I, was from a family of modernisers and innovators, with wide business and cultural interests, who used their money to fund the capital's theatres, ballets and orchestras and new building projects. The Duke had commissioned the Art Nouveau artist and architect Theodor von Postels to design the building, which is now a popular tourist destination. The façade on the lower two storeys is decorated with delicate wrought iron and stucco, and between them and the third floor is a wide tiled mosaic frieze, in rich shades of purple and blue, depicting landscapes, rivers, seas, industrial towns and factory chimneys. The fifth floor at the top, with its floor to ceiling windows, was rented out to artists' studios.

Residents had a lift, modern plumbing and electricity, and their own bathrooms and telephones (forty thousand homes in the city had telephones by then), for which they paid the Duke five hundred roubles' rent a month, an unimaginable sum for most in the capital. The Reisners' flat, number 42 on the third floor, consisted of five spacious rooms – bedrooms for the children and their parents, a large drawing-room overlooking one of the building's two courtyards, planted with flowerbeds and lilac trees, and Mikhail Andreevich's study. Forty years after his death, Przhiborovskaya was told by one of the building's residents that the flat was still known as the 'Professor's flat', and it would be Larisa's home for the next eleven years.

Behind the Leuchtenberg Building were rows of allotments and wooden hovels, occupied by poor day labourers, tailors and domestic servants, and Great Gunpowder Street was famous for its bars and brothels, which the children walked past every day on their way to and from school. Nine-year-old Igor, small, sharp and freckled as his mother, was sent to an elite boys' *gimnazium* catering to the sons of doctors, lawyers and professors, and eleven-year-old Larisa was enrolled in A.R. Balabanova's private academy for girls.

The years when their father had struggled to support his family were over, and his large salary allowed them to take skiing trips and holidays on the Black Sea. Ekaterina Alexandrovna followed his academic successes with pride, and celebrated them with parties, and home was an oasis of culture. She held literary soirées and poetry readings, and at the age of forty she began to write short stories, and had several published. Larisa and Igor were encouraged to think independently, and to raid the bookshelves for the latest science and history books and works of foreign and Russian literature. They loved animals, and had a dog, a fox terrier called 'Foxy', and there were skating and horse-riding lessons, trips to the Hermitage Art Gallery, the opera, the ballet and the theatre, and everything a cultured family could give their children.

After her working-class school in Berlin, Larisa found her prim conservative academy 'agony', and she made few friends there. She was known as a show-off and troublemaker, who enjoyed goading her teachers with her socialist views, and her mother was called in frequently about her behaviour. But she did her homework and worked hard, especially at Russian literature, and after school and at weekends, she and Igor were free to explore the world outside the Leuchtenberg Building and play on the streets.

Despite her years in Siberia, the Russia of St Petersburg must have been virtually a foreign country to her. Capital of the Tsarist Empire, and one of the most beautiful cities in the world, with its canals and broad aristocratic squares and graceful bridges across the mighty River Neva, it was a beacon of wealth and power in a sea of Russian poverty, and a jumble of the old and the new. Horse-trams still trundled along Great Gunpowder Street to the Bolshoi Prospect, but the street was already being dug up for the new electric trams. Built on a vacant lot on the corner was the new two-story *Art Moderne* Nemetti Theatre, with its popular productions of Gorky, Chekhov, Ibsen and Shakespeare, which were performed outside in the gardens in the summer. At the far end was the Alexandrovsky Park, with its tennis courts and fairground, much loved by Blok, who recorded in his diaries riding its rollercoaster eighty times in six weeks, in search of new thrills. Further off were the Zoo, the Cirque Moderne, the new roller-skating rink, and the Coliseum Cinema.

Russia's first cinematograph had opened in 1896, in St Petersburg's Acquarium Variety Theatre, where stunned audiences had watched the Lumière Brothers' film of Tsar Nicholas's coronation. Over a hundred Russian films had been made since then – several adaptations of the classics, including Tolstoy's *Anna Karenina* and Pushkin's *Evgeny Onegin* and *Queen of Spades*, but mainly horror and action movies and slapstick comedies for the masses, accompanied by barrel organs and accordions. Ticket prices were kept low, and audiences were a lively democratic mix of workers and intellectuals, aristocrats and students. New picture houses opened and were invariably packed, and by 1907 there were seven on the Bolshoi Prospect alone.

For Blok and his fellow Symbolist poet Andrei Bely, the supercharged close-ups and special effects of the early silent cinema represented all the speed and energy of the city. Leonid Andreev, himself a pioneer of colour photography in Russia, predicted a brilliant future for the cinematograph, the new 'writing with light:'

> There will be no limits to writers' freedom. Their imagination will be enriched, new dramatists, new talents and geniuses, as yet unknown, will emerge. A cinema Shakespeare, abandoning the inconvenience of spoken words, will deepen and broaden language to such an extent, and find such new and unexpected combinations, that action will become as expressive as speech.[15]

The Reisners were keen cinema-goers, and in *Requiem* Larisa recalled the magic of her early trips as a child – 'breathing a sigh of happiness as the lights flickered in the darkness, and the ship set sail from the shore'.

She was also discovering the rough side of the capital and its street life, wonderfully evoked in the memoirs of her contemporary the poet and biophysicist Alexander Chizhevsky. 'King of the St Petersburg Side' was the hooligan 'Vaska the Cat', who claimed to be the illegitimate son of the capital's Governor-General, General Kleigels. Great Gunpowder Street was patrolled by gangs of wealthy merchants' sons, 'in their high patent-leather boots, belted side-buttoned Russian shirts, and fashionable "Moscow" caps', who would buy sulphur and potassium from the chemists to make rockets and firecrackers, and set them off in the allotments behind the Leuchtenberg Building.[16]

Years later, Larisa described to a friend how she had picked up her revolutionary fighting skills 'in the wonderful fights on Great Gunpowder Street, in which I was considered an unparalleled expert, even by the boys. There were lots of fights on the street. Every other building was a bar, and at nights you avoided the pavements and walked along the middle of the road'.[17]

At the age of twelve, she was a tall active child. Despite the damage to her feet from her years in exile, she loved dancing and sports. Mikhail Andreevich, a keen tennis player, gave the children lessons at the Alexandrovsky Park courts,

---

15   Leonid Andreev, 'First Letter on Theatre', in *The Film Factory* (trans. & eds. Ian Christie and Richard Taylor), 1988, pp. 27–31.
16   Alexander Chizhevsky, *Vsya zhizn* (All Life), Moscow, 1974, pp. 49–50.
     Lev Nikulin, 'Gody nashei zhizni' (Years of Our Life) in *Larisa Reisner v vospominaniyakh sovremennikov* (Larisa Reisner Remembered by Her Contemporaries), ed. Yury Tomashevsky, Moscow, 1965, p. 35 (from now on LRRC).
17   Lev Nikulin, 'Years of Our Life', LRRC, p. 50.

and in the winter there were trips to the nearby ski resort of Kuzmolovo. The allotments behind the Leuchtenberg Building would be flooded to become the *Mon Plaisir* skating rink, and at the first sign of frost she would dash out with her skates and whirl round the ice, jumping over the blackened cabbage heads to practise her new moves.

Reisner remained under close police surveillance at the University, and he limited his activities there to discreet support for individual student causes. He was a popular and generous teacher, who paid the fees of his poorer students, several of whom he would support financially for the rest of his life, and all this was recorded in his criminal files. But accepting the job had lost him many of his old comrades, who accused him of selling out, and most of his academic colleagues hated his politics and resented his appointment. And his politics would cause him and his family yet more grief in the years to come.

A year into his new post, the story began to circulate at the University that the authorities were turning a blind eye to his socialism because he was an agent of the secret police. This was then repeated as fact in the academic history journal *The Past*, edited by the Reisners' friend from Finland Vladimir Burtsev, revered by socialists for his work exposing police spies in the revolutionary movement, and was soon picked up by other academic and political publications in Russia and abroad.

Burtsev was now running his well-funded and staffed 'Detective Bureau' in St Petersburg, known as the 'revolutionary police', which had recently achieved the spectacular coup of unmasking the leader of the Socialist Revolutionaries' Battle Organisation, Evno Azev, as a highly paid police double agent, involved in the assassinations of the Grand Duke Sergei and the Minister of the Interior von Plehve. It was only after the Revolution that Burtsev was exposed as a former police agent himself, and Reisner discovered that this man, who he had trusted as a good socialist and a good friend, had been gathering information against him all along. But as Karl Radek wrote:

> The great world of learning is essentially a tiny world of learned men. There is no muck, meanness or pettiness scholars won't use against an enemy. So the old gossip-monger Burtsev latched onto this bit of slander, and added his own jealousy and private grudges. For years Reisner struggled for his political honour against the 'one-eyed monster' from Peer Gynt – against slander, lies, whispering campaigns and insinuations that couldn't be challenged or brought to legal proceedings. At home, anxiety and despair took over. Larisa understood why the flat grew emptier, why her father paced up and down for hours, why his voice was heard less often, and why he built a wall between the university and his family.

His students organised protest meetings, and urged him to take Burtsev to court. But defending himself would have meant acknowledging his links with the revolutionary movement, which would have cost him his job, and possibly put him in jail. In desperation, he published his pamphlet *To Public Opinion. My Case Against Burtsev*, which ended, 'This is how the slander against me was hatched, a professor and teacher of the young, whose only compensation for all he has suffered is knowing that his conscience is clear'.

But the mud stuck, as it was intended to. Although he remained one of Russia's most respected academic authorities in constitutional law, he found himself increasingly ostracised by his colleagues and former comrades, and for a while he was close to suicide. Torn between work and politics, he retreated into his family.

The Reisners were fiercely protective of their children, and committed to their education. Fifteen-year-old Larisa was moved from the Balabanova Academy to the more academically challenging D.T. Prokofieva girls' *gimnazium*, next to Igor's, and in addition to their school work, they had their own study programme at home with their father, reading books on sociology, philosophy and politics with him, and translations of the Greek and Latin classics. Both were regularly *otlichniki*, or top of the class, and their school reports were celebrated with family parties.

In 1910, Russia was plunged into mourning by the death of Tolstoy – who Tsar Nicholas called the 'evil genius of Russia'. A year later, the Tsar had put Russia's fate in the hands of his 'holy man' the peasant Rasputin, who preached 'redemption through sin', and claimed to have the powers to heal his haemophiliac son and heir, the Tsarevich Alexei.

After five years of savage reaction, the protest movement was on the rise again, and throughout 1911, Russia was swept with assassinations, strikes and student riots. Over four hundred terrorists and suspected terrorists were hanged that year. All universities were placed under police control, and 125 professors resigned in protest.

In September, Socialist Revolutionaries shot dead the Prime Minister, Pyotr Stolypin, outside the Kiev Opera House, after ten unsuccessful attempts on his life. Three months later, Burtsev's Detective Bureau sensationally exposed the role of the secret police in the assassination. This latest exposé of Burtsev's gave new weight to his allegations against Reisner, and those close to the family saw a new reserve and severity in their dealings with the world. But they had a loyal ally in their friend Andreev, who they had visited regularly since leaving Finland, and Reisner wrote the introduction to the first edition of Andreev's *Collected Works*, published in 1912. That year he also brought out his two-volume work *The State*, a collection of his law lectures and writings, which was favourably reviewed, and did much to restore his reputation at the University. And as the protest movement gathered momentum again, he began to emerge from his isolation, joining a strikers' support group in the city, raising hardship funds for the families of sacked workers, and speaking at student meetings.

Several of his students were said to be in love with Larisa, and with her large grey eyes, dimpled cheeks and long auburn hair, she was never short of male admirers. There was her skating partner Nikolai Totsky, who appears in *Requiem* as 'Urs', a Buddhist and pacifist who practised yoga. She was seen with another of her boyfriends by the young poet Georgy Ivanov, who was working as a courier for her father's publisher, and came to the flat to drop off some proofs. 'When no one opened the door, I let myself in', he wrote, 'and saw standing against the tall windows of the drawing-room a young naval cadet and a teenage girl, locked in a passionate embrace. She had her hands on his shoulder-straps, and he was carefully clutching her waist, like the couple in the English painting "The First Kiss". I don't know if it was their first, but it went on a very long time'.[18]

Larisa's cousin Ekaterina Sheremeteva told Przhiborovskaya her aunts saw her as a 'princess', bookish and strong-willed, who called herself a Marxist and a poet, and claimed to have read *Capital* when she was fourteen. Whatever the truth of this, she took her poetry very seriously, and her archives in Moscow's State Lenin Library contain two thick notebooks of her early verses. Like her father, her main inspiration was Blok, and the first poem in her first notebook *My Songs* ('dedicated to Goga'), was 'For Blok'.

She was becoming a writer in the 'Silver Age' of Russian literature – of Andreev and Gorky, of Blok and the Symbolists, and the new 'Acmeist' poets, Osip Mandelstam, Nikolai Gumilyov and Anna Akhmatova, who stood for a new 'Apollonian' clarity against the vagueness and 'Dionysian frenzy' of the Symbolists. The Symbolists saw poets as priests of an esoteric art, and women as their muses, elusive and mysterious, like Blok's 'Eternal Woman' – the 'myrrh-bearers', Akhmatova called them. Akhmatova wrote as a modern woman, witty, elegant and passionate, with an emotional intensity and technical perfection that have been compared to Pushkin's. Born Anna Gorenko, she published her first poetry collection under her adopted Tatar name in 1912, and from then on her future was assured, and she was lionised and imitated. The first woman writer with a significant readership in Russia, she inspired thousands of young women to be poets, who honoured her in their verses. Larisa first went to one

---

18   Georgy Ivanov, *Peterburgskie zimy* (Petersburg Winters), Moscow, 1928, p. 265. Republished Moscow, 2001.

of her poetry readings in St Petersburg when she was sixteen, and it would be the start of her lifelong love affair with her work.

In April 1912, three thousand miners at the British-owned Lena goldfields in Siberia (almost half of them women) came out on strike against their inhuman working conditions, and two hundred and seventy were shot dead by the army, leaving an equal number with life-changing injuries. The massacre set off riots and strikes across Russia, and Larisa joined her father at the large angry demonstration in the capital, which was violently broken up by the police. A month later, workers in Moscow marked the socialist holiday of May Day with a mass strike in honour of the Lena victims, ending in thousands of arrests.

The Tsar's new Minister of War, the imposing and incompetent General Sukhomlinov, a distant relative of Ekaterina Alexandrovna's, known as 'Rasputin in uniform', declared on coming to office 'I haven't read a military manual in twenty-five years!', and spent ten million roubles kitting out his officers in gold braid, in the belief that wars were won by the best-dressed troops. 1912 ended with the Russian army's brutal and disastrous occupation of Northern Persia, and the executions of over 1,200 Persians by tsarist forces.

It was in that year that a group of young Moscow poets calling themselves the Futurists, led by Vladimir Mayakovsky, burst on the scene to give a voice to the fightback, mocking the art for art's sake preoccupations of the Acmeists and Symbolists, attacking conventional rhyme and metre, celebrating the end of the old Russia with their invented 'trans-sense' language, and the rough slang of the streets. 'Gentlemen poets, aren't you tired of writing about palaces, love and lilac blossoms?' Mayakovsky wrote.

Larisa poured out a mass of poems about Russia's revolutionary struggles, few of them completed, raiding the family library in search of new subjects. She read works of politics and history, and immersed herself in the classics of European literature – the novels of Zola and Dickens, the poetry of Rainer Maria Rilke, Goethe and Schiller, and the plays of Shakespeare. And inspired by Shakespeare's great female characters (and perhaps by the female narrator in Akhmatova's 'Reading Hamlet' cycle), she started work on two essays about his tragic heroines Ophelia, 'passionate and powerful, struggling like Hamlet through a morass of lies', and the 'sorceress' Cleopatra.

It was Andreev who encouraged her to write her first play, for his journal *Wild Rose*. Apart from a few short stories filled with drunken overstatement and all-round despair, Andreev had virtually abandoned fiction to write for the stage – realistic plays about Russian life, and symbolist dramas – and the subject he suggested to her was the Greek legend of the lost island of Atlantis.

For the next eight months she worked on 'Atlantis' under his guidance, reading Plato's account of the story in his last *Dialogues*, and Thucydides' *History of the Peleponnesian Wars*, for its reports of floods and cataclysms in the Atlantic. But her main sourcebook was her father's two-volume *History of Ancient Socialism and Communism*, by the German historian and anthropologist Robert von Pöhlmann, a study of early utopian 'communist' cultures in South America and ancient Greece.

In Andreev's despairing vision of the world, the legend was the story of a once mighty civilisation descending into decadence and destruction. She made her play a parable about oppression and resistance, and its hero, a poor fisherman's son, a model of revolutionary courage, who dedicates his life to his people, and ultimately dies for them.

'Atlantis' opens as his lover dances with their newborn baby at the seashore, conjuring the rising waters of the ocean to retreat, and ends as he helps her and the people of the island to build boats and escape. 'Call him Happiness. Let him know the Golden song of Love and Creativity', he tells her as she sails off to safety with their son. And when he is killed by the island's rulers, he dies happy in the knowledge that they have left for freedom and a better life.[19]

19   'Atlantis' was published online in Russia in 2018 by the University Electronic Library.

CHAPTER 2

Student Life

In the summer of 1912, at the age of seventeen, Larisa left her *gimnazium* with top marks in all her exams except mathematics, with the gold medal awarded to Russia's best students. Jewish quotas were still in place at the universities, and women were still barred from full-time higher education. But in 1905, they had been allowed to attend university lectures with the special permission of the authorities, as 'unregistered auditors', and her gold medal won her a place as an external student at St Petersburg University, for courses in Law and Philology. She was also awarded a full place at St Petersburg's prestigious and progressive Psychoneurology Institute, with its policy of 'unrestricted admission to Jewish and women students'.

The Institute had opened in 1907, next to the University's Medical School on Vasilev Island, one of several dozen such institutes established in Russia over the past ten years, attached to the main universities, but funded by private wealthy liberal donors, and freer of police control. Its director was the neuroscientist Professor Vladimir Bekhterev, who the Reisners had met in Finland, known throughout the world for his research on the brain, founder of the new discipline of Psychoreflexology, forerunner of modern behavioural psychology.

Bekhterev had studied in Paris with Freud's mentor the neurologist Jean Charcot, and in St Petersburg with the great physiologist Pavlov, and he had developed his own theory of human reflexes, independent of Pavlov's, focused on the brain's role in the development of social relations. He saw psychoneurology as the key to understanding people as 'biosocial beings', and to creating a properly functioning society of 'harmonious personalities', free of class and social injustice, and in numerous popular and academic works, published in Russia and abroad, he explored the political implications of these new ways of studying the brain. He wrote of the 'golden idol of capital, that fearful enemy of humanity, which paralyses all strivings to mutual aid'. And at a conference of neurologists and psychiatrists in St Petersburg in 1909, he called on his colleagues to 'search for higher norms of life than under capitalism, and to place service to truth and goodness at the forefront of all our endeavours'.

Bekhterev recruited some of Russia's finest lecturers to his staff, many of them socialists, and his friend Reisner lectured in Law. The Institute was also a clinical treatment and research centre, with its own neurology, psychiatric and epilepsy hospitals and children's clinic, and its drug and alcohol rehabilitation programmes. As well as students' broad programme of courses in history, philosophy, languages and literature, psychology, biology and physics, they attended his lectures on Psychoreflexology, and he encouraged them to join him in all his research projects. He took personal responsibility for their welfare, welcomed Jews and women, and set up a Jewish Fund, which offered free places to those without money.

The Institute was known throughout Europe for its pioneering research, and its enlightened holistic approach to learning, its tutorial system similar to that at Oxford and Cambridge, its excellent staff-student relations, and its lively political atmosphere. Despite frequent threats to sack Bekhterev and his 'anti-government professoriate', the Ministry of Education was reluctant to antagonise his powerful supporters abroad and risk international outrage, or to offend his wealthy donors in Russia, and even the Tsar was known to be an admirer of his popular writings on the brain.[1]

In the months before term started, Larisa sat up until dawn wrestling with her Shakespeare essays and 'Atlantis', her 'verse play for reading'. Five acts and eight scenes long, with its ballet scenes and realistic sea settings, and enormous cast of over forty characters, it was written in the lofty ornamental style appropriate to its subject matter, and her editor at *Wild Rose*, Solomon Kopelmann, had demanded drastic cuts. She spent the month of August with her aunt in Lublin, reworking it according to his instructions. To her mother she wrote:

> You know the joy and grief it's giving me. The worst thing is I just can't lose as much as he wants. Every line seems essential, as if it's all cast from one block ... I grind and polish – god knows what it costs me, I'll return it to him covered in blood and bruises. At least Andreev doesn't find too much to criticise in the first two acts. If Kopel wants more cuts I'll refuse. I feel with my whole being that it would be against my artistic principles ... For heaven's sake write and tell me how it will be published – will it really be in pieces, in instalments?[2]

In September she returned to St Petersburg for the start of the academic year, and her ambitious programme of courses. Bekhterev called his classes at the Institutute 'laboratories of ideas', and she joined his 'Immortality Project', investigating how people's behaviour affected others after their death, and took new forms – what he termed the 'transference of psychoneurological energy'.

---

1 For valuable information about Bekhterev's work at the Institute, see John McKay, *Dziga Vertov: Life and Work*, 2018.
2 Quoted in Eleonora Solovei, *Larisa Reisner. Ocherk zhizni i tvorchesta* (*Larisa Reisner. A Sketch of her Life and Work*), Moscow, 1985, pp. 29–31.

The University was a far less welcoming place for women, and she was the only one on her Philology course. The student Vsevolod Rozhdestvensky recalled her first appearance in the lecture hall. 'We were waiting for our professor to arrive, when a tall elegant young woman walked in, wearing a plain grey suit of English cut, a white blouse and man's tie, with her braided hair wound round her head like a crown. There was something proud and un-Russian about her, with her regular features and sharp playful eyes'.

A few students catcalled, and blushing with embarrassment, she made for the seat next to him and took out her exercise-book and pencil. Professor Zelinsky arrived and delivered his lecture, pretending not to notice her, and she scribbled away so furiously that her pencil broke, and she asked Rozhdestvensky peremptorily for a knife.[3]

She continued to cover her shyness in haughty silence, until one day she strode up to him at the student noticeboard, raised her hand in salutation, and questioned him earnestly about the poetry he was writing. Her awkwardness vanished, and she became part of his group of poet friends – four from the University, Georgy Maslov and Anna Regat, Viktor Trivus and Vladimir Zlobin, and Igor Ilinsky, Semyon Roshal and Mikhail Koltsov from the Psychnoneurology Institute.

Some like Larisa were from élite St Petersburg families, others had to work to support themselves. Rozhdestvensky, the son of a village priest, tutored schoolchildren. The Jewish Roshal and Koltsov both had their fees paid by the Institute, and covered their rent by loading timber on the railways. Roshal was from a poor Jewish family in the town of Orienbaum, fifty miles from the capital. Seventeen-year-old Koltsov, born Moisei Friedland, the son of a Jewish shoemaker from Kiev, had escaped the Jewish quota by renaming himself after the great Russian peasant poet of the 1830s, Alexei Koltsov. Anna Regat was the non-Jewish name adopted by Elena Tager, born into a family of St Petersburg Jewish intellectuals who had converted to Chistianity. The poet Osip Mandelstam, in his second year at the University, studying Romance Languages, had travelled to Finland in 1911 to be baptised into the Finnish Methodist Church – the famous 'Finnish baptism' used by Jewish intellectuals wishing to enter the universities. The Jewish Boris Pasternak, studying in Moscow, had been pragmatically baptised into the Orthodox Church at birth by his nanny.

In 1912, Larisa's father's tennis partner the young artist Vasily Shukhaev, who had a studio on the top floor of the Leuchtenberg Building, painted the portrait of her that now hangs in Moscow's Museum of Literature. She is depicted

---

3   Vsevolod Rozhdestvensky, 'Yunost nashikh dnei' (The Youth of our Days), LRRC, pp. 15–42.

as an icon, sitting before a half-open window against a majestic background of rocks and sky, her long fingers clasping an open book, and she is mysterious and strangely stiff and unyouthful. Rozhdestvensky wrote that none of her friends thought it looked anything like her, and that despite her sometimes imperious manner, students found her not so daunting after all, with a passion for dancing, tennis, ice-skating, horseriding and books, light and serious.

The law student Lydia Rosenblum, whose University fees were paid by Larisa's father, remembered the women students meeting in the canteen to discuss their work and their latest outfits, competing to be the best dressed. She recalled Larisa arriving at a student party once in a pink and orange striped silk dress with a ribboned sash, and begging to swap it for her plain white blouse – 'I'd have let her have it, but it would have been too small for her!'[4]

But her closest student friendships were with men, and she would remain friends with Rozhdestvensky, Ilinsky and Koltsov for the rest of her life. And in taking on men's rights and privileges, she was also sharpening her formidable talent for puncturing male egos, which she would later use to such effect in her writings.

Ilinsky remembered an ambitious young sociology professor at the Psychoneurology Institute 'delivering a lecture loaded with phrases such as "cumulative collective aggregates", and in the discussion afterwards, he sought the opinion of Larisa Mikhailovna. She replied gravely, with modestly lowered eyes, that his lecture "shone with rare erudition, but had neglected to mention the work of Stoll and Schmidt on demographic complexes". Pride forced the professor to reply that although familiar with their work, he found little of value there in comparison with the Anglo-American school'. The secret being that 'Stoll & Schmidt' were manufacturers of German bathroom goods, and Ilinsky imagined him searching for them in the libraries of Berlin forever afterwards.[5]

Ilinsky wrote that most of the students were in love with her, and Vladimir Zlobin had even followed her home once to beg her to marry him, and she had shown him the door. Rozhdestvensky described their friendship developing over the next year into a 'student romance,' and their long walks around St Petersburg together, exploring the islands in the white nights of summer, rowing on the River Neva, sitting on the steps of the Embankment discussing the poetry of Mandelstam, Bely and Blok.

Like thousands of young women in Russia then, Larisa was in love with Blok, with his dreamy fallen angel looks, poet of St Petersburg and the 1905

---

4 Rosenblum in conversation with Przhiborovskaya (Przhiborovskaya 2008, p. 97).
5 Igor Ilinsky, 'Granyonyi talant' (A Cut-glass Talent), LRRC, pp. 119–23.

revolution. 1905 had been a spiritual cataclysm for him, of symbols and allusions, sacred, blasphemous and erotic, guided by his muse, his elusive 'Eternal Woman'. The defeat of the revolution had brought his mystical misty St Petersburg crashing to earth in wild nights of drink and music and gypsy women in the city's bars and brothels, inspiring some of his most beautiful poetry – of 'terrible caresses', and 'sacred traditions profaned in secret singing'.

Larisa opened Rozhdestvensky's eyes to the revolutionary language of these poems, and said they spoke the voice of the people. 'Her generous, romantic, complex nature was shaped both by the culture of the past, and by the experiences of struggle and exile', he wrote. She spoke of poetry as a sacred language, the language of the soul. He also saw her using poetry to mask her emotions and enhance her aura of glamour and mystery – 'which annoyed some, especially her tendency to hide behind unanswerable riddles, delivered with a sardonic smile'.

Her own poems then were mainly on weighty themes connected to her studies. Her 'Song of the Red Blood Corpuscles', published in Rozhdestvensky's memoirs, was written in the fashionable new 'biological' style, heavy with scientific metaphors:

> Driven eternally by the auricles' beat,
> Our untroubled people
> Drink from the ocean of inhaled strength
> And the oxygen of the sun ...[6]

As she struggled on with 'Atlantis', she was irresistibly drawn to the visual and verbal vividness of the Acmeists. They had shown her new ways of seeing the world, and they would influence her writing long after Russia was plunged into revolution. She was also repelled by this glamorous cotery who saw poetry as a refuge from the horrors of life in Russia and its struggles.

In 1912, urged on by Rasputin and his Minister of War General Sukhomlinov, the Tsar embarked on another disastrous costly expansionist war in the Balkans for control of the Ottoman Empire, which left over 120,000 dead, most of them Russians. Demonstrations, strikes and terror attacks exploded across Russia, and students rioted and occupied the universities. Reisner spoke at a student occupation of St Petersburg's Law Faculty, before the police broke in and made

---

6 Rozhdestvensky's student poems and later poetry published in I. Vasileva, *V. Rozhdestvensky. Ocherk zhizni i tvorchestva* (V. Rozhdestvensky. A Sketch of his Life and Work), Leningrad, 1983.

hundreds of arrests. He then led the campaign to defend them, and gave evidence at their trials.

That winter, he offered his services to the socialist Samsonievsky Society, which ran night classes for factory workers, travelling by horse-cab to the capital's Nevsky shipyard and the vast Obukhov and Putilov armaments plants, and to the munitions factory in Sestroretsk twenty miles away, giving lectures in shabby workers' halls on literature, philosophy and politics, learning about the latest strikes, making new contacts in the revolutionary underground.

1913 opened with a blaze of celebrations for the third centenary of the Romanov dynasty – 'to inspire reverence and popular support for the glorious history of the Autocracy, and the mystical union between the Tsar and His Orthodox subjects'. The streets of St Petersburg were lined with monumental portraits of tsars and double-headed Romanov eagles and imperial coats-of-arms, and all Nicholas's power and wealth were on display at his dazzling banquets in the Winter Palace for his princes, grand dukes, generals and government ministers. In February, his family proceeded in the royal carriage from the Palace to the Kazan Cathedral, for a grand service of blessing, then set off by steamer along the River Volga to the ancient town of Kostroma, site of the coronation in 1613 of the first Romanov, Tsar Mikhail, where a model 'Potemkin village' had been built for him.

This spectacle of tsarist insanity and wastefulness triggered a wave of political strikes across Russia, intended to paralyse the regime – on the trams and railways, in the factories, mines and postal services. In March, the new socialist holiday of International Women's Day was celebrated in Russia for the first time, backed by the Social Democrats. Five thousand women in St Petersburg occupied the Stock Exchange, demanding access to the universities, equal pay and the vote, before the police arrived to arrest them, and there were women's demonstrations in Moscow and the cities of Samara, Tbilisi and Kiev. Two months later, a quarter of a million in the capital celebrated the workers' holiday of May Day with a mass strike. 'The searches and arrests turned the workers' quarters upside down', Lenin wrote. 'The government seemed to lose its wits, and the gentlemen factory-owners behaved as if they had never had any wits at all, first punishing the strikers with lockouts and jail, then offering them bribes and concessions. And the workers laughed at the impotence of the Tsar and his capitalist gang'.

The upheavals found their expression in an explosion of new art forms, and a new language of protest and resistance. The Futurists mocked bourgeois propriety and philistinism at their poetry events in workers' clubs and on the streets. Vsevolod Meyerhold, artistic director of St Petersburg's Imperial Alexandrinsky Theatre, staged his avant-garde productions of the Russian classics.

The Ballets Russes production of Igor Stravinsky's ballet 'The Rite of Spring' opened that May in Paris, and produced riots. Artists became set-designers and poets, poets became artists, and the painters Natalia Goncharova, Mikhail Larionov and Kazimir Malevich were changing the face of European art with the new visual language of abstractionism. Malevich's famous 'Black Square', marking the 'zero-point of art', first appeared on the curtain of the Futurists' opera 'Victory Over the Sun', performed that summer in St Petersburg's Luna Amusement Park – alternating with Mayakovsky's verse drama 'Mayakovsky. A Tragedy', directed by the author, who played himself as a blaspheming parody of Christ, with his supporting actors wearing white hoods, their faces covered in cardboard boxes.

Two years later, Malevich's 'Square' was exhibited at the Futurists' first exhibition in the capital, hanging in the place traditionally reserved for the icons. The opening broke up in a brawl, and the exhibition moved on with great success to Berlin, Munich, Amsterdam, Brussels and London.

None of this turmoil was visible in the Acmeists' journal *Apollo*, printed on the finest paper, filled with beautifully crafted poetry inspired by images from 'Helleno-Christian culture', whose end, the Apollonians believed, was near. 'Life was suffocatingly hard, reality was loathsome, and all hopes were pinned on the fall of tsarism', wrote the poet Vera Inber. 'There was no beauty anywhere, just its surrogate, aestheticism, which allowed a generation of Russia's intelligentsia to sip reality through a straw and find it bearable'.[7]

The Reisners' friend Andreev was drinking heavily by then, and when he became unable to care for eleven-year-old Vadim, they offered to look after him. He moved in with them in the autumn of 1913, and after the chaos in his father's house, he found it hard at first to adjust to the orderly routine of their lives, and their daunting insistence on perfect table manners – 'it was a sin to use the wrong fork, a great sin to put one's elbows on the table, and a mortal sin, never forgiven by anyone, to eat with an open mouth'. But he soon felt part of the family and was joining their conversations. 'It was as if they weren't a family of four, but one person', he wrote. 'Every joy or sorrow was a joy or sorrow shared by all'.

He immediately loved Ekaterina Alexandrovna, for her attentiveness to everything that was important to him, especially his love for his father. He was sent to the same school as fifteen-year-old Igor, who showed him 'the authority that comes with academic success. No one could toss their head like him, or

---

7   Vera Inber, 'Evolyutsia lebedya' (Evolution of a Swan); first published in 1927 in the journal *Red Virgin Soil*, republished in Inber's *Complete Works*, Moscow, 1966, vol. 4, pp. 274–5.

emerge with dignity from a difficult situation, or quieten an over-excited classmate with a glance'. Mikhail Andreevich gave him socialist pamphlets to read and told him about the strike movement, and took him to his workers' classes in poor suburbs of the city Vadim had never heard of, where he met factory workers for the first time, in their caps and overalls.

Reisner spoke with great emotion, without notes, Vadim wrote, and his classes were always packed. His lectures were carefully prepared to be accessible to his students, but he never talked down to them, and Vadim remembered the thrill of recognition in the audience when he spelt out the revolutionary message of H.G. Wells's novel *The War of the Worlds*.

'Being a "Reisner" filled me with pride', he wrote. 'It was with the Reisners that I felt for the first time a recognition of my childish self, and became someone people spoke to seriously, as an equal. Breathing in the tender severe air around me, I began to live with interests, their likes and dislikes, and learned more from them than from anyone else in my life'.

He remembered family evenings after dinner:

> Igor, the star, would talk like a grown man about politics, music and the theatre, frowning and waving his arms, and Ekaterina Alexandrovna would hush him with a joke and a story. Mikhail Andreevich would sit carefully balancing a saucer under his glass, murmuring the occasional observation. Larisa would sit silent and aloof, with lowered eyes, looking up suddenly to utter a clever rather mannered aphorism, then falling back into enigmatic silence.

Five years earlier, they had been children playing on the beach, and when Vadim wrote his memoirs of the Reisners in 1919, she was already a famous writer and revolutionary.

> In 1913, she was a young girl who had recently left the *gimnazium*, and was writing decadent verses and dreaming of revolution, because in the Reisner family it was impossible not to, but enjoying even more the radiance of her youth and her unusual beauty – her large grey eyes and her pale hands like white butterflies, flying up to adjust her hair, which was wound round her ears like shells.
>
> Even the coarsest objects seemed to gain a new tenderness in her presence. I remember the pride I felt when I walked along the narrow streets of the St Petersburg Side with her. Not one man passed without stopping to observe her, and according to the author's own statistical evidence, every third would stand rooted to the spot as we disappeared into the crowd …

Few men escaped the fate of falling desperately in love with her. But any who dared speak of their feelings would be permanently banished, like a heretic from church ...

It was Larisa who showed him that the most important thing in life was to write poetry. Like her father, she wrote in a trance of inspiration. He remembered coming home from school to find her 'pacing the twilit drawing-room like a ghost, in a long white shirt, her loose hair falling over her face, hurrying to the desk to scribble a line with a pencil, then pacing again, gazing through the frosted window, murmuring "The youth, in love with the ringing dawn ..."'.

'Her voice and the rhythm of her steps were sweet music to me', Vadim wrote, 'and seized by this creative atmosphere, I began to write poems too, not casually, but as a matter of necessity'.[8]

She would read her work at meetings of the University's new Poetry Circle. The Circle was small, Rozhdestvensky wrote, but it took its role very seriously. 'We dreamed of liberating poetry from the language of Symbolism, which had recently enslaved us, and revealing to the world a new expressive freely intonated poetic language. Our programme was ambitious, but we would settle for nothing less, for in the naivety of our youthful enthusiasm, we considered ourselves the arbiters of taste'.

The group put out a scruffy poetry magazine, *Bohème*, printed at the University and edited by Larisa, whose opening statement declared: 'We are bohemians, restless, rootless, turbulent, forever seeking and not finding, creating new idols, and abandoning them in the name of a new god'.

Published in this first issue was Mandelstam's poem to Larisa, 'Madrigal':

> The room is filled with blue tomacco mist.
> A mermaid stands before us, shimmering with seaweed,
> Ashamed she hasn't learnt the art of smoking.
> The burning embers scald her parted lips.
> She doesn't notice her dress smouldering,
> As the ashes fall on its green silken wisps ...[9]

New writers were recruited, who met to read their works in each other's homes, shabby student rooms and comfortable flats like the Reisners'. (Blok was given a free subscription, but declined to contribute). Rozhdestvensky recalled her

---

8   Andreev 1966, pp. 76–7.
9   From Mandelstam's *Complete Collected Works*, Moscow, 1994, p. 176.

declaiming in elated tones her poem about St Petersburg, the Tsars' capital, where Pushkin had offered a prayer for Russia with his dying breath:

> Peter's granite
> Barely covered the swamps,
> And Benckendorff ruled
> Where once ruled the Graces ...[10]

Other poems of hers were inspired by her visits to the Hermitage Gallery, and by the new 'artistic' school of poetry, with its heady blend of the macabre and the gothic, in the style of Gogol, Andreev and Edgar Allan Poe. In 'The Hermitage', she evoked the demonic imagery of Mikhail Vrubel's painting 'The Gorgon' to depict the artist in tragic conflict with reality, unable to escape through aestheticism:

> The exhausted day subsides,
> Fearing to squander the April warmth.
> The dead Vrubel on the wall
> Breaks the curdled seal of horror ...
>
> There is no limit to toil or desire.
> The Gorgon's head on the canvas
> Laughs grotesquely through its groans,
> And the hand clenches in fury to a fist ...

Her parents were boundlessly supportive of her writing, and the publication of her first poem in *Bohème* was celebrated with a week of family parties. But friendly student discussions were a good antidote to too much praise, and her various and unusual themes and images came in for a great deal of criticism from her fellow poets.

Bohème also made contact with young poets in Moscow, among them the economics student Lev Nikulin, from the well-known Jewish acting family in Ukraine the Olkonitskys, who like others had changed his name to escape the Jewish quota. He sent Larisa his poems, but it would be three years before they met in person, and in those years they communicated through letters and poetry. 'Her language was bright and romantic and full of paradoxes, and

---

10 This and the next poem are published in Rozhdestvensky's memoirs.
    The hated Count von Benckendorff, special adviser to Tsar Nicholas I, founder of the Third Section, the Secret Police, who in 1837 orchestrated Pushkin's death at the age of thirty-eight in a duel.

she was proud of her "male mind", although she wasn't without sentimentality either', he wrote.[11]

Nikulin thought she often allowed her love of beautiful writing to cloud her judgment, and she did not always appreciate his criticisms of her poetry – 'who does?' But she enjoyed the sharp and often noisy meetings of the Poetry Circle, at which students would praise and tear apart each other's work. She had learnt from her mother how to hold her own in discussions, and Rozhdestvensky was impressed by her ability to keep her cool when arguments became heated.

In the winter of 1913, as she was putting the finishing touches to 'Atlantis', she was exploring the city's nightlife with her friends, and reading her poems at the Stray Dog Café, the wildly popular hangout for the capital's poets, artists, musicians and dancers, later the setting for a long section of her novel *Requiem*.

The Stray Dog had opened a year earlier, in the disused wine cellars of a mansion on the Square of the Arts, near the Summer Gardens, home to the aristocratic Dashkov family, philanthropists and patrons of the arts. Its proprietor, the theatre director Boris Pronin, was known for his 'magical art' productions, and he made the decor a magical stage-set for his cast of 'stray dogs' – lit with coloured lanterns and heated with a blazing log fire, its walls and ceilings covered with paintings of fantastic birds and flowers by the Ballets Russes set-designer Sergei Sudeikin, inscribed with verses from Baudelaire's *Fleurs du Mal*.

Anna Akhmatova and the poet Nikolai Gumilyov presided, Akhmatova in black silk, Gumilyov in his frock coat, and guests stayed from midnight until dawn, and signed their names in a thick volume bound in pigskin. For the élite, entry was free. Everyone else, known as the 'pharmacists' – including the usual scattering of police spies – paid a membership fee of twenty-five roubles, roughly the average Russian worker's annual wages.

The Café was famous for its *tableaux vivants*. Gumilyov's friend and first biographer Pavel Luknitsky recalled its spectacular staging of Herod's Massacre of the Innocents, for which 'twenty orphans were borrowed from the local orphanage to pass between the tables, dressed in white, with golden wigs and silver wings, holding lighted candles in their hands'.[12]

Tamara Karsavina, premiere ballerina of the Ballets Russes, 'goddess of the air', danced on a giant mirror to Couperin's 'Pastorale', arranged for cello and piano. There were 'Musical Mondays', with piano recitals of Ravel, Debussy and Schoenberg, and the shimmering soundscapes of Rachmaninoff and Alex-

---

11 Lev Nikulin, *Vospominaniya i vstrechi* (Memories and Meetings), Moscow, 1939. Republished in his book *Lyudi i stranstviya* (People and Travels), 1962, pp. 90–1.
12 Vera Luknitskaya, *Nikolai Gumilyov. Zhizn poeta po materialam domashnego archiva semi* (Nikolai Gumilyov. Life of the Poet from the Family Archives), Leningrad, 1990, p. 129.

ander Scryabin. Larisa's contemporary at the Psychoneurology Institute David Kaufman performed his Scryabin-inspired 'sound collages', composed at the Institute's Laboratory of Hearing he had set up with Bekhterev.[13] The young composer Ilya Satz, a distant cousin of hers, played his compositions for 'prepared piano', an early form of *musique concrète*. And she described marathon poetry readings – 'twenty-year-old epicureans warming their backs against the great fireplace, whose jaws could heat all the poets in the world, waiting in agony to read their verses, endlessly similar to each other and to their authors, with their dishevelled hair and faces of debauched night animals, like those in Van Gogh's "Café de Nuit"'.

In those years before the world was plunged into war, the Stray Dog was an escape into decadence, where people came to have sexual adventures and swap partners. Akhmatova's meditation on the fate of Russia, 'Poem Without a Hero', published after her death, opens with a gathering of poets partying the night away as Russia hurtles to its doom. In her 1913 poem 'Cabaret Artistique', she described wild nights at the Stray Dog:

> We're all harlots and libertines,
> We drink too much and we don't care.
> The walls are covered with birds and flowers
> That will never see the light.
> I put on my skinniest skirt to make me more svelte ...[14]

Akhmatova was known as the 'Russian Sappho', and fell in love with men and women, including the beautiful dancer and actress Olga Sudeikina. When the first Russian translations of Sappho's 'Fragments' were published in the eighteenth century, lesbianism was traditionally seen in Russia as confined to actresses, criminals and prostitutes, and she had been read as a heterosexual poet. But new translations in the 1890s had given lesbian love a name, and there was a rage for her poetry among liberated women in the capital.

Homosexual acts between men, 'sodomy' in the Penal Code, were officially punishable by five years' hard labour in Siberia – with three years' jail for lesbianism and 'perversions', and a whole range of 'unnatural' positions in heterosexual sex. But the law was rarely enforced, except in cases of child abuse and rape. The 1905 revolution had opened up previously taboo issues of gender

---

13 John MacKay writes fascinatingly about Kaufman's 'sound experiments' with Bekhterev in MacKay 2018.
14 All Akhmatova's poems quoted are from her 8-volume *Complete Works*, Moscow, 1998–2005. Gumilyov's are from his 3-volume *Collected Works*, Moscow, 1991.

and sexuality. The works of Oscar Wilde were widely read in St Petersburg, men could be seen openly cruising the streets, picking up soldiers and students for sex, and there was a flourishing homosexual life at the court, in the Imperial ballets and theatres, and in the city's bars, bath-houses and cafés.

The Stray Dog was at the centre of the capital's new gay cultural scene. The impresario Sergei Diaghilev, director of the Ballets Russes, visited with his dancers, and his friend the aesthete, musician and poet Mikhail Kuzmin, author of Russia's first gay male novel, *Wings*, sang his homosexual love songs there. The peasant poet Nikolai Klyuev openly had male lovers, including Blok's young protégé and disciple Sergei Esenin, who had recently arrived in the capital from his village to make his name as a poet. Mayakovsky, who later read his poems at the Stray Dog, described himself as 'omnisexual'.

Outside St Petersburg, homosexuality was widely seen as a 'foreign disease', which thrived only in the western environment of the capital. In St Petersburg too, many were fiercely hostile to the new permissiveness. Blok visited the Stray Dog occasionally with Esenin, but he preferred to send his wife there to read his poems, and in his diaries he described it as a 'dead place'. He disliked Gumilyov and Akhmatova, personally and as poets, and he was revolted by Diaghilev and his queer crowd: 'He says art is a stimulus to sensuality, and he's not the only one ... Everything about him is significant and dreadful, including his "active" homosexuality ... A terrible impression, a terrible epoch. Reality has so far outstripped imagination ...'[15]

Akhmatova and Gumilyov had been married for three years, and they had a two-year-old son. But apart from their frequent public appearances, and despite sharing a flat with his half-sister and his elder brother and his wife, they lived virtually separate lives.

Before marrying him Akhmatova had told a friend, 'Gumilyov is my destiny. I swear by all that is holy that this unfortunate man will be happy with me'. None of her family attended the wedding, believing neither of them was serious about the marriage and it would be disaster, and he left her soon afterwards to travel in Africa for two months. He spent the night she was giving birth getting drunk in bars, and the baby had then been sent to live at his grandmother's estate, far from the capital.

Akhmatova's childhood friend Valeriya Sreznevskaya, who had first introduced them, saw Gumilyov as irresistibly attracted to her, and envious of her talent and popularity. 'They weren't a pair of cooing turtle doves. Their relation-

---

15   Sjen Scheijen, *Diaghilev. A Life*, 2010, p. 145.

ship was more like a secret duel, between her affirmation of her status as a free woman, and his desire to remain independent and not submit to her enchantment – powerless alas against this eternally elusive, many-sided woman, who refused to submit to anyone'.[16]

His affairs were his main weapon against her, but they rarely lasted. 'You couldn't call her beautiful, but all my happiness is in her', he wrote in 1912 in his poem to her 'I Know a Woman. Silence'.

Akhmatova saw her place in his affections differently in her poem 'He Loved' a year later:

> Three things he loved in the world,
> White peacocks, evensong,
> Faded maps of America.
> He didn't like bawling infants,
> Or raspberry jam with his tea,
> Or women's hysteria.
> And I was his wife.

Gumilyov was her greatest admirer and her fiercest rival. Worldly, brilliant, successful, teacher and leader of poets, by 1913 he had published four volumes of poetry, philosophical and intensely personal, glowing with colour and adventure, many written during his travels in Abyssinia (modern Ethiopia), where he had hunted lions and elephants, and was entertained at the court of Ras Tafari, the future Emperor Haile Selassie. Hundreds of his poems were written to women he fell instantly in love with, often several at a time, and just as instantly lost interest in. And as in most of these poems they were a generic 'she', they could be re-dedicated from one to the next – 'behaviour that strikes our modern sensibility as frankly tasteless', writes his new Russian biographer, Valery Shubinsky.[17]

He divided them into two types, powerful independent ones like Akhmatova, and younger sexually inexperienced ones, preferably virgins, according to Akhmatova, the more unavailable the better.

In *Requiem*, Larisa described the night of poetry and lust when she first caught his eye at the Stray Dog:

---

16   Sreznevskaya's unpublished memoirs quoted in Luknitskaya 1990, p. 136.
17   Valery Shubinsky, *Nikolai Gumilyov. Zhizn poeta* (Nikolai Gumilyov. Life of the Poet), St Petersburg, 2004.

He is sitting with the beautiful people, under an arch painted with twining grapevines, discussing God and love over endless cups of black coffee. He is ugly, with a long narrow face and ruthless sullen brow, like one of Velasquez's portraits of the Spanish princes. His slightly squinting eyes have a fixed bewitching gaze, and his sensual lips move constantly, scanning verses about the night, the death of hope, and a white silent monastery. There is no window covered in virginal hoar-frost the poet cannot melt with his breath, no enchanted garden, flowering in the northern spring, from which his bold hands cannot pluck a bunch of lilac, damp with dew, drunk on the sun ...

He is looking at her with an aching tenderness, an almost physical pain. When this unknown girl, nervously clutching her poems, blushing with embarrassment, is asked to read, all the scars his critics left on his soul when he was starting as a poet throb sweetly, and make them equals ...

High above the crowd, he smiles at her. 'What's she writing about?' he asks his companion.

'No idea, something odd, she must be a socialist'.

It was the start of his two-year campaign to seduce her. He had made clear his views of her poetry and her politics, but mixed messages were the key to his success with women. And in the words of his hero the Italian poet Gabriele d'Annunzio, 'Neither the strength of Hercules nor the beauty of Hippolytus has the power to attract women like fame'.

As a student in St Petersburg in 1905, he had been involved in socialist circles and had read Marx. But after discovering the works of Nietszche and d'Annunzio in his twenties, with their cult of beauty and hatred of the 'herd', he had described himself like them as 'apolitical'. D'Annunzio's heady mystical sensuality and appetite for violence had a huge influence on the Acmeists, particularly Gumilyov, and he had travelled to Rome the previous summer with Akhmatova to meet him. Both poets were ardent patriots and devout Christians, Gumilyov of the Russian Orthodox variety. Both saw the Poet as a Man of Destiny, who turns his life into his own poetry manifesto, and both played out their apolitical politics on the same grand scale.

The Belgian-born revolutionary Victor Serge first met him in Paris, three months after the Bolshevik Revolution. 'We were both trying to get into Russia, but for different reasons', Serge wrote. He was planning to leave for Petrograd to work with the Bolsheviks. Gumilyov was working for the Provisional Government in exile, and had volunteered to fight with the French Expeditionary Force in Russia to bring the Bolsheviks down. '"I am a traditionalist, monarchist, imperialist and Pan-Slavist," he said. "Mine is the true Russian nature, formed by Orthodox Christianity." And on these subjects we had many excellent discussions, and became fierce antagonists and firm friends'.[18]

Serge saw him as hopelessly ill-equipped for his role as saviour of Russia, and behind all the mystical bombast and machismo he saw a deeply sensitive tormented man – his loneliness and insecurity and hunger for approval, his need to be close to death to feel alive.

He had first attempted suicide in 1905, when Akhmatova first refused to marry him, driving her even further from him. Two years later, as a student in Paris, he had been involved with a circle of decadent poets who dabbled in the black arts – 'my old friend the Devil sings his last song to me' – and he had poisoned himself in the Bois de Boulogne (a forester rescued him). In 1909, he fought a duel with the poet Maximilian Voloshin, on the spot chosen by Pushkin for his fatal duel, after discovering that the mysterious woman he had been writing passionate love letters to had been Voloshin's fictional invention. He was fighting for his honour, and fired at Voloshin but missed; Voloshin confessed he didn't know how to use a gun. His third suicide attempt was a year later, after Akhmatova finally agreed to marry him, and told him she wasn't 'innocent'.

Like the colourful d'Annunzio, despite living on the edge, beyond the conventions of bourgeois morality, he held extremely conservative views of women. Poetry, philosophy and politics were to be discussed with men. Women, even powerful successful ones like Akhmatova, were expected to practise the Christian virtues of suffering, silence and self-sacrifice.

The writer and anthroposophist Margarita Tumpovskaya, with whom he had the longest of his affairs, who was deeply involved with him when he met Larisa, wrote of the 'chaos' of his emotional life:

> He takes a long and difficult path to the peace and unity he achieves in his art, and he finds them in constant change and movement ... He perceives the world not through thought or feeling, but through sensation. Not content with even the most vivid elements he can discover in real earthly life, he extends them to their limits, taking his poetry into the world of fantasy and hallucinations, which for him are simply extensions of reality ...[19]

Later after she had left him, Tumpovskaya commented sharply on his 'banal' attitude to women – 'submissiveness and happy laughter were all he wanted'.

---

18   Victor Serge, *Memoirs of a Revolutionary* (trans. Peter Sedgwick), 1978, pp. 59–60.
19   Tumpovskaya quoted in Luknitskaya 1990, p. 145.

Akhmatova would write many poems over the years about their tormented relationship – 'My husband, my executioner, whose house is my prison'. 'A whip hangs over the bed, to stop me singing my songs'. She told her friend Lydia Chukovskaya she had understood his attitude to sex after reading Freud – particularly the incest themes in much of his poetry, 'always trying to reproduce the same sexual setup as in childhood, the child marrying the mother, the mother oppressing the child and so on'.[20]

As an inexperienced eighteen-year-old, Larisa must have been completely out of her depth with his complicated relationship with Akhmatova and love life. But replacing her heroine would have clearly been unthinkable, and her alter ego in *Requiem* was cold and aloof with him, which made him more determined to conquer her.

The Acmeists and their Olympian dramas were a gift to the Futurists' mad punk performances at the Stray Dog. The poet Vasilisk Gnedov first read his *Death to Art* on its stage – fifteen one-line poems reduced from one line to one word, and finally the wordless 'Poem of the End', the title alone on a blank page, delivered with a sharp swing of the arm. There was 'Marinetti Week', to celebrate the visiting Italian Futurist poet Filippo Marinetti, and Mayakovsky made his debut there in 1913.

Since joining the Bolsheviks in Moscow six years earlier, at the age of fourteen, Mayakovsky had been arrested three times for his political activities, and had spent six months in jail. He was now touring Russia with the Futurists' manifesto, 'A Slap in the Face of Public Taste', which dumped ideas of 'good' and 'bad' writing, along with syntax, punctuation, 'Pushkin, Tolstoy, Dostoevsky and all the rest of them, from the steamship of modernity'.

He became a familiar figure at the Stray Dog, with his painted face and top hat and striped orange blouse, lying on a huge Turkish drum, banging it when his fellow Futurists read their work. Crowds gathered for his performances as he stormed the stage, hurling insults, mocking verse and metre and 'beautiful' writing, and women fainted when he declaimed his epic poem 'A Cloud In Trousers', published that year:

> Your thoughts
> in their brain of porridge
> like a bloated official on a greasy sofa,
> I'll mock them to death with a dripping shred of my heart.

---

20 Lydia Chukovskaya, *The Akhmatova Journals*, 1968, p. 28.

The poet strides the earth, with the sun as his monocle, holding Napoleon on a lead like a lapdog. He 'brandishes dirty fists at bright joy'. He is 'pure raging meat'. 'Or if you prefer I'll be absolutely tender – not a man, a cloud in trousers!'[21]

The Futurists' war with the Acmeists was the prelude to many literary battles after the Revolution, in which Larisa would defend them against the old guard. But for all their power and honesty, their assault on the great literature of the past was alien to her, and they never had any detectable influence on her writing.

In December, her Shakespeare essays were published as booklets by the Riga publishing house Science and Life, under the male pseudonym 'Leo Rinus'.[22] Her biographer Eleonora Solovei saw them as 'little better than school essays', but there were more family parties, and when a radically cut 'Atlantis' was finally published in *Wild Rose* in January, the celebrations lasted until the spring. But according to Rozhdestvensky she had already lost interest in the play by then, and would refuse to discuss it at Poetry Circle meetings. Getting it published had taught her the discipline she would later need as a writer. But she had buried its message of struggle and resistance in the language of an older generation of writers. Thousands of revolutionaries like her hero had sacrificed their lives to their beautiful ideals, and the only function of her heroine had been to be his muse and the bearer of his son. The Futurists wrote for the stage, not the printed page, and showed that plays were meant to be acted, not read. They were loud, cartoonish, grotesque, visceral and full-on, and they were finding new audiences in the factories and on the streets, turning the mood of despair into one of dynamism and hope – 'catching the rhythm of action, attack and destruction, fighting for their place in the sun', wrote Trotsky.

21 Mayakovsky poems quoted from his 3-volume *Selected Works* in English (trans. Dorian Rottenberg), Moscow, 1985–7.
22 'Zhensky tipy Shekspira: Ofelia i Kleopatra' (Shakespeare's Female Characters Ophelia and Cleopatra), *Nauka i zhizn* (Science and Life), nos. 25 and 34, Riga, 1913.

    Leo Rinus, eighteenth-century ancestor of her father's, Rector of Jena University, dedicatee of many of his works.

CHAPTER 3

Poets and War

Throughout the first months of 1914, almost half of Russia's workforce was out on strike. By May, mass street demonstrations had reached their highest levels since 1905, with barricades up in the cities. A month later, the strike movement had collapsed in a surge of anti-German feelings.

On 28 June, the Tsar's escalation of tensions with Austro-Hungary in the Balkans came to a head in Sarajevo, with the assassination of the Archduke Franz Ferdinand, heir to the Austro-Hungarian throne. On 28 July, Austria declared war on Serbia, and the Tsar ordered the mobilisation of the Empire's armed forces. On 2 August, Germany invaded Belgium, and declared war on Russia. 'Russia is ready!' declared the Minister of War General Sukhomlinov.

In Berlin, the Kaiser declared that he forgave his political enemies – 'I know no parties now, only Germans!' – and the leaders of the Social Democratic Party, the largest party in the Reichstag and the mighty Socialist International, with a membership of over a million, voted in support of his new War Budget, declaring 'civil peace' until the war was over, and 'the class struggle adjourned'.

Thousands in newly russified Petrograd were caught up in the war frenzy. The Tsar was greeted by crowds of his subjects on their knees outside the Winter Palace, singing the anthem the *Te Deum*, and soldiers marched off to the front singing war songs. The giant cast-iron horses on the roof of the German Embassy were thrown onto the street, German shops were wrecked and looted, and Russians with German names like the Reisners were suspected of being enemy agents.

Even the revered Georgy Plekhanov, whose writings had introduced Russia to the works of Marx in the 1880s, became an ardent patriot. Mayakovsky described his excitement in the first weeks of the war at its 'noisy decorative aspects', and although banned from the front as a 'subversive element', he volunteered as a draftsman at Petrograd's Military Automobile Institute, producing patriotic posters and verses. The Symbolist poets Fyodor Sologub and Vyacheslav Ivanov, although too old to enlist, appealed to Russia's 'young conscience' to 'join the battle for God's truth', and saw the war bringing about Russia's long-awaited 'miracle of transfiguration'. For Gumilyov, the war was a necessary cleansing of the old order, a chance to test his courage and discover the mystery of his soul, and he enlisted immediately as a private in the Empress Alexandra's élite Cavalry Regiment of Uhlans, and left for the East Prussian front, accompanied by Akhmatova.

Akhmatova and others did benefit poetry readings to raise money for the wounded. The only major poet in Russia to speak out against the war from the start was Blok, who called it 'the worthy crown to the lies, filth and vileness in which our homeland is drowning'.

Of the sixty-five million soldiers mobilised from the thirty combatant countries over the next four years, the largest number, fifteen million, were Russians, a third of the adult male population. And of the nine million killed in battle, three million were Russians, mostly workers and peasants, fighting in the inferno of the trenches, away from their families for months, even years at a time, completely untrained to survive the new weapons of tanks and poison gas, and gassed to death in their thousands.

Fatally weakened by the Tsar's adventures in the Balkans, the army suffered its first major defeat two weeks after war was declared, when the invincible Russian 'Steamroller' was thrown into Eastern Prussia, and was smashed after three weeks of bloody fighting, with the loss of over fifty thousand lives.

In his place of exile in neutral Switzerland, Lenin analysed the class interests of the war, as a dynastic struggle for foreign markets and colonies – 'launched to divide and decimate the proletariat of all countries, by sending the wage slaves of one state against those of another, to the profit of the bourgeoisie'. The major capitalist states were fighting to divide the resources of their colonies and the smaller weaker nations between them, he wrote in his pamphlet *Imperialism. The Highest Stage of Capitalism*. The imperialist war must be transformed into a revolutionary class war against capitalism, and he called on soldiers to fraternise and desert, and turn their guns on their real enemies, the criminals responsible for the slaughter.

He would repeat this message over the next three years in thousands of articles, letters and pamphlets, smuggled out of Switzerland across Europe into Russia, and to frontline soldiers in the warring countries. He was supported by the small left anti-war minority in the International, led by Liebknecht and Rosa Luxemburg in the German party, and by radicals in the French, Serbian, Bulgarian and American socialist parties. Luxemburg called the International 'a stinking corpse', and its politics 'the politics of the swamp'. Social Democracy was dead, Lenin said. Marxists must reclaim the name of internationalism by building a new anti-war communist one. But they were isolated and arguing virtually alone, against the great majority of socialists who had turned patriots.

The Reisners were acutely depressed by the collapse of the German socialist party, and they lost many of their old friends in Russia, including Andreev, who was woken by the war to write patriotic propaganda, and ordered poor Vadim home.

Soon after he left, the family fostered another boy, twelve-year-old Lev Dauge, the son of their Latvian friend Pavel Dauge, a dental surgeon in Riga, who had translated the works of Marx and Engels into Latvian, and was deeply involved in Latvia's Bolshevik underground, facing the daily threat of arrest, and he asked the Reisners to give Lev a safe home in Petrograd.

Lev quickly became part of the family, and people meeting him with Larisa and Igor for the first time would assume he was their brother. A year later, the Reisners adopted him and he took their name, and he lived with them until he was seventeen, two years after the Revolution, when he volunteered as a junior seaman in the Baltic Fleet – registering himself in his papers as 'Lev Mikhailovich Reisner', with the surname and patronymic of his adopted father.

Sadly, though, there is nothing in Larisa's published writings about him, and the only evidence of their relationship is a photograph of them together at the front in 1920. Her cousin Ekaterina Sheremeteva told Przhiborovskaya she created a rift between the two families by being rude to his father, which was considered particularly inexcusable as it was Dauge who had arranged for his Riga publishers to publish her Shakespeare essays.

Sheremeteva spoke of her passionate fiery relationship with her mother, and their frequent rows and reconciliations. And she quarrelled with her mother's elder sister. 'Dearest Auntie, please forgive me', she wrote to her after staying with her in Lublin. 'I know I was unbearable, but sometimes I'm so overcome with grief and rage I can't see clearly, and I don't want to. It's a sort of madness, and your harsh words to me in those dark lonely moments were nothing compared to the shame I've felt and the tears I've wept. Be happy and healthy and beautiful, and kiss Uncle for me. Your Lyalya'.

There were also complaints of her rudeness from the Reisners' neighbour in the Leuchtenberg Building Vladimir Svyatlovsky, the Duke's business manager. 'You think because I'm female I'll be upset by your criticisms of my little hooligan', her mother wrote to him. 'No Volodya, no one can offend me on the "children issue". Despite all the trouble she's made, starting at her first *gymnazium*, I never stop hoping she'll become a decent person one day'.[1]

Arguments about the war at the University were often ending in fistfights. The Poetry Society's magazine *Bohème* had been closed by military censorship, but students were exempt from conscription until they had finished their courses. Bekhterev spoke at anti-war meetings at the Psychoneurology Institute, and Larisa's friend Semyon Roshal at the Institute had immediately joined the Bolsheviks. But many more students were signing up at officer training schools, and leaving for the front.

---

1 Przhiborovskaya 2008, pp. 86, 149–151.

By the end of 1914, patriotism was turning to anger and despair. The ill-led ill-equipped tsarist army was being cut to pieces by the Germans, and Russia's defeat seemed beyond question. Soldiers blamed 'dark forces' at the court and the evil Rasputin and 'Bloody Nicholas'. The Tsar blamed the Jews – 'nine-tenths of Russia's troublemakers are Jews' – and mass conscriptions of Muslims and Jews turned into massacres.

Petrograd's hospitals filled with the wounded and dying, and the capital became a harsh, hungry, xenophobic place of hoarding, speculation and rocketing food prices, crowded with spies and speculators and refugees and the starving unemployed, with thousands of orphaned and abandoned children on the streets. Patriotic songs and posters were filled with Christian images of female sacrifice, of women serving their country as 'sisters of mercy', and sending their sons and husbands to die in Russia's 'holy war'. The reality was broken families and motherless children, as women took over men's jobs, driving the trains, trams and buses, toiling all day in the munitions factories.

Two weeks into the war, Mayakovsky had abandoned his government propaganda work, and was calling on Futurists to invent new words for the horror and suffering – 'exploding with the force of landmines'.

The young literary theorist Victor Shklovsky, in his 1914 pamphlet 'The Resurrection of the Word', called the Futurists demystifiers of poetry, whose stripping away of the labels attached to the world by social convention was the essence of great art, expanding the limits of language, offering new opportunities to investigate and change the world. Shklovsky later developed these ideas in his essay *Art as Device*, published two months after the Revolution, in which he first formulated his ground-breaking 'defamiliarisation' theory of art. Art was 'thinking through images', he wrote. 'The purpose of the image is not to bring meaning closer to our understanding, but to create a special perception of the subject – not "recognition," but its own "vision"'.

At the age of nineteen, Larisa knew she was going to be a writer. The problem was knowing what to write about. Rozhdestvensky reported that she was working on an opera libretto, 'Mukhomor' ('Fly Agaric'), a satire on the poet and self-styled religious prophet Dmitry Merezhkovsky, and his druggy band of followers. But she complained to Rozhdestvensky that like her characters in 'Atlantis' they were just mouthpieces for ideas, and she was unable to bring them to life:

> 'I've forgotten how to understand simple natural things', she said, 'I always have to sharpen and complicate them'.
>
> 'But how is that?' I asked her. 'You write about sunsets and nature, don't you love our Finnish sand dunes and lakes?'

'No, I don't, it's just a trick of the heart. I try to convince myself I do, but I'm actually indifferent to nature'.

'And people?'

'People are different. But again I want them to be complicated and extraordinary, not as we are now, but as we'll be in the future, which I love and don't know yet. But I don't want to talk about people, I'll get carried away and there'll be no stopping me, I'd rather listen instead'.[2]

In the autumn of 1914, Gumilyov had been thrown headfirst into the bloody battles for Eastern Prussia and German-occupied Poland and Lithuania, and by December, his regiment had driven the German army from the Polish towns of Ivangorod and Radom, south-west of Warsaw.

His elder brother Dmitry, who was conscripted, suffered shellshock, from which he never recovered. Gumilyov was miraculously uninjured in battle, and despite being a poor horseman, with bad eyesight and weak lungs, frequently invalided out with bouts of bronchitis and pneumonia, he fought with exceptional courage for virtually the entire war. He loved the danger and discipline of battle, and war was an inexhaustible source of poetry for him, filled with fantasy, testosterone and adventure. War exalted his Christian faith, and he called himself a 'warrior poet', who found meaning in transcendent moments of beauty at the front. 'We haven't eaten for four days. But there is no need for earthly food in this bright terrible hour, the Lord's word sustains us more than bread', he wrote in his poem 'The Offensive'. He described his first winter at the front as the best time of his life, even better than Africa, and he dreamed of celebrating the new year with a Russian victory parade in Berlin. According to his biographer Shubinsky, he was 'in heaven'.

He returned to the capital in January after the winter campaign, where his bravery in battle was rewarded with Russia's highest military decoration, the St George Cross, and he stayed with Akhmatova and his sister-in-law at their old flat. (His brother as a conscript would spend most of the war at the front). 'Words don't open a woman's heart, what she loves is a hero', he said, and after five months without them, he had his pick of them. He resumed his affair with Margarita Tumpovskaya, romanced the writer Marietta Shaginyan, slept with Akhmatova's friend the dancer Tatyana Adamovich (who was apparently under the impression he wanted to marry her), and seduced Adamovich's young dance student Anna Engelhardt, who was studying the new Dalcroze 'Eurythmics' method with her.

---

2   Rozhdestvensky, 'The Youth of our Days', op.cit., p. 21.

Larisa would see him at the Stray Dog reading his war poems in his cavalry uniform, serialised the following year in the *Stock Exchange Gazette* as *Notes of a Cavalry Officer* – a d'Annunzian hymn to blood and death, about the beauty of dying in battle, and men's tragic acceptance of their fate. He was a hunter pursuing a noble sport, as he had been in Africa hunting lions, who saw Germans as 'game', and he celebrated in religious, almost erotic tones the healing release of killing: 'Murmuring a prayer to the Virgin Mary, instantly forgotten in the face of death, I have only one thought, mighty and alive like passion, rage, ecstasy – either I kill him, or he will kill me'.

Within two months, the Stray Dog had been closed by war censorship, and dozens of literary magazines and journals had been caught in the ever-tightening censors' net, and replaced with cheap jingoistic rags.

Gumilyov's patriotic outpourings had a huge influence on Russia's impressionable young at the University, and lost him his admirers among Larisa's friends in the Poetry Circle. But Rozhdestvensky recalled her smiling her enigmatic smile when his work was attacked at meetings, and changing the subject to a new literary project she wanted to discuss with them.

That winter she had persuaded her parents that they should put out a new anti-war literary magazine, and try to get it past the censors. Her father arranged with his publishers, the liberal Suvorin publishing house in Moscow, to handle sales there and in the capital, and her mother pawned the family silver at the pawnshop on the Bolshoi Prospect – 'consisting of three silver teaspoons', Larisa wrote in *Requiem* – and approached the family's friend Vladimir Svyatlovsky for funds.

Svyatlovsky's employer Duke Leuchtenberg had been appointed an *aide de camp* to the Tsar, and Commander in Chief of the Eastern Front. Svyatlovsky had opposed the war from the start. An economics lecturer at Petrograd University, literary critic and poet, in 1905 he had been elected to the central bureau of St Petersburg's professional trade unions, which campaigned for improved housing, sanitation and healthcare for the city's workers, and he was editor of its journal. After the revolution, he was appointed chair of the highly successful Mutual Credit Publishing Company, which funded numerous progressive publications, and the company would be the magazine's main backer.

It was also common knowledge in the Leuchtenberg Building that Svyatlovsky was in love with Larisa's mother – which presumably explains her combative attitude to him. Several scenes in *Requiem* are set in his flat, with its large library and collection of Napoleonic memorabilia, and describe their meetings and dramas:

> Today Vladimir Vladimirovich calls her on the phone. 'Kitty darling, I'm desperate, I need to see you, please come over'.

'No I won't!'
'I'll hang myself from the chandelier!'
'Hang yourself then!'
That night he waits for her under the trees as she comes skipping over the frozen pavement.

'Let's talk business. If you're thinking of calling your magazine *Robespierre* or *Marat*, don't, it will only annoy people and make you enemies, and you'll crash after the second issue. And there won't be another revolution!'

'Dearest Volodya, let's be honest, you'll become a government minister, and we'll lash you to death in our mad magazine'.

They face each other like enemies, she dark and slender, he wiry and filled with energy, his hair sticking up on end like a beast of prey.

'Idiot!' she says, and in the darkness he can barely see her smile, but what a smile ...!

The name finally chosen for the magazine was *Rudin*, after the vacillating philosopher hero of Ivan Turgenev's novel of the same name, and its main targets were to be his modern equivalents – not deluded patriots like Gumilyov who were dying in the trenches, but Russia's armchair patriots at home, and the socialists who had abandoned socialism to become apologists for the war.

The editorial office was in Mikhail Andreevich's study, and Larisa invited her friends home to discuss the venture over tea – an experience Rozhdestvensky found both exciting and exacting: 'An apparently peaceful discussion was in fact a real test of a person. But having passed the test, one would automatically be initiated into the "Rudinists," and forever in the Reisners' favour'.[3]

Most of *Rudin's* first 'initiates' were from the Poetry Circle. But several of the thirty writers it published were established poets, including Mandelstam, who had recently published his first anthology, his fellow Acmeist Sergei Gorodetsky, and Sergei Esenin, who Rozhdestvensky remembered attending an editorial meeting in Professor Reisner's study.

In the bitter cold of February 1915, Gumilyov fought in Lithuania and northwest Poland, where his regiment suffered massive losses, then joined the Great Russian Retreat from Poland to the River Bug, the border with Ukraine. After a month in the saddle he collapsed with bronchitis, and was invalided out to a field hospital in the rear. But a week later he discharged himself and returned to the front.

---

3   Quoted by Eleonora Solovei in her article '*Rudin*', in the journal *Neva*, 1957, no. 3.

In May, he was fighting the Austro-Hungarian army in Galicia, when Italy switched sides to the Allies, and he celebrated the Italian people's heroic struggles against Habsburg Austria in his 'Ode to d'Annunzio':

> The she-wolf at her column
> Snarls in the crimson blaze.
> Italy's fate lies in the fate of her poets ...

That summer, the bungling General Sukhomlinov was sacked as Minister of War. By then the German and Austrian armies had advanced far into Russia's borders, overrunning Russian Poland, Lithuania and most of Latvia, making some two and a half million people refugees. Wage cuts, rampant speculation and soaring living costs brought new misery to the cities, and women in Petrograd's poor suburbs began to riot and loot the food shops.

Demonstrations in support of them were violently broken up by the police, and turned into demonstrations against the police themselves, and the University became the forum for endless student meetings.

The poet Vera Inber described a packed student meeting she went to one evening after classes at the Psychoneurology Institute, 'in a cooling auditorium lit by the late sun', where Larisa gave a talk entitled 'Towards which goal and by which route must humanity travel?' 'Her language, bold, picturesque and original, frothed like unfermented juices, but was material for real wine', she wrote.[4]

Five years older than Larisa, Inber was from a prosperous Jewish family in Odessa, whose father, the owner of a scientific publishing house, was an uncle of Trotsky's. Trotsky's family was from the nearby town of Kherson, and he had lived with the Inbers for six years while he was at Odessa high school, and had later hidden in their house from the police. In 1910, while he was living in exile in Austria, Inber had fled Russia into voluntary exile, and had lived for the next four years in Switzerland and France, where she studied at the Sorbonne in Paris, and published her first poetry collection, *Sad Wine*. Her first meeting with Larisa was the start of a warm friendship between them, and it was Inber's poetry and revolutionary politics Larisa wanted for *Rudin*.

The magazine's purpose, it proclaimed ambitiously in its first issue in July, was to 'brand with the scourge of polemic, satire and ridicule the lies, hypocrisy and hideousness of Russian life'. *Rudin*'s opposition to the war was exceptional in those days of savage press censorship, and it was possibly Reisner's polit-

---

4   Vera Inber, 'Evolution of a Swan', LRRC, p. 269.

ical isolation and his interest to the police that allowed it to get its barbs past the censors. Published and edited by Larisa, assisted by her father, it appeared at first sight quite innocuous, with its soft large-format cover, and the title wreathed around the silhouette of Turgenev's hero, with his high collar and flowing hair. But in the sixteen pages inside, his heroics were thrown back at him, and in poems and stories, political and literary articles and feuilletons, most written anonymously or under pseudonyms, *Rudin* satirised the bankruptcy of tsarism, lampooned government figures, and attacked Russia's most respected liberals and socialists who had turned patriots. (Despite its veiled 'Aesopian' language, it would have been obvious to its readers who they were).

Several pieces were illustrated by caricatures, inspired by the satirical journals of the 1905 revolution. One showed the former Marxist Plekhanov, dripping with gold, in the embrace of a fat banker. In another, members of the 'Beauty' literary group huddled in a tree like sinister fairytale sirens. A favourite target was Burtsev, who was depicted as a rat crawling from a naturalistically drawn skull, representing the defeated 1905 revolution.

The first issue opened with Larisa's 'Sonnet to Rudin', signed 'E. Nitzman':

> Ludicrous, reckless, alone,
> He died on the barricades.
> Now an impartial court
> Will finish that unwritten chapter ...[5]

Other poems and articles were published under the names 'Rikki-Tikki-Tavi' (from Rudyard Kipling's *Jungle Book*), and 'I. Khrapovitsky' (the name of her maternal grandfather). Her mother contributed sketches and stories as 'E. Vlast', and her father published dozens of articles under a variety of pseudonyms, attacking the war, state terror, and the anti-Semitic Black Hundreds press. Blok was given a free subscription, and called *Rudin* 'dirty and sharp'.

As chief editor, Larisa visited the printing press to supervise production, managed the magazine's complicated finances, and was responsible for ensuring that the fourth page carried the obligatory 'Passed by the Military Censors' stamp. But it was *Rudin's* poetry that took most of her attention. Readers sent in unsolicited verses, which she would read closely, then throw open to discussion at friendly editorial meetings, similar to those of the Poetry Circle.

Rozhdestvensky recalled a great deal of laughter and argument at these meetings, and that students who had passed the stern-looking young woman in

---

5 Larisa's poems and articles for *Rudin* are in Larisa Reisner. *Selected Works*, ed. and introduced by A. Naumova, Moscow, 1965 (from now on sw), and in Solovei, 1985.

the University corridors would be astonished to see her showering an opponent with questions, or sighing comically as she read the letters of readers shyly submitting their first works.

She wrote to Lev Nikulin in Moscow, asking him to send his poems, and he forgot about them until the following summer, when they finally met in person, and he became one of *Rudin*'s most regular contributors.

Her own poems for *Rudin* were mainly sonnets on grand historical themes, set in an atmosphere of revolutionary sacrifice and struggle. She wrote of the French revolutionaries Camille Desmoulins and 'victorious Marat, crowned by haughty Gorat after a duel', and of Pushkin, punished for his association with Russia's first doomed revolutionaries, the Decembrists. In 'The Bronze Horseman', the poet vows to avenge Pushkin's death:

> Divine Arab!
> Today the rising slave
> Counts your losses,
> And reads the epic Decree
> Banishing you to the Caucasus ...

According to Nikulin, 'these poems frankly failed to meet the needs of the situation'. She set herself high goals as a poet, but despite their sometimes appealing rawness, the tone was too bombastic and full of big ideas, drawing heavily on the Acmeists' repertoire of myths and allegory, and lacking the playfulness and originality of the Futurists. She was much more original and interesting as a prose writer. In her articles for *Rudin* on Russia's contemporary literary scene, she abandoned images borrowed from others for a quieter more truthful voice, and her bold accurate judgements show a powerful polemical voice in the making.

For all the magazine's radicalism, the Futurists were not invited to contribute, possibly for fear that they would wreck it with one of their 'interventions'. But in her essay 'From Blok to Severyanin and Mayakovsky', she wrote appreciatively of Mayakovsky's 'rage, his love, his hunger for life and freedom', and she contrasted his poetry with the 'cosmetic beauty' of the Symbolist poet Igor Severyanin, 'who once dreamed of a crystal grave and the fantastic funeral of his soul, and now exposes his soul for money, and isn't too well paid for it'.

In 'Bryusov and the Eternal Female', she wrote of the Symbolist poet Valery Bryusov's decline into mystical sensuality, and accused him of promoting the mass-produced pornography that had flooded the market since the 1905 revolution. 'The Russian Jungle' was a more forthright attack on the brutal version of 'free love' glorified in Mikhail Artsybashev's play 'The Law of the Wild'. She praised Evgeny Zamyatin's sharp political satires about life in the Russian provinces. And in 'Out of the Frying Pan', she wrote of her old mentor Andreev, 'the great nihilist who became a patriot, and broke the promises he made in a moment of pathetic self-mockery'.

The Futurists were the only poets calling explicitly for the overthrow of the old order – 'seeing what is approaching over the mountains of time'. But literature, art and poetry were all being hurled into the new world, because the old one was collapsing. The tsarist regime, weak and incompetent and on the brink of collapse, unable to give its citizens even the most basic liberties, was drawing thousands to the revolutionary movement.

CHAPTER 4

In Petrograd

In September 1915, the Tsar appointed himself Chief of Staff of the Army and set off for the front, leaving his wife and Rasputin in the capital in charge of matters of state. Gumilyov still believed fervently in Russian victory. But by the autumn the army had suffered such catastrophic losses that the German High Command had virtually discounted the Eastern Front until the winter, and in October he was discharged from his unit.

He spent the next two months studying for his officer's exams at the Tsarskoe Selo Military Academy outside Petrograd, making frequent trips to the capital to stay with Akhmatova in their old flat, picking up his affairs with Anna Engelhardt, the dancer Tatyana Adamovich and the long-suffering Margarita Tumpovskaya, and pursuing Tumpovskaya's friend the young poet Maria Lyovberg, who had recently published her first collection, *Moonlit Nights*.

Reviewing her poems in the Acmeists' journal *Apollo*, he wrote, 'They betray the author's complete lack of experience, they're just modernist clichés, but with the energy of the sun, linked to revery and a severe melancholy, which has nothing to do with grief'. There was a more menacing edge to his mixed message wooing technique in his poem to Lyovberg, 'The Serpent', the story of the mythical Volga dragon who kills beautiful young girls and throws their bodies in the river – 'Ah times were different then. The earth cast spells with the heavens. Wonders of wonders were dreamt, miracles of miracles ...'[1]

He returned to the front in December as an officer cadet, fighting in a series of inconclusive and massively costly battles in Belorussia (now Belarus), and he returned in January to Petrograd to be awarded a second bar on his St George Cross.

Larisa went to the celebration party Akhmatova and his friends the poets Mandelstam and Sergei Gorodetsky organised for him at the Stray Dog, at which he read from *his Notes of a Cavalry Officer*. His biographer Pavel Luknitsky recalled the magic of that night – 'the blazing open fire, the candles, the cigar smoke, and Gumilyov's sweet words of triumph, far from the raging snowstorm outside, and the slaughter at the front.' She described the scene in *Requiem*, and it was probably that night that she first slept with him. She wrote of the first rushed days of their affair, tearing him from his adoring fans before

---

1 Gumilyov's article quoted in Luknitskaya 1990, p. 143.

he returned to the front. They went ice-skating, and to the Hermitage Gallery, where they both loved the Persian miniatures, and they took long walks around the city discussing poetry, and he told her of his travels in Europe and Africa. His late father had sailed the world as a surgeon in the Russian navy, and adventure and travel were in his blood. From his first two journeys to Abyssinia, he had brought back elephants' tusks and 'savages' artefacts' and panther skins to decorate his room ('I liked their spots'). His third journey, in 1913, had been as guide to an ethnographical expedition sponsored by the Russian Academy of Sciences to the holy city of Harar, a historic centre of Islamic culture, famous for its bookbinding.

The first European expedition to Harar had been led in 1854 by the British explorer Sir Richard Burton, disguised as an Arab merchant, and the poet Arthur Rimbaud had worked there in the 1880s as a coffee trader and gunrunner. Gumilyov and the Russians were welcomed as guests of the Governor, Ras Tafari, who gave them manuscripts and bookbinding tools to take back to St Petersburg, and he took Larisa to the Kunstkammer Museum of Anthropology to show her the displays, which are there to this day, with his photographs of Ras Tafari on the wall, and a map of his travels. Then he was back at the front, with its raids, attacks and retreats.

Their affair continued over the next thirteen months during his brief leaves in the capital, and was sustained by long rapturous letters, over thirty of which were published in a 1980 edition of his previously unpublished works, although correspondence to and from the front took weeks to arrive, and was often lost, and they refer to several others.[2]

'I dream of you every night. I gallop across the fields crying your name to the wind', he wrote to her.

'It's an eternity since I heard from you', she wrote to him. 'I try to forget you, but just when you seem decently buried, I'm suddenly reminded of you by a stray word, the scent of my perfume'.

'Only the most fervent scribbler could write in the trenches', he wrote. 'There are no chairs, the ceiling leaks, the table is covered with rats that growl at you when you approach them, and at night I lie in the snow looking up at the stars, drawing lines between them in my head, tracing the outlines of your sweet face looking down at me from the heavens'.

They were both fighters, proud, theatrical and aristocratic, in love with danger and incapable of compromise, and the language of their letters was both

---

2 *Nikolai Gumilyov. Neizdannyie stikhi i pisma* (Nikolai Gumilyov. Unpublished Poems and Letters), YMCA Press, Paris, 1980, pp. 129–151. All quotes here from the letters are from the book.

passionate and formal, and they were both *'vy'*. The war had brought him closer to Akhmatova, and they had a long affectionate correspondence, in which she was 'Anya' and he was 'Kolya', and they were *'ty'*. Larisa was *'ty'* only in his poems to her, and his biographer Shubinsky suggests that she was the most 'literary' of all his relationships with women.

On his breaks from the front he was working on two new plays, his marionette drama 'Child of Allah', and his verse play 'Gondla'. The first, inspired by the British director Gordon Craig's marionette version of 'Hamlet', was the story of the fourteenth-century Persian poet Hafiz, and his love for a mythical Persian maiden, or 'Peri'. 'Gondla' was based on a ninth-century Icelandic saga, with echoes of Pushkin's fairytale poem 'Ruslan and Ludmila'. But the violence and incest themes were his, as was its hero Gondla, a hunchbacked warrior poet born in Christian Ireland, sent as a baby to pagan Iceland to be raised as a symbol of the union between Paganism and Christianity. The play opens with his wedding to his half-sister, the beautiful Princess Leri, half-Celtic, half-Icelandic, part wolf, part swan, who joins him in his mission for peaceful coexistence, which they achieve after sadistic scenes of her gang rape by jealous Icelandic warlords, and his suicide.

The women in his life were frequently involved in disputes about the identities of the unnamed subjects of his poems, and Margarita Tumpovskaya and Anna Engelhardt both claimed to be the inspiration for his spirited dreadfully punished heroine. But 'Gondla' was his love poem to Larisa. 'Leri' was his private name for her, used by no one else, and she wrote to him as 'Hafiz', waiting in a frenzy for his next letter telling her he was still alive, escaping from the horror into their private world of myths and magic and poetry.

By early 1916, over seven million Russian and German soldiers had been killed, injured or taken prisoner, without achieving any significant military victories. 'Chaos at the front reigns supreme', said the Tsar's cousin the Grand Duke Nicholas, who had replaced him as the army's Chief of Staff.

Rosa Luxemburg and Karl Liebknecht spent most of the war years in jail. But in brief breaks in their sentences in January, they attended the illegal founding meeting in Berlin of the new underground Spartacus League, which called on workers to build mass strike action against the war. Humanity faced the choice between barbarism and socialism, Luxemburg said.

In April, the Tsar was forced by liberal pressure in the Duma to arrest the disgraced General Sukhomlinov, and jail him in the Peter and Paul fortress for high treason. He then ordered a massive new conscription drive to replace the dead, starting with first-year university students. Larisa's friend Semyon Roshal from the Psychoneurology Institute was conscripted into the navy, as a junior officer at the Kronstadt garrison, and he would stay with her family when he was on leave in the capital. But Rozhdestvensky, Ilinsky and many others were drafted into the army and sent to distant fronts, and it was a year before she would see them again. Seventeen-year-old Igor, who was still at school, was still exempt.

That spring, Gumilyov was promoted to junior lieutenant in the Empress Alexandra's Regiment of Hussars, known as the 'Holy Regiment', dashing, reckless hard-fighting cavalry officers and adventurers, who were sworn to secrecy about their operations. But he was known to have fought in a series of bloody battles on the Austrian front. He then collapsed with pneumonia, and spent six weeks in the officers' hospital run by the Empress Alexandra in a wing of the royal palace at Tsarskoe Selo. Much of the hospital's resources was spent on training her and her two elder daughters as nursing assistants, and Gumilyov organised sickbed visits for the Tsarevich Alexei and the younger princesses Maria and Anastasia. On Anastasia's birthday in June, he presented her with his 'Ode to Her Majesty Her Royal Highness the Princess Anastasia on Her Fifteenth Birthday', signed by sixteen fellow Hussars.

Margarita Tumpovskaya had by then finally realised that he was serious about Larisa, and wrote to him at the hospital to end their affair. Defying the doctors, he rushed to her flat in the city and begged her unsuccessfully to take him back, and he was then pronounced unfit for service. But he demanded a reexamination, and was soon back with at the front, fighting with the Hussars in western Latvia.

That summer Britain and France were saved by another sacrificial Russian offensive in Galicia, which cost over a hundred thousand Russian lives, and left the Russian army no longer able to fight. As *Rudin*'s mailbag bulged with contributions and requests for new subscriptions, the censors grew increasingly vigilant, and in June it was banned from being sold in the capital's working-class districts, on the personal orders of the new Governor-General, General Adlerburg. It was still sold elsewhere, mainly at station kiosks, but more articles were censored, and Larisa and her father had to battle daily for its survival. Its finances became increasingly precarious when the Suvorin publishing house in Moscow withheld payment, and in July she went to Moscow to plead in person with the director, Efremov, for the money owed.

It was then that Lev Nikulin finally met her. In their three-year exchange of letters, he had imagined her as 'a literary bluestocking, with pince-nez, mannish clothes and a cigarette in her mouth', and he was astonished by the youthful voice on the telephone summoning him to her hotel without delay. She was staying at the old merchants' Loskutnaya Hotel, where her family always stayed when they were in Moscow – 'in a large room with velvet drapes at the windows, and a samovar and spice cakes on an oval redwood table. And when I stepped through the door and saw the smiling young woman sitting at the writing-desk, with golden plaits wound round her high forehead like a crown, I was literally deprived of the power of speech'.

But they were soon discussing the poetry of Mandelstam and Mayakovsky, Akhmatova and Gumilyov, and passing judgement on Moscow's literary 'Parnassus'. 'I was delighted by her sharp independent judgements, in such contrast to her musical voice and laughter. "My god, what a shocker, how can you like such drivel! Is the old potbelly still churning them out?"' They discussed *Rudin*, and Nikulin told her he was puzzled by its attacks on Burtsev, and she vehemently defended its savaging of her father's tormenter. And he would see her proved right a year after the Revolution, when the malevolent Burtsev emigrated, and became a fierce enemy of the Bolsheviks.

Then it was business, and he accompanied her to the offices of the Suvorin company. Ignoring the stacks of unsold *Rudins* on the floor, withered by the sun and stamped 'Return', she persuaded the taciturn Efremov to hand over all the money owed, and afterwards she took Nikulin to a chamber-music recital at the house of a family friend, a well-known violinist. The evening was a disaster, he wrote. She held forth loudly about their snobbish hosts, and they were shown the door. And when he suggested a trip to the theatre next evening, she insisted they go to the circus and the Apollo dance-hall instead, 'where the proletarian atmosphere was more to her taste'.[3]

Apart from family trips to concerts and the opera, music and Russia's rich musical culture seem not to have played a big part in her life. Asked in a writers' questionnaire after the Revolution to name her favourite composers, she wrote 'Beethoven, Scryabin – I like "bad" music, movie pianists, barrel organs, street bands'. 'Beethoven for cultural solemnity and legitimacy, proletarian music for emotional release', as Richard Stites succinctly summarises revolutionaries' musical tastes in his excellent book on Russian popular culture.[4]

Like others, Nikulin often found her impossibly loud and opinionated. But in their three-year exchange of letters he had never been afraid to stand up to her, and he would become one of her severest critics and dearest friends.

Later that summer, she invited him to stay with her family, and she showed him around Petrograd's nightlife. Since the Stray Dog closed, its proprietor Boris Pronin had opened a new club, the Comedians' Halt Cabaret, in the vaults of a mansion on the Field of Mars, exquisitely decorated in the same style, which he would wander round with a stray dog in tow, as a reminder of the old place. One night she took Nikulin to a poetry reading there. Gumilyov and

---

3   Nikulin, 'Years of Our Life', LRRC, pp. 55–7.
4   Richard Stites *Russian Popular Culture*, 1992, p. 46.

most of Petrograd's poets were at the front, and Nikulin described a succession of 'powdered, howling Acmeists' reading their verses, and Mayakovsky declaiming his poem 'War and Peace' 'with the power of an exploding bomb'. They left in the small hours, and took a cab home, and as they drove through the sleeping city in the rain, 'she exploded with rage at "those aesthetes with their poems about hussars and estates, publicly taking the sins of the world on their shoulders, privately fighting to advance themselves and live comfortable lives. I want to write poetry about biology and scientific issues, from a sense of protest!"'

The Troitsky Bridge across the Neva had been raised to let the ships through, and they waited with crowds of cabs and carriages filled with revellers heading for the gypsy taverns in the poor suburbs. As they discussed poetry and politics, a crowd of pedestrians – homeless people and seasonal workers, bricklayers, plasterers and carpenters – waited sullenly for the bridge to come down, and prostitutes went from carriage to carriage in search of customers. When the queue finally began to move, a man in a smart cab dashed to the front to be first across. 'And as our carriage drew level with the workers, she said, "Here are the *real* people! One day they'll be the masters, and won't have to give way to gentlemen in top hats!"'[5]

In August, Gumilyov collapsed at the front with bronchitis, and spent two weeks recuperating in a sanatorium in the Crimea, where he finished writing 'Gondla', and had flings with two young Moscow University students on holiday there. He spent the remaining two weeks of his leave in the capital with Larisa.

They played tennis, and went to the Zoo and to the cinema (he preferred films to the theatre), and he told her he dreamed of taking her to the magical island of Madagascar. According to Shubinsky, she told his friend the poet Andrei Petrov that he was taking her to a 'house of assignations' on Gorokhovaya Street for sex – 'but I was so in love with him, I would have gone anywhere with him'. He also spent long periods on his own, writing, reading the Holy Scriptures and praying in church.

Soon after he returned to the front, she set off with a group of student friends on a steamer trip along the River Volga. Their first stop was the Tsar's Potemkin Village outside Kostroma, from where she wrote home, 'Darling Mother, I left with an unforgiven guilt. But my soul has brightened this morning with the weather, and I beg you again to forgive me'.

Her mother must have been deeply distressed by her relationship with Gumilyov, and he may well have been the cause of their quarrel. But she had

---

5 Nikulin, 'Years of Our Life', LRRC, pp. 58, 71.

raised her to be independent and fight for what she wanted, and at the age of twenty-one she had more freedom than women of her mother's generation could have dreamt of. Perhaps part of her 'unforgiven guilt' was for the opportunities she took for granted that her mother had fought so hard to give her. Perhaps she just needed to be away from her family for a while, to see the future more clearly.

She would return two years later to these little towns and villages on the Volga, when they were the scenes of some of the bloodiest battles of the Civil War. But even in the dull ferment of 1916, she saw the signs of the approaching revolution.

From the town of Kineshma, fifty miles south of Kostroma, she wrote to her parents:

> My darlings, it's impossible to describe – the dark nights, the will-o-the-wisps, the water rustling under the paddles, the saffron yellow shores, the tall undergrowth, the eternally pacified snow-white churches, arched by rainbows. We needn't fear for Russia. All along all the moorings of this vast river, in every sentry-box and little market village, things are irrevocably decided. People here know everything, forgive no one and forget nothing. And when the time comes, they will exact punishment such as has never been seen before ...
>
> Sometimes I'm overcome by hopeless presentiments – if only the string doesn't break too soon, and these calm and terrible deeds don't remain just words. But everywhere things are stirring – beyond the yellowing forests, the islands and rapids. And the elements are never mistaken ...
>
> Please write. You belong with these people, with their longings and griefs.[6]

In October Gumilyov returned to the capital to study at the Nikolaev Cavalry Academy for his lieutenant's exams. He was under strict curfew, and they had time for only a few rushed meetings. One morning he was waiting for her outside the Leuchtenberg Building when she left for her lectures, and afterwards he delivered his poem 'To Her Highness Larisa Mikhailovna Reisner' to her flat, a spoof on his ode to the Princess Anastasia – 'The tram groans and howls as it carries you off to the Institute. How sweet your little Faust's cap is on your childish face, I'm insanely in love with you'.[7]

---

6 *SW*, p. 512.
7 Poem quoted in Luknitskaya 1990, p. 135.

Like the fifteen-year-old princess, she was his child muse. But she was no longer the naive teenager she had been when they first met. She was editing *Rudin* virtually single-handed, recruiting contributors, challenging and cajoling the censors, and managing its increasingly strained finances. The money from Efremov had covered its next issue, but he had soon stopped paying again, and by the autumn the magazine was barely surviving. Debts mounted, and clashes with the censors became more frequent, with more blank spaces, often whole pages, where passages had been deleted. A facsimile of Reisner's precious letter from Karl Liebknecht's father Wilhelm, friend of Marx and Engels, founder of the German Social Democratic Party, was removed from his article 'The Liebknechts. Heroic Dynasty of Fighters and Leaders', in which he prophetically foretold 'Karl's fiery death'. Larisa challenged the censors with him, unsuccessfully, and the censors' blue pencil struck his broadside against the Tsar's fourth highly reactionary Duma from the same issue. They protested again without success when his article 'Shakers and Feelers', about Burtsev and his fellow provocateurs in the secret police, was removed from the eighth issue, and the ninth was laid out but never published.

In November, when the family had nothing left to pawn, *Rudin* was forced to close, and her father had to sell a large number of his books to clear their debts to Svyatlovsky's publishing company. Poems, articles and letters continued to pour in, and readers telephoned to ask why their copies had been held up. '*Rudin* is dead', she told them.

Gumilyov failed his fortifications exams at the Cavalry Academy, and left for the Latvian front in November still as a junior officer in the Hussars. A month later, he was back in the capital to celebrate the publication of 'Gondla', 'Child of Allah', and his book of war poems, *Quiver*, dedicated to the dancer Tatyana Adamovich. There were more assignations at the Gorokhovaya Street hotel, and he spent much of his leave alone, writing and praying. Then he was back at the front, fighting in the battles for the River Dvina.

Once, when his unit came under heavy fire, he was seen lighting a cigarette and smoking it in a rain of shells, and he was reprimanded for his 'senseless bravery'.

'Leri, Leri, proud girl, why are you avoiding me?' he wrote to her at the end of December.

> It's two weeks since I left, and still no word from you. Don't forget me so quickly, I don't deserve it ... To survive here it's necessary to imagine another existence which is bright and beautiful, and you are beautiful. My love for you has freed me from all the blindness of this life ...

He is enchanted by her, then he demolishes her:

> You have bright beautiful honest eyes, but you are blind. Strong young legs, but no wings. A powerful elegant mind, but with a strange emptiness at the centre. You are Daphne turned to Laurel, a princess turned to stone …

'But never mind!' he went on, to soften the blow.

> Everything will be different in Madagascar. And on a warm night under the blazing stars, in a thicket of red rosewood trees beside a bubbling spring, you will tell me wonderful things I have glimpsed only in my dreams. Goodbye Leri, I kiss your dear, dear little hands. Your Hafiz.

In her reply, to 'Warrant Officer Gumilyov, Fourth Squadron, Fifth Hussars' Regiment', she made light of his cruel assessment of her:

> Darling Hafiz, you destroy me. Next time send me a sonnet about janissaries, seven-headed Cerberuses, whatever you like, dear friend, so long as the fantasies spread their peacocks' tails over our Madagascar, where we can rediscover the joy of existence and the purity of our souls. I wait for you. Your Leri.

By the end of 1916, entire Russian regiments were deserting, killing their commanders and seizing their weapons and commandeering trains. The villages starved as the peasants were called up. Soldier peasant bands looted the landowners' estates for food, and the cities were paralysed by strikes. Thousands more students were conscripted, and Nikulin was drafted into a medical unit in Belorussia.

That winter there were more women's food riots in the capital, and soldiers were leaving their barracks to join them, marching through the streets with them with red flags. People spoke of Rasputin's drunken orgies with Alexandra and her ladies-in-waiting in the Winter Palace, and liberals in the Duma were calling for her to be jailed for treason. Even Gumilyov had fallen out of love with the royal family by then. In his poem 'The Peasant' that winter, he evoked the sinister blaspheming presence of 'the *muzhik* from the swamps, with his sly talk and his gold cross on his chest, who came to our proud capital, God help us, and bewitched the Empress'.

On 30 December 1916, Rasputin was murdered by courtiers close to the Tsar, who saw his death as the monarchy's only hope. Shaken by war and rotten from within, the regime was slipping into chaos. Revolution was stirring.

The Poetry Circle survived a few months longer, and put out a new poetry anthology that winter, *Arion*, but Larisa did not contribute to it. Instead she began writing for Gorky's popular new anti-war literary journal *Chronicle*.

Chronicle published the first two volumes of Gorky's autobiography, *My Childhood* and *In the World*, the first stories of the young writer Isaac Babel, and works by many of Russia's greatest poets, including Blok, Esenin and Mayakovsky, despite Gorky's objections to Futurism – 'There is no Futurism in Mayakovsky, just Mayakovsky the poet, a great poet!' he said. Larisa contributed poems, literary reviews, and translations of the poetry of Rilke and Schiller. There were essays on literary criticism, semiotics and linguistics by the theoretician of Futurism, Victor Shklovsky, translations of stories by Jack London, O. Henry, Romain Rolland and H.G. Wells, and articles from Berlin and Paris on women's liberation, psychoanalysis and aesthetics by the exiled revolutionaries Alexandra Kollontai and Anatoly Lunacharsky.

Philosopher, playwright and essayist, Lunacharsky was both a revolutionary Marxist and a 'seeking Marxist'. Since joining the revolutionary underground in 1898, at the age of eighteen, he had spent long spells in exile and jail, and had worked with Lenin and the Bolsheviks in Switzerland, and in 1909 and 1910 he had lectured on Freud and art history at Gorky's two socialist schools for Russian workers in Italy, later the models for his Circle of Proletarian Culture for Russian workers in Paris.

Gorky spoke of 'this man of astonishing cleverness and talent, with a great future, well placed to advance revolutionary thought'. But unlike Kollontai and Lunacharsky, he and most of *Chronicle*'s contributors believed Russia was too poor and backward for a socialist revolution. The journal delivered a stinging attack on Gumilyov's *Quiver* poems – 'war isn't the milky-white marble of Abyssinia, people are dying!' But it spoke the language of pacifism, not class war. Gorky was deeply hostile to what he called 'Bolshevik extremism' – 'which is leading millions and millions of virtually illiterate, politically uneducated Russians who don't know what they want in socially dangerous directions'.

As the only anti-war publication since *Rudin*, *Chronicle* was highly vulnerable to censorship, and he stressed that writers must avoid the crude personal attacks the tsarist press used against its enemies, which 'distort the truth, and arouse dark hatreds in people', and would lead to its inevitable closure. He saw the common ground on which different political viewpoints could meet as Science, 'which is democratic, and must be accessible to all', and serious attention was paid to *Chronicle's* science section, which was edited by the distinguished biologist Professor Timiryazev.

Larisa went to noisy editorial meetings in Gorky's flat, and to the writers' workshops he was running in the factories with Mayakovsky, Esenin, Babel and

Shklovsky, where they shared their literary skills with workers, and encouraged them to write for the journal. Despite Gorky's well-known views on the Bolsheviks, the police agents present at these gatherings described them in his enormous criminal files as 'recruiting grounds for the revolution', and made special reference to his religious beliefs, and his views on the war and the 'Jewish question'.

Gorky spoke of the 'poison of anti-Semitism', and was a lifelong campaigner against all forms of religious and racist persecution and oppression. As a teenager he had been deeply affected by the infamous 1884 pogrom he had witnessed in his home town Nizhny Novgorod, and he had turned against the Orthodox religion in which he had been raised, with its hatred of Jews and women, to practise his own socialist religion, which he called the 'religion of rebellion'.

Gumilyov's Orthodox faith was the inspiration of his life and his poetry. He had prayed devoutly since he was young child, and his constant companion in battle was his officers' manual, with its ideals of selfless service to the Fatherland – 'ascending to the heights of Russia's Christ-loving army'. But for all his nationalism and religious fervour, he was no anti-Semite. This was noted by his friend and political adversary Victor Serge (who wasn't Jewish, although he was often assumed to be), and by his numerous Jewish friends and lovers. 'He thought I was Polish, but when I said I was Jewish he wasn't bothered', Margarita Tumpovskaya said after they met.

Religion had simply never been part of Larisa's life. 'I'm not tempted by other worlds, I don't want people having the currency to buy into some higher power', she told Nikulin. On Gumilyov's nameday, St Nicholas Day, the 6th of December (which he shared with the Tsar), she wrote to him that she had lit candles for him in church – 'just for luck':

> On Kamenny Most, before you reach the taverns and the fat policeman yawning on the bridge, there's that funny little toy chapel to Saint Nicholas, not so much a chapel as two stone hands clasped round some miraculous stained-glass windows, and not just one Nicholas, but three. The priests didn't know which was the most important, so I lit candles to all three ...
>
> Oh my Hafiz, I miss you all the time. There's a poets' evening tomorrow at the university – a lot of silly students and professors hiding from the front, and you won't be there ...

Letters were arriving from the front from Rozhdestvensky, Ilinsky and Nikulin, but it would be a month before she heard back from Gumilyov. In January 1916, her long poem 'Letter' was published in *Chronicle*, written in the voice of a trench soldier numbed by war – 'a poet in love with Tasso, who has learnt to disembowel human flesh':

> Your letter is with me,
> It is still sealed, I have not read it.
> I am a dead weapon in the hands of the maddened horde.
> Your talk of love cannot wash away the blood ...[8]

When she finally heard from him later that month, he wrote that he had returned from the battlefield to find two letters from her waiting for him:

> How sweet you are in them. When I read them I remembered you saying I don't take enough from you. How unforgivably childish of me, I don't deserve you. I love you, that's why I wrote those crazy things to you ...
>
> A book is taking shape in my head, written just for you. Its title will be *Leri And Love*, in big red letters like the summer sun, and the chapters will be 'Leri and the Snow', 'Leri and the Persian Lyric', 'Leri and My Childhood Dream of an Eagle' ...
>
> Everything I know and love I want to see through your eyes, as if through coloured glass. Your soul has its own special colour, which people can't see yet, just as the ancients couldn't see blue ... I remember your every word, every gesture, but it's too little, I want more, more, more from you ... You promised to send me your picture. I hope it arrives before I hop off home to count the railings in the Summer Gardens ... Write to me. I kiss you. Your Hafiz.

He spent the first week of his leave at his mother's estate with Akhmatova, seeing their son and discussing a divorce, and on their return to the capital he stayed with her at their flat.

The new Comedians' Inn Cabaret had a proper theatre, which was staging Pronin's production of his marionette drama 'Child of Allah', and Akhmatova told her friend Lydia Chukovskaya about her encounter with Larisa there after a performance one night. 'I was putting my coat on when suddenly Larisa appeared, two tears in place on her cheeks. I shook her hand. "Thank you, you're so generous", she said, "I'll never forget that you gave me your hand". What was that about? A pretty young girl, why so self-deprecating? How could

---

8 Larisa Reisner, *Selected Works* (edited and introduced by A. Naumova), Moscow, 1965. Referred to in the footnotes from now on as sw. Quotes from her books in sw are not footnoted, p. 528.

I have known she was sleeping with Nikolai Stepanovich? And even if I had, why wouldn't I have shaken her hand?'[9]

Despite her policy of keeping a fastidious distance from his affairs, she must surely have known about Larisa by then. According to Chukovskaya, it simply never occurred to her he would be interested in this socialist who wrote bad poetry – 'her poems were totally worthless, thank goodness she had the sense to stop'.

He told her about Larisa soon afterwards, 'as an emancipated woman', when they were discussing the divorce on a tram, and announced that he planned to marry her – 'Larisa Reisner will be happy to have me!' He then proposed to her, and his biographer Shubinsky reports her saying she cared too much about Akhmatova to upset her, to which he replied with a wry smile, 'Unfortunately nothing I do seems to upset her!'

Eventually she accepted, and her archives contain a mass of unpublished poems and love letters she wrote to him then. She wrote of the 'one unrepeatable moment in a person's life when they meet their true double, inhumanly beautiful, standing under the open skies'. 'Sweet husband Hafiz, like a Jaguar', she wrote after a visit with him to the Zoo, where he was mesmerised by the panthers, deadly and defeated in their cage.

Her next letter from him at the front came with his three 'Canzonas' he wrote to her (published the following year in his collection *The Pyre*):

> Only love survives for me,
> Calling with the string of an angelic harp,
> Piercing my soul with the blue rays of paradise.
> I have seen the sun of the night.
> It is for you alone that I live on this earth …

On 20 January, her rapturous review of 'Gondla' was published in *Chronicle* – 'Gumilyov creates a kingdom of pure abstract ideas above the mortal transitory world. With a pagan boldness reminiscent of Plato, he gives limitless freedom to art, an ideal existence that does not fear eternity and cannot be destroyed. The fate of the universal moment lies in the poet's hands, which give immortality to love and joy …'[10]

A week later, she discovered that he had also proposed to Anna Engelhardt.

According to Shubinsky, 'Gumilyov didn't abandon women, he simply interchanged them'. Since Tumpovskaya left him, he had been taking three women

---

9   Chukovskaya 1994, p. 62.
10 Article quoted in Luknitskaya, p. 149.

to his dream destinations – Larisa to Madagascar, Anna Engelhardt to America, and Engelhardt's friend Olga Arbenina, an actress at the Alexandrinsky Theatre, to Egypt (he called them 'Pieretta and Columbine'). Arbenina was deeply in love with him, and Osip Mandelstam was in love with the beautiful Arbenina, and they fell out over her. Arbenina was then ousted by Engelhardt ('a most disagreeable, quarrelsome person', Akhmatova told Chukovskaya, 'he thought he had finally found someone he could keep in her place, but she was a tank'), and for the next eight months he had been sleeping with Larisa and Engelhardt without either of them apparently knowing about each other.

She wrote immediately to him at the front to end the affair. Since he was known never to meet a woman he didn't want to sleep with, she must surely have had her suspicions about all the time he spent praying and reading religious books. But there could be no jealousy between poets, jealousy would have been bourgeois and beneath her, and she wrote to him in a noble, generous tone, without reproaches, thanking him for everything he had taught her, and for 'the strange feelings that connected us, like love. Bless you, your life and your poetry. I often think we'll meet somewhere again. My beloved, may you experience and create miracles, and be better and purer than ever. Your Leri'.

Either her letter never reached him or he decided to ignore it, or it crossed with his, in which he begged his 'beautiful golden Lerichka' not to be angry with him for not writing earlier, explaining that he had been out on manoeuvres, 'shooting at Germans and being shot at'. He complained about the shambles on the Eastern Front, and told her he had applied to join the Russian Expeditionary Forces in Persian Azerbaijan, to fight the armies of the Ottoman Empire. He then wrote of his poetry: 'How I regret the years I wasted listening to ignorant critics, trying to write poems that were heartfelt and sincere, instead of practising my rondeaus, rondels, lays, virileys and so on. I must act the cavalryman and embrace my Hussar happiness, knowing that the joy of creativity comes from my love for you, and without you I would not dare to write ...'

Five years later, she told her mother she had never loved anyone as deeply as she had loved him, and she would have died for him. But she was clearly in no mood to be wooed back by his rondels and virileys, and the end of the affair left her in a deep depression. She fought it with work, firing off articles and essays to *Chronicle* on art and literature – the paintings of Goya and Velasquez, the poetry of Rilke, the novels of H.G. Wells. Her archives contain files of notes she wrote then, ideas for more essays, translations from German, scraps of poetry, and she would write poetry for the rest of her life. But the aesthetic detachment of her old literary idols had finally lost its appeal for her, and from now on her poetry would be in her journalism.

CHAPTER 5

Red Kronstadt

Two and a half years into the war, a million soldiers had abandoned their sectors and were pouring home to join the ranks of the revolution, breaking into arsenals, sacking estates and killing the landowners on the way. In the cities, they were drafted into the factories, and were joining the women in the bread queues, raiding shops and warehouses. Hunger riots and political strikes gathered unprecedented strength and ferocity, and on 27 February, fifty thousand workers at Petrograd's Putilov arms factory came out on strike.

The capital filled day and night with demonstrators, and strikes and demonstrations quickly spread across Russia. Nine days later, thousands of women in Petrograd celebrated International Women's Day in an event of civil disorder unparalleled in Russia, looting bakeries and wrecking factories, breaking into the barracks and arsenals, persuading the soldiers to hand over their weapons and join them, marching through the streets with makeshift placards saying 'Bread!' 'Increase Our Rations!' 'Our Children Are Starving!'

The Tsar was at his military headquarters south of the capital, and was kept informed of events by his wife. 'A hooligan campaign', she wrote to him, 'a lot of silly girls and boys running round shouting that they have no bread. It will surely pass'.

He returned to Petrograd on 14 March, expecting a warm welcome from the Duma, and was told that the autocracy had collapsed, and the country was being run by the new Provisional Government of the Duma. Two days later, he was forced to sign the abdication papers, bringing an end to the Tsarist Empire and three centuries of Romanov rule.

The Provisional Government, businessmen and landowners, announced an impressive programme of reforms, in education, hospitals and the army, and set out to restore morale in the officer class to keep Russia in the war. The Treasury and postal services, the High Command and the Secret Police were still in the hands of tsarist functionaries. And occupying (appropriately) the left wing of the Tauride Palace, holding the balance of power, was the newly resurrected Petrograd Soviet, the Soviet of Workers' and Soldiers' Deputies. 'The Provisional Government has no real powers', said the Prime Minister, Prince Lvov. 'Its orders are obeyed only if they happen to fall in with the wishes of the Soviet of Workers' and Soldiers' Deputies'.

Soldiers handed over the keys to the arsenals to arm the Bolsheviks' new volunteer militia the Red Guards, formed to defend the Soviet, and as exiled revolutionaries poured back to the capital that spring to work with the Soviet, thousands rallied to the Bolsheviks' slogan 'Peace, Bread and Land'.

According to Akhmatova, the March revolution passed Gumilyov by – 'he simply didn't notice it'. In April, he finally received his orders to leave the Eastern Front, not for Azerbaijan, but for the Greek port of Salonica, to fight with the Russian brigades defending the Serbs against Bulgaria. But another bout of bronchitis sent him back to Petrograd, and by the time he recovered his orders had changed, and he was appointed Military Attaché to the Provisional Government's embassy in Paris.

He travelled there via Sweden, Norway and England, and he spent three weeks in London, discussing poetry with G.K. Chesterton, Aldous Huxley, Virginia Woolf and other members of the Bloomsbury set, and was interviewed by the journal the *Russian Literary Triquarterly*, in which he deplored the Futurists, and their 'contempt for the past and the spiritual in Russia'.

The last things he wrote to Larisa were two postcards, one from Stockholm, with his poem 'Sweden' (later published in *The Pyre*), the other from Oslo, saying 'Have fun. Stay out of politics'. 'Leri' was now 'Larisa Mikhailovna', and 'Hafiz' was 'N. Gumilyov'.[1]

All university courses in Russia had been indefinitely suspended in March, and her mother worried that her father would be out of a job, and she wouldn't finish her studies. 'The mistakes I made in raising you were appalling, and the revolution played its part, interrupting your education and making you rootless', she wrote to her later. But although the revolution meant the end of her formal education, it was also opening up a whole new world of opportunities for women, and from now on she would be getting her education from the revolutionary movement.

Thousands of women were being thrown into politics for the first time, and longstanding revolutionaries like Kollontai became some of the Bolsheviks' most effective activists and public speakers, demanding a proper political commitment to their rights and equality. They soon represented such a powerful force in the Party that Kollontai proposed setting up Party women's sections, like those in Germany, to report back to the leadership on their needs. A majority of women members rejected this though as unnecessary and divisive, and Larisa would probably have agreed with them. Like many young women who became politically active that spring, she believed the best way for them to make a place for themselves in the reorganisation of power was to put aside their differences with men and work with them as their equals.

---

1 Quoted in Luknitskaya 1990, p. 192.

In March, she joined the educational programme of the Petrograd Soviet, teaching literacy and literature in the workers' clubs in the poor suburbs, as her father had done, encouraging them to write about their lives and discuss each other's work. A month later, she attended the meeting to launch Gorky's new socialist paper *New Life*, with the *Chronicle* writers Blok and Esenin, Isaac Babel, Shklovsky and Mayakovsky, the literary critic Kornei Chukovsky (brother of Akhmatova's friend Lydia), the Marxist historian Yury Steklov, editor of the Petrograd Soviet's new newspaper *Izvestiya*, and her student friend Mikhail Koltsov from the Poetry Circle.

Koltsov had joined the Red Guards in March, and was in the special unit appointed by the Soviet to arrest the Tsar's ministers still in the Winter Palace. But Steklov was the only Bolshevik on the editorial board. Gorky wanted *New Life*, like *Chronicle*, to represent a diversity of political views, revolutionary and non-aligned. Shklovsky recalled that first meeting. 'Reisner spoke. Steklov was amazed, and kept saying "So she's a Marxist!"'[2]

On 16 April, Lenin returned to Petrograd in his famous 'sealed train' from Switzerland, filled with revolutionaries, and delivered his message to the Soviet to overthrow the Provisional Government and prepare for the seizure of state power. Lunacharsky returned a week later, in a second train full of revolutionaries, and took over the Soviet's culture and education department, and became a regular contributor to *New Life*.

Larisa wrote articles for the paper about her teaching work for the Soviet, and attended daily editorial meetings at its offices on the Nevsky Prospect. The Bolshevik journalist Nikolai Demidov described first meeting her there with Mayakovsky, and being invited back to her home to meet her family and 'Sima' Roshal, who was on leave from Kronstadt.[3]

In March, in a repeat of the October 1905 uprising, Kronstadt's sailors had shot the most brutal of their commanders and declared the 'Kronstadt Republic', electing the new Bolshevik Revolutionary Committee to run the garrison's affairs, chaired by Roshal, with decisions taken at daily mass meetings in the town square. Kronstadt was now a major centre of Bolshevik power, in close contact with Bolsheviks at Helsingfors (now Helsinki), the main base of the Imperial Baltic Fleet. Roshal spoke of his comrades' work on the Revolutionary Committee, and the fighting mood of the sailors. Then they discussed the

---

2 Victor Shklovsky, 'Bessmylneishaya smert' (A Most Absurd Death), in *Gamburgskii schet. Stati, vospominaniya, esse, 1914–1933* (Hamburg's Debt. Articles, Memories, Essays), Moscow, 1990, p. 356.
3 Demidov in conversation with Przhiborovskaya 2008, p. 219.

turmoil in the capital, and their frustration with Gorky, and his appeals in *New Life* for peace and reason.

Lenin later accused Gorky of allowing his politics to be ruled by his 'moods and feelings', and Trotsky complained of his 'fastidious hand-washing' – 'Gorky approaches the revolution with the caution of a museum curator'. Larisa deeply appreciated writers' debt to him. He had funded two anti-war publications, and had helped countless workers to get their work into print, including many from her classes. But she had talked enough about revolution, she needed to see it for herself.

Her teaching work for the Soviet took her around Petrograd, to the munitions town of Sestrorestsk, the Estonian capital Reval (now Tallinn), and to Kronstadt, and in over a dozen articles and sketches for *New Life*, she reported on the new workers' culture – the street theatre groups, the factory wall newspapers, the songs and poetry. Many of the paper's contributors dismissed these rough new proletarian art forms. She celebrated them as 'the creative pulse of the revolution, which is making culture the property of the people, the true inheritors of the treasures of the past'.[4]

It was at 'Red Kronstadt' that she met some of the revolution's bravest fighters, and Roshal's comrades on the Revolutionary Committee – Nikolai Markin, Chair of the Bolshevik committee in the Navy, and the two Ilin brothers, in charge of the Committee's education work, Alexander, the 'Genevan', and Fyodor, two years older, Chair of the Kronstadt Party and Soviet, better known by his underground name Fyodor Raskolnikov, who recruited her to give literature classes in the sailors' clubs and on the ships.

An Asian communist who met Raskolnikov in 1917 described him as 'tall, handsome and athletic, with blue eyes and close-cropped hair, who looked more like an English student than a Russian Bolshevik, quick, direct, incisive, uninterested in theoretical problems, with a sharp and active mind'.

Although just three years older than Larisa, he already had a wealth of revolutionary experience behind him. While she had been agonising over Acmeism, he had been suffering jail and persecution and the marginalised life of the underground. His Party name, from the Nietzschean underground superman hero of Dostoyevsky's novel *Crime and Punishment*, spoke of his attraction to the implacable being of pure will, defending the right of the strong to destroy those who stand in his way, and his life had been a story of Dostoyevskyan suffering and redemption. Proud, sensitive, highly strung, prone to fits of ela-

---

4   From Larisa's article 'The Transformation of the People's House', *New Life*, 19 September, 1917. SW, p. 586.

tion and despair, a fighter and hardened Bolshevik, who loved poetry and literature, he was a powerfully romantic figure, and she fell wildly in love with him.

She is likely to have known the brothers already in fact, as their mothers were distantly related. Antonina Ilina was an aristocrat, the daughter of a general. Their father, Fyodor Petrov, was a popular St Petersburg parish priest with socialist views, hated by his superiors in the Church. He had been a widower when the couple met, and since ordained Orthodox priests are forbidden to remarry, their sons had to be registered as illegitimate, with their father's patronymic, Fyodorovich, but their mother's surname. Illegitimacy was a terrible stigma in tsarist Russia, and the Church's mistreatment of the boys' gentle deeply religious parents turned them both into resolute atheists at an early age.[5]

In Raskolnikov's brief autobiography, he described their brutal education at Prince Oldenberg's charitable boarding-school for the sons of poor priests, where they were starved and beaten, and leading the other boys in a riot there in 1905, when he was thirteen. He then came to the dark heart of their story, two years later, when their father was finally destroyed by his superiors in the Church. A parishioner of his was paid to accuse him of raping her, and unable to defend himself or bear the disgrace, he slit his throat with a razor on the eve of his trial.

His death left the family destitute. The boys' mother worked as a saleswoman in a wineshop to support them, and when seventeen-year-old Fyodor passed the entrance exams to St Petersburg's prestigious Polytechnic Institute with top marks, she went into debt to pay his fees. He immersed himself in his economics studies and was soon awarded a full scholarship, and he began attending student Bolshevik meetings and reading Lenin and Marx. He joined the party in 1910, writing articles under his new name Raskolnikov for its newspaper *Star*, and two years later for its new daily paper *Pravda* (Truth). His brother Alexander, a gifted chess player, wrote articles on chess for *Star* and *Pravda*, and he

---

5 Details of Raskolnikov's life in the *Granat Encyclopaedia*, op. cit. Nikolai Sukhanov, *The Russian Revolution 1917* (trans. Joel Carmichael), 1955.; *Makers of the Russian Revolution* (trans. David Bellos, eds. G. Haupt and J.J. Marie), 1974, pp. 206–7.; E. Saul Ross, 'A Secondary Bolshevik,' *Russian Review*, April 1973, vol. 32, pp. 131–42.; Vladimir Savchenko, *Otstupnik. Drama Fyodora Raskolnikova* (Renegade. The Drama of Fyodor Raskolnikov), Moscow, 2001. (A fictional biography, drawn from the archives).; On his brother: Alexander Morozov, *A. lin Zhenevsky. Revolyutsioner, istorik, shakhmatist, literator* (A. Ilin the Genevan. Revolutionary, Historian, Chess-player, Author), St Petersburg, 2006.

joined the party in 1912 aged seventeen, in his last year at school, for which he was immediately expelled.

That May, Raskolnikov was arrested and jailed in St Petersburg's political prison the 'Crosses', and was then sentenced to three years' exile in the northern penal colony of Arkhangelsk. He escaped from jail with false papers, and lived abroad for a year, first in Paris then in Berlin, where he was rearrested in 1913 as a Russian spy. He was waiting in jail to be deported back to Russia, when the Tsar announced another amnesty for political exiles, to celebrate the Romanov centenary, and he returned legally to St Petersburg, where he worked underground with the Bolsheviks, and was elected editorial secretary of *Pravda*. In August 1914, two days after war was declared, the entire *Pravda* editorial board was arrested or conscripted, and he was drafted into the navy.

Given the brothers' closeness, Alexander must have been an important figure in Larisa's life, but unfortunately there is nothing in her published writings about this interesting man.

Unlike Raskolnikov, he escaped arrest in 1912, and a wealthy Bolshevik supporter paid for him to leave Russia for Switzerland, to study natural sciences at the University of Geneva, where he adopted his underground name the 'Genevan', and became chess champion of Geneva. The city was Lenin's base in exile for many years, and he became close to him and his circle of Bolsheviks. Lenin was a keenly competitive chess player and played regularly with him, and he gave him a briefcase for his lists of players, inscribed with the words 'To fellow-exile A.F. Ilin from V.I. Ulyanov',[6] which he would describe for the rest of his life as his most treasured possession.

He returned to St Petersburg in the spring of 1914, and a month after war was declared, he was conscripted into a flame-throwing unit on the Polish front. That autumn he was asphyxiated by poison gas in the battle for Warsaw, and after two weeks in hospital he was sent back to the front, where he suffered a serious head injury. Crippled and shellshocked, he regained his memory and his ability to walk by teaching himself to play chess all over again, and he became an even better player than before, and a lifelong advocate of the healing powers of the game.

Raskolnikov survived the war without injury. As a conscript with higher education, he was trained as an officer at Petrograd's élite Naval Academy, and sailed as a junior commander on two cruises to the Far East, to Korea and Japan. He was sitting for his final officer's exams in Petrograd when the March revolution broke out, and unable to complete them, he returned to Kronstadt a week

---

6   Lenin was the underground name of Vladimir Ulyanov.

after the uprising still as a sub-lieutenant. His brother, as a semi-invalid, had been assigned to non-combatant duties in the navy, and he arranged for him to join him there, and together they organised classes for the sailors, and edited the garrison's new party paper, *Voice of Pravda*.

Popular with his men, a gifted public speaker and journalist, Raskolnikov brought to his work in Kronstadt the outstanding organisational and leadership skills he had learnt in his years in the underground. He and Roshal worked so closely together on the Revolutionary Committee that they were known by the sailors as one person, 'Raskolnikov Roshal', and by the spring of 1917, the town's garrison, shops and factories were all ready to pass to the Committee's control.

Unfortunately for Larisa, he was also known to be in love with the brilliant and charismatic Alexandra Kollontai, who visited Kronstadt to speak about workers' power and women's liberation at packed sailors' meetings on the battleships.

Kollontai was a heroine and role model for young activists like Larisa, and an even more formidable rival than Akhmatova, a figure of great stature in the Party, entrusted by Lenin to smuggle his 'Letters From Afar' into Petrograd when she returned from exile, and a trailblazer for the new liberated sexuality of the revolution, whose passionate love affair with the sailor Pavel Dybenko, Chair of the Bolshevik Committee at Helsingfors, was the subject of much shock and disapproval from her Party comrades. She was an aristocrat, forty-five years old, divorced, with an adult son. He was seventeen years younger, from a family of illiterate Ukrainian day-labourers. But as she had written six years earlier in her pamphlet *Sexual Relations and the Social Struggle*: 'A professor can marry his young working-class student, or a doctor his young cook, and they will be praised for raising their status. But god help the woman professor or doctor who marries her student or cook – and if he is handsome and has "physical qualities", so much the worse!'

In Kollontai's life and writings, she challenged the double standard of the old family under capitalism, based on private property, which made women the property of men. She wrote of the revolution in people's feelings about sex, and she imagined the more equal and civilised sexual relationships possible under socialism, when private property was abolished, and the state could take full responsibility for mothers and their children. And in the process she saw a new kind of marriage partnership developing, 'between two members of the workers' state, bound by comradeship and mutual respect. In the socialist future, there is no doubt that love will become the cult of humanity'.

Kollontai's message to women was to initiate relationships with men on their own terms. And in the heady days of spring, Larisa finally won Raskolnikov from her rival, and they became lovers and comrades in the struggle.

Returning from the Eastern Front that summer, the Minister of War Alexander Guchkov reported, 'The disorganisation is such that one might believe oneself to be in a madhouse'. 'The army is drowning in its own blood', reported General Brusilov, Commander of the South-Western Front.

Inflation soared to over 400 percent, and bread rations in the cities were reduced to 100 grams a day. In Moscow, railworkers led a general strike in the city, and millionaire factory-owner Pavel Ryabushinsky slashed his workers' wages – 'so that the gaunt hand of famine and destitution will seize the false friends of the people, the soviets, by the throat'. 'We have entered the zone of collapse', a Bolshevik delegate told a Moscow factory conference. 'We no longer have the strength to live under these conditions', a trade union official informed the Provisional Government.

Strikes and anti-war demonstrations in the capital reached massive proportions, with thousands filling the streets day and night. In June, ministers frantically opened negotiations with their supporters in the Petrograd Soviet, from whom they picked their new Minister of War, the ambitious young lawyer Alexander Kerensky. Kerensky toured the battlefields, fuelled by morphine and cocaine, delivering patriotic speeches about victory, honour and the oath. But when he ordered more soldiers to the front, in Russia's last desperate offensive in Galicia, most in the capital refused to leave their barracks, and those who did were killed in their thousands when the offensive collapsed a few days later.

In the countryside, the peasants' revolution was past the point of no return. In the cities, strikers were breaking into the bakeries and demonstrating for Soviet power. On 3 July, fifty thousand Red Guards and workers from Petrograd's Putilov arms factory appeared on the streets, armed by the Bolsheviks, demanding workers' control over pay and production, the arrests of the bosses, and the immediate transfer of power to the soviets. They were joined by workers from other factories, an entire machine-gun regiment, a division of armoured cars, and women support troops, nurses and runners. Barricades went up, and there were pitched battles with the police, and several buildings were set on fire, including the Ministry of Religion and the notorious Litovsky Prison, which was burnt to the ground. Fearing revolution was imminent, five ministers resigned from the Provisional Government, and the Prime Minister Prince Lvov was replaced by Kerensky, who pledged to restore 'Russia's full economic and political stabilisation'.

Raskolnikov was appointed to lead the armed detachment of sailors defending the Kshesinskaya Palace, where the Bolsheviks had installed their military headquarters. But his men were in a mood to fight. On 7 July, twenty thousand sailors and workers sailed from Kronstadt to the capital and marched through the streets, gathering supporters on the way, demanding that the Bolsheviks take power. Many believed the sailors had left Kronstadt on Raskolnikov's orders, then saw him rapidly lose control of the situation, attempting helplessly to intervene as they broke into a session of the Soviet at the Tauride Palace. Trotsky ordered them back to their barracks, insisting that power must pass in an orderly fashion to the Petrograd Soviet, and most eventually left. But hundreds of revolutionary leaders, including Trotsky and Raskolnikov, Lunacharsky, Kollontai and Dybenko, were arrested and jailed as agents of the German government, which was claimed to have orchestrated and funded the insurrection. Lenin escaped arrest, and went into hiding in Finland. 'We are searching for him', Kerensky said.

Regiments were drafted from the front into the capital to crush the rising, and over two hundred were killed in the 'July Days' by forces still loyal to Kerensky. But his war strategy had been disintegrating even as he took office, and the Russian army fought its last battle on 21 August, when the Latvian capital Riga fell to Germany.

Foreign businesses in Russia had been badly affected in March, and the British and French governments were openly calling for a military dictatorship as the only alternative to another revolution, under the newly appointed Chief of Staff, General Kornilov, former commander of the Petrograd garrison, who had been in charge of suppressing the July rising, and vowed to 'hang every member of the Soviet'. On 9 September, twenty thousand of Kornilov's troops, joined by fifty British and French officers dressed in Russian uniforms, marched on Petrograd to restore law and order and seize power from Kerensky. Workers patrolled the streets, machine guns were moved into position, more barricades went up, and forty of Kornilov's generals were arrested by Red Guards in the Astoria Hotel, where they had been prematurely toasting his victory.

The defeat of Kornilov's *putsch* without a shot fired was a triumph for the Bolsheviks, who already held the majority of seats in the Petrograd and Moscow Soviets, and were emerging as the only viable alternative to the drug-addled Kerensky's foundering government. Trotsky and Lunacharsky both joined the Party in jail, and were elected to its Central Committee. They were released with Raskolnikov and others in the last week of September, Lunacharsky as deputy mayor of Petrograd, Trotsky as Chair of the Petrograd Soviet, the post he had occupied twelve years earlier, reminding cheering delegates that in 1905 they had been smashed – 'This time we are stronger than ever!' Raskolnikov, Roshal and Markin returned to Kronstadt, now under the control of the Revolutionary Committee, to keep its members in touch with Bolsheviks in Petrograd, and Raskolnikov was appointed to liaise between the Party and Lenin in his hiding place in Finland.

After eight months of bourgeois liberal rule, the Bolsheviks were ready to take power. More Red Guards and women fighters, nurses and stretcher-bearers appeared on Petrograd's streets, and soldiers and sailors in the garrisons were instructed by Trotsky to take orders only from the Soviet. By 23 October, Red Guards had seized the main railway stations, the central Post Office, the Ministry of Religion and the State Bank, and Kronstadt's sailors were preparing to sail down the River Neva to defend the Second All-Russian Congress of Soviets, where power was to pass to the Bolsheviks.

On the 24th, members of the Central Committee were summoned to the Smolny Institute, formerly Catherine the Great's School for Girls of the Nobility, now the headquarters of the Bolshevik General Staff. The guard was strengthened, and extra bullets were laid on, and cables were sent to Dybenko and Raskolnikov at Helsingfors and Kronstadt to send 'regulations' to the capital. 'The sailors will sail at dawn', Raskolnikov cabled back.

On the evening of the 25th, as the Congress of Soviets prepared to open in the Smolny, the Battleship *Aurora*, escorted by a flotilla of gunboats, anchored in the Neva and aimed its cannon at the Winter Palace, where the Provisional Government was in session. Lenin then emerged from hiding, and at 9.30 that night, against the sounds of muffled blanks from the *Aurora*, he informed the Congress that the Provisional Government had been overthrown, and the Bolsheviks were in power.

CHAPTER 6

Bolshevik Russia

Lenin spoke again in the early hours of the 26th, to announce Russia's withdrawal from the war, and to ask for delegates' endorsement of the new government, the Commissariat of People's Commissars. He was elected Commissar of the People's Commissars, or President. Trotsky was Commissar of Foreign Affairs. Lunacharsky was Commissar of Education, and Kollontai was Commissar of Social Welfare, the government's only woman. Raskolnikov was appointed commissar of the Naval General Staff of the Petrograd Military Committee, and his brother Alexander chief commissar of Red Guard reservists in Moscow and the surrounding textile towns, with their militant mainly female workforce.

Raskolnikov was reported to have led the detachment of sailors appointed to arrest the remaining members of the Provisional Government in the Winter Palace, and there were several accounts of Larisa's activities that night. According to Vadim Andreev, she sailed to Petrograd with Raskolnikov and the sailors on the *Aurora*, and it was she who gave the orders for the cannon blanks to be fired at the Palace, signalling the birth of the new Russia. Victor Shklovsky claimed she joined the detachment of Red Guards who stormed the Peter and Paul Fortress – 'Not a difficult assault. But the fortress had to be approached. To have faith that the gates would open'. Vera Inber reported that she presented herself for duty to the Bolshevik Central Committee, huddled in a small side room in the Smolny, and when asked 'What can you do Comrade?' replied, 'I can fight, ride, write reports from the front, and if necessary die'.[1]

As Lenin said, 'There are days when decades happen'. Many in the new government had imagined it would survive no longer than a few days, but within a fortnight, soviets had taken power in towns and villages across a vast area of Russia and eleven time-zones – from Moscow to the Baltic, the Volga and industrial Eastern Ukraine, from the Siberian border to the Central Asian tsarist protectorates of Tashkent, Samarkand and Bukhara, and the oilfields of the Caspian.

But the Bolsheviks were already facing their first battles with the counterrevolution. Kerensky saw the new government as a temporary inconvenience that could quickly be dealt with. The day after the Revolution, he appointed himself Supreme Commander of the Armies of the Republic, then set off for the Tsar's

---

1   Vadim Andreev, *Childhood*, 1966, p. 70; Shklovsky, 'A Most Absurd Death', 1928, p. 356; Inber, 'Evolution of a Swan', 1966, p. 280.

military headquarters at Gachina, twenty miles from the capital, to mobilise tsarist commanders and cadets to defeat the mutinous rabble. On 27 October, the cavalry commander General Krasnov marched seven hundred Cossacks of Kerensky's 'Savage Division' from Gachina on Petrograd. Raskolnikov led a detachment of Kronstadt sailors who fought on the front line of the city to drive them back, and thousands of men, women and children, in temperatures of 25 degrees below zero, poured through the streets with rifles, picks and shovels, to dig trenches and build barricades in its encircled suburbs. Over three hundred died in the battles for the capital, but by the 31st Red Petrograd had been saved, in the Bolsheviks' first military victory. Raskolnikov and his sailors then left for Moscow, where they fought to defend the Soviet with his brother's Red Guard reservists.

The Reisners' landlord, Duke Leuchtenberg, who had led a unit of Cossacks in the battle for Petrograd, fled to Berlin. Kerensky also avoided arrest, and escaped to Paris. General Krasnov was arrested, but was soon released, after giving his word as an officer not to take up arms against the Bolsheviks. He then headed south to the Don and Kuban regions, where he was joined by General Kornilov, who had escaped from jail, Kornilov's Chief of Staff Admiral Kolchak, hero of the Russo-Japanese War, and Generals Denikin, Alexeev, Yudenich and Kaledin, who with Allied support, set about building their volunteer army of counterrevolutionary White Guards.

Dozens of arrested former tsarist officers were released in the months before the revolutionary police force the *Cheka* was set up, and the Bolsheviks soon regretted their benevolence. 'The greater our terror, the greater our victories', Kornilov said.[2]

Once the Whites were driven from the capital, the government now had to battle with the old ruling classes, who mobilised to make Soviet Russia ungovernable. The Committee to Save the Country, formed immediately after the Revolution, paid civil servants a month's wages to come out on strike, and factories, government offices and schools, the railways and the army were paralysed by sabotage. Striking officials in the new commissariats wrecked premises and looted funds, and the huge wine cellars of the Winter Palace, guarded by one sober Bolshevik sailor, threatened to drown the Revolution in a haze of the tsars' alcohol.

Mayakovsky was in the Smolny with Lenin the night the Bolsheviks took power, and the theatre director Vsevolod Meyerhold immediately joined the

---

2 The *Cheka* was the Extraordinary Commission for the Struggle Against Sabotage and Counterrevolution, established in December 1917.

Party. Blok and the poet Andrei Bely were both members of the left Socialist Revolutionaries, who were close to the Bolsheviks. Bely wrote in Messianic terms of the Revolution, predicting that history would view the new proletarian state as one of the great pinnacles of human achievement, like the birth of Christ – 'ushering in a new culture of eternity'. Blok, when asked if writers could work with the new government, replied simply, 'Yes they can, and they must!'

Most of Petrograd's writers were in shock at the lightning speed events. The day after the Bolsheviks took power, Gorky issued a long statement in *New Life* denouncing them for the chaos they would unleash, calling them 'socialist Napoleons who suppress free speech, and put Russia's proletariat in mortal peril', and Lenin angrily refuted Gorky's charge that 'the 24,000 members of the Bolshevik Party will be unable to govern Russia in the interests of the poor, and against the rich'.

Many writers felt nothing but disgust and loathing for the workers occupying the tsars' palaces, and fled abroad. Others stayed in Russia as open enemies of the Revolution and 'internal emigres', denouncing those who worked with the regime as traitors. Leonid Andreev died in Finland in 1919, cursing the Revolution. The poet Dmitry Merezhkovsky called October a victory for 'Beast Nation' – '150 million fools, all of them lice-ridden'.

Only a handful of intellectuals supported the Bolsheviks in those early days. The journalist Boris Malkin reported that a week after the Revolution, Petrograd's writers and artists were invited to the Smolny to meet the new commissars: 'At 7 o'clock in the evening, representatives of the capital's intelligentsia assembled at the Smolny, seated on one sofa – Blok, Mayakovsky, Meyerhold, and Larisa Reisner'.[3]

Lunacharsky's Commissariat of Education was the first to start functioning after October, launching a nationwide literacy programme, turning palaces into museums, and opening new public libraries, 'to feed hungry readers with books'. Lunacharsky set up departments of further and polytechnic education, an art department, and a literary and publishing department, which sponsored the new State Publishing House, *Gosizdat*, and he appointed Blok, Kornei Chukovsky, Larisa, and her comrade Mikhail Koltsov to its editorial board, preparing mass editions of the works of Gorky, Tolstoy and Pushkin on the cheapest paper. Blok and Larisa were against publishing them in the new simplified spelling and orthography proposed by the Provisional Government. But they were outvoted by Lunacharsky and the majority, and the reforms became

---

3   Quoted in Eleonara Solovei, *Larisa Reisner*, 1985, p. 39.

law the following summer. (Eleven years later, Lunacharsky even campaigned unsuccessfully for the Cyrillic alphabet to be replaced with Latin).

All the Reisners were swept up in the historic events of October. Larisa's mother worked with Lunacharsky as secretary of his Commissariat's Reading Commission. Nineteen-year-old Igor, who had missed out on university in the turmoil, worked with Trotsky at the Commissariat of Foreign Affairs. Their father rejoined the Party, and as Russia's leading authority on constitutional law, he was appointed by Lenin to write the first Soviet Constitution, the Declaration of the Rights of Working People, passed the following summer, which enshrined in law the dictatorship of the proletariat, making Russia the first workers' state in the world.

He worked on at the Commissariats of Justice, Labour, Health and Education on their formidable programme of new legislation – nationalising property, doing away with the old tsarist ranks and titles, abolishing censorship and the Jewish Pale, reforming Russia's collapsing hospitals and schools. Free healthcare was promised to all citizens in state-funded hospitals, and free education to all children between the ages of eight and fifteen in their native languages, including Yiddish. Ethnic minorities were to have full educational and occupational equality, and racial diversity was celebrated, with new Jewish Sections of the Party established – the *Evsektsii* – staffed mainly by former members of the Jewish Bund. The Bolsheviks declared war on anti-Semitism and all forms of racism and nationalism, and the large number of Jews in the government spoke for itself.

Reisner had a major role in the drafting of the first law of the Revolution, the Labour Law of November 1917, which cut the working day to eight hours, increased wages, introduced equal pay for women and banned them from heavy work in the mines and factories, and outlawed child labour. His vast knowledge of church-state relations was also used in the drafting of one of the Revolution's most difficult and contentious laws, the Law Separating Church and State, passed in February 1918.

On coming to power, the Bolsheviks had declared their intention to create a 'scientific state'. Science was central to the Marxist conception of history. Just as scientists investigated how one form of matter turned into another, Marxists sought to understand the laws that turned one form of society into another. Reisner laid the groundwork for the new law in a series of articles and philosophical essays on religion for the popular and academic press, and his pamphlet *Who Needs Soviet Power?* He called for a new science-based education programme to draw people away from the Orthodox Church, purveyor of the most reactionary ideas of the tsarist state. At the same time he stressed that monasteries and churches and their contents were not to be touched in the Bolsheviks' mass expropriations of buildings for housing, and that despite the Party's explicitly atheist programme, religion was no bar to membership.

The novelist and playwright Mikhail Bulgakov was reported to have studied Reisner's atheist writings closely in the 1930s when he was working on his novel *The Master and Margarita,* and to have made him the model for his character Woland – the mysterious Bolshevik professor who arrives in Moscow with his demonic retinue and an enormous talking cat, and a 'faith-shaped hole in his soul filled with atheism'.

Two days before the Revolution, Gorky had issued an appeal in *New Life* for Russia's precious heritage to be preserved: 'Citizens, do not touch one stone! This is your history, your pride!' Lunacharsky's Commission for the Preservation of Artistic and Historic Monuments recruited Red Guards to guard the capital's museums and palaces, and he appointed Larisa to head its team cataloguing the imperial treasures in the Hermitage Gallery in the Winter Palace, the largest art collection in the world, to ensure that they were passed intact to the worker's state.

She was the first journalist to enter the Palace after October, still with Catherine the Great's 'Rules of Conduct' on the wall:

1. Leave all ranks outside the door. Likewise hats and large swords.
2. Be cheerful. Spoil, break and soil nothing.
3. Argue without heat or temper.
4. Eat delicately and drink in moderation, so that each may find his feet when departing.

In her article for *New Life* 'In the Winter Palace', published four days after the Revolution, she cast a sardonic eye at the tsars' possessions, now the property of the people:

> In the evening, covered with the first November snow, the Palace looks as serene and undisturbed as the white square outside ... Inside, nothing breaks the elegant proportions of its halls and galleries. The windows reveal the magnificent perspectives of the Neva, the pale sky, the Stock Exchange, the Peter and Paul Fortress, and the stoves and chandeliers are positioned to complement them ...
>
> At the heart of the building lies the ballroom, closed in on itself, gleaming with gold and malachite. The city, with its factory hooters and church bells, feels unimaginably distant. The domed rotunda lies as in the sleepy waters of the ocean depths, in an illusory realm of stairs, corridors and mirrors, which replace the windows with artificial light ...

It's most oppressive and unpleasant here, where the tsars have lived for the last hundred and fifty years. Some tasteless portraits and watercolours daubed by god knows who, furniture in the fashionable 'modern' style – in a dwelling built for demigods! My god, the sideboards, writing-desks and wardrobes! It's the taste of a stockbroker with a family photograph album and 'five cosy rooms!' You long to shove all this rubbish in the fire, in honour of the one nice old Florentine candelabra.

Even the Alexander II period is smeared with bad taste. Down a secret stairway leading from his dressing-room, is a passageway his maids of honour had to pass with shawls over their faces to reach their quarters. For it's a harem of nude Dianas and Venuses, muses and shepherdesses, dancers and marquesses. The Hermitage will be proud of these Bouchets, Watteaus and Fragonards. But the frames are all double – press a button, and the chaste magnificent goddesses turn into obscene playthings, with two crude botched-up nudes in pride of place, displayed as if in a butcher's shop. Pure pornography ...

The March revolution did little damage to the Palace. Then Kerensky moved in to take Nicholas's throne, and set up his offices in the best rooms ... Now everything is covered in ink stains, dust and cigarette ash. Kerensky's carelessness with the Romanovs' property smells bad. Why did he sleep in the Tsar's bed, and wipe his feet on luxuries belonging to the people? Why, after the Tsar had fled to Tobolsk, did he order his billiard table and balls to be set out for his own private game?[4]

When the crowds stormed the Winter Palace to arrest the Provisional Government, they had destroyed several paintings and sculptures in their rage at finding Kerensky gone. But she reported that several of the old servants she spoke to, who had bravely stayed on to defend the Palace, said they preferred the Bolsheviks, with their boots and guns and alien ways, to the Tsar and Kerensky. 'They don't insult us, and they smell more real', one told her. 'The masters liked to smother themselves in perfume, because they had no smell of their own'.

Compared to *Rudin*'s savaging of the powerful, her swipes at Kerensky seem fairly mild, and despite *New Life*'s policy of not attacking individuals by name, the article was published as she wrote it. That day she left Petrograd with a journalist's pass for Gachina, from which Kerensky's forces had just been driven back, and she returned a day later to find that the piece had produced storms of

---

4 'V Zimnem Dvortse' (In the Winter Palace), *New Life*, 29 October, 1917. *SW*, pp. 452–60.

protests from his supporters in Russia. Gorky had issued a public apology, and she was allowed the right to reply.

In her 'Letter to the Editors' she wrote: 'The paper has apologised for publishing through an oversight several references to A.F. Kerensky not as a politician, but as a private individual. I care nothing for Kerensky as an individual. I wrote of him only because his occupation of the Palace was an essential part of the picture'.[5] She then left *New Life* before she was fired.

5 *SW*, p. 461.

CHAPTER 7

'Unforgettable 1918'

The Revolution set off storms of diplomatic activity across the world. The governments of Britain, France and America immediately refused to recognise the new regime, and British and French officials met for secret talks in Paris to plan joint military action in Russia. The most profitable parts were to be divided up between them, with local soviets overthrown, and replaced with new British- and French-backed Committees of the Constituent Assembly, embryos of Russia's future national government. Britain, the senior partner in the alliance, claimed the oil of the Caucasus, and the strategically vital Baltic countries. France was to get the industrial Eastern Ukraine, and the Crimea, with its access to the Black Sea.

Isolated and impoverished, surrounded by hostile capitalist states, the Bolsheviks' survival depended on revolutions spreading to the advanced capitalist countries of the world, which would share their wealth and resources with Russia. And the first to follow Russia's example was to be Germany. 'Without a revolution in Germany we're doomed', Lenin said.

Fraternisation literature was smuggled to German soldiers at the front, appealing to them to desert and rally to the Bolsheviks' defence. The government simultaneously approached Germany for a separate peace, and on 18 November, a delegation from the Commissariat of Foreign Affairs arrived in the town of Brest-Litovsk, on the Russian-Polish border, to negotiate a ceasefire with the German High Command. By withdrawing from the war with Russia and eliminating its Eastern Front, Germany could focus its forces against France and Britain, and the armistice was signed a fortnight later, followed by negotiations for a permanent peace.

The talks continued until the end of December, when the Germans delivered their punishing conditions – for thousands of miles of territory in the west, including Ukraine and Finland, and a huge share of Russia's oilfields, industrial centres and farming land. The terms were rejected, and the Bolsheviks broke off the negotiations, issuing desperate appeals to workers in Germany to rise up and support them.

Germany's socialist leaders, allied to conservatives in the Reichstag, had survived the disgrace of 1914 and tightened their grip on the party. Thousands tore up their party cards to work underground with the Spartacist League for the revolution that would save Russia and spread to the rest of the world, and throughout January, mass strikes and anti-war demonstrations across the country brought an estimated forty million people onto the streets. 'It has happened! The head of German imperialism is on the chopping block! The armed fist of the proletarian revolution is raised!' headlines in *Pravda* declared.

By the end of the month, two hundred workers in Berlin had been jailed, with fifty thousand drafted into the army. On the point of being annihilated, the Bolsheviks sent a new delegation to Brest-Litovsk, headed now by Trotsky, Commissar of Foreign Affairs. The talks were soon deadlocked again, and on 18 February, the German government announced the start of its new offensive on Ukraine – 'to restore order in Russia, and wipe out the oriental pestilence of Bolshevism'.

Trotsky agreed to continue the talks, and on 23 February, after prolonged and bitter arguments that threatened to split the Party, the Central Committee voted to accept Germany's final predatory conditions, which shocked even the German negotiators – for Latvia, Lithuania, Belorussia and Finland, most of Poland and Ukraine, Bessarabia (now part of Moldova and Ukraine), and large parts of the Caucasus. The Bolsheviks were to pay Germany 300 million gold roubles in war reparations, and completely demobilise their army, and Germany prepared to overthrow the Soviet government by force if the terms were not ratified.

On 3 March,[1] nine days after the Treaty was provisionally signed, Britain and France announced the start of their economic land and sea blockade of Soviet Russia, and a *'cordon sanitaire'*, to stop the Bolshevik infection spreading West. A week later, the British warship *Glory* arrived at the Arctic port of Murmansk, followed by large detachments of French and American troops. Combined British and French forces were arming and training the counterrevolutionary White Guards assembling near the Finnish border and in the Don region in the South, and German troops were already occupying Ukraine and threatening Petrograd.

In anticipation of the German invasion, the capital was moved seven hundred miles east to Moscow, the historic capital of Russia. On 12 March, two million of Petrograd's citizens, along with factories, schools and hospitals, received their evacuation orders, and Larisa, Igor, Lev and their parents left Great Gunpowder Street for their new home in Moscow.

Most of the new arrivals in this mass resettlement programme were housed in the homes of the wealthy businessmen and aristocrats who had left the country or fled south, planning to sit things out until the German offensive. Those

---

1 In February 1918, Russia adopted the Western calendar, thirteen days ahead of the pre-revolutionary Julian one. Larisa refers interchangeably in her writings to the old and new dates for the Revolution, 25 October and 7 November.

who stayed lived a despised, 'declassed' existence, on the lowest rations, forced to share their homes with the workers.

The Reisners were allocated three small divided-up rooms in a luxurious mansion on Vozdvizhenka Street in Central Moscow, home of the late Count Sheremetev, leader of Moscow's Assembly of Nobles, who had voluntarily bequeathed the building to the Moscow Soviet on his death. It had then been hastily turned into municipal housing, and renamed the Fifth House of Soviets.

The top floor was occupied by the workshops and offices of the Red Seamstress sewing factory. On the ground floor was Sheremetev's marble columned reception hall, with its grand piano and library, which became a reading-room and club, where concerts and meetings were held. The rest of the rooms had been arranged mathematically, to give each resident a minimum of nine metres of living space, with little attention to the building's architecture. Corridors had been turned into rooms, with large rooms carved up into smaller ones, and doors and partitions at odd angles. Nine families lived there – teachers, factory workers, party officials, pensioners, single women with children – as well as a huge drifting population of new arrivals to the city, desperate for accommodation. Over seventy people shared the single telephone, bathroom and kitchen, and as in most Moscow homes then, even those of the wealthiest, there was no gas or geyser. Cooking had been done by servants on vast coal-burning ranges, which the new residents now had to keep going to heat the building and provide the hot water. Stove space was limited, and people either cooked on small primus-stoves in their rooms or ate in Moscow's new public canteens, set up to make the best use of scarce food and fuel supplies, and liberate women from the kitchen. Children under sixteen were fed there for free, and by 1920 over ninety percent of Moscow's population were eating in the canteens, and a majority were in communal housing.

Communal living went some way to relieving Moscow's acute housing shortage, and was seen as better way of living than the old bourgeois family arrangements, and as a rough and ready model for the future society, bringing people together from different generations and class backgrounds, fostering feelings of collective responsibility and respect.

Few in Moscow were as well housed as the Reisners, and all were thinking of the hard hungry days ahead.

The government moved into the Kremlin, where the Seventh Party Congress opened on 16 March, to debate the Brest-Litovsk Treaty with Germany. Lenin appealed to delegates to ratify the German terms, as a 'breathing space' for Russia's exhausted people. The seven Central Committee members of the Left Opposition group, headed by Radek and Kollontai, opposed 'this obscene "peace"', under which Russia was to give more than half its territory to its aggressors. The Treaty was 'a "breathing space" only for German imperialism', their programme said. Germany's demands were a declaration of war, which imposed a duty on revolutionaries to rebuild the army and fight.

Lenin argued that to continue the fighting would pass the death sentence on the Revolution – 'We'll surrender Imperial Petrograd and Holy Moscow, but we'll save the Revolution!' 784 delegates voted with him to ratify the Treaty, with 261 voting against.

Encouraged by this disunity, the British and French governments then opened talks with their old enemy Germany, for a new joint British-French-German intervention in Russia. For Lloyd George's Minister of Munitions, Winston Churchill, it was crucial that Germany was reintegrated into Europe to fight the 'foul baboonery of Communism', and 'strangle Bolshevism in its cradle'. 'Our threat now isn't the Boche, it's the Bolsheviks', said the Chief of the British Imperial Staff, Sir Henry Wilson.

The end of the war had left some fifty thousand well-armed Czech troops stranded along the Siberian and eastern railways, waiting to be allowed home. The Czecho-Slovak National Council had long seen tsarist Russia as its saviour against Austro-Hungary, and had received generous loans from France to recruit its army to the anti-Bolshevik cause. Many of the Czechs had complained of being badly treated by the Russians, and it was Churchill who saw that they could be used as an anti-Bolshevik rather than an anti-German force.

In March, after lengthy negotiations between the British, French, Soviet and Czecho-Slovak governments, it was agreed that they could return home via the eastern port of Vladivostok, on the Sea of Japan, Russia's main naval base in the Pacific, on condition that they surrender their arms. The Czechs assembling in Vladivostok were ordered by their commanders not to do so, and in May, Czech legions overthrew the soviet and installed a Constituent Assembly Committee.

Gateway to Siberia, with its vast untapped resources of coal, oil and precious minerals, Vladivostok was a huge prize for the Czechs, and triggered a wave of revolts in other key cities in the east, engineered and financed by Britain and France, in which sixty thousand Czechs, White Guards and foreign troops were met by some thirty thousand ill-equipped and largely untrained Red Guards and volunteers.

As the Allied Intervention struck into the heart of the country, the economy was put on a war footing, mass conscription was introduced, and the war became a war of total social mobilisation. Thousands went off to fight with the Bolsheviks. *'Agit-trains'* toured the country, exhorting people to defend the Revolution, and Trotsky, now Commissar of War, travelled to thousands of fronts on the armoured train in which he lived throughout virtually the entire Civil War, mobilising the disintegrating tsarist regiments into the new Red Army – 'conjuring the Red Army literally out of nothing', Lenin told Gorky.

That spring was the turning point in Larisa's life. She joined the Bolshevik Party, and in May, a week after her twenty-third birthday, she registered her marriage to Raskolnikov in one of the Bolsheviks' new state 'red wedding' ceremonies.

Raskolnikov's bravery in the battles for Petrograd had earned him a place in Lenin's inner circle, and in January 1918 Lenin had appointed him to read the government's statement of its withdrawal from the Constituent Assembly (he described the episode vividly in his memoirs *The Tales of Sub-Lieutenant Ilin*). Promotion quickly followed, to Vice Commissar of the Navy, and in April Larisa resigned from the Commissariat of Education to work with him at the Naval Commissariat, as a commissar of the General Staff.

His Menshevik friend Nikolai Sukhanov, who was close to the Bolsheviks, described him as 'a man of action and natural leader, popular, principled and highly regarded by his men, a convinced socialist and extreme Bolshevik, who unlike many others, is still completing his socialist education'.

According to Ekaterina Sheremeteva, her parents had tried to talk her out of marrying him, and thought he would never be good enough for their daughter, however hard he worked on his education. And the unspoken issue was surely class; despite being distantly related, their social backgrounds were very different. Her father had written the Soviet Constitution, making workers Russia's new ruling class. But he was known to clash with many of the new worker commissars, zealous class warriors, who saw the aristocratic Reisner as the class enemy, and Raskolnikov was famously rude and derisive with those he considered phonies and snobs. Nor did he endear himself to Larisa's mother, who saw him as controlling and mentally unstable, and feared he wanted to separate her from her family. 'We have seen his hatred of us, however hard you try to deny it', she wrote to her later. 'Some say his sickness is incurable, but I think they exaggerate, the Party will save him'. Her mother's friend the poet's wife Nadezhda Mandelstam called him 'alien in every respect'.[2]

For Larisa he was a hero of the Revolution, a model of Bolshevik courage and integrity, and it was their differences that attracted them, and would make their relationship an increasingly tempestuous one over the years.

In her novel *Requiem* she wrote: 'There is a secret sadness in the lives of those who cross from the right to the left shores, especially if they leave without

---

2 Sukhanov, *The Russian Revolution 1917*, 1955, p. 275; Przhiborovskaya 2008, p. 92; Mandelstam, *Hope Against Hope*, 1971, p. 108.

repentance for their birth, their roots, their name, and the cruel dominance of their class. Only war and struggle can purge and level this. Only under shared bullets can private battles be forgotten, and can people become brothers'. This is where the story ends, as the narrator looks back on her old life, the comfortable flat, the books and poetry, and joins the great collective struggle for the Revolution.

She faced an uncertain future with Raskolnikov, without home or security. And in the tangled passions of the Revolution, the old patriarchal attitudes to women survived – what Lenin called 'the lingering filth of bourgeois marriage'. Raskolnikov worshipped his 'divine wife' and his 'warrior Diana', as he called her in his published letters to her when they were apart. He also wrote of their frequent fights when she would demand a divorce, and he was seen by several of her friends to treat her roughly.

There is nothing in her published writings about their relationship – what they fought about, whether they slept with other people, or needless to say, anything so mundane as who did the housework. The new woman of the Revolution spurned 'subjective' female preoccupations and emotions. 'Larisa had no time for women who sighed into their pillows complaining of their helplessness', Nadezhda Mandelstam wrote. 'With her and her circle, it was the cult of strength. "We have to create a completely new type of Russian woman", she said. "The French revolution created its type, and we must do the same"'.

Not that she was above using her feminine charms when it suited her, according to Mandelstam. She claimed to have helped Raskolnikov capture three White officers that summer by luring them to their room, where they were arrested without a shot fired – although Mandelstam suspected she might have made the whole thing up, 'to enhance her reputation as a fearless revolutionary'.[3]

Behind her talk in *Requiem* of 'brothers' were the challenges she faced as a woman at the Naval Commissariat. Raskolnikov's Kronstadt sailors were some of the Bolsheviks' most loyal supporters, committed politically if not always in practice to women's equality. She was also working with those trained by the Imperial Navy, exhausted by four years of war, disinclined to take orders from the new commissars, let alone from a woman. Those who fought with her later recalled her tenacious battles to impose her authority on men desperate to cling to their power. But she wrote nothing of this, or of the obstacles to women's freedom after the Revolution – the age-old chauvinism, the inad-

---

3 Mandelstam 1971, p. 111.

equate contraception and unwanted pregnancies, the millions of women widowed in the war, toiling all day in the factories while their children lived on the streets.

Like Rosa Luxemburg, she was never involved in the politics of women's liberation. And because she operated mainly in the world of men, it might seem to us now that much of what she achieved was at the cost of experiencing herself as a man. But her writings were filled with the new possibilities opening up for women after October, and many believed she served the cause of their liberation where she was, fighting for the Revolution.

The Bolsheviks' vision for women was both utopian and deeply practical. As Commissar of Social Welfare, Kollontai made women and children her priority, setting up new state maternity hospitals, children's homes, creches and nurseries, canteens and laundries, and she was consulted by Larisa's father at the Commissariat of Labour on the drafting of the Labour Law of November 1917. The state took responsibility for women when they were pregnant, and in advance of every other country in Europe, they were allowed sixteen weeks' paid maternity leave. Any woman, married or not, could have a friend take paid time off work to attend the birth and help with the baby afterwards. New mothers were to work no more than four days a week, and factories were to provide them with properly run creches, and warm rooms and regular time off to breastfeed their babies.

The law was followed in December by the Bolsheviks' new Marriage Law and Family Code, which declared war on the old oppressive patriarchal family, and razed to the ground the old tsarist marriage law, under which women were little better than slaves. The church-sanctioned beating of wives was classified as a 'counterrevolutionary offence', punishable by jail, and sex crimes were defined as 'any acts which violate an individual's right to life, health, freedom and safety'. Homosexuality and same-sex marriage were legalised, and women now had the right to initiate divorce, a simple matter of registering the end of the marriage, allowing couples to part when either partner wanted, often informing each other by postcard. The law made both parents equally responsible for their children until they were eighteen. But the state would take care of them if they were unable or unwilling to do so, and the stigma of illegitimacy was removed by allowing mothers to choose which surname they and their children took after marriage.

The poverty and isolation of the workers' state made most of this early progressive legislation impracticable in the short term – 'more valuable as evidence of our determination to bring about socialism than as reality', according to Kollontai. Almost eighty percent illiterate, denied for centuries any access to knowledge or power, women were being told overnight to take paths they had never travelled before, and live at the cutting edge of the male world, when most longed only to rebuild their shattered families. But for thousands of women like Larisa in their teens and twenties, those early days of the Revolution were an intoxicating mix of political and personal liberation.

Strong, proud and idealistic, the 'new women' of October came of age when it finally seemed possible to shut the door on the conventional ethic of female submission that had held back women of their mothers' generation. Over seventy thousand women would fight with the Red Army in the Civil War, in male regiments or in new communist women's battalions. 'Happiness wasn't a cosy flat with a gramophone, a successful marriage or a pretty dress, happiness was working with the wounded, the stricken and the dying', wrote Alexandra Bulygina, a nurse at the Urals front. 'The Revolution wasn't the time to be growing rubber plants or doing satin-stitch embroidery', wrote Asmik Papyan, leader of a women's espionage unit in Central Asia. 'We can laugh at ourselves now for rejecting love, reckoning it would get in the way of our work. Perhaps we did err too far in that direction, but I know we couldn't have won in those unbelievably hard days if we hadn't been able to overcome our personal cares and attachments', wrote Adelaida Prokhorova, a single mother from Moscow, who left her three-year-old son with friends to fight with Bolshevik forces in Ukraine.[4]

Under the new Marriage Law, the old bourgeois sexual morality was dead and buried. 'Sexual relationships no longer have to be seen as a lifetime of conjugal bliss', Kollontai wrote. In the chaos and freedom of the Revolution, people had affairs, then were separated or split up and moved on to new ones. Other relationships survived. For long periods Larisa and Raskolnikov would be thrown apart by the Revolution, and would live completely separate lives. But despite their frequent rows and separations, their marriage would last for the next five years.

Her new home with him was the Red Fleet naval hostel, formerly the Loskutnaya Hotel, where they ate with the men in the dining-room, now a makeshift canteen, and had the same room she had been in when Lev Nikulin first met her two years earlier. When he visited her there that summer, the main staircase was guarded by armed sailors, and 'instead of the samovar and spice cakes on the table in her room, were a crust of stale black ration bread mixed with straw, a small polished Browning pistol, a Maxim machine-gun, and the yellow wooden box of a field telephone'.[5]

---

4 These and other women's memoirs are in *Pravda stavshei legendoi* (Truth Becomes Legend), ed. M.D. Konyushenko, Moscow, 1969, pp. 90–116.
5 Nikulin, 'Years of Our Life,' *LRRC*, pp. 55–74.

The Naval Commissariat had set up its Moscow headquarters in the mansion of the former oil magnate Shamsi Assadulaev, near the House of Soviets on Vozdvizhenka Street. She was taught to shoot in the basement, and was licensed to carry a gun, and she set up her desk in Raskolnikov's office in Shamsi Assadulaev's ballroom, with its grand piano and chandeliers and gilded chairs, working with her new secretary, Misha Kirillov, on the Commissariat's voluminous correspondence, issuing travel warrants and filing reports. All the different departments of the new Red Navy had their offices in the building, and Nikulin remembered the corridors echoing with the tramp of sailor's boots, and gazing out of the windows with her at the vigilant city, dreaming of action.

One night, as they were walking back to Vozdvizhenka through the patrols of the Arbat, in a silence broken by gunshots, he told her he had seen a phial of cyanide in a chemist's laboratory, sealed with a skull and crossbones. '"Then get it for me if you can," she said. "I'll need it if I fall into the Whites' hands. I'm a woman, and they're animals."' (He refused).

Two years earlier, while Raskolnikov had been mobilising sailors to the Bolsheviks, the 'Rudinists' had been huddled in rooms denouncing the old world in their poems. Now they were experiencing its bloody end in war and revolution, wrestling with the new possibilities opening up for literature. Two weeks after the Revolution, the new Proletarian Cultural and Educational Organisation, *Proletkult*, had been established, with the backing of Lunacharsky and the Commissariat of Education, and she went to the writers' workshops it was running in the factories, at which Blok, Bely and Mayakovsky discussed poetic composition and technique with workers.

Much of the poetry emerging from these workshops celebrated the cosmic sweep of the Revolution in the rhythms and images of Blok and the Symbolists. Blok had worked with the Bolsheviks immediately after October, with Larisa at the Commissariat of Education, and with her father at the Commissariat of Justice, as head of his Commission Investigating the Crimes of the Tsarist Government, transcribing interviews with the former accomplices of Rasputin and the Tsar. He had then shut himself away to turn his experiences into his epic 'The Twelve', published the following January, a verse account, part celebration, part satire, written in startling staccato rhythms reminiscent of Mayakovsky, of twelve Red Guards marching through the streets of Petrograd in a blizzard, rifles in hand, to defend the Revolution. Nikulin remembered sitting with Larisa and their friends in the café in the Hermitage Gardens, drinking pink saccharine-sweetened water and discussing 'The Twelve' late into the night – 'and who wasn't discussing "The Twelve" then!'

Blok's next masterpiece, 'The Scythians', was both his warning to the Western governments not to attack Russia – 'but if it's war you want, we'll fight' –

and his appeal for peaceful co-existence – 'old world, we welcome you. Join us as friends, share our comradely peace and toil'.

That summer the Czech campaign began in earnest, and the Volga towns and villages Larisa had visited two years earlier were now on the front line of the first major battles of the Civil War. In June, the Czech legions and the British-backed Cossack forces of Admiral Kolchak captured the central Volga town of Samara, overthrowing the soviet and replacing it with a Constitutional Assembly Committee. Encouraged by this success, British and French military advisers in Russia then urged an immediate offensive on Bolshevik-held Saratov, Simbirsk and Kazan, and in one Volga town after another, Constituent Assembly Committees quickly took power.[6] Nationalised and municipalised enterprises were returned to their old owners, workers and Bolsheviks were killed in their thousands, along with those who sheltered them, and there was an epidemic of public lynchings.

When Nikulin visited Larisa at the Red Fleet in July, the room was packed with sailors, commanders and journalists poring over piles of telegraph tapes announcing the latest White advances on the Volga.

> 'The Revolution can't fail!' she said. 'The Left Socialist Revolutionaries are just flirts – and you're no better!' She took a copy of the paper the *Evening Hour* from the table, in which a poem of mine was published, and sighed comically: '"I met my sweetheart on the stairs ..." Well I hope you met her for the last time! There's fighting on the Volga, British submarines are attacking our gunboats – it's civil war, we have to shoot counterrevolutionaries, it's unavoidable, starvation is worse!'[7]

By mid-July, the Czechs and Kolchak's forces were closing in on the industrial city of Ekaterinburg, capital of the Urals, where the Tsar and his family were being held under house arrest. His guards had been instructed to keep him alive, so he could be tried. But in the chaos of the retreat and evacuation, local *Cheka* officials ordered him to be killed before the Whites arrived and released him, to rally support for the counterrevolution in Russia and abroad.

On the night of 17 July, he was shot dead with his wife, his four daughters and young son and four servants, and the massacre signalled the start of the 'Red Terror' – 'the armed sword of the Revolution, to crush the hydra of the counterrevolution and the White Terror'. Nine days later, the Whites entered Ekater-

---

6 Lenin's birthplace Simbirsk, renamed Ulyanovsk after his death, has remained Ulyanovsk since the end of the Soviet Union.
7 Nikulin, *People and Travels*, 1962, pp. 95–7.

inburg, and slaughtered twenty-five thousand of its citizens, then advanced on their main target, Kazan.

The key to the entire lower Volga, for four centuries the Moghul stronghold in Europe, captured in the eighteenth century by the serf army of the Cossack Pugachev, Kazan was now the financial base of the counterrevolution, where the Whites had banked Russia's gold reserves and hoards of securities, stocks and platinum. As the Bishop summoned the faithful to defend the Church, and the University placed itself at the patriotic disposal of the Whites, the resurrected bourgeois press predicted their unstoppable advance west into Central Russia.

Defending the city in those days, when the Red Army was no more than an idea in Trotsky's brain, were two units of the new Fifth Army, supported by a couple of hundred barely trained local Red volunteers, and Raskolnikov was hastily assembling his Kronstadt sailors to join them there.

Before leaving however, he was sent south by Lenin on a dangerous secret mission to Novorossiisk, Russia's main port on the Black Sea, threatened by General Denikin's White armies, to supervise the scuttling of eleven destroyers and a dreadnought of the Black Sea Fleet. 'Let me tell you the man in charge is Comrade Raskolnikov, who workers here and in Petrograd know well from his agitation and Party work', Lenin told a conference of trade unionists in Moscow when informing them of the operation.

Two days after he left, Victor Shklovsky visited Larisa in their room at the Red Fleet, crowded with commanders and journalists discussing his latest cables from Novorossiisk. Shklovsky had worked with the Provisional Government before the Revolution, and had joined an underground group in October plotting to overthrow the Bolsheviks, and he had then fled to his native Ukraine to escape arrest. But that summer Gorky had arranged for him to return to Moscow to work with the government as a journalist. 'I met Larisa Mikhailovna at the Loskutnaya, she was married to Raskolnikov at the time', he wrote. 'The fleet was practically in the Moscow River, it was horribly crowded. I had been in the enemy camp, but when I had reconsidered things and come back, she greeted me as the finest comrade. With her benign northern bearing, that was somehow good'.[8]

A week later Raskolnikov had completed his mission in Novorossiisk, and was back in Moscow, where he was appointed to the Revolutionary War Council of the Eastern Front, with orders to leave immediately under its operational command for Kazan.

---

8   Shklovsky, 'A Most Absurd Death', 1928, p. 357.

In late July, Larisa joined him and a detachment of sailors on the two-hundred-mile train journey east, along tracks wrecked by sabotage, to the Volga city of Nizhny Novgorod, where his Kronstadt comrade Nikolai Markin had hastily improvised a small flotilla from a number of river vessels and destroyers transferred there from the Baltic Fleet. So began her life on the Volga, the longest river in Europe, the vital transport route connecting European Russia to the oilfields of Central Asia and the Caucasus, and the Caspian Sea.

For the next two years, she would sail on the great warships of the new Volga Naval Flotilla, as commissar and cavalry instructor, flag-secretary, war correspondent and reconnaissance officer, fighting with Raskolnikov and the sailors in the battles for Kazan and Tsaritsyn, the defence of Astrakhan, and the liberation of Azerbaijan. And her first weeks on the Volga were a foretaste of what was to come.

Commissars, Party members, had the same rights as the soldiers and sailors, but many more duties, and had to be tough and tireless and fight with the men, and inspire confidence and respect. And as the new Red Navy's only high-ranking woman commander, she had much to prove.

Thousands fought with the Red Army, but almost none joined the Red Navy. Sailors' lore was filled with superstitions about women on the ships bringing storms and shipwrecks and bad luck, and she was generally the only one on board. She was known and trusted by most of Raskolnikov's men, who formed the core of the new Flotilla, and she evidently made full use of her status as his wife, signing herself 'Commissar Raskolnikova' in her military correspondence. But new recruits were constantly arriving, who saw her as too bourgeois and educated for the job, and demanded she discuss the 'marriage question', she later told Nikulin. Women at the front were expected to stand up for themselves, and she had had to learn to give as good as she got, with her fists if necessary – 'remembering the wonderful fights on Great Gunpowder Street when I was twelve'.

By the first week of August, the Flotilla had covered the two hundred miles to Kazan, where the Eastern Front set up its headquarters in the Siberian Guesthouse, and watched helplessly as combined Czech and White forces attacked from the land and river, the front disintegrated, and officers of several newly formed Red regiments went over to the enemy.

Throughout the turmoil, in moments snatched between battles, she was writing her 'Letters from the Front', later published as her book *The Front*, the story of the Flotilla's two-year campaign from Kazan to the Caspian, its defeats, retreats and victories. 'Raskolnikov's warboats slipped across the sandbanks and traced a red line along the Volga, and there Larisa Mikhailovna found her style as a writer', Shklovsky wrote. 'It wasn't a "woman's" style, or the journalist's habitual irony. Irony is a cheap way of being clever. She held dear what she saw, and she took life in earnest. A little too earnestly perhaps. But life then was as overloaded as a freight train'.[9]

The 'Letters', published in *Izvestiya*, daily paper of the Petrograd Soviet, and the Marxist literary journal *Red Virgin Soil*, were written in the language of the journalism of the Revolution, born in the hard years of exile and the underground, when hundreds of illegal publications had kept the struggle alive. *Izvestiya* and *Pravda*, daily paper of the Party, were now the official papers of the government, printed in mass editions across the country, and her 'Letters' reached a readership of millions – intellectuals, workers and the newly literate.

The first, from Kazan, opens with the retreat from the advancing Whites:

> Doors slam on empty rooms littered with abandoned papers and possessions ... Women stand in doorways saying goodbye to their loved ones, while the servants sweep out the revolutionary rubbish. All the bitterness of our defeat is there, as the dust flies up from the doormats and they bang their brooms, throwing out our still warm traces ...
>
> And when the first White shells hit our headquarters, containing those who will be the last to go, by which time there will be nowhere for them to go, we leave without looking back, trying not to think of our armoured car, or the terrible washed-out road it must pass, or won't pass ...

Raskolnikov was staying with the other commanders until the last minute, and on the morning of 6 August, under a crescendo of shells, she left him and headed off with a party of sailors, with some top secret documents and a portable printing press hidden under her navy coat, which she was to deliver to the first Red detachment they met.

> All words are forgotten at such moments, all the formulae that help us keep our presence of mind, leaving just a sharp cutting grief, and a vague 'in the name of' something, which makes us leave or stay ...
>
> Leaving with us is a flood of poverty – soldiers, families and children, carts laden with samovars and pots and pans and winter coats, pouring across the golden summer fields in the rain to escape the Czech liberators ...

---

9   Shklovsky, 'A Most Absurd Death', 1928, p. 359.

Beyond the city the noise of the shells stopped, and the rain turned to a downpour. She had no idea if Raskolnikov was still alive, but there were reports that the Commander of the Eastern Front, General Vatsetis, had escaped capture with a handful of fighters, and had joined what remained of Soviet forces defending the small railway town of Svyazhsk, thirty miles west of Kazan, on the opposite shore of the Volga.

> I don't remember how many we were, falling in the mud and getting up again, driven on by exhaustion and the rain, only that we were heading for what we hoped was Svyazhsk ...
>
> Why Svyazhsk? The name of this little station on the banks of the Volga, which would later play such a vital role in our recapture of Kazan, is remembered now as something elemental, the furnace in which the nucleus of the Red Army was forged in the heat of the retreat. I don't know if our commanders had identified it as the base from which they would consolidate their power, or if its name was simply thrown into the escaping crowd. But it was there that the flood of refugees was heading.

On the third day, they were resting in a cottage when they had a visit from the village policeman. Their sailor guide quickly explained that they were holidaymakers, 'looking for a nice dacha with all conveniences and a good view of the river'. Then with one leap, they all dashed out and across the fields. They spent the rest of the day sheltering under haystacks from the rain. Stumbling off into the night, they met a line of carts carrying a detachment of Bolsheviks from Kazan to Svyazhsk, and she handed over her documents and printing press.

After travelling an hour with them they crossed the Volga, and finally reached Svyazhsk, where she learned at the headquarters of the Revolutionary War Council that Raskolnikov had been arrested. 'Don't worry, I expect he's escaped to Paris!' a dashing former tsarist commander told her. 'Next minute, red-faced and angry, he was covered in hot tea, but it didn't change anything'.

Desperate for news of him, she volunteered with a sailor named Misha to travel the forty miles back to Kazan and reconnoitre behind enemy lines. The commander of the Red Latvian Rifles scribbled their passes for the Red patrols, after she told him Raskolnikov was Latvian too – 'on his mother's side' – and he found horses for them, and army greatcoats, boots and trousers.

She was a good rider and mounted easily, but her horse was huge, and she was soon in agony.

> But my meeting with my chestnut stallion 'Beauty' was the start of a tender three-year friendship between us. We had left the Volga and were

approaching a small railway station, when suddenly he shied and looked back at me with burning eyes and trembling ears, and refused to move ... Then in front of our noses three bolts shot past, one after another, three dusty red explosions, three deaths ...

They rode back through the forest to the next village, where the Third Latvian Rifle Brigade, under their commander Yanis Yudin, had set up their headquarters in an abandoned dacha. The Whites were a few miles away, waiting to attack, 'and in those last hours of Yudin's life, pulsing like a bursting vein, we spent several sharp oath-filled minutes'.

After they had rested and eaten, a soldier brought down from the attic 'a chic pink Parisian corset, some gold-braided courtier's trousers, a suit for Misha, and to my joy, a nice black dress. A soldier tried on the corset, and the courtier's trousers were soon on the proud backside of the messenger boy, and Misha and I left this fancy dress party as a respectable bourgeois couple. "Good luck, until we meet again", Yudin said, secretly convinced we wouldn't come out of the forest alive, while death stood behind his back, mocking him in the darkness'.

After walking for miles through the silent forest, they reached a peasant settlement, where piercing screams were coming from the bath-house. They were invited in, and a young Kirghiz woman was in labour on the floor. 'She had been there for three days, but new faces and the touch of unknown hands soothed her nerves and encouraged her will to live, and with a terrible shudder, the baby was born'.

The next day they attended the christening as his godparents, and the grateful father drove them in his cart through the forest back to White Kazan:

> It was only five days since we left, but it was as if ten years had passed. Everything was different: the officers, the ladies from educated families in nurses' uniforms, the *gimnazium* boys guarding the offices, the open shops, the rollicking hysterical gaiety of the cafés – the whole tawdry transient rash on the body of the defeated Revolution.

Men with rifles and white armbands roamed the streets, and raided buildings for suspects. Red prisoners were paraded through the city, and the pavements were littered with corpses, with their Party cards pinned to their chests. Close to the centre, their cart stopped to make way for a truck loaded with the naked bodies of shot workers, rumbling past a fence plastered with posters saying 'All Power To the Constituent Assembly'. 'Little did those who put that constitutional lie there realise that such images would soon be appearing on our popular revolutionary posters'.

Assuring them he was taking them 'somewhere safe', their driver delivered them to the house of Kazan's Police Superintendent, 'where Misha and I fell into our roles as a White officer and his wife, in our own private theatre of the absurd.'

> The main part of the house was the set for a comedy of merchant manners, with its waxed floors and its icons and geraniums at the windows ... Huddled below the Superintendent's family lived seventeen workers' families. The Revolution had temporarily disturbed relations between those on the upper and lower floors, and the Superintendent's roots, patriarchally drawing their nourishment from the basement, had suffered several nips and blows that even threatened his daughter's dowry. The last straw was when one of the workers expropriated her fluffy white goat for his children to play with ...
>
> Then in July, God intervened in these sordid human affairs, and the unruly lodger was led away, never to be seen again. After that, everything returned to normal. The new authorities threw cartloads of the workers' bodies in the Volga, and the Superintendent happily licked his lips at the grief in the basement, where people dared not weep or make a sound.
>
> It was as God and the Bolsheviks were going at it tooth and nail that we moved in with him. At first he bristled, like a hedgehog caught snacking on a live frog in broad daylight, starting his tasty treat through long habit with its shuddering hind legs. But after he had drunk tea with us and cursed the Bolsheviks, he seemed satisfied with our politics, and accepted us as his lodgers. Then he went off to town to celebrate at the Whites' headquarters and report another worker from the basement.

Next morning Misha left for town with their money and papers to reconnoitre for news of their comrades. He was not back that afternoon, when the Reds began firing from the outskirts. 'Shells flew over the house and exploded on the street. Boom! My heart did a mad happy dance for our red devils, and the Superintendent, leaving his lofty strategic considerations for another time, put on a spare pair of trousers, and disappeared with his family and the goat into the bath-house'.

> It was then that I first met the residents of the basement, standing at the top of the stairs – men, children, women with babies, resting their heads against the low doorpost, gazing at the barrage in the sky ... We understood each other without words. The wife of the worker arrested last night asked me my name in a whisper. 'No, your comrade escaped, it said in the

paper, you shouldn't be here!' She moved her baby, struggling to reach her thin breast, and listened to the bombardment outside, lost to everything but the symphony of explosions shaking the house ...

A day later, the Reds had been driven back and Misha had still not returned. The Superintendent advised her to visit the Whites' headquarters in town for information, and she tricked her way in with a false identity, based on some mythical relatives and a lost passport.

> How good the White regime is on the third day of its creation! What sweet faces the typists have, cheerfully tapping away on their Remingtons ...
> Smartly uniformed officers stand to attention at the doors to the main office, like those guarding the Imperial bedchamber. Through these doors appear if not generals, then at least captains or majors, with their luxurious whiskers and dazzling white shirts. And modestly blending in with all this military business, gilding the epaulettes with their brilliance, is the occasional teacher and academic. How flirtatiously they flaunt their university badges! On my next visit, I saw a well-known professor, with the thick grey hair and soft-brimmed hat fashionable among learned lovers of the 'sensitive radical young', gabbling in a low voice to a disdainful junker about 'unreliable elements' in his neighbourhood ...

She made two more visits there over the next two days, and learnt from a sympathetic secretary that Misha had been arrested, but that Raskolnikov had escaped and was still alive. More workers from the basement were arrested, and the Superintendent was growing increasingly suspicious of her, and on the third morning she made her escape, with her pass hidden in a crust of bread.

The wife of an arrested worker gave her a ruble note, and she slipped out to the gate, where she was stopped by the Superintendent, who escorted her to the Whites' headquarters to be interrogated by Lieutenant Ivanov, 'the "Mademoiselle Fifi" of White Guard Kazan, famous for flogging workers on the soles of their feet "for the Revolution"'.

Much of what followed has to be pieced together from her letters and conversations later with her family and friends. Outside Ivanov's office, she exchanged looks with a group of Red sailors before they were led off to be shot, then it was her turn. She was strip-searched by a woman guard, who removed her underwear and put it on the pile of clothes on the floor of those before her, then took her in to Ivanov, 'in his white tunic, with his clean white hands and pale eyebrowless eyes and shaven head, white as a boiled egg'.

> Sitting next to him at a green baize table was a French officer. I don't remember his face, just something cold and sneering about him, not missing a thing, so he could turn it all later into an amusing story for his fellow officers. Opposite them sat the stenographer, with his straight parting and fountain-pen, fixing a flourishing tail to the capital letter of my name

For two hours Ivanov questioned her about Raskolnikov, her 'relatives', and her missing passport – 'switching from mocking courtesy to animal shrieks, nudging the French officer and winking at my underwear, folded neatly by his inkwell'. She later confided to Nikulin how she had fought to wrestle him off as he tore at her clothes and repeatedly kicked and punched her, cutting her head open, while the Frenchman looked on. 'Then an extraordinary thing happened. There are moments of mad fairytale happiness in life, and on that grey morning, which I glimpsed through the hopeless bars of the window, I experienced a miracle'.

Ivanov left the room with the stenographer and the Frenchman to fetch a prosecutor, and the sentry stepped out of the door to calm his nerves with a smoke, leaving her briefly on her own. Next to this door was one tacked with felt and bolted firmly shut. Ripping off the tacks, she pushed back the bolt with all her strength and ran down the stairs to the street, where she stopped a cab.

Looking at her bloody head and torn clothes, the driver whipped his horse to a gallop, and took her back to his wife, Avdotya Markovna – 'red and white and three girths wide, warm and comforting as buns fresh from the oven, and she took me in her arms and I howled like a piglet on her boundless motherly breast. Then after feeding me and covering my bare shoulders with her peasant shawl, she listened to my story from beginning to end, and cursed Ivanov so roundly that the roosters scratching in the yard crowed with joy'.

Her name was already on the Whites' counterintelligence 'Find and Kill' lists, but her peasant disguise allowed her to slip through their patrols. She was then driven by a peasant to the next village, where she met up with a detachment of Yudin's Cossacks.

> That peasant also saved my life that day, the happiest day of my life. After we had trotted on in silence for several miles, he said in the same voice as that of Avdotya Markovna and the cab driver and all the poor in Russia who were unquestionably on our side in those first days of the Revolution, with its retreats and defeats, who helped thousands of comrades scattered on its wide roads to survive: 'Time to get out now, girl. Enough pretending, I know what you are. Go to the village on the left, your people are there. The black cloud on the right is the Czech cavalry'.

Back in Svyazhsk next day, she learnt that poor Misha had been shot in Kazan, but Raskolnikov had escaped to Kronstadt, where he was mobilising ships and sailors to sail to Svyazhsk. She had learnt nothing about him in Kazan. Her mission there had accomplished nothing and had cost Misha his life, and she was reprimanded for her carelessness.

CHAPTER 8

Svyazhsk

By the late summer of 1918, Bolshevik fortunes were at their lowest ebb. On 2 August, the first British troops landed in the northern Pacific port of Arkhangelsk, under Captain Ironside, 'Baron Ironside of Arkhangel' (immortalised in the novels of John Buchan as Richard Hannay). A day later, British naval forces in the Pacific landed at Vladivostok, and were soon joined there by the first U.S. and Japanese troop landings. The British Expeditionary Force in the Caucasus, led by Major General Dunsterville (Rudyard Kipling's 'Stalky'), had set up a government in Baku, capital of Azerbaijan, to take control of its oil. British ships patrolled the Caspian Sea and the Arctic coast around Murmansk. The French Fleet was in the Black Sea, and the Czechs were still holding Kazan and the Volga towns of Simbirsk and Samara, and threatening Kursk, Voronezh and Tsaritsyn.

Although the war with Germany had officially ended with the Brest-Litovsk Treaty, the German army had now effectively joined this joint Allied-Czech-White Russian force to bring down the Bolsheviks. As Germany's High Command launched its last desperate offensive against Paris, its forces were moving along the railway-line to Murmansk, and occupying a 350-mile line along the Gulf of Finland. The German-backed army of General Krasnov occupied large parts of Ukraine, and Hetman Skoropadsky's puppet German government in Kiev was slaughtering communists and Jews.

Anti-Semitism was at the heart of the Western governments' propaganda against the Bolsheviks, and Jews were the main targets of the White armies. In Winston Churchill's article 'Poison Peril from the East', in the paper the *Evening News*, he called for an international crusade against 'Jewish Bolshevik Russia' – 'a poisoned Russia, a plague-bearing Russia, a Russia of animal hordes, of typhus-bearing vermin that slay the bodies of men, and political doctrines that destroy the health and soul of nations ... The mob are raised against the middle classes to murder them, plunder their houses, debauch their wives, and kill their children ...'[1]

That August, peril was everywhere. Daily bread rations in the cities were cut to an eighth of a pound, and the Revolution, scourged by hunger, typhus and cholera, strangled by the Intervention and the Allied Blockade, was collapsing into the chaos of counterrevolution.

---

1 Churchill reworked these passages in *The Aftermath. 1918–1928*, the fourth volume of his six-volume history of the First World War, *The World Crisis*, 2003.

Its fate was being decided at Svyazhsk, where a few hundred Bolshevik volunteers were defending the bridgehead over the Volga, barring the Czechs' access to the river route from Kazan to Nizhny Novgorod, and the railway line to Moscow. 'When the Red units hastily thrown together to fight the Whites fled from Kazan, the best and most class-conscious of them were drawn to Svyazhsk', Larisa wrote. 'And there they stopped, and decided to make a stand'.

> By the time the deserters from Kazan were almost at Nizhny Novgorod, the dam erected at Svyazhsk had already stopped the advancing Czechs, and their general, who tried to take the railway bridge across the Volga in a night attack, was ambushed and killed. Thus in this very first clash between the nucleus of the new Red Army and the Whites, who had just taken Kazan, and were consequently stronger in weapons and morale, the Czech offensive had had its head chopped off ...
>
> Neither the Whites, flushed from their victory in Kazan, nor the Reds, rallying around Svyazhsk, had any idea of the historic importance these first skirmishes would have.

Her essay on the 'glorious epic of Svyazhsk', the second chapter of *The Front*, was considered by many to be the most brilliant of the 'Letters'. But her glowing praise of Trotsky made it unpublishable in Soviet Russia, and the chapter was missing from *The Front* in her *Complete* and *Selected Works*. 'Svyazhsk' was republished online in Russia in 2017, to celebrate the centenary of the Revolution, and my translation is from that.

On 8 August, two days after the fall of Kazan, with the Eastern Front in chaos, Trotsky's legendary armoured train arrived in Svyazhsk, with its radio telegraph office and printshop, and two hundred communists he had picked in Moscow for their courage and endurance. 'They travelled slowly, smashing the resistance of the railworkers in their path', wrote Victor Serge. 'They were organised with strict military discipline, and were constantly on alert'.

> After stopping at Svyazhsk's little station, the engine drove off, making clear its passengers intended to stay, leaving the carriages containing the headquarters of Trotsky's General Staff, its revolutionary tribunal, and all departments of an army that didn't yet exist. And it was there that the advance of the Whites and Czechs was halted against a line of hastily dug trenches, behind which stood nothing but a will of iron.[2]

---

2   Victor Serge, *Year One of the Revolution* (trans. Peter Sedgwick), 1992, pp. 192–4.

By the first week of August, Raskolnikov had manoeuvred twelve ships from Kronstadt up the Mariinsky canal system and along the Volga to Svyazhsk – four gunboats and seven river steamers, hastily refitted as warships and mounted with machine-guns, and the Flotilla's staff ship the *Summer Tide*, the former tsarist pleasure boat on which the royal family had sailed up the Volga during the Romanov centenary celebrations.

In the two weeks since Larisa left him in Kazan, they had both narrowly avoided death. Now they were thrown together in the battles for Svyazhsk:

> There were almost no medical supplies, god knows how the doctors dressed the wounds. But the desperateness of our situation banished fear and shame. Soldiers passed the injured and dying lying on stretchers in the open, but death held no terrors. To lie on the ground in an army coat caked with blood and mud, with a face that was no longer human – it was expected every minute, and was taken for granted.

Fighting with units of Trotsky's new Fifth Army were local Red Guards from the towns and villages along the Volga, and Raskolnikov's Kronstadt sailors, most of them barely trained, many still in their teens. Two hundred thousand in the new Communist Youth League, the *Komsomol*, almost half its members, fought on the front line of the Civil War. The youngest from Kronstadt was fourteen-year-old Alexander, known as 'Lyutik' ('Buttercup'), cabin-boy of the *Summer Tide*, who had sailed to Svyazhsk with Raskolnikov wearing a child's sailors outfit found on board, of naval jacket, cap and striped jersey, armed with a revolver.[3]

As commissar, Larisa was responsible for all the sailors' welfare, and she had to instil discipline and respect, and fight with them to the end. And with every new group of recruits arriving at the front, she had to fight the same battle to prove herself as a woman, and win their trust. Trotsky and Victor Serge both wrote of her great courage in battle, and sailors who fought with her recalled her steely flair for handling herself in the hard-drinking male world of the front, her fight to be listened to and respected, and the endless trials and 'tests' they subjected her to. 'She passed the first test. That was at Svyazhsk', wrote the *Komsomol* journalist Lev Sosnovsky.[4]

'Svyazhsk was the furnace in which the nucleus of the Red Army was forged, at the height of the retreat and panic', she wrote,

---

3 Larissa Vasileva, *Kremlin Wives* (trans. Cathy Porter), 1994, pp. 46–7.
4 Lev Sosnovsky, 'V pamyati Larisy Reisnera' (In Memory of Larisa Reisner), in *Lyudi nashego vremeni* (People of Our Time), Moscow, 1927, pp. 76–7.

> the crossroads from which the tide of the revolutionary offensive began to roll in all directions – in the East to the Urals, in the North to Arkhangelsk and Poland, in the South to the Caucasus, the shores of the Caspian and the Persian border ...
>
> I can see it now, this Svyazhsk where not one soldier fought under compulsion, where everything that was alive was fighting to defend the Revolution, bound together by voluntary ties of discipline in a struggle that had seemed to hopeless at the outset ... Those who slept on the station floor, in straw littered with broken glass, were afraid of nothing. No one asked when it would end. Tomorrow didn't exist, there was only a brief hot smoky today, and we lived for it as we live at harvest time ... The days seemed so rich, so utterly unlike previous life. As soon as one passed it seemed like a miracle. And it was a miracle ...

Despite the disastrous failure of her intelligence work in Kazan, she was appointed Commissar of the Reconnaissance Division of the Flotilla's General Staff, and she worked closely with Raskolnikov's comrade Nikolai Markin, commander of the battleship *Vanya the Communist*.

The eighteen-year-old machine-gunner on the ship Vsevolod Vishnevsky first met her when she arrived on a scouting mission:

> She came alongside on a destroyer launch, dashing and cheerful in her black navy jacket and fleet cap, and we decided to set her a test, and sent her into the path of the Czechs' machine-gun battery. We gave her full speed, and she left, and we watched this female there, then ordered her back. 'Why? It's too early, we must go on!' she shouted.
>
> From then on we were firm friends, and afterwards we did much reconnaissance work with her. This person had knowledge and strength. People couldn't believe it. 'Look at her, what a woman!' they said.[5]

In the lulls between battles, she escaped to the *Summer Tide* to write. The commander Ilya Berlin recalled her making herself at home in the Imperial state-room, using one of the Empress Alexandra's diamond rings to scratch out her name carved on the porthole and replace it with her own. And there she worked on her 'Letters', caught up with her paperwork, and wrote letters home.[6]

To her mother she wrote:

---

5 Vsevolod Vishnevsky, 'Ostalas v pamyati na vsyu zhizn' (Remembered All My Life), LRRC, pp. 103–4.
6 Ilya Berlin, 'Delo sluzheniya naroda' (The Business of Serving the People), LRRC, pp. 77–82.

> I'm writing in a rush from a madhouse. I miss you so much darling. How are you? Are you terribly hungry in Moscow? I worry endlessly about you. It's very hard to write here. At night Fedya and I make mad raids against the Whites' flotilla. We've already sunk three of their ships and two barges, under the nose of their battery. I've learnt to ride for days on end. Any free time is here on the Summer Tide, where the sounds of shooting are like a dream. Why don't you come and visit for a few days? I kiss you. Your Lyalya.

Sick with worry, Ekaterina Alexandrovna made the dangerous journey east to stay with her on the Summer Tide. 'I'm terrified for her', she wrote to her father in Moscow. 'All this *Sturm und Drang* will doubtless be good for her soul, if she survives, but she seems doomed, and I can't save her. Our little aristocrat stands on the bridge, yielding to none of the sailors in cool courage, and they silently follow her'.[7]

Her friend Vsevolod Rozhdestvensky, who was fighting with the Red Army on the Southern Front, also visited her on the ship that summer, as did the unlikely figure of the poet and future emigre Vladislav Khodasevich, who reported seeing little Lyutik guarding her door with his loaded revolver – wearing what he assumed to his horror must be the dead Tsarevich Alexei's sailor suit.[8]

Trotsky's new Red Army and Navy emerging from the Bolsheviks' straggling bands of beaten fighters were born of a revolutionary passion bordering on fanaticism. Larisa wrote of Trotsky's miracles of recruitment and organisation at Svyazhsk – 'refusing to yield an inch, inspiring fighters with his ruthless authority and icy calm'.

> But there is another force in revolutionary war, without which victory is impossible, and that is the romanticism of the Revolution, which inspires people to throw themselves straight from the barricades of 1917 into the harsh discipline of the army, without losing the light step learnt from street battles and political demonstrations, or the quick thinking gained from decades in the underground. It means swimming against the tide, beating back the exhaustion of the four years of war and the stormy waters of the Revolution, which is sweeping away the hated discipline of the old Imperial army like so much flotsam. Ultimately it's the revolutionary instinct that is the supreme judge. Trotsky possesses this instinct. The

---

7   Her letter in sw, p. 514. Her mother's letter in Sofia Zhitomirskaya, 'The Music of the Revolution', *Literary Paper*, 1975.
8   Quoted in Vasileva, *Kremlin Wives*, 1994, p. 47.

revolutionary in him is never pushed aside by the soldier, the leader, the commander.

Trotsky is a huge presence in Svyazhsk, Raskolnikov is virtually invisible, and her passionate admiration for him led many to believe they were lovers in Svyazhsk. According to a popular Russian online compendium of 'state secrets and scandals', the story went round the front that she had spent nights with him on his train before Raskolnikov arrived, and he had entered his boss's carriage once to find her naked in his bed – but he 'understood and forgave them'.[9]

Victor Serge wrote of Trotsky's powerful sexual charisma – 'his superb military bearing, broad chest, and jet-black hair' – and his enemies have tried unsuccessfully to portray him as a serial womaniser. In the new freedoms and collective living arrangements of the Revolution, several married commissars had affairs, even second families, often forced by the housing crisis to cohabit under the same roof. Trotsky's brother-in-law Lev Kamenev, Chair of the Moscow Soviet, who was married to his sister, moved his second wife in to live with them for a year before they divorced. Trotsky, like Lenin, was known for his abstemious ways. His manner with people was brisk and business-like, he didn't smoke and rarely drank, and fitness was an obsession with him – 'our health is our revolutionary capital, it's a sin to squander it'. He had been married to his second wife, Natalya Sedova, for fifteen years, was a devoted father to their two sons, and was known to have had only one romantic adventure outside his marriage, at the age of fifty-two, with the Mexican artist Frida Kahlo.

Clearly he and Larisa had a deep friendship. But their nights of passion in Svyazhsk seem highly improbable, and were most likely the product of Raskolnikov's jealous imagination.

Countless lurid stories about her sexual adventures have been told over the decades, and have survived in Putin's Russia. In 2017, the centenary of the Revolution was marked by the big-budget Channel One TV series 'Trotsky', available on Netflix, a grotesque concoction of historical falsifications, pornography, and blatant anti-Semitism, with Trotsky the sadistic leather-clad agent of an international Jewish cabal seeking world domination, and Larisa his accomplice and leading groupy, in heavy makeup, writhing and groaning with him on his military train as its speeds towards Svyazhsk, where in an orgy of depravity, they call every tenth sailor from the ranks and have them shot.

---

9 *Entsiklopedia tain i senzatsii gosudarstevnnykh perevorotov* (Encyclopaedia of Secrets and Sensations in State Upheavals), 1998.

'Trotsky' is advertised to Western audiences as 'the epic biography of this complex and tumultuous historical figure'. Viewers in Russia and abroad have reacted with horror to its sinister rewriting of history, with calls for its directors never to work again, and an international campaign for Netflix to drop the series.

In the recently opened Lev Trotsky Museum in Svyazhsk, set on the site of the old railway station, in a mock-up of his train, there are models of them alone together in his carriage. He is writing at his desk, she is standing behind him, gazing out of the window, fully clothed in her naval uniform, with excerpts from her 'Letters from the Front' on the walls.

But there were worse things to be accused of than sleeping with the great Trotsky, and she clearly enjoyed playing up to her image as a seductress. 'I know they say I've slept with all the commissars, but I swear it's not true, only a few of them!' she later told his friend and fellow commissar Adolf Joffe.[10]

In *The Front*, Trotsky is simply the genius of the Civil War, and she wrote equally warmly of Svyazhsk's less known heroes, his commanders and comrades. His close friend Markin, founder of the Red Fleet, 'who loved danger, and was drawn to it like a boy'. The Fleet's Chief of Staff, Semyon Lepetenko, 'one of the most courageous and self-sacrificing soldiers of the Revolution, whose biography could provide this book with its best chapter'. Svyazhsk's chief of communications Arkady Rosengoltz, 'softly spoken, with his pale gentle face and totally unmilitary appearance, despite his army greatcoat and the enormous pistol at his belt'. And Ivan Smirnov, of the Revolutionary War Council, 'the incarnation of the revolutionary ethic at Svyazhsk, and its communist conscience'.

> Even non-Party soldiers meeting Comrade Smirnov for the first time responded immediately to the exceptional warmth and purity of his personality. He probably had no idea how they feared to be seen as weak or wanting before this man who never raised his voice, who was always simply himself, calm, modest and cheerful. Everyone knew that at the worst moments he would be the strongest, the most fearless …
>
> With Trotsky it was the sacred demagogy of battle, to die with our last cartridge gone, oblivious to our wounds, his words and gestures evoking the most heroic episodes of the great French Revolution. With Comrade Smirnov at our side, it seemed to us that we could be calm when we were against the wall, being interrogated by the Whites in some hell of a prison.

---

10   Nadezhda Joffe, *Back in Time. My Life, My Fate, My Epoch*, 1995, p. 91.

> That was how we spoke of him in the cold nights, whispering to each other as we huddled close together on the floor.

Great causes turned people into heroes and made them invincible, she wrote, and Svyazhsk was the final bastion for which they were prepared to die. 'We are the eternal unforgettable 1918, and the long years leading up to it', she wrote to her mother that summer, 'and we are happy, for we have seen it, red, pure, naked, rejoicing in the face of death'.[11]

> Each day Svyazhsk held out, against an enemy vastly superior in weapons and numbers, increased its strength and confidence. And the fantastic faith that this godforsaken town could be the starting point for a new offensive against the Whites gradually began to take the shape of reality ...
> Planes come and go, dropping bombs on the station, and our machine-gunners on the roofs fire back, and they fail to damage them. Then a soldier in a ragged army cape, civilian hat and patched shoes, one of the heroes of Svyazhsk, takes his watch from his pocket and grins, 'At 0.300 hours, or 04.00, or 06.20, I'm still alive. Svyazhsk is holding out. Trotsky's train is still here, with a light in the window of the Political Department. Good. Another day over'.

Nikolai Kartashov, a commander on the *Vanya the Communist*, first met her a few miles from Svyazhsk, after his platoon had captured the villages of Berezhnye Morkvashi. The men were resting on deck when three riders appeared, bearing carbines and sabres. They dismounted, and Markin invited one up to the captains' bridge and introduced the tall young woman to his disconcerted officers as 'Larisa Mikhailovna Reisner, commissar and war correspondent'. She asked Markin the position of the Whites' ships, and inspected them through her field-glasses, then warmly congratulated Kartashov's platoon for their brave attack on the enemy.

Below deck, the sailors could be heard discussing her with their usual noisy obscenities, and unable to contain herself, she asked Markin to invite them up.

> They crowded round, astonished and curious, and she said, 'Comrade sailors! The pick of the bunch! I'll never forget how the Whites dealt with our brothers in Kazan. But we'll have our revenge! I wish you great success, and I'll be with you at the front!'

---

11 Quoted in Solovei 1985, p. 40.

This brought cheers of applause, and she went on, smiling, to rebuke them for their language – 'which insults all our heroic working women and mothers. If you want to curse, curse the White Guard filth!' She followed this with a stream of choice oaths, which were greeted with more cheers, and shouts of 'Bravo, cavalryman! Good woman!' Then she went ashore, swung onto her horse, waved and trotted back towards Berezhnye Morkvashi.

That evening she was back on a destroyer launch, accompanied by a commanding officer, Captain Neuberg, and she asked Markin's permission to scout out the Whites' ships. Neuberg objected that it was too dangerous, but she overruled him, and they returned to their launch. As they cut down the fairway at full speed, she stood smiling at the helm, waving her cap, shouting 'If anything happens, open fire!' Then they disappeared from sight.

They returned safely, to more loud applause from the sailors, and she thanked them for saving them with their answering fire. '"I think we put the heat on the Whites!" Then turning to the despondent Neuberg, she said, "The tragedy is that our captain is unwell". Neuberg muttered that he had never met such an Amazon, she wasn't a woman dammit, she was a sailor in skirts, and Markin reassured him it was only frightening the first time – "Look how easily Larisa Mikhailovna did it!"'

'Her raid on enemy territory produced unheard-of excitement and love for this fearless young woman', Kartashov wrote. 'To the day I die, I shall never forget the shining memory of Larisa Mikhailovna, an extraordinary communist, and the bravest of the brave'.[12]

Little by little the situation at Svyazhsk improved:

> Reinforcements began to arrive from villages deep in the rear, at first one by one, then in small detachments. Before long new armed communist combat units were arriving, and an enormous spider's web of telephone and telegraph wires began to operate at Svyazhsk's tiny station – this barely discernible dot on the map of Russia that the Revolution was clinging to in its hour of despair.

By the last week of August, Svyazhsk's fighters were preparing to take Kazan. An aeroplane arrived, and a garage truck for five cars. A small airfield was laid, and Trotsky's train was joined by another, with three hundred cavalry soldiers

---

12   Nikolai Kartashov, 'Bravo kavaleristu!' (Bravo Cavalryman!), LRRC, pp. 83–7.

on board. 'It's fascinating to see the changes in people when they arrive at the revolutionary front', she wrote. 'They blaze up like a straw roof lit on all sides, and when the fire cools they have turned to steel, fireproof and indestructible'.

On the night of the 26th, under cover of darkness, the 'leading lights of White Guard Russia', Commanders Kappel and Fortunatov, launched a surprise cavalry attack on the nearby village of Tyurlema, before moving on to the small railway station of Shikhrana, on the line to Moscow, killing sentries, destroying tracks and telegraph poles, blowing up the Red armoured train sent to intercept them. With the Red sector cut in half and the army thrown into panic, the regiment holding the front by the river, headed by their commissars and commanders, scattered and fled, and invaded the ships of the Flotilla.

Trotsky then gathered together everyone on his train – office-boys, clerks and paramedics, anyone who could hold a gun – and threw them into battle. The Bolsheviks' only hope lay in these five hundred hastily armed recruits, facing over a thousand Whites, and Larisa was appointed by Trotsky to lead a dangerous mission to reunite those cut off at Tyurlema with the General Staff.

Eight years later, an anonymous sailor she recruited to the mission recalled the operation in the Red Army paper *Red Star*:

> The enemy is advancing along the Volga, to the rear of our Flotilla. Our orders are to get through and make contact with those cut off. Larisa picks me and a sailor lad called Vanyushka Rybakov (just a boy!), and someone else whose name I don't recall, and the four of us set off. Night. Shivering with cold, loneliness and the unknown. But she marches ahead so confidently.
>
> At the village of Kurochkino the Whites spot us and open fire, and we have to spread out and crawl – a tight spot! And Larisa is smiling, and her hidden anxiety only makes her voice more velvety. Then we escape from their firing line, and we're through.
>
> 'Are you tired, Vanyushka my lad?' In her concern for us she reaches an unattainable height, and we want to kiss that marvellous woman's hands, black from the mud of the road.
>
> She strides along so quickly we almost have to run to keep up with her. By morning we're at the Whites' camp at Tyurlema, piled with dead bodies. Dropping on our feet with exhaustion, we make for Shikhrana, where we meet up with the Red Latvian Rifles. They make contact with Trotsky's train, and the front has been tied up, and that smiling woman with the pale face was the knot that tied it.
>
> 'Look after my boys, comrades. Me? No, I'm not tired!'

> Then more scouting near Verkhny Uslon and the Morkvashis, and as far as Pyany Bor. Sixty miles on horseback without stopping.
> Pleasures were few then. But the smile never left Larisa Mikhailovna's face in those tough campaigns. Then Tsaritsyn, Baku, Persia ...[13]

The battle for Svyazhsk lasted many hours, and the Whites finally retreated, thinking they were up against a formation of crack troops unspotted by their scouts.

Next day, Trotsky ordered the soldiers who had panicked and deserted at the start of the siege to be arrested, and twenty-seven were shot, including eight Bolsheviks. There was no alternative, Larisa wrote:

> Among those who were killed were good comrades, who had suffered years in prison and exile before the Revolution, and had served the Republic honourably. And of course, it was a tragedy. But many had seen Party members as exempt from the law, who could desert and get away with it ... If it hadn't been for Trotsky's exceptional courage, communists' prestige in the army and the Revolutionary War Council would have been finished for good.
>
> All who lived the life of the Red Army then, and grew strong with it in the battles for Svyazhsk and Kazan, knew that its solidarity and iron spirit would never have been forged, the fusion between commanders and the rank and file would never have been achieved, if on the eve of storming Kazan, where hundreds would lose their lives, the Party failed to demonstrate before the eyes of the whole army that it was prepared to make this great and terrible sacrifice for the Revolution: that the laws of comradely discipline were binding for the Party too, and that it had the courage to apply these laws ruthlessly to its own members.
>
> When soldiers saw communists being punished for cowardice, not just former tsarist officers and ordinary privates, it made the least class-conscious of them and most likely to desert pull themselves together and join those who went without compulsion into battle, knowing it was not only the fate of Kazan that was being decided, but the fate of the entire Revolution.

The night after the executions, she joined Trotsky and Raskolnikov on the destroyer the *Endurance*, at the head of a squadron of gunboats sailing with their lights out in battle formation to Kazan. Slipping through the narrow entrance

---

13   'N.', 'Pod Tyurlema' (Outside Tyurlema), *Red Star*, 14 February, 1926. *SW*, p. 517.

to the harbour, they fired at a caravan of fuel barges, which went up in flames. The Whites fired back, grazing the *Endurance*'s bows and breaking its rudder-chain, and it rammed one of its own gunboats. But engineers managed to repair the damage as they sailed back to join the rest of the ships, which were pounding the enemy's batteries on both sides of the river, and the squadron returned without losses.

On 30 August, Lenin was shot at point-blank range in Moscow as he was leaving a factory meeting, and Trotsky had to return. One bullet had penetrated Lenin's neck, close to his brain, the other punctured his left lung. But he was soon back at work at the Kremlin with both bullets still in his body, and he would survive for another six years, his health increasingly undermined by blackouts, headaches and insomnia.

The Socialist Revolutionary leader Boris Savinkov, Minister of War in the Kerensky government, was arrested, and confessed that gun and bullets had been provided by the British, and the ensuing reprisals saw a significant escalation of the Red Terror, with hundreds of Socialist Revolutionaries, suspected terrorists and 'class enemies' rounded up by the Moscow *Cheka* and shot.

After two days, Trotsky was back in Svyazhsk, having assured Lenin of the success of the Volga campaign. By then some ten thousand soldiers and sailors had assembled on the far bank of the Volga for the final assault on Kazan, under the command of the Fifth Army and the Volga Flotilla – consisting now of six gunboats, eight armed steamers, twenty destroyer launches and a floating battery, supported by an air detachment of six planes.

Drafted into Svyazhsk were the Red Army's first 'International Battalions' – prototypes for the International Brigades in the Spanish Civil War – including the Karl Liebknecht Regiment, the Red Tartars, and the Latvian Rifles. Larisa was appointed commander of the Hungarian former prisoners of war of the new Karl Marx International Battalion. In a letter home, signed 'Commissar Raskolnikova, Espionage Division, HQ of the Fifth Army, Svyazhsk', she wrote:

> My darlings, I've trained thirty Magyars for dangerous assignments, and found them all horses and weapons. We speak German, and we've been out scouting together, and we've already arrested a Czech commander ...
>
> Life speeds madly. In three or four days we'll take Kazan. There are lots of soldiers and lots of guns, and we suffer horribly from dirt and lice. Eternal thanks for the scissors etc. Please send my hat and autumn coat as soon as you can. I left all my things in Kazan and I'm freezing, and I look like nothing on earth. I kiss you all, your daughter at war with the bourgeoisie.[14]

---

14 Quoted in Solovei 1985, p. 42.

On 4 September, workers at Kazan's arsenal rose up against the Constitutional Assembly Committee, and were massacred. Young men were marched off to the front to fight the Bolsheviks, the prisons filled with fresh corpses, and more convoys of fugitives poured from the city with their possessions. Next day, the Volga Flotilla and the Fifth Army went on the attack.

After four days of bloody battles on both sides of the river, Markin led his sailors into the city with units of Vladimir Azin's 28th Cavalry Regiment, and together they knocked out the Whites' artillery and stopped the executions. Attacked on three sides, the Whites fled, abandoning quantities of weapons.

Kazan was the Eastern Front's first victory in the Civil War, and its fighters were showered with praise. A week later, the youthful new First Army under Mikhail Tukhachevsky drove the Czechs from Simbirsk, 150 miles south. The Whites' gold reserves moved east from Kazan to Samara, and from there ever eastwards, a security without a base. The exhausted Czech forces looked for support from the Japanese troops pouring into Siberia. But by then the Whites were already facing twelve Red armies, stretching from the White to the Black Sea.

CHAPTER 9

Reds and Whites

In September 1918, the main forces of the Flotilla left Kazan for the next stage of its campaign, driving the Whites from the upper reaches of the Volga, and its tributary the Kama. Sailing mainly at night, they fought in desperate daily battles for the towns and villages along the shores. And in breaks in the fighting, she escaped to the *Summer Tide* to write. She wrote with a dreamlike intensity of shellshocked sailors who had seen their comrades die, of 'times when the smallest thing seems full of ominous significance and tests us to our limits',

> when the rising sun prophesies a long terrible day, and the nights are endless and crimson like a bad dream. At such times, it's easy to understand people's ancient superstitions about the cry of a bird, the sound of a falling stone, the rustle and rattle of inanimate things ... All the icy concentrated forces of reason are needed then to stop the men abandoning their posts, and banish these spectres that are more dangerous than the visible enemy ...

She wrote of a young nurse struggling for her life after being hit by an enemy shell:

> She is barely out of her teens, with the sweet high voice of a child, and her small freckled nose is bloody with shrapnel, and her left eye, her cheek and her chin are covered in bandages ... No one has been granted to see the true face of the Revolution yet, but in those terrible days it was the face of that girl, her one grey transparent eye trembling with dark flecks like the leaves of wild poplars in autumn, her soft peasant lips covered in a pink foam of blood ...

She is a powerful presence in all her writings, but at the same time invisible, and a picture of her life at the front has to be assembled from the memories of those who fought with her, from her letters home, and her later conversations with friends.

Raskolnikov published five books about the Revolution and the Civil War, filled with warmth and drama and his personal memories and observations – *Kronstadt and Petersburg in 1917*, *Men of Kronstadt*, *Memoirs*, *Stories of a Flotilla Commander*, and *The Tales of Sub-Lieutenant Ilin*. In *The Front*, he is simply

'Flotilla Commander', *'Flotkom'*. After the first and most personal of her 'Letters', from Kazan, they are no longer her story or his, they are the collective story of the Revolution, and each page is filled with unforgettable characters, and has hundreds more behind them.

> There were so few in tsarist Russia who cut through the old orthodoxies, and threw themselves into real working struggles. And now there were hundreds of thousands of them, and I had the good fortune to meet many of them in our Flotilla. History will never be able to do justice to our sailors' daily acts of heroism. The names of those whose courage, modesty and discipline, all given of their free will, helped to create our Flotilla, are still barely known – those who at critical moments stepped out from the crowd and showed true leadership and authority, who knew their heroic role, and inspired others to rise to their level.

There was noble Markin, hero of Kazan, and romantic Vladimir Azin, commander of the legendary 28th Cavalry Regiment. Gun-layer Eliseev, 'his eyebrows singed off after he sank one of the enemy's ships from six miles away'. The sailor Andrei Babkin, who helped lay the mines that blew up one of the Whites' torpedo ships – 'feverish and desperate from the illness that would soon kill him, regally squandering his precious talents and his indomitable carefree spirit'. And the peasant Ivan Ivanovich, gun-position officer on the *Summer Tide*:

> Standing on the bridge in his felt boots, lit up by the magical brightness of the shells, a smile appears on his face after each explosion ... Never before has a peasant in felt boots stood on this proud high bridge, with its complex machinery and its circling telegraph levers on the masts, above the shells and the ten-inch rifles, above the whole of Russa, the whole of humanity, smashing the world to pieces and starting again with the Revolution ...

She wrote of quiet times, 'when the men rest on deck, hang their washing on the line, write letters home, and play with the two little puppies we rescued from our last battle', and of brief shore leaves. She led foraging expeditions with Raskolnikov to the abandoned estates along the river for food and fuel, and helped herself to their wardrobes, and she was photographed on shore in one of her expropriated outfits, a loose embroidered cotton shift and ribboned sunhat. On duty, she wore the sailors' uniform of striped jersey, cap and boots, and commissar's leather jacket. They recalled her striking appearance, riding at the head of mounted reconnaissance missions, and on board the warships, revolver in hand. And between battles, they would crowd onto the *Kashin*, the *Speedy* and the *Intrepid* for her lectures on literature – 'Songs of October', 'The Poetry of the Factories', and 'Stories from the Villages and their History'.

A major part of commissars' work at the front was to spread culture and literacy. Almost seventy percent of Russia's adult population were illiterate when the Bolsheviks took power, most of them peasants and women. 'Without literacy there can be no politics, only rumour and gossip', Lenin said, and the Commissariat of Education declared its intention to make the entire population literate by the year 1923. The Commissariat's Commission to Liquidate Illiteracy, *Likbez*, sent hundreds of *agit-trains* to the frontline towns and villages, with books, printing presses and teams of teachers, and over forty thousand reading rooms and literacy 'liquidation points' were set up across the country.

Theatres, cinemas and circuses closed during the Civil War, and troupes of actors, dancers and circus performers travelled on *agit-trains* to the front, staging political skits, '*agitki*', in dugouts and hospitals, and mock 'trials' of White generals. Artists produced posters of heroic revolutionaries and evil capitalists, and journalists reported from the battlefields, and soldiers' telegrams from the front were turned into posters and articles often within hours of arriving. These were then brought to the towns and villages by the national network of the new Russian Press Agency, ROSTA, and were displayed on factory walls, on *agit-trains* and in empty shop windows.

A genius of ROSTA's poster art was Mayakovsky, who called this new mass medium art form 'a documentary record, in colours and words of the most difficult three years of the revolutionary struggle serving a hundred-million-strong giant of a people'. The most popular of ROSTA's Civil War journalists was Larisa's old comrade Mikhail Koltsov, who toured the Northern Front on the Red October *agit-train*, with its teams of fighters, teachers, actors and journalists, writing articles illustrated by his brother, the cartoonist Boris Efimov. And coordinating this vast nationwide propaganda campaign at the Commissariat of Education was Raskolnikov's brother Alexander.

Lenin called film 'the most important of all the arts'. Studios were in ruins, stocks had been lost and destroyed, distribution networks had collapsed, but the Commissariat of Education's State Film Trust, *Goskino*, set out to replace the old tsarist melodramas with high quality productions. Mayakovsky acted in and wrote screenplays for over a dozen films made during the Civil War. ROSTA camera crews travelled to the fronts, shooting and showing documentary *agitki* newsreels of the battles, and these first Soviet productions would revolutionise world cinema.

The director Lev Kuleshov, who filmed the battles with Kolchak's armies in the Urals, found a new language of visual metaphors to express the clash between the Reds and Whites, in an editing technique he called the 'montage of attractions' – which conveyed the meaning of a scene by condensing time and space into multiple dramatically charged images and narratives. The most brilliant of ROSTA's frontline filmmakers to use the 'Kuleshov effect' was Dziga Vertov, the adopted Futurist name of Larisa's contemporary at the Psychoneurology Institute David Kaufman, who toured the fronts on the Red October train as head of the Moscow Film Committee's 'Kino-Week' newsreel collective, with his own carriage equipped with cameras, makeshift labs and projectors, shooting, developing and projecting films on the battlefields. In the autumn of 1918, the Red October brought Vertov and his crew to Svyazhsk, and their films of the battles featured Trotsky prominently, but unfortunately not Larisa.[1]

Montage would reach its highest form in the 1920s and 1930s in the masterpieces of Kuleshov's star pupil at the State Film School, Sergei Eisenstein. After October, twenty-year-old Eisenstein had volunteered with Petrograd's Red Engineers' corps, working on the defences of the city. He had then set off on an *agit-train* for the North-eastern Front, where he learned his craft as film director, writing, designing and acting in plays in the frontline towns and villages.

The language of montage entered the graphic arts, architecture and literature. In *The Front*, Larisa used the new editing techniques to cut from battles and crowd scenes to closeups of individuals, from the beauty of the Volga landscape to passages of haunting sadness. Here she describes the river Kama at dawn,

> flowing through steep yellow ravines, dividing between little islands, reflecting the silver outlines of the pine trees on its silky surface. Our noiseless battleships cut across the landscape like wild war horses of the sea, without breaking the enchanted silence. A clump of ducks skim over the water, and hundreds of swans spread their wings in the shallows, pierced by the first rays of the autumn sun. Far in the distance, an eagle circles over a white church …

These scenes are set against some of the most tragic episodes of the Civil War, and the mass graves of the White Terror:

---

1   Dziga Vertov's brother, Boris Kaufman, left Petrograd after October for Paris, where he worked as cameraman on Jean Vigo's films 'Zéro de Conduite' and 'L'Atalante'. In 1942 he moved to Hollywood, where he worked as director of photography for Elia Kazan's 'On the Waterfront', which won him two Academy awards, and for Sydney Lumet's '12 Angry Men' and 'The Pawnbroker'.

How much bestial cruelty the Whites inflicted as they retreated. The names of hundreds of little towns and villages along the river are written in the history of the Revolution with blood ...

The wives and children of those killed don't run abroad to write their memoirs about the cruelty of the *Cheka*, or the burning of their ancestral estates with their Rembrandts and libraries. No one trumpets to sensitive Europe about the thousands shot by the Whites along the Kama, whose bodies are washed up on its uninhabited shores. Can any of you who sailed on the *Speedy*, the *Intrepid* or *Vanya the Communist* remember a day when a soldier in his army greatcoat didn't float silently past, his head shaved against typhus? A village where you weren't greeted with sobs of grief from hundreds of starving widows and orphans?

She wrote nothing of her own battles with the sailors to establish her authority. But brutal times demanded brutal discipline, and the Kronstadt sailor Victor Shamov, a gunner on the battleship the *Kashin*, recalled her ruthless teaching methods.

In the last week of September, Shamov led a landing-party of sailors to drive the Whites from the little town of Chistopol, fifty miles south of Kazan. The rest of the ships were far behind, and the town was defended only by a few members of the exhausted landing-party, who were unable to spy out the Whites' positions. The commanders had seized a stable of trained and saddled cavalry horses, but none of the men could ride. And since Larisa rode excellently, like a man, and was often taken for one, she was appointed by Raskolnikov to turn a group of them into a new cavalry intelligence unit.

Shamov recalled the cold wet morning when 'word went round the ship "Our Darling" is on board – that's what we called her. We lined up for inspection, and she moved along the line with Raskolnikov, congratulating us on our courage and fighting spirit'. She then ordered a grumbling Shamov and seven others to be released from their duties while she left to pick horses for them, and they waited horrified for their first lesson.

She returned that evening in the pouring rain, and to much laughter from the men on deck, she ordered them to their horses, and instructed them in the basics of riding, grooming and feeding. As darkness fell, she swung into the saddle of her chestnut stallion, and Shamov and the others scrambled up as best they could. Then after lining them up in pairs, she led them away from Chistopol and ordered them to trot. Shamov described them bouncing up and down with their rifles bumping against their backs, begging to rest. 'Instead, she ordered us to gallop. What happened next is hard to describe. Some of us fell off our horses into the mud, some clung to their necks, some slid onto their rumps.

The reins slipped from our grasp, we lost sight of each other in the darkness'. After galloping for several miles, she stopped and waited for them to catch up, then without asking how they felt, turned back towards the town, making them first canter then gallop again. When the straggling line of dejected riders finally returned to their ship, she congratulated them on their success. 'We had barely managed to stay in our saddles and were beaten to a pulp, and this didn't please us', Shamov wrote.

It was dawn by the time they had fed and groomed their horses and fallen into a deep sleep, from which she ordered them not to be disturbed. And when they woke in agony next morning, she told the cook to give them extra helpings of breakfast.

The exercise was repeated two days later, less painfully, and the third time she led them into an attack against some White scouts, who took them for experienced riders and hid in the woods, and they returned to their ship as heroes. She was soon sending them off on scouting missions behind enemy lines without her, and her new unit earned the praise of even the great cavalry commander Azin.

Shamov next met her outside the little town of Elabuga, a hundred miles north of Chistopol. His landing-party from the *Kashin*, covered by the *Speedy* and the *Mettlesome*, were to infiltrate the enemy's rear and cut off their retreat across the Kama. Scouts worked around the clock, checking their assessments of the Whites' firing lines, and it was raining heavily when they disembarked in the darkness. 'We quietly unloaded our supplies and prepared for battle, soaked but confident, writing letters to our loved ones at home, promising to have our revenge on the Whites and return victorious'.

Then a cutter came ashore, and Larisa disembarked. Presenting herself to the commander, Gritzai, as an officer of the Fleet's General Staff, she announced that she would be fighting under his command, and introduced herself to the sailors, who greeted her with frank suspicion. Pretending not to notice, she joined the middle of their line, and moved off with them through the forest. 'With no maps to guide him, Gritzai led us through thick mud', Shamov wrote. 'Larisa marched ahead, ignoring the rising chorus of oaths against the commander and his Fleet representative. And when we finally reached a dry spot, she asked Gritzai's permission to use the break for some reconnaissance – she knew no rest, that woman!'

Borrowing a peasant shirt from one of the sailors and tying it with a belt, she tousled her hair, threw off her boots and smeared her feet with mud, then turned to Shamov. 'Well my old friend, you'll make a good shepherd!' After helping him to disguise himself and approving his appearance, she told him to take orders from her on the way and led him off through the forest. 'I was captivated by her resourcefulness and courage', he wrote. 'There wasn't a trace of fear on her face'.

Their convincing disguises allowed them to enter the Whites' camp unchallenged, where they saw chaos and collapse, and officers being shot on the spot for the slightest disobedience, 'with a mass of unburied corpses, "for the edification of others"'. She had given Shamov an extra assignment, and got back before him, and she was waiting anxiously for him when he finally returned, and embraced him warmly in front of the others, covering him with praise.

She went on to fight with his detachment in the battle for Elabuga, where they reached the enemy lines earlier than expected, and attacked before waiting for the signal. 'The Whites scattered and surrendered, and we returned to our ships victorious', Shamov wrote. 'And by then the men's suspicion of her had turned into admiration, even worship'.

> Larisa Mikhailovna feared neither bayonet attacks, shells nor gunshots. Calm and brave in all circumstances, she was a model of revolutionary courage, inseparable from us in battle, moving from platoon to platoon, encouraging and advising us, and the sailors and commanders listened to her ... She won our hearts, and she knew it, and that we loved and trusted her, and that she had contributed to our victory.[2]

Sailing from Elabuga up the widening Kama, meandering around islands and through muddy yellow ravines, the Flotilla reached the village of Pyany Bor ('Drunken Forest'), where the ships met an overwhelming force of Whites, and Markin's ship *Vanya the Communist* was hit by enemy fire. Larisa left with Raskolnikov on the *Intrepid* to order him back. 'But it was too late. A hail of shells hit the *Communist*, and a minute later, golden tongues of flames were licking the engine and it was billowing smoke. Then its siren called for help'.

Red launches got through under heavy fire and rescued thirty sailors. But Markin and the rest of his crew were drowned.

> And the artillerists mourned him, and the silent helmsman at his wheel, and the lookouts in their towers, their windows streaming with tears. Markin had gone down with the *Communist*, with his selflessness and generosity, his fierce curses, his almost animal instinct for the enemy's presence, his iron will, his goodness and heroism.

---

2 Victor Shamov, 'Nasha Lyubov' (Our Darling), *LRRC*, pp. 88–96.

'Markin was all of one piece, of the purest dye', Trotsky wrote. In the hectic days of October, Markin had helped his family with their rations and accommodation, and had babysat for his two sons in the Kremlin while he and his wife were at work. Later, during the Civil War, 'whenever I heard that the man at the danger point was Markin, I felt heartened and relieved'.

> But now his hour had struck. When I received the telegram informing me of his death, I felt as if a column of granite had come crashing down before me.
> His photograph, in his ribboned sailor's cap, was on the children's table. 'Boys, boys, Markin is dead!'
> The two little faces twisted in pain before me, and in the silence of the night, the little bodies shook under their blankets ...[3]

One of the survivors brought back to the *Summer Tide* was the young machine-gunner Vsevolod Vishnevsky, who a month earlier had been setting Larisa 'tests' outside Svyazhsk:

> Our ship went down. Thirty of us survived. Larisa Mikhailovna gave us coffee and spirits and bandaged our wounds, and comforted us with her tender motherly care. 'What happened?' she said. The men pushed me forward and I spoke. She listened, then came up to me and kissed me on the forehead. The others sniggered, and she silenced them with a look. It was all so simple, but it has stayed with me all my life.[4]

Years later, Vishnevsky would be a successful screenwriter and playwright, and his memories of Larisa are from the speech he recorded in 1933 for actors rehearsing the second production of the play for which he is best known, his romantic Civil War drama 'An Optimistic Tragedy', about her life on the Volga – a commissar and intellectual and 'girl', who fights to win the respect of a rough crew of sailors and turn them into a communist fighting force, and dies defending the Revolution.

She mourned Markin in her long poem 'Requiem', published in the Flotilla's paper *Red Sailor* thirteen months after his death, on 7 November 1919, the second anniversary of the Revolution:

---

3   Trotsky, *My Life*, 1975, pp. 304–6.
4   Vishnevsky, 'Remembered All My Life', *LRRC*, pp. 103–4.M.

The destroyers return to the sea,
Like swans leaving for the south,
Sending the fallen crusaders
A host of iron-winged blizzards ...

Upwards, upwards, frozen Markin,
Tear the ice from your wounds,
Pouring in a red stream
Into the boundless ocean ...[5]

It was the only poem she published after the Revolution, written far from the front, in a break in the fighting, in the lofty ornamental style reminiscent of her student poetry. Her 'Letters' are written in a different voice, hammering from the heat of battle a new poetry of working-class struggle and resistance, and the voice is always thrillingly hers, bold, instinctive, filled with images from myth, art and poetry, by turns intimate and formal, tender and sardonic, sweeping us along in the narrative.

Her first two 'Letters', from Kazan and Svyazhsk, were published in *Izvestiya* in October, and reviews were clamorous in their praise. *Pravda* wrote of her exceptional identification with her characters, and the brilliance of the writing. 'No one has described the Civil War with such emotional depth and subtlety, or discovered so many new facets to this epoch', wrote the journalist Lev Voikov in the Kronstadt paper *Red Baltic Fleet*.

On 16 October, on a morning sharp with the first frost, the Flotilla reached the little frontline town of Sarapul, two hundred miles north of Elabuga, recently cleared of the Whites. The quays and jetties were packed with jubilant Red soldiers waving red flags, and a rough brass struck up the *Marseillaise*. But on shore the sailors were surrounded by crowds of sobbing women, who told them that when the Whites retreated they had loaded six hundred workers onto a battery barge, armed with long-range weapons, and sailed them up the river to be killed.

Raskolnikov and Larisa both left gripping accounts of the operation to rescue them, Raskolnikov in his *Tales of Sub-Lieutenant Ilin*. She described sailing north with him on the battleship the *Speedy*, with a division of torpedoes flying white flags, planning to trick the enemy into thinking they were part of Admiral Stark's White Volga Flotilla.

---

5 'Rekviem. Na gibel voennogo korablya *Vanya-kommunist*' (Requiem on the Sinking of the Warship *Vanya the Communist*), *Krasny Voenmor* (Red Sailor), 19 November, 1919. sw, p. 319.

They caught up with the 'barge of death' at the village of Galyany, where the Whites had made their encampment:

> The floating grave, armed with long-range weapons, guarded by sentries, waited motionless under the left shore ... How to move it, trapped between the narrow banks of the river, was another matter ...
>
> But as luck would have it, just then the Whites' tugboat *Dawn* came steaming towards the pier. Our *Flotkom*, in his White naval officer's cap, addressed the captain imperiously through his loud-hailer: 'In the name of Admiral Stark, Commander of this Flotilla, I order you to approach the barge with the prisoners and attach it to the tug, then follow us along the river!'
>
> The *Dawn's* captain, trained by the Whites not to question orders, turned it towards the barge, and we held our breath ... But spurred on by his shouts, the *Dawn* performed magnificently. The sentries on the barge weighed anchor, and it inched forward, and the *Flotkom* calmed the confused crew: 'In the Admiral's name I order you to proceed! We'll sail ahead and cover you!'
>
> Then unhurriedly, so as not to attract the suspicion of the White officers on shore, we sailed on to Sarapul.

Four hundred of the six hundred survived, barely alive, and they were welcomed back to Sarapul with their rescuers with storms of tears and applause. Sarapul's main street was renamed Raskolnikov Street, and a day later a Flotilla landing party drove the Whites from the village of Galyany, which was renamed 'Raskolnikovo'.

Larisa's adopted brother Lev, now a junior naval commander in the Baltic Fleet, joined her in Sarapul for the celebrations, and they were photographed together in the town. She is seated, in civilian clothes, beaming at the camera, he is standing behind her in his naval uniform, with his arm resting protectively on her chair.

The division then rejoined the main forces of the Flotilla, which sailed north to the factory towns of Izhevsk and Votkinsk, where they fought with local Red Guards and units of the Second Army against the forces of the Kama Constituent Assembly Committee. Trotsky reported that forty-eight British soldiers fighting in Kotlas, a hundred miles north of Votkinsk, had gone over to the Red Army, and within a week, all three towns were in Bolshevik hands.

By the end of October, the Flotilla had driven the Whites all the way up the Kama to Ufa, and had liberated all the territory from Kazan to the Urals. And as ice began to form on the river, the ships prepared to leave for Nizhny

Novgorod for the winter. The end of the autumn campaign was celebrated on the 7 November, the first anniversary of the Revolution, and in a cable to the Kremlin, Raskolnikov and Larisa pledged 'on this day of workers' liberation, that the Volga Naval Flotilla will fight until the plunderers have been destroyed, and the Great World Socialist Revolution has been brought to a victorious conclusion'.[6]

---
6 The telegram is in the Central State Archive of the October Revolution (acquired in 1992 by the new State Archive of the Russian Federation). *SW.*, p. 325.

CHAPTER 10

From Moscow to the Caspian

Leaving the rest of the Flotilla in Nizhny Novgorod, they travelled back to Moscow, where Raskolnikov was awarded the Order of the Red Banner, the highest military award of the Red Army, and was appointed to the Revolutionary War Council of the Republic. He then left for Kronstadt, to assess the threat to Petrograd, and Larisa moved back into her family's cold cramped flat in the House of Soviets.

It was an exceptionally harsh winter. A third of Moscow's citizens were fighting at the front, and terrible stories about Russia were published in the Western press to demonstrate the horrors of Bolshevism. 'The Bolshevists are rounding up young girls and placing them at the mercy of the soldiery, and eighty to ninety percent of the new commissaries are jews', a British officer in Moscow wrote in the *Times*. As Lenin said, 'The poets of the lie are boundlessly imaginative'.

The random looting of possessions in the first months of the Revolution was now managed in a more orderly fashion by local soviets. But people in the cities still had barely enough to eat. The transport system was virtually at a standstill, cutting off Central and Northern Russia from the wheat-producing areas of the South, and drastic rationing had been introduced. Larisa and her father both held senior posts at the commissariats, and Igor had a highly responsible job at the Foreign Commissariat in its Eastern Affairs Department. But like Lenin and his wife Nadezhda Krupskaya, in their small unheated flat in the Kremlin, the Reisners were on the basic 'labour rations' of an eighth of a pound of bread a day.

Shklovsky was living in Petrograd, the 'Northern Commune', where conditions were even harder:

> Ink froze in the inkwells. The streets were covered in ice and were unusable. No cars or trams. Dead horses lay on the ground with no one to cart them away, and were hacked up with pocket-knives and carried off in pieces ... The plumbing froze, and buckets of excrement were dumped in the courtyards in front of the buildings. Men became impotent, women stopped menstruating. Well-dressed men urinated on the Nevsky Prospect. The common procedure for a burial was to find a sledge, call on a friend or relative for help, and pull the body to the cemetery.[1]

---

1 Victor Shklovsky, *Sentimental Journey* (trans. Richard Sheldon), 1970, pp. 144–45.

Shklovsky, on his diet of oats and potato peel, gave lectures to factory workers on translation and literary theory, and a linguist friend of his 'worked under a tent of tarpaulin and rags on his thousand-page *magnum opus*, on the similarities between the Japanese and Malay languages'.

Boris Pasternak remembered meeting Larisa at a Moscow barracks that winter, and discussing the poetry of Rilke with her. Poetry and writing were her escape from the cold and hunger and her cramped living conditions, and it was during her five-month break from the front that she started on her novel *Requiem*, her first and only work of fiction, about her life before the Revolution.

Despite the victories on the Volga, the Bolsheviks seemed doomed to be annihilated without a revolution in Germany, and after four years of war, in which over two million had lost their lives at the front, people in Germany were at breaking point. The collapse of the Western Front in September 1918 had triggered an upsurge of mutinies and desertions, setting off strikes, riots and demonstrations across the country, which culminated on the 9th of November in another general strike in Berlin. On that day the Kaiser fled into permanent exile in Holland, with his lesser princes and grand dukes and his General Staff, leaving his Chancellor, Prince Maximilian of Baden, to supervise the transition to the new Germany. A day later, the Chair of the Social Democratic Party, Friedrich Ebert, became President of the new German Republic, and on the 11th an Armistice was signed with the Allies. Talks then opened in Versailles for a permanent peace treaty. The First World War was over.

The collapse of Imperial Germany was widely seen in Russia as the start of the longed-for world revolution. It was in this optimistic mood that thousands of women from all over the country poured into the Kremlin on 16 November, for the First All-Russian Congress of Peasant and Working Women. They spoke of fighting on the Volga and in Petrograd and Siberia, and of working in the factories to support their children. The organisers reported on their work with the commissariats, setting up state nurseries, laundries and canteens, and Kollontai gave her speech on the new family life of the Revolution, later published as her pamphlet *Communism and the Family*. Lenin then took the stage, to deafening applause, and delivered a rousing attack on women's unpaid drudgery in the home:

> Despite all our liberating laws, woman continues to be a domestic slave, because petty housework crushes, strangles, stultifies and degrades her, chains her to the kitchen and nursery, and wastes her labour on barbarically unproductive tasks. The real emancipation of women, real communism, will begin only when a mass struggle, led by the proletariat, is waged against this domestic economy. Do we devote enough attention to this

question, theoretically indispensable to every communist? No, of course we don't.[2]

The Congress ended with a resolution to establish nationwide Women's Commissions, similar to the Party's Jewish Sections, on the lines of the women's sections Kollontai had recommended two years earlier, responsible for caring for orphans and setting up children's homes at the front, and for organising creches, canteens and laundries in the cities – 'to liberate women from the kitchen and the cradle'.

It is not known if Larisa attended the Congress. But her appointment in December as the Red Navy's first woman Political Commissar is an indication of the new opportunities opening up for women in the Civil War. In the frontline towns, they learnt to shoot and left for the battlefields, and they were especially valued for their propaganda and espionage work. Kollontai was one of the Red Army's most popular frontline speakers, and Larisa was famous for her naval intelligence missions. On the home front, women were everywhere, as factory and union organisers, and in high-level government jobs. One of those who rose to high office was the Moscow factory worker Varya Kasparova, chief organiser of the Party's Political Department, in charge of coordinating the work of the Political Commissars.

Political Commissars, Party members, were appointed in a personal supervisory capacity to every officer of the tsarist General Staff who had thrown in their lot with the Bolsheviks, and they were the key to Trotsky's strategy for building the Red Army. Joseph Stalin argued that the advantages of using the tsarist commanders' superior military knowledge and experience were outweighed by the risk that they would turn traitors, and the issue had been the cause of the first major political clash between them, in September 1918, in the strategically vital beleaguered steppe city of Tsaritsyn. Commissar of Nationalities between 1917 and 1924, Stalin had adopted his Party name 'Man of Steel' when he was first elected to the Central Committee in 1912, and it was at Tsaritsyn that he discovered his taste for military ways of working.

On the river route connecting Greater Russia with the food and fuel supplies of the Lower Volga and the Northern Caucasus, with its large powerful industrial workforce, Tsaritsyn had elected its Bolshevik Soviet to power in September 1917, five weeks before the Revolution in Petrograd. Eight months later, the city was attacked by the German-backed forces of General Krasnov,

---

2 'V.I. Lenin i pervyi sezd rabotnits' (V.I. Lenin and the First Congress of Women Workers), in *O Vladimire Iliche Lenine. Vospominaniya, 1920–1922* (Memories of V.I. Lenin, 1920–1922), Moscow, 1963, p. 197.

then over the next eighteen months by the armies of Generals Denikin and Alexeev and Baron Wrangel.

In May 1918, Stalin had arrived in the Northern Caucasus with an armed guard of battalion strength, to organise the transport of grain to Moscow. A month later, at the start of the Whites' first assault on the city, he had taken over military operations, and Trotsky was soon inundated with complaints about his chaotic command structure. He and his second in command, Kliment Voroshilov, Commander of the First Cavalry, refused to serve under the former tsarist officer Trotsky had appointed as Commander of the Southern Front, and had had him arrested, and Trotsky arrived in Tsaritsyn in September to find them in charge of a powerful 'NCO opposition to Moscow' – mainly to Trotsky himself:

> In these circles, graduates of the Military Academy, senior officers and Moscow 'specialists' were referred to with loathing. But since the commanders had no military knowledge themselves, they all had their own 'specialists' close at hand, who being naturally of the second order, clung tenaciously to their posts, against those who were more capable and better informed.[3]

Trotsky ordered reinforcements from the rear and the city was saved, and he persuaded Lenin to order Stalin tactfully back to Moscow. A special train was sent to collect him, and Voroshilov was sent to fight in the Caucasus and Ukraine as Commander of the new Tenth Army.

Stalin never forgave Trotsky for his public humiliation in Tsaritsyn, and in an early salvo against him in 1925, he would honour his role in its defence by renaming it Stalingrad.[4]

Political Commissars had to develop their own leadership style with the old officer class. Larisa was considered to have a special understanding of the former tsarist commanders, who in Radek's words 'needed someone dynamic to help them identify with the Revolution', and in the tense political climate of the winter of 1918, she was appointed to work with the new Commander of the Naval Forces of the Republic, the aristocratic Admiral Vasily Altvater.

Like her father, Altvater was descended from generations of Baltic German barons, and he was widely believed to be the illegitimate son of the last Tsar, Alexander III. Before the Revolution he had served with Admiral Kolchak, and he had fought with Kolchak's White armies in the Urals after October. But in

---

3 Trotsky, *My Life*, 1975, p. 458.
4 Renamed Volgograd in 1961, in the 'de-Stalinisation' of Russia after his death.

January 1918, he went over to the Bolsheviks, joining their delegation at Brest-Litovsk as their chief naval technical adviser, and he had served the Red Navy honourably in the months that followed.

Their shared German ancestry was clearly a deep bond between them, and it was possibly in recognition of this that Larisa signed the first draft of *Requiem*, 'L. v. R' – 'Larisa von Reisner'. She had earned Altvater's respect for her record on the Volga. Now she had to breathe the ideas of the Revolution into him, and encourage him to continue fighting with the Bolsheviks.

The Brest-Litovsk Treaty had delivered thousands of miles of Russian territory to Germany, and the armies of Britain and Germany were now vying to establish governments in the Baltic states of Latvia, Lithuania and Estonia. On 12 December, a British squadron arrived at the Estonian capital, the Baltic port of Reval (now Tallinn), and Raskolnikov was appointed by Trotsky to lead a perilous naval reconnaissance mission there. In his *Tales of Sub-Lieutenant Ilin*, he described vividly his disastrous journey to Reval, 'on a state of alert against its British "guests"', and the months that followed.[5]

On 15 December, his crew left an ice-bound Kronstadt on the destroyer the *Spartak*. A few miles from Kronstadt, they were approached by the British warship the *Calypso*, and Raskolnikov was recognised by an old schoolfriend of his on board, who was fighting with the British. As the *Spartak* retreated it ran aground, and he and his men were arrested at gunpoint. The crew were sailed to a British prison camp on the remote island of Norgen in northern Norway, half way to the North Pole, where five would die of starvation. He was taken under armed guard by naval launch to Britain's Scottish naval base at Rosyth, and from there by train to London, where he was interrogated at Scotland Yard by the head of British military intelligence, Sir Basil Thomson, prosecutor of suffragettes and Marxists, Irish and Indian nationalists, high-level German spies, and 'Bolshevik Jews'. He was then taken to Brixton Prison, where he was held in solitary confinement, with a sign on his cell door saying 'Prisoner of War'.

Headlines in the British press celebrated the capture of the 'First Sea Lord of the Bolshevist Admiralty', and hardline anti-Soviet members of Lloyd George's cabinet, led by Winston Churchill and the Leader of the House of Lords, Lord Curzon, called in Parliament for no negotiations with the Bolsheviks, and for him to be jailed indefinitely. But Lloyd George went over their heads to approach Moscow for talks, and Larisa joined the Soviet team, led by Trotsky and Altvater, who met British Red Cross officials in the Kremlin to discuss his release, in exchange for nineteen British officers jailed in Arkhangelsk.

---

5 Raskolnikov, *Tales of Sub-lieutenant Ilin* (trans. Brian Pearce), 1970, pp. 144–49.

'Raskolnikov's wife is also a personage of considerable importance in the Soviet government', a Red Cross official cabled back to the Foreign Office.

1918 was the year of the deadly influenza pandemic, the greatest human disaster in history, which claimed an estimated fifty million lives worldwide, far exceeding the deaths so far from the Covid virus. In Britain, the press was banned by war censorship from publishing information about the disease to avoid spreading panic, resulting in widespread ignorance of its early symptoms, with over two hundred thousand recorded deaths, and a quarter of the population affected, and Raskolnikov saw solitary confinement as the safest place he could be.

He worked hard at improving his English, reading the prison library's tattered copies of Shakespeare, Dickens, Thackeray, Conan Doyle and the Bible. His cell was unheated, and London was in the grip of one of the coldest winters on record, but he found the climate 'very mild'. 'They don't have proper frosts here, just rain and fog and damp flakes of snow, which melt as soon as they touch the ground. The fat red-faced warders pant and clutch their bundles of keys and rub their hands, gasping "Siberia! Siberia!", and I shake my head and laugh at the poor fellows'.

Much had been written in the Soviet press about the Revolution's galvanising effect on anti-colonialist struggles in India and Ireland, and on the British left. In November the Hands Off Russia! campaign had been formed, to coordinate resistance to the Intervention, and 1918 saw mass demonstrations across the country against war, capitalism and 'imperialist plunder'. After four years without rights, over two and a half million workers, led by the industrial unions of the miners and the transport workers, came out on strike for better pay and conditions. Soldiers, sailors and airmen mutinied, Bolshevik-style Workers' Councils sprang up, and the Shop Stewards Movement, established during the war, campaigned for the Bolshevik peace initiative. In January 1919, Glasgow dockers on 'Red Clydeside' began their month-long strike for the eight-hour day, declaring the strike the start of the 'socialist revolution' in Britain, and the army cracked down on the strikers with tanks and machine guns. 'There is no doubt we are up against a Bolshevist movement in Glasgow, London and elsewhere', said the First Lord of the British Admiralty, Sir Eric Geddes.

At Raskolnikov's second interrogation, on 16 January at the Admiralty, he was informed by Foreign Office officials that Rosa Luxemburg and Karl Liebknecht had been killed the previous day in Berlin while resisting arrest.

The strikes in Germany had continued throughout the winter of 1918. Luxemburg and Liebknecht were both released from jail and spoke at factory meetings, and workers' and soldiers' soviets took power in Hamburg, Keele and Berlin – named by the Spartacists 'capital of the German Socialist Republic'.

The new Social Democrat-led government quickly set out to restore law and order, and bring the soviets under its control. On 16 December, Germany's first legal Congress of Workers' and Soldiers' Soviets was held in Berlin, at which a majority supported Social Democrats' call for a new parliament, to take its name from Germany's ancient cultural centre of Weimar, home of Goethe and Schiller, far from the turmoil in Berlin.

Members of the small new Spartacist League were divided on whether to take part in the elections. Although realising they would be a farce, Luxemburg and Liebknecht were for using them as a propaganda platform. But they were hugely outvoted by those who argued that 'two men on the street are worth a thousand votes', and called for the Spartacists to dissolve themselves into the new German Communist Party, which would lead a mass armed uprising against the state.

Luxemburg and Liebknecht saw this as a huge tactical error. Revolution could not be forced from above, Luxemburg said, it could be achieved only through workers' united will, and she argued that they needed more time to develop their solidarity and fighting skills before taking to the barricades. But both supported events as they unfolded, and attended the founding meeting of the Communist Party on 30 December. Communists immediately occupied the offices of the Social Democrats' paper *Vorwärts*, and published their own revolutionary issues for two weeks, before government troops fought their way into the building and shot them dead.

President Ebert then ordered the far-right paramilitaries of the *Freikorps*, the 'bloodhounds of the revolution', to finish off the resistance. Over five hundred communists were arrested in Berlin, and on 15 January, the 'chief criminals', Luxemburg and Liebknecht, were dragged from their underground hiding places for a brief preliminary hearing, then driven off separately, supposedly to jail, and had their skulls smashed on the way in a barbaric display of revenge. Four days later, elections opened for the new Weimar Republic.

Trotsky's biographer Isaac Deutscher has called their murders 'the first triumph of Nazi Germany'. The months that followed saw a surge of support for the new nationalist German Workers' Party in Munich, precursor of the Nazi Party, and for Hitler's Brownshirt gangs in Bavaria, modelled on the *Freikorps*, who were attacking Jews, workers and communists on the streets.

For the Bolsheviks, the defeat of the German revolution was another catastrophe in an already catastrophic situation. In Poland, the vital bridge for their revolutionary message to Germany and the rest of Europe, its Chief of Staff had declared the country's independence from Russia, appointing the charismatic Marshal Pilsudski President of the new Polish Republic, whose legions were fighting the Red Army for Western Belorussia and Western Ukraine. Britain had meanwhile announced its backing for a new combined Kolchak-Denikin-Yudenich offensive against Soviet Russia, and a swift advance on Moscow – 'to deprive Bolshevism of its basic vital centres, and crush it in one blow'.

Raskolnikov learned from his guards of February's packed Hands Off Russia! rally at the Albert Hall, chaired by its founder George Lansbury, future leader of the Labour Party, at which London dockers declared their refusal to load ships with munitions to 'arm the White Terror'. The Soviet government still clung to the hope that the world revolution would simply take longer to mature.

In March, fifty delegates from Europe, China and America broke through the Blockade and the war zones to attend the founding congress in Moscow of the new Bolshevik-led Third (Communist) International, the Comintern, to replace the moribund Socialist International, and pledged to 'fight with every available means, including armed force, for the overthrow of the international bourgeoisie, and the creation of an International Soviet Republic, as a transition stage to the complete abolition of the state'.

But with the German left struggling to survive the loss of its two most brilliant leaders, and the Allied armies in control of most of Russia, it was a small and impotent affair. Two weeks later, hopes were raised when soviet regimes took power in Munich and Budapest, but they were short-lived, and as daily reports reached the Kremlin of new threats to Moscow, 'the plots and the Intervention and the Blockade and the looming famine made the government lose its head', Victor Serge wrote.

Hundreds were accused by secret *Cheka* agents of being 'anti-Soviet' or 'anti-Party', and several senior former tsarist commanders were arrested on slim evidence as foreign agents. And in April, four months after Larisa became Altvater's commissar, he was summoned to appear before a revolutionary military tribunal.

The tribunals had been set up by the *Cheka* in 1918, to defend the Revolution against 'counterrevolutionary forces, saboteurs and profiteers' in the armed forces. But Altvater was never informed of the charges against him, and her request as his commissar to give evidence at his hearing was denied. She and others close to him were in no doubt that it was the fear and uncertainty that led to his fatal heart attack two weeks later, at the age of thirty-six. Trotsky wrote in *Pravda* of 'the huge loss to our comrades in the Fleet of this tireless, competent honest worker', and in two long obituaries in *Izvestiya* and the Kronstadt paper *Red Baltic Fleet*, she paid tribute to his 'irreproachable integrity', and questioned the circumstances of his death.

She must have come under scrutiny herself over the affair, and her father was facing increasing criticism at the Commissariat of Justice. Although admired and respected as the author of the Soviet Constitution, he was seen by many of his colleagues as an old liberal, if not worse, and he had abandoned much of his Party work to write stage plays and publish articles on the new Soviet theatre. Igor would join the Party only in 1944, seven months before the end of the Second World War.

Altvater's death was a major blow to the negotiations for Raskolnikov. But in late April, the Soviet government undertook to improve the conditions of the nineteen British prisoners in Arkhangelsk, in preparation for their release, and on 1 May, he was transferred from Brixton Prison to a hotel in Gower Street near the British Museum, run by a Mrs Florence Mills. 'Your repatriation is almost complete', Larisa cabled him there. 'You'll receive funds for clothes etc. from the Danish Trade Delegation in London, who we'll reimburse in Moscow'.

After his five months behind bars, he enjoyed his freedom in London, shopping in Oxford Street for a new suit and felt hat to replace his sailor's uniform, attending a meeting of the British Labour Party in its dingy headquarters in Drury Lane, visiting the British Museum, the Zoo and the Royal Opera House, for a performance of 'Tosca'.

Two weeks later his holiday came to an end, and he was escorted by armed British police back to Russia. On 17 May, Larisa headed the large delegation of Soviet officials and journalists who gathered at the Russian-Finnish border station of Beloostrov to welcome him back. A band played the *Internationale*, and he was released from his police escort to exchange salutes with the nineteen British officers, led by a Major Goldsmith of the British Expeditionary Force in the Caucasus, who *Pravda* reported Larisa escorting personally off the train. Raskolnikov then expressed his 'boundless joy to be back in the Socialist Fatherland', and gave a short speech on the world situation after Versailles – 'pregnant with dangers of a new war'.

The Versailles peace talks had thrown up major disagreements between France and Britain over the issue of Russia. The French argued that the security of the post-war world depended on destroying the Bolsheviks. The British believed that without some accommodation with the Soviet government there could be no stable peace – 'and we will leave half of Europe and Asia in flames', Lloyd George said. But both were agreed on the need to inflict maximum damage on the Germans. Under the final terms of the Treaty, ratified in June, Germany was stripped of all its colonies and occupied land, and three-quarters of its army. The Brest-Litovsk Treaty was annulled, and German troops were ordered out of Ukraine and Russia's occupied territories, and the Weimar government was ordered to pay France and Belgium $25 billion in war reparations.

Hitler drew mass audiences to his rallies with his speeches about Germany's 'bleeding borders:' 'Wrecked and prostrated, Germany will rise up against Versailles and avenge the Fatherland. Sixty million men and women, their souls aflame with rage and shame, burst forth with the common cry "We will have arms again!"' The French had called for Germany to be broken up into separate states, and saw the Treaty as too soft on the Germans. 'This isn't peace, it's just a twenty-year armistice', said France's Marshal Foch, Supreme Allied Commander during the war.

In a letter to her mother in Moscow, Larisa described the weeks after Raskolnikov's release as the happiest in their marriage: 'It's hard to describe, it's not just a sudden burst of "happy feelings," it's something straight and true – England has made a man of him!'[6]

But his freedom was a small victory in an otherwise dire situation. By the spring of 1919, Soviet Russia was being invaded by the armies of fourteen states, led by Britain, France, Germany and America, and headlines in London, Paris, Berlin and Washington were celebrating one White victory after another. 'We're actually dead, we're just waiting for someone to bury us', Trotsky said.

French troops were fighting with Pilsudski's Polish legions in the West, occupying much of the disputed territory east of the River Bug, recognised by Versailles as part of Russia, but claimed as Poland's 'historic heritage'. A major White offensive in Ukraine had broken through to the industrial Donbas region in the east, and Germany's puppet government in the capital, Kiev, had been ousted by the ultra-nationalist Symon Petlyura, President of the Ukrainian National Republic, responsible for the slaughter of over fifty thousand of Ukraine's Jewish, Polish and Russian men, women and children.

The British government of occupation in Baku, capital of Azerbaijan, had taken control of the oil of the Caucasus. The British-backed army of General Yudenich had occupied all the territory along the Baltic Coast as far as Pskov, twenty miles from the Estonian border, and was threatening Petrograd. British-armed forces had driven the Red Army from Latvia, and occupied the capital, the Baltic port of Riga. Britain was arming the forces of Admiral Kolchak, Commander of the Eastern Front in the Urals and Siberia, and had named him 'Supreme Ruler of Russia'. And the armies of Denikin and Baron Wrangel, backed by a British tank corps and a squadron of the RAF, were advancing along the Volga for the Whites' fourth assault on Tsaritsyn.

In early June 1919, Larisa left Moscow by train with Raskolnikov and his commanders and her secretary Misha Kirillov for Saratov, two hundred miles north of Tsaritsyn, where the greatly enlarged Flotilla was assembling to support the city's local army units and workers' defence forces.

---

6 *SW*, pp. 514–15.

As Political Commissar, she was responsible for the welfare of Saratov's increased number of sailors, and Kirillov remembered her swiftly arranging for the sailor Andrei Babkin to be sent to a sanatorium when he collapsed with tuberculosis and started coughing blood. It was in Saratov too that she first met Altvater's successor as Commander of Naval Forces of the Republic, the equally aristocratic Admiral Behrens, when he came to inspect the ships.

In the nine months she worked with Behrens as his Commissar, she developed a deep respect and affection for this 'philosopher with the soul of an aristocrat':

> Behrens is constantly offended by the boorishness of the Revolution, which he treats like a devoted elderly grandee managing a badly behaved prince. But as a rationalist, he was convinced from the start by the irrefutable logic of October, and was prepared to draw the necessary conclusions from its great barbaric truths ... And suddenly this man, who thought the world had nothing more to offer him, discovered the last, most tender love of his life – for youth and creativity, and for the cruel beautiful angel splashed with the people's blood, which had come to judge the whole world ...
>
> The Revolution made Behrens roll up his lacy cuffs and dig with his own hands the grave of his conquered class. And he has no doubts that our little Flotilla, crammed to the bows with heroism and sacrifice, must and will win.

The admiration was evidently mutual, although Behrens was less complimentary about Raskolnikov, who he described as 'a decent enough fellow who does his best, and tries to supplement his lack of naval skills with a great deal of reading and discussion with specialists'.

According to Misha Kirillov, 'Larisa could get even the most anti-revolutionary officers to work with her'. And one of these was the new navigator of the *Summer Tide*, Nikolai Struisky:

> Struisky had been mobilised virtually by force, and he arrived in Saratov believing everything he read in *The Stock Exchange Gazette*, and that the Bolsheviks were all German spies ... But after the first shots, all that changed ... And at our victorious welcome at a little town liberated from the Whites, as the workers pressed the hand of our new 'Red officer' arriving in this foreign land, he realised to his horror that he was in tears, and that these people weren't a bunch of spies, but the whole of Russia. And that this Russia, of the workers and soviets, of its deserters, Jewish agitat-

ors, peasant women and young boys, was the one he would fight for to the end, braving the danger and hunger and the lice, not knowing how things would turn out, just that this was his country's only hope for justice and a future ...

The Tsaritsyn front covered a huge area of over thirty square miles, with the Volga patrolled by ten cruisers of the Flotilla, five destroyers, and a battery barge armed with heavy artillery. By the second week of June, the ships had anchored twenty miles from the city, and she described fighting in desperate daily river battles for the surrounding towns and villages:

> British planes roar overhead. Constant bombing day and night. It's a lottery of misfortunes. One of our destroyers is pierced in the heart by four shells. We watch it go down with a hideous shriek, scattering debris over the Intrepid, whose hull is shattered. The commander and three of his crew are wounded, and the sailors struggle to defend themselves and repair the damage as the barrage intensifies ...

As Stalingrad, Tsaritsyn would suffer the greatest casualties of the three-and-a-half-year Nazi occupation of the Soviet Union, and of the entire Second World War, when over a million soldiers and citizens died defending the city. Tsaritsyn in the summer of 1919 was described by Voroshilov as the 'red Verdun' – the eleven months of trench warfare in the First World War, in which three-quarters of a million French and German soldiers lost their lives.

Hundreds of women volunteered as fighters in the eighteen-month battles for the city, including Voroshilov's twenty-year-old wife, Ekaterina Davydovna. Born Golda Gorbman, from a poor Orthodox Jewish family in rural Ukraine, she had joined the strike movement in 1905, as a factory worker in Odessa, and had met Voroshilov a year later in exile in Siberia. Since exiles were allowed to cohabit only if they were married in church, she converted to Christianity and changed her name, and from then on she was at his side throughout the entire Civil War, fighting with him in the first battles for Tsaritsyn, then in the Caucasus, Poland and Ukraine.

Stalin's innocent second wife, nineteen-year-old Nadezhda Alliluyeva, spent their honeymoon working as his secretary in the blood and bullets of Tsaritsyn. Others organised creches, orphanages, canteens and women's soviets on the front line, or like Larisa worked as intelligence officers.

The officer Fyodor Novitsky sailed with her and Raskolnikov and a group of commanders late one night at the head of a squadron of torpedo boats with their lights out, to assess the threat to the city. They had stopped a few miles away to discuss their next move, when shells flew over their heads and exploded on the shore, and deciding the risks were too great to sail on, they ordered the ships back. 'It was during this tense and sensitive military episode that I first witnessed a woman soldier at the front', Novitsky wrote.

> Although I generally don't approve of women fighting on the front line, I confess I came to love and admire Larisa Mikhalovna. Not once did she lose her calm or cheerfulness under fire. Her very appearance, standing at her full height in full view of all the sailors, helped to keep order and maintain morale. And as well as all her other gifts were her remarkable powers of observation, her ability quickly to analyse the military situation, and more importantly, to describe it with great skill on paper.[7]

On 23 June, White and British forces launched their all-out assault on Tsaritsyn. A detachment of sailors from the Flotilla left to support the city's Red Guards and defence units, and she watched from the river as the first frontline troops moved along the shore:

> It's hard to write about them now, to remember the little figures marching to their deaths, however the battle turned out …
> For hours the terrible music of war raged on the river. Our flagship was the *Karl Marx*. The air was thick with gunpowder, and each ship fought separately, one to one with the invisible enemy. The Whites passed like fantoms in the night, pounding the shore with their shells. Fountains of water shot up, and columns of red tore the blackness, lighting the forested cliffs with flashes of gold. It seemed the explosions would never end, and slam shut the door of the baking oven …

By dawn, the roads out of Tsaritsyn were crowded with people escaping, and the Flotilla was in headlong retreat. 'The ships disappeared up the river in clouds of smoke and wreckage, and Behrens sat alone in his cabin, grieving like a father who had lost his son'.

British warships patrolled the Caspian Sea, vital to Britain's oil interests in the Caucasus, and the Flotilla's next mission was to support local defence forces at the port of Astrakhan, the southernmost point of Russia, the Red Fleet's only access to the Sea, under Bolshevik control since January 1919, but encircled by Whites, backed by British air and naval forces. With the Volga cut off at Tsar-

---

7 Fyodor Novitsky, 'Na minonostse' (On the Torpedo Ship), *LRRC*, pp. 89–91. First published in *Izvestiya*, 11 February, 1926.

itsyn, blocking their access south, they had to travel there by train, via Saratov and Pokrovsk, and the journey took three weeks, along railway lines pummelled by White raids, littered with wrecked trains, following the course of the Volga – 'widening as it approaches the salty waters of the Delta, dividing into thousands of sleeves whose shoulders are lost in the mist'.

They arrived in mid-July, and spent the next eight months there, while the Flotilla underwent a major reorganisation, and was merged with the river and sea-going forces of the Astrakhan Caspian Flotilla to become the new Volga Caspian Naval Flotilla, under Raskolnikov's command.

She wrote of Astrakhan's poverty, its mosques and mosquitoes, the smell of raw sewage and the sea, and its polyglot population of Kalmyks, Tatars and Russians, Chechens, Georgians, Daghestanis and Turks, and Armenian refugees fleeing the Armenian genocide in Turkey. The headquarters of the new Flotilla was in the Kalmyk quarter, where 'grave old men in silk robes and white stockings sit dreaming in doorways, their faces glowing in the sun like their Buddhist deities'. She visited the oases in the sands where the Kalmyks tended their ancient orchards and vineyards, destroyed in a British bombing raid. And in Astrakhan's naval hospital she met the remains of a family killed in another British raid, a mother and her baby son, whose leg had been amputated. She met the airman defending the town in the Bolsheviks' single broken-down little plane, numb with grief after the death of his son – 'going up four times a day, despite all warnings, throwing his metal tears to the ground'. She wrote of the troop trains rumbling across the steppe, bringing dead and wounded back from the front. And she paid her respects to the great glass coffin displayed in the park, 'overflowing with carnations, lilies and roses, the most beautiful mass revolutionaries' grave I have ever seen'.

> Astrakhan is torn and naked, as towns are only in the East. Yet how many unbelievable sacrifices for Soviet Russia have been made here, at the rusty gates to Asia. And how precious every stone is to the Revolution, every bend in its roads ...
>
> In defending Petrograd, people were fighting for its monuments sanctified by the Revolution. Everything inspired their resistance – Red Kronstadt, the rundown factories defying cold and hunger to produce weapons for the Red Army, the Winter Palace, containing nothing now but the tsars' paintings. Every step of the proletarian forces marching off to fight for Petrograd evoked an iron response from the rest of Russia, and will never be forgotten ...
>
> But how much heroism has been needed to defend Astrakhan. People are inspired neither by revolutionary tradition nor by love for the town,

but by a sense of duty. And it's not just some cold abstract duty, it's the collective will not to abandon the Caspian to the British.

The new Volga Caspian Flotilla was now defending a vast area, from the Lower Volga to the Northern Caspian. She fought with Raskolnikov in a raid on White Cossacks in the village of Solodniki, twenty miles from Astrakhan, and she sailed two hundred miles north with him on a mission to deliver oil from the British-occupied Caspian oilfields at Guriev in Western Kazakhstan (now Atyrau).

To her parents she wrote:

> Our sailors saved a wonderful Kalmyk Buddha from a bombed shrine on the blazing steppe, and I pray to it when my Fedya is in dangerous places ... He has just taken two more torpedo boats to Tsaritsyn, where he is probably in a mess, and my heart bleeds for him. On our train journey here with our Operational Division, the Whites had smashed everything in their path. If we lose Tsaritsyn, Astrakhan will be cut off. But we'll hold it to the end, and it will be our second Kazan. And despite all the dangers and setbacks, Fedya and I are infinitely happy ...[8]

By the summer of 1919, Crimea and most of Ukraine had fallen to the Whites, and Kolchak's armies were in control in Siberia. Petrograd was in mortal danger from the British-backed forces of Yudenich, and Red soldiers were hungry and exhausted. But the Whites had little popular support, and autumn brought a dramatic improvement in the Bolsheviks' fortunes.

In October, in an epic replay of the October 1917 battle for Petrograd, seven hundred thousand of its citizens under Trotsky's leadership drove Yudenich's army from nearby Tsarskoe Selo. By November, Kolchak had evacuated his Siberian capital east from Omsk to Irkutsk, and Denikin's troops were in full retreat from the Caucasus. The Southern Army, under General Frunze, was clearing the Whites from Turkestan, and by the end of November, the Whites and British had been driven from the outskirts of Astrakhan. Writing in the official Blue Book of the British Army, the Chief of Staff, Sir Henry Wilson, complained of 'the insurmountable difficulties of formulating a Russian policy, since in no Allied country has there been sufficient weight of public opinion to justify armed intervention against the Bolsheviks'.

Having secured these areas of Central Asia, the Soviet government set out to build relations with the Muslim countries on Russia's borders, and its first

---

8   SW, p. 514.

venture in foreign diplomacy was in Afghanistan, gateway to British India, for a century at the centre of the 'Great Game' between the tsarist and British empires for control of their eastern dominions, now the key to the Bolsheviks' complicated relations with British Imperial power in Asia. Igor Reisner had worked with the Commissar of Foreign Affairs, Georgy Chicherin, on the first exchange of letters with Afghanistan's reforming King Amanullah on establishing diplomatic relations, and in the autumn of 1919, at the age of twenty, he left Moscow as First Secretary of the new Soviet mission in Kabul.

As Bolshevik defeats turned into victories, women's heroic role in the fighting was rewarded with a new Party Women's Department, the *Zhenotdel*, responsible for everything that concerned their lives. *Zhenotdel* activists travelled to the new Soviet republics in Central Asia to campaign with local women against polygamy and child marriage, setting up girls' schools and women's literacy classes and creches, and an energetic team of Moscow organisers arrived in Astrakhan to open a new women's club and library.

Larisa worked with Kirillov setting up reading groups in the town and Kazakhstan's new Union of Journalists, organising lectures, concerts and poetry evenings at the Flotilla's social club. After the years of fighting, the exhausted sailors could finally rest and relax, and Kirillov directed them in a series of plays, including his 'Astrakhan version' of Goethe's tragedy 'Egmont', without lights or costumes, about the hero's struggle against foreign oppression.[9]

Larisa wrote articles for the Flotilla's paper *Red Sailor* – 'What Tomorrow Promises Me', 'On the Front Line', and 'Poets of the Red Fleet'. On 7 November, the second anniversary of the Revolution, the paper published her poem 'Requiem', on the death of Markin, and her obituary of her friend and comrade Semyon Roshal, tortured to death by White Ukrainian officers on the Rumanian front:

> I remember Roshal in Petrograd in the bitter cold of winter, in his torn coat, without boots, walking the endless streets from his room in the poor suburbs to the Psychoneurology Institute. As a poor Jew, he couldn't get a residence permit, and could often barely afford to eat. A convinced Bolshevik from the age of eighteen, he organised meetings at the University and at Kronstadt. Then Great October, when Kronstadt became his tribune ...
> The murderers broke Roshal's limbs and tore his flesh, and thought the cold tortured body they threw on the road was Roshal, and that Roshal

---

9   Mikhail Kirillov, 'Shchedroe serdtse' (A Generous Heart), LRRC, p. 129.

was no more. But they were wrong. Roshal will never be killed. Let them count the White Guard strongholds wiped off the earth by Red Roshal, the invincible merciless avenger, and they will fear our corpses. Yes, the dead will rise from their graves, and Roshal will march at the head of our Revolution, mightier than in life ...[10]

In January 1920, the Supreme Allied Council in Paris announced that the economic Blockade of Russia was to be lifted. According to the British diarist Lord Riddell, owner of the *News of the World*: 'The Allies now understand the impossibility of fighting the Bolsheviks in Russia. No nation is prepared to continue supplying the Whites with troops and money. A more promising tactic is seen as the exchange of goods on the basis of reciprocity between the Allied countries and the Russian people'. Or as Lloyd George put it more succinctly to Parliament, 'The moment trade is established with Russia, Communism will vanish'.

The Blockade would remain in place for another fourteen months, but the decision had been forced by another series of Allied defeats. By January, the Red Army had driven the Whites from Tsaritsyn, and from the Don and Kuban regions in the South. Kolchak had been killed, and Yudenich had fled to Paris, leaving the remains of his scattered army to die of starvation and disease. In April, Polish forces had captured Kiev in a surprise attack, but a month later they had been thrown back by Tukhachevsky's Thirteenth Army. Astrakhan was meanwhile celebrating more Bolshevik victories in the Caucasus. Workers had overthrown the White government in Ashkhabad, capital of Turkestan, and expelled British forces from Azerbaijan, replacing the British government in Baku with a Soviet one, which proclaimed the city capital of the new Soviet Republic of Azerbaijan.

On 1 May, the day before Larisa's twenty-fifth birthday, the Flotilla left Astrakahan by train for Baku, for a victory May Day parade through its streets:

> Marching in front are the local regiments who have come over to us from the British, with their smart English uniforms and English weapons ... Then our regiments appear, in their ragged uniforms, blackened by the sun, but marching easily and naturally at the correct marching pace ... They have crossed the whole of the Republic to the Caucasus at this pace, without swaggering or dawdling or any special drill, and the earth thun-

---

10 'Doroga iz Oranienbauma v Kronstadt' (The Road from Oranienbaum to Kronstadt), *Krasnyi Baltiiskii Flot* (Red Baltic Fleet), 1919, no. 5. SW, pp. 428–30.

ders with their iron rhythm ... Every oil worker, every bourgeois from Baku, knows their path won't stop here, and that the human flood rolling through Baku will go further, beyond the borders of Azerbaijan ...

Beyond Azerbaijan's borders, however, lay Persia, historically the buffer between Russia and British India – 'the vital bastion of Empire against the deadly advance of the Muscovite', in the words of Britain's new Foreign Secretary Lord Curzon, former Viceroy in India.

Britain had set the terms of its aggressive policies against Soviet power in Asia in August 1919, with its Anglo-Persian Agreement with Iran, which gave the British Anglo-Persian Oil Company exclusive drilling rights in all Persia's oilfields, including those in areas under Russian influence, and offered the Shah unlimited funds and arms for a new army on the borders with the new Soviet Central Asian republics, from which to launch another British invasion of Russia. Lenin called the treaty 'banditry and a swindle', and appealed to 'Iranian workers, peasants and nationalist forces to intensify their struggle against the robbers and oppressors'. And in May 1920, guided by Raskolnikov, the Soviet government took the high-risk decision to seize the Persian port of Badar-e Anzali, in Gilan Province, Britain's main base on the Caspian, occupied by British naval forces and a squadron of Denikin's ships.

Larisa described sailing south from Baku to Anzali with Raskolnikov and the Flotilla's High Command on the destroyer the *Karl Liebknecht*. But as always, she completely wrote herself out of the operation. Boarding the British ships, the commanders ordered the officers at gunpoint to surrender, then went ashore to inform the Persian authorities that the Bolsheviks were in power. A day later, Red soldiers and sailors entered the town, shelling British military positions and Denikin's vessels. Within a few hours, the entire White Fleet had been captured, and the hopelessly outnumbered British occupation forces, led by Major-General Sir Charles Crutchley and Brigadier-General Bateman-Champain (who had brought his wife and three children and their English nanny with him to Anzali), were forced to enter into humiliating negotiations with Raskolnikov.

'For the first time in the East, regular British troops were defeated in open battle', Larisa wrote. 'In Anzali, the power of Imperial Britain clashed with the power of the workers' state, and lost'.

> This wasn't just anywhere, it was Persia, weakened by its forced alliance with Britain, duped into signing all sorts of extortionate treaties. And now the British were leaving Persia in shame ...
> For the local population, their departure was the source of much amusement. People dropped their normal business for the day, and sat on

> the piers, watching their old masters meekly obey our *Flotkom's* orders to board a cutter for our warship the *Karl Liebknecht*, where they hoped to wangle an honourable capitulation ... At the rear of the departing British convoy were various luxuries, including a special bath and a grand piano, the private property of the Brigadier, none of which escaped their mocking eyes ... Oh, Eastern people see things, and having seen the weakness of the occupying forces, they'll never forget it!

Soviet forces in Anzali inherited fifteen warships and six sea-planes from the British, and quantities of ammunition. Denikin's troops left in ships, and the British in cars, and the Sikhs, Turks and Gurkhas who had fought with the British escaped on horseback or on foot.

> Not one foreign ministry in Europe would have bothered to send us a note if these 'coloureds' had disappeared off the face of the earth, and they shook with fear when they fell into the hands of the 'terrible Bolsheviks'. But not only were they given their freedom, they were treated with a brotherly respect they had never known from their masters in India, and they left us as our friends, returning to their ruby lands with stories of a new transformed world ...

The Chair of Tehran's Council of Ministers, the Anglophile Vossugh ed-Dowleh, fled to Baghdad, and his government was replaced with one that demanded the withdrawal of both Soviet and British forces from Persia, and approached Moscow to exchange ambassadors. Lenin cabled Raskolnikov thanking him for the brilliant success of the operation, and Raskolnikov cabled back: 'Having captured the Caspian Sea for the Soviet Republic, the Red Navy sends greetings from its Red shores to the beloved leaders of the international proletariat, Lenin and Trotsky. The people of Persia of all classes welcome Soviet Russia as the liberator of the East from the world bourgeoisie'.[11]

Other reports from Anzali suggest somewhat less enthusiasm for the Bolsheviks, who were seen by many as just another army of occupation. But Britain's defeat did enormous damage to its prestige in the East, and Bateman-Champain was sacked for his incompetence.

'The Caspian is now a free Soviet sea, surrounded by friendly republics', Larisa wrote. 'Miracles were needed to wake the poor of Persia from their age-long

---

11   Both telegrams are in the Archive of the October Revolution, quoted in A. Naumova's introduction to *sw*, p. 25.

sleep, and the first of these was the defeat of the British in Anzali. The second was the arrival in the town of Persia's national hero Kuchek-Khan, and his meeting with us on our ship'.

For three years Kuchek-Khan had been hiding in the forests and mountains of the Gilan and Qazvin provinces, building his Jangali army to drive out the British, and she joined the crowds who gathered on the shores of the Caspian to hear him speak, surrounded by his Jangali warriors:

> The English had offered a bag of gold for his head, and now here was his precious head, black against the sky. And old men fell before him to kiss his incorruptible hands, and fanatics left their prayer-mats and merchants their stalls, and the bootblack boy stood on his box to get a better view, and thousands of the poor and dispossessed poured from all corners to hear his message, which spread from neighbour to neighbour, from one leafy orchard and watering-hole to another, across the barren hills to the borders with Mesopotamia and India ... Without radio or telegraph, the people of Persia knew of Britain's fruitless bloody imperialist war in Egypt, and of the packed secret meetings on the Afghan border the British were powerless to stop, and they were beginning to throw off their slaves' chains and think for themselves ...

Kuchek approached the Bolsheviks in Anzali for talks with Moscow, and in June he was appointed President of the new Autonomous Soviet Socialist Republic of Iran, the first such republic outside Soviet territory, based in the Gilan capital, Rasht.

With the liberation of Anzali, the Flotilla had completed its final mission, and one by one its warships were demobilised and converted to oil tankers, carrying the oil of the Caspian back to Russia's wrecked factories:

> For six years, the old fighters had suffered heart-attacks from the shells shaking their mighty engines. But by the time they left Baku they had achieved the apparently impossible, and had pushed open the locked doors of the East with their armoured fists. Now they were sailing back not as fearsome dreadnoughts, but as powerful working vessels, slow caravans pushing into the hungry factory heart of Russia.

She and Raskolnikov stayed another two weeks in the town, exploring its narrow streets, taking car trips to the surrounding countryside, with its camel caravans and rice fields and water buffalo, its rose gardens and groves of pomegranates and dense mysterious smells:

> How close this magical country and its people feel to us. A line of men walk past a cluster of straw-thatched mud huts built on airy wooden stilts. Their golden faces are framed by their long black hair, cut in a square line above their eyes, and their light barefoot walk is nothing like ours. But as they turn back to watch us they seem so familiar. They are fishermen and peasants, slender from poverty and endless toil, supple as the stalks of their beloved rice …
>
> The sun blesses the mountains and the emerald chessboard of the rice fields, where little girls wade timidly through the water on their thin legs, not daring to lift their veiled faces or muddy hands from their work, breathing in the sweet air, shot with the barely noticeable shivers of malaria …

For two years she had pushed herself to the limit, enduring danger, hunger and exhaustion, and in Anzali her prodigious energy finally gave out. The stagnant water and tropical temperatures were the ideal environment for the malarial mosquito, and by the time she left Persia, she had already suffered the debilitating fevers and headaches and drenching sweats of her first attacks.

CHAPTER 11

Rabfaks and Commissars

They returned to Moscow in June 1920 as heroes. Raskolnikov was awarded his second Order of the Red Banner for the Persian campaign, and was promoted to Commander of the Baltic Fleet. He then left immediately for Kronstadt, where his brother was working as a commissar of the General Staff. Larisa was appointed Director of the Fleet's Political Department, and she stayed in Moscow for a month with Kirillov, organising with the Commissariat of Supplies to take a train wagon of food to Petrograd's writers.

The Moscow headquarters of the grandly named Administration of Fleet Personnel, on Malaya Znamenskaya Street, where she lived and set up her office, was in the palace formerly owned by the Tsar's close friend Prince Dolgorukov, who had followed the royal family into exile (and when arrested was found to be loaded with weapons and millions of roubles in cash). Nearby were the Hermitage Gardens, where she and Lev Nikulin and their friends had sat in the café after the Revolution discussing poetry. Nikulin had recently returned to Moscow from two years at the front, and was working as political commissar of one of its military units, and it was at the gates of the Gardens that he saw her again that summer – 'sitting in an open motorcar, with a sailor at the wheel, looking youthful and sunburnt in a cotton summer dress'.

He drove back to her office with her, 'a large vaulted room on the ground floor, resembling a battle headquarters, full of guns, flags and war photographs, packed with the usual crowds of sailors, commissars and journalists'. They escaped to the garden to talk, and remembered their friends who had lost their lives in the Civil War. Roshal and Victor Trivus had died fighting with the Red Army. Georgy Maslov had been killed fighting with the Whites in Poland. Rozhdestvensky and Victor Shklovsky had both fought with the Red Army in Ukraine, Rozhdestvensky as commander of an engineers' unit, and Shklovsky had been wounded in battle. Her student admirer Vladimir Zlobin had emigrated to Paris.

Nikulin told her about fighting the armies of Kolchak and Denikin in the Urals and his native Ukraine, and his frontline journalism, as editor of the soldiers' paper *Red Fighter*. She spoke of the battles for Tsaritsyn and Svyazhsk, and her mission in Kazan, that had almost cost her her life – 'I cursed you then for not getting me that cyanide, that *was* an emergency!' 'I was enthralled by her stories', Nikulin wrote. 'Everything was charged with her romanticism, her unusual metaphors, her unexpected word associations, and the aesthetic habits of her youth'.

He visited her every evening after work, and they discussed poetry – the Futurists and Acmeists, the neo-classicists and neo-romantics, the 'Imaginists' and 'Nothingists', and their beloved Blok. 'We've been so cut off!' she said.

One night he had to light matches for her during a power cut, while she typed a letter to the head of the *Cheka*, Felix Dzerzhinsky, interceding for a jailed Kronstadt sailor, and her letter was successful, and the sailor was released.

Nikulin was so captivated by the atmosphere at Malaya Znamenskaya Street that he resigned from his Moscow unit, and applied to leave with her for Petrograd. Kirillov signed his travel documents, and in July he joined them on the train from Moscow, with her wagonload of food and a battalion of sailors.

They were eating stale pancakes and drinking carrot tea in their packed compartment with the sailors, he wrote, 'when one of them, unfamiliar with Larisa's character, told a rather indecent story about a young lady, and the "young lady" calmly poured her glass of hot tea over the joker's head, much to the satisfaction of all present, especially Comrade Gromov, a brave and gallant commissar at the Kronstadt garrison'.[1]

Kirillov had also contracted malaria in Persia, and they were both delirious with fever when they reached Petrograd, and had to be rushed straight to hospital. A week later, she was well enough to join Raskolnikov in the cold splendour of the Admiralty Building, symbol of the tsars' naval power, now the headquarters of the Red Navy.

For much of the next five months Raskolnikov would be working at Kronstadt, and she would be there on her own, living in Petrograd virtually as a single person. Nikulin described their two rooms, at the end of a long dark corridor hung with paintings of sea battles and stern tsarist admirals. Their small bedroom glowed with the colours and memories of the front. On the walls were exotic fabrics, ships' signal flags, an old naval cadet's broadsword and a revolver. The floor was covered with a white felt Caspian nomads' tent, and low oriental tables gleamed with crystal scent bottles, majolica plates, bronze jugs and boxes and Kalmyk Buddhas. She filled the space with her writing, working on a wide sofa in a disorder of rough drafts, books, dictionaries and maps, turning her 'Letters from the Front' into a book.

The Fleet had its office in the large beautiful room next door, with its three tall windows overlooking the River Neva and the Winter Palace, and it was there that the artist Sergei Chekhonin (one of Andreev's artists on *Wild Rose*) painted the watercolour portrait of her that hangs now in Moscow's Tretyakov Gallery. The Civil War had turned her into a stern and disciplined fighter. Now she was

---

1 Nikulin, *People and Travels*, 1962, pp. 97–101.

a poet in a flowing shirt, gazing out at the austere grandeur of St Petersburg's distant domes and spires.

Most of Petrograd's leading writers had rallied to the Bolsheviks by then. Gorky's works had been the first to be published after October by the new State Publishing House, and in the spring of 1918, at the start of the Civil War, he had buried his differences with the government, and joined the Executive of the Petrograd Soviet. Lunacharsky made him head of the Commissariat's Commission for the Preservation of Artistic and Historic Monuments, and he worked with the Soviet and the Commissariat helping writers who had left Russia after October to return, sorting out their rations and accommodation, and finding them work.

One of the first whose return he organised was Gumilyov, who had left Paris for Petrograd that spring not to fight the Bolsheviks, but to work with them. 'I hunted lions in Africa, and fought the Germans for three years, I doubt the Bolsheviks are more dangerous', he told his friend Victor Serge.

He had finally divorced Akhmatova to marry Anna Engelhardt (known as 'Anna II'), and they were living with their baby daughter at the House of the Arts, the writers' hostel and meeting place set up by Gorky on the Nevsky Prospect, in the former home of the Eliseev brothers, owners of St Petersburg's fashionable Eliseev bakery and grocery store. Bakeries had been the first businesses to be nationalised after the Revolution, and the Eliseevs had immediately emigrated with their families, and their home now provided accommodation for over two hundred writers, including Gumilyov, Mandelstam and Andrei Bely, Nikolai Klyuev, Marietta Shaginyan and Victor Shklovsky.

The building had been known as one of the most luxuriously appointed private homes in St Petersburg. Shklovsky recalled its sixty-seven rooms, previously occupied by the two brothers and their families, exquisitely decorated in the popular *Art Nouveau* style, its modern bathrooms and its Swedish gym, with all the latest equipment. Shklovsky's first room there had been in the servants' quarters in the basement, known by the Eliseevs as the 'monkey-house'.[2]

The House of the Arts had a library and a cheap canteen, and Gumilyov paid for his family's accommodation by running its programme of art shows, poetry readings and writers' workshops, held in the austere marbled hall where the brothers had conducted their banking business. Shklovsky gave lectures on 'The Theory of Plot', and Gumilyov's poetry classes were invariably packed with aspiring young poets, he wrote. 'He organised the versifiers. He took bad

---

2 Shklovsky, *Sentimental Journey*, 1970, p. 238.

poets and made them less bad, and banned them from writing about flowers in spring, or any of the crap in mass-produced verse'.

Gorky had made Gumilyov chief editor of the French department of his *Gosizdat* World Literature series, which published cheap paperback editions of the foreign classics. Most writers supplemented their meagre rations by translating for Gorky and teaching in the factories. Larisa's salary from the Fleet allowed her the luxury of writing, but *The Front* would not appear in print until four years later. With paper and ink in short supply, publishers' main priority was to produce literacy material and propaganda posters, and Lenin was not optimistic about the immediate prospects for literature in Russia, given its poverty and mass illiteracy.

But as the Civil War drew to an end, people were hungry for entertainment. Towns and villages across the country staged huge theatrical pageants and parades – Lenin called them 'festivals of the oppressed' – flying the new Soviet red hammer and sickle flag, emblem of the poorest in society, the workers and peasants. Buildings were covered in posters celebrating the heroes and heroines of the Revolution, and a new *samizdat* factory journalism of wall newspapers and leaflets was publishing workers' songs, stories, poems and plays.

In Moscow, Mayakovsky was running poetry readings, lectures, plays and concerts at the new House of the Press, opened by Lunacharsky in the palace of the exiled Gagarin family, former patrons of the arts. Larisa's father was a director at Moscow's boldly experimental new Meyerhold Theatre, which was giving free tickets to workers for its shows – political satires and cabaret acts, full of pantomime and circus acrobatics. The director of Moscow's new Vakhtangov Theatre, Chekhov's friend and mentor Evgeny Vakhtangov, was developing a more naturalistic intuitive acting style in his productions, precursor of what came to be known as the 'Method'.

Most of Petrograd's theatres, circuses and cinemas were still closed, and unemployed actors and circus performers joined street theatre groups, like those in the French revolution, performing Civil War-style *agitki* about brave Bolsheviks and imperialist gangsters. The 'Blue Blouse' drama collective staged its 'living newspapers' in the factories and garrisons, acting out the day's news and heroic episodes from the Civil War, and Nikulin's *agitprop* verse drama 'On the Volga', about Larisa's escape from Kazan, was performed by a sailors' theatre collective at Kronstadt.

As head of the Fleet's Political Department, she appointed him chief editor of the new Kronstadt paper *Red Baltic Fleet*. She set up and supervised a new political education programme there, and she taught literature and ran writers' workshops in Petrograd's new workers' colleges, the *rabfaks*.

The Revolution had rapidly to create a new generation of intellectuals, and the *rabfaks* had been established in 1919, in consultation with Lenin's wife Nadezhda Krupskaya, who had taught factory workers before the Revolution, to prepare them to enter the universities. There were free courses in the arts and sciences, history, economics and Marxist philosophy, and the only qualifications required were to be proletarian and literate. Most of her students were from the army or the factories, in their teens or early twenties, almost half of them women, and she later dedicated *The Front* to them – 'our future professors, statesmen and writers, working by day and studying by night, hungry for knowledge, selling their last pair of shoes to buy the works of Lenin and Marx'.

She was a popular teacher, loved and revered as the heroine of the Volga. But her 'Letters' were not universally popular. Many said they found some of the writing hard to follow, with too many words, and that she should write more like she spoke, and the rough drafts of *The Front* in her archives show the pains she took to make the book version more direct and accessible.

She invited the aspiring young writers in her classes to the Admiralty, to meet Petrograd's established writers who were seeking a *modus vivendi* with the new regime, and they would all sit round the long oval conference table discussing their respective roles in the Revolution, finding common ground. An enthusiastic speaker at these meetings, who shared with them his 'long painful political journey', was Gumilyov's close friend the poet Sergei Gorodetsky, a former Acmeist and patriot, now an ardent Bolshevik, who had written for *Izvestiya* during the Civil War, and had worked briefly with Larisa in Baku. But her most honoured guest was Blok.

In Blok's diaries that summer, he wrote of his long horse rides with her around Petrograd's islands, discussing politics and poetry, and they became a familiar sight together on their horses. His aunt and first biographer, Maria Beketova, deplored the liberties she took as a young writer, lecturing the revered Blok to 'rise above his environment', and believed she was 'on a mission to recruit him to the Party'.[3]

This is hardly likely, given his recent painful and highly public clashes with the Party. The previous spring, after a series of attacks in the press on his masterpieces 'The Twelve' and 'The Scythians' for their religious imagery, he had been arrested for his alleged counterrevolutionary activities. The charges had almost immediately been declared a mistake and dropped, but the ordeal had

---

3   Maria Beketova, *Aleksandr Blok. Biograficheskii ocherk* (Alexander Blok. A Biographical Sketch), Moscow, 1990, p. 190.

shaken his faith in the Revolution, and he was telling friends he felt increasingly drained and unable to write.

Larisa was said to have been reprimanded by her local party for her bravado show of support for him, parading round the hungry impoverished city on her horse. There was talk too of her large collection of expensive outfits. She was famous for her style and elegance and her love of dressing up, and she was allowed to take her pick from the Petrograd Soviet's vast storerooms of expropriated clothes – including allegedly two fur coats and several hats from the Imperial wardrobe.

Commissars and commanders who had survived the horrors of the Civil War returned from the front as 'beloved comrades', and lived significantly better than those under them who had suffered equally, and there was growing anger at this privileged new Party élite. Sailors at Kronstadt were hearing of their commissars' slap-up three-course banquets on the staff ship the *Falcon*, with roast goose and pounds of butter and rice. And although neither Raskolnikov nor his brother were ever accused personally of abusing their position – 'we ate the same cabbage soup as the men, to emphasise the democratic nature of our authority', Alexander said – Raskolnikov was widely blamed for turning a blind eye to the looming crisis.

Leading Party members lived rent-free, and Nadezhda Mandelstam commented bitterly on Larisa's freeloading life at the Admiralty, 'with her large staff of servants and magnificently prepared meals', and called her 'not much of a fighter'. (Mandelstam herself had spent much of the Civil War in the Ukrainian city of Kharkov, where she told a friend, 'the money we starved on in Moscow was enough to buy us luxury').[4]

Larisa's writing too had its vocal critics. Many of the new proletarian writers saw her 'Letters' as too poetic and refined to be accessible to the masses, too close to the language of poets like Gumilyov and Akhmatova who dreamed of returning to the old Russia. According to the *Komsomol* journalist Lev Sosnovsky, the summer of 1920 was her 'second test:'

> We were all workaday and prosaic. There was so much poetry in Larisa, so much emotion and romanticism. Wasn't there too much colour and elegance in her writing? To us who were stumbling around in real life, it sometimes seemed as if the object of her creativity was just this continual juggling of contrasts and images.[5]

---

4 Clarence Brown, *Mandelstam*, 1978, p. 75.
5 Lev Sosnovsky, 'In Memory of Larisa Reisner,' *People of our Time*, 1927, p. 90.

Neither Akhmatova nor Gumilyov accepted her invitations to the Admiralty. Akhmatova refused to have anything to do with the regime, and turned down all Gorky's offers of work. Gumilyov worked with the Bolsheviks, but never disguised his contempt for them. Larisa told Nikulin of a strange encounter she had with him in the Summer Gardens, where she was resting on a bench soon after she left hospital, and he walked straight past her murmuring verses, his eyes fixed on the far distance. Blok found his poetry after the Revolution cold and soulless, and in his diaries he described an angry altercation between them at a party he went to with her at the House of the Arts, where Gumilyov accused him of 'serving the cause of the Antichrist'.

Her worship of Akhmatova survived the Revolution, proud and defiant, suffering for her art. She had been housed in a flat in the beautiful baroque Fontanka Palace, nationalised to provide accommodation for Petrograd's writers, scholars and artists, and when she visited her there soon after she arrived from Moscow, allocating writers their food rations, she found her living in poverty, dressed in rags, boiling soup in a borrowed saucepan. She had an extra sack of rice sent round and a basket of clothes, and found her a job as a librarian at Petrograd's Agronomy Institute, and Akhmatova told her friend Lydia Chukovskaya she had been in the demeaning position of accepting charity from Gumilyov's former lover. But somehow in these difficult circumstances, they managed to talk about him for the first time. Larisa was a 'wounded animal', Akhmatova said, still traumatised by the way he had treated her. She told her she had loved him, and he had only wanted her because she was a virgin, and Akhmatova described her to Chukovskaya as 'very large, with broad shoulders and hips, like a waitress in a German tavern. "I'd give anything to be Anna Akhmatova", she said. Three windows overlooking the Bronze Horseman, three windows overlooking the Neva. Stupid words!'[6]

Nikulin thought she overestimated her power to turn political enemies into friends. She had learnt her negotiating skills with the tsarist commanders at the front. Away from the front, he saw her as a soft touch for all sorts of shady characters and their stories – including 'an "extremely experienced journalist of the pre-revolutionary school" she stubbornly recommended to us at the *Red Baltic Fleet*, who had proposed to Rasputin's daughter, "to get inside information"'.

With the open enemies of the Revolution, she was not so accommodating. A popular meeting place for Petrograd's future emigres and 'masters of thought' was the Russian Institute of Art History on St Isaac's Square, in the palace of the

---

6 Lydia Chukovskaya, *The Akhmatova Journals*, 1968, p. 62.

art historian and philanthropist, the former Count Zubov. Since the Institute was nationalised a week after the Revolution, Zubov and his friends had been involved in endless disputes with the Commissariat of Education in Moscow over its funding, and the management of Petrograd's nationalised art galleries and palaces, and Lunacharsky had appointed Larisa to negotiate with them on his behalf. But the talks had quickly broken down, and she took to dropping in unannounced on their meetings.

That summer, Moscow was filling with delegates to the Second World Congress of the Comintern. The opening day, 20 July, was a national holiday, and Nikulin drove with her in her military car to Petrograd's Tauride Palace, for the latest cables from the Kremlin, through streets packed with cheering crowds of demonstrators with red banners and brass bands.

A world away from the celebrations, the Institute continued with its programme of meetings on aesthetics and religion. Asking the driver to stop at St Isaac's Square, she marched Nikulin inside, where the religious philosopher and medievalist Professor Karsavin was delivering a learned disquisition to his rapt audience on the evils of socialism, and the primacy of self-fulfilment and self-respect. When he spoke of the 'sublime nature of the inner experience', she let out a loud guffaw and stood up to speak, but was drowned out by a chorus of jeers and catcalls, and they left and drove on to the Tauride.[7]

At its founding congress the previous spring, two months after the defeat of the German revolution, with the Intervention tearing great chunks out of the workers' state, the Comintern had been little more than a Bolshevik pipedream. But although still cut off from trade and diplomatic relations with the rest of the world, against unimaginable odds, the Bolsheviks had survived, and there were high hopes that the German left could overcome its setbacks and save them.

Delegates were forced by the Allied Blockade to travel to Russia with false passports, via Finland and the Estonian port of Reval, and three from France had drowned when their boat tried to sail past a squadron of British warships. But over two hundred communists and socialists from forty countries gathered in the throne-room of the Kremlin's Imperial Palace for the opening session – including the late Rosa Luxemburg's lawyer, Paul Levi, representing the German Communist Party, thirty communists from India, China, Japan and Korea,

---

7 Lev Nikulin, *People and Travels*, 1962, p. 105.
    Lev Karsavin (1882–1952), brother of the ballerina Tamara Karsavina. His star student and disciple at Petrograd University, Alisa Rosenbaum, emigrated six years later to the United States, where she reinvented herself as Ayn Rand, heroine of the American right, author of the books *The Virtue of Selfishness*, *The Fountainhead*, and *Atlas Shrugged*.

the communist Scottish trade union leader Willie Gallacher, hero of 'Red Clydeside', and four members of the American Communist Party, led by the journalist John Reed.

Heading the Comintern's sixty-two strong Russian delegation were its co-founders Lenin and Trotsky, and its Chair and Secretary, Grigory Zinoviev and Radek, and the topics under discussion were Poland, colonialism, and the prospects for revolution in Europe. Trotsky and Lenin were in high spirits, and gave the keynote speeches, on the international situation since Versailles, and delegates were given copies of Lenin's pamphlet *Leftwing Communism, An Infant Disorder*, and Trotsky's book *Communism and Terror*, written on his military train during the Civil War. Both were translated into four languages, but were aimed primarily at the Germans. Lenin spoke first, to deplore communists' failure in Germany to connect with the revolutionary mood in the factories, blaming this on ultra-leftists' reluctance to work with the trade unions. Trotsky then spoke to defend the Soviet government against criticisms of its 'revolutionary excesses' by moderate socialists in Germany and elsewhere, who had opposed the Comintern's founding statement on armed force. Unless the embattled workers' republic took up arms against its enemies, it would be smashed, he said. He was followed by Radek, who called on workers throughout the world to 'rise up and bury Versailles with their bayonets'.

Six weeks later, thirteen delegates, headed by Radek, Zinoviev and John Reed, took this message to Baku, for the Comintern's hastily convened First Congress of Peoples of the East, at which over two thousand communists from China, Japan, Korea, Persia, Turkey and the Soviet republics of Azerbaijan and Kazakhstan – fifty-five of them women – affirmed 'the mutual destiny of the colonial peoples of the world with Soviet Russia', and their 'undying opposition to capitalism and British imperialism'.

Britain's Foreign Secretary Lord Curzon called in Parliament for 'immediate action against the hurricane of Bolshevik propaganda, intrigue and conspiracy against Britain's interests in Asia', and ordered increased supplies of funds and arms to British-backed forces in Persia fighting to destabilise Tehran's pro-Soviet government. In Larisa's *Izvestiya* article 'About Persia and the English', she mocked the increasingly unpopular Curzon – derided by colleagues as 'a pompous gasbag', and 'a Rolls Royce kept to deliver the occasional parcel to the station' – reminding him of Britain's recent humiliation in Anzali: 'What do Curzon's foolish words mean to Persia's veiled women, its poor and dispossessed? Let him threaten Tehran and Moscow with his fine speeches, ringing with empty diplomatic phrases. They are powerless against the rage of the East, plundered and raped by the European imperialist powers'.

She followed this with her *Izvestiya* pamphlet *What They Lived For*, a series of sketches based on material found on the *Summer Tide*, anti-Semitic letters and telegrams and Black Hundreds leaflets left on the ship by the Tsar and his family on their tour of the Volga during the 1913 Romanov celebrations – 'parasites and living corpses, trying to escape the vast spiritual emptiness of their lives, until it finally caught up with them'.[8]

Nikulin reported that she was also writing a play (of unknown fate), set in a town the Bolsheviks are forced to abandon, whose heroine, the wife of a communist fighting with the Red Army, defies her family to join him at the front. 'I watched her dictate it to the typist, a lady of the old school, who typed obediently, with an expression of pained dismay at its conclusion', he wrote.

One burning hot Saturday in August, Nikulin visited the Palace Embankment, cooled by a fresh breeze from the Neva, where she had joined crowds of workers who had given up their weekend to chop up a barge for firewood to heat Petrograd's children's homes that winter. He spotted her with her work brigade, led by a team of factory women in their caps and overalls, and she ran up the steps to meet him, 'in a torn cotton dress, with a shawl over her hair, laughing and wiping her wet face with her hand'. An hour later she was back at the Admiralty, writing her article 'Voluntary Labour Day' for *Red Paper*.[9]

On her horse rides with Blok around the city, she was discovering the new Petrograd of the Revolution. Przhiborovskaya quotes from a long (unsourced) letter she wrote that summer to Trotsky in Moscow: 'Dear Friend, I'm writing to you from the depths of an ocean that has drowned Petersburg in oblivion ... You can't imagine the silence. The suburbs are destroyed, the streets have turned to rubble. After five years, the ruins of the North are like the ruins of Asia ...'[10]

She developed this theme in her essay 'In Petersburg', published in September in *Red Paper*, later a quiet reflective coda to *The Front*:

> Terrible stories about Petrograd reached distant parts of the Republic during the years of the revolutionary war – that it was a dying city, and was staying alive only to fight the Whites, who were advancing from all directions ...
>
> Yet a thousand signs bear witness to its regeneration. The noble symmetry of its squares and avenues have a new spartan simplicity, resting from the hurrying crowds under their soft carpets of weeds ... This isn't the

---

8   'O Persii i angliiskikh' (About Persia and the English), and *Chem oni zhili* (What They Lived For), *SW*, pp. 436–40 & 463–5.
9   Nikulin, 'Years of Our Life', *LRRC*, p. 64. 'Subbotnik' (Voluntary Labour Day), *SW*, pp. 443–6.
10 Przhiborovskaya 2008, p. 320.

sleep of death, it's the dizzying exhaustion of convalescence, the silence of the Field of Mars, where people come to honour those killed in battle. Petersburg has not died, it has saved its history and its monuments to the Revolution, and every Red soldier on all of our ten fronts played their part in defending it ...

Paralysed Siberia, the Volga, cut off at the joints, Ukraine, falling away in rotting chunks – nowhere inspired such desperate hope and anger as Proletarian Petersburg. This was why those fighting on the Volga, on the shores of the Caspian, in the malaria swamps of Astrakhan, cried out to it in the despair and emptiness, praying for it in the face of death, as for the most precious thing in the world – the birthplace of the Revolution, empty and wild, slowly recovering its strength after the death agony of the old epoch and the birth of the new one, blessed by eternity.

Editing *Rudin* had given her a love of the technical side of publishing, the rough proofs and smell of hot metal, and she would visit the printshops to make last-minute changes to her articles, working with her usual conscientiousness and attention to detail, and with an intensity that brought on another series of malaria attacks. She would ignore the warning signs, Nikulin wrote, and the chills and headaches would strike suddenly, followed by days when she could barely lift her head, shivering, vomiting and blue with cold, then drenched in sweat, until the fever broke, and she would rally until the next attack.

She took a break from work in September, when Count Zubov threw a grand fancy dress ball for his friends at the Institute of Art History. The Institute hired costumes from the Mariinsky Theatre, home of the Imperial Opera and Ballet, and Nikulin described her getting a ticket to this strange event, dressed in an eighteenth-century ballgown and white periwig. She watched amused and enraged as Zubov toured the ballroom chatting to his parade of antiquated St Petersburg snobs, and afterwards she fired off a long piece of doggerel about him for Nikulin:

> The Count bares his teeth,
> The mother weeps for her son,
> And the old world rises from the dead ...[11]

A week later, she and Gorodetsky attended the inaugural meeting at the House of the Arts of the All-Russian Union of Poets, chaired by Blok. He opened by

---

11   Quoted in Nikulin, *People and Travels*, 1962, pp. 109–10.

reading from his long unfinished poem 'Retribution', which he had started writing in 1905, setting the epic events of the Bolshevik Revolution against the story of three generations of one family. He then spoke of the 'difficulties of this wild unnatural word combination of our new "Union of Poets"':

> Fortunately though we have with us two of Petersburg's most indigenous citizens, Larisa Reisner and Sergei Gorodetsky. We haven't seen them for a long time, but we know they are listening to life's heartbeat – difficult but elemental, great and alive. For they are connected to life, and life in Russia means the Revolution.[12]

By the autumn of 1920, the Red Army had regained virtually all Russia's tsarist borders, and thousands of the Revolution's enemies were escaping to join anti-Soviet emigre groups in Berlin, Paris, New York and London. But victory against the massed armies of the world had come at a terrible cost, and the government now had to deal with the misery and chaos left by six-and-a-half uninterrupted years of war, counterrevolution and foreign invasion.

An estimated fourteen million had died in battle or from starvation or disease, and the survivors were at the end of their strength. Transport, industry and farming barely functioned, railway-lines were smashed, mines were flooded, factories were deserted, shops were empty and boarded up, families were scattered, and thousands trekked across the country in search of lost loved ones. Millions of women were widowed, and children were orphaned or abandoned to the streets when their mothers became unable to feed them. And as men returned from the front, women were generally the first to lose their jobs.

In the villages, wealthy peasants and former landowners subjected to the requisitioning of War Communism hoarded and speculated, and refused to exchange their grain for worthless paper money, and the Red Army put down one rebellion after another. In the factories, hungry workers suffering the further hardships of labour conscription seethed with anger at the privileges and capitalist management methods of the 'specialists' – the engineers and managers trained under the old regime, who were being brought back to run industry in a desperate bid to increase production.

Little of this was seen by the foreign socialists and journalists and the merely curious who visited Russia as the Civil War drew to an end, to see the great socialist experiment. They were welcomed with great ceremony, and were entertained by Gorky and his wife, the actress Maria Andreeva. And in late

---

12   Alexander Blok, *Collected Works*, vol. 6, Moscow, 1962, p. 437.

September Larisa met the writer H.G. Wells at a party in their cold flat, heated with a small stove burning broken boxes.

Wells had first visited Russia in January 1914. His second much publicised trip was financed by the *Daily Express*, which had commissioned him to write five articles from Petrograd and Moscow, where he was to interview Lenin, and he was accompanied this time by his nineteen-year-old son George, 'Gip', who at his insistence was learning Russian, and was interpreting for him.

Larisa met them again at a reception Gorky hosted at the House of the Arts, where guests dined on bread and sausage and slivers of chocolate, and the toasts were led by the anti-Bolshevik journalist and future emigre Alexander Amfiteatrov, who raised his glass to Wells with the words, 'You see before you well dressed people in this elegant place, but it's all a sham! If we were to take off our outer clothing you would see our dirty underwear, which is falling to bits and hasn't been washed for months!' To which a furious and embarrassed Gorky replied, 'It seems to me lamentations are out of place. The Revolution is invincible, and will transform the world!'[13]

The following day Wells left for Moscow, and Larisa wrote a long unfinished letter to him there:

> Honoured Mr Wells, we are deeply moved by your visit. You have seen our wrecked cities, our suffering, our creative spirit, and we await your verdict on us with trepidation. We trust your honesty, your ear for the truth. In your writings you have dreamed up mighty utopias, and predicted the death of the old order in the battle waged in the outer darkness between the Elois and Morlocks ... All you have written about has come true. The Morlocks have descended on the young workers' state with their technology and Blockade ... But the sleeping world has woken. The Revolution has destroyed centuries of stagnation in its flame, creating this miracle of miracles we dreamed of as children, and wept for as we approached adulthood ... How sad then that you met the relics of our old intelligentsia in Petrograd, and didn't see the heroism and sacrifices of our people far from the cities, in the towns and villages at the front ...[14]

The letter trails off and was never sent, and the worshipful tone doesn't ring entirely true. Wells was never a Marxist. He was a member of the British Labour Party, characterised by Lenin as 'a capitalist workers' party born of workers'

---

13 Henri Troyat, *Gorky* (trans. Lionel Blair), 1991, p. 149.
14 The letter was published in the magazine *Druzhba narodov* (Friendship of the Peoples), 1967, no. 4, p. 246.

struggles, but existing to contain them within the capitalist system'. He wrote of 'tiresome class war fanatics', and called *Capital* 'a monument to pretentious pedantry', and in his *Daily Express* article 'Dreamer in the Kremlin', about his meeting with Lenin, he portrayed him as 'a small man, with a brownish face, whose feet barely touch the ground, who writes shrill little pamphlets full of misconceptions'.

Four years later, after Labour came to power in Britain under the anti-Soviet Ramsay MacDonald, Trotsky wrote of 'these insufferable drawing-room Fabians of independent means', 'this civilised Gulliver arriving in the land of the communist Lilliputians', with whom Lenin had found time in his gruelling schedule to discuss politics, in English, in which he was fluent, 'and had the honour of being lectured by Wells on how to run Russia'.[15] (On his next visit to Russia in 1934, he interviewed Stalin in the Kremlin, and George Bernard Shaw called Stalin 'an excellent listener', and the garrulous Wells 'the worst listener in the world').

His articles, later published as his bestselling book *Russia in the Shadows*, brought the *Daily Express* eighty thousand new readers, and he was often able to go beyond his banal observations to report more truthfully on what he saw. He wrote of 'the rottenness of imperialism', and its legacy, 'the vast irreparable breakdown in Russia'. He called the Bolsheviks the legitimate rulers of Russia – 'the only government possible at the present time' – and he expressed his deep admiration for the flourishing state of culture and the arts, in the midst of poverty, war and foreign invasion.[16]

Damned by Trotsky and the British left, Wells was demonised by the Tory press as a 'crypto-Bolshevik'. The attack was led by Winston Churchill in the *Sunday Express*, who wrote of 'the Bolshevik cancer eating into the flesh of this wretched country, the monstrous growth swelling on the emaciated body of its victims ... And the philosopher romancer Mr Wells proposes that the cancer is the only thing to pull the body round ...'[17]

The Civil War wasn't over. The economic Blockade was still in place, Allied 'assistance' still poured in to the White armies, and the Red Army had recently suffered a major defeat in Poland, where Pilsudski's legions had driven Tukhachevsky's Thirteenth Army from Warsaw. But British forces had been cleared from central Persia, the Whites had lost control of Russia's eastern borders, and

---

15 Trotsky, 'H.G. Wells', *Portraits*, 1977, pp. 56–64.
16 Wells, *Russia in the Shadows*, 1920, pp. 11, 12, 35–49.
17 Winston Churchill, 'Mr Wells and Bolshevism,' *Sunday Express*, 5 December 1920. Republished in *The Collected Essays of Winston Churchill*, vol. 2, pp. 81–2, Library of Imperial History, London, 1976.

the invading armies were losing the will to fight. Few in Russia that autumn doubted that final victory was in sight, and the start of better times was celebrated across the country with a round of festivals and parties.

In September, the first All-Russian Chess Olympiad opened in Moscow, organised by Raskolnikov's brother Alexander. 'The players had been scattered to the four winds, and we drew up our lists not knowing who was alive or dead, or who could still play', he wrote. 'They were billeted in unheated rooms in one of Moscow's military training hostels, and several went on strike, refusing to play until their rations were increased'.

Mayakovsky organised concerts and grand theatrical productions at Moscow's House of the Press, and writers in Petrograd decided to follow Count Zubov's fancy dress ball with one of their own at the House of the Arts. The director of the Mariinsky Theatre agreed to allow them too to hire costumes, and for weeks literary Petrograd talked of little else.

It was in October that Larisa met her old friend Rozhdestvensky again, who had returned from the front earlier that month, and was working as a junior commander in one of Petrograd's garrisons, supplementing his income by translating French and German poetry for Gorky's World Literature series, and sharing a room at the House of the Arts with Shklovsky and the poet Nikolai Tikhonov.

'Early one foggy morning, as I was crossing the Dvortsoi Bridge on my way to work, I heard the rustle of car tyres, and saw Larisa's familiar smiling face at the window, dashing and glamorous as ever, in her naval jacket and cap', he wrote. As they drove across the Vasilevsky Island to his garrison, she brushed aside his questions about her life at the front, and insisted they discuss poetry instead. And when she dropped him off at work, she made him promise to bring his friends to the Admiralty to drink coffee and read their latest poems.

He took up her invitation the next day, and arrived at the Admiralty with the poets Mandelstam and Mikhail Kuzmin. They were so in awe of its echoing splendour they could barely keep up with the sailor escorting them along the endless corridors to her room, and shy sensitive Kuzmin almost fainted from nerves. She made a dramatic appearance, wearing a heavy Cossack gown embroidered with gold brocade, with her hair wound round her head like a halo – 'resembling one of the Buddhist figurines in her room', Rozhdestvensky wrote. But she soon had them in fits of laughter with her stories about the British in Persia and the Whites in Kazan. Then the talk turned to the fancy dress ball, and the all important question of what to wear for it. Mandelstam made an emotional plea for her to go as Artemis the Hunter. Rozhdestvensky challenged her to settle for nothing less than Leon Bakst's precious 'Columbine' costume, worn by Tamara Karsavina in Diaghilev's original 1910 Ballets Russes production of 'Carnaval', which they knew was not for hire. (Diaghilev liked to cast actors as well as dancers for his ballets, and Pierrot had been played by Meyerhold).

Rozhdestvensky was to go as Tomsky, from Tchaikovsky's opera 'The Queen of Spades'. He described waiting stiffly for her at the House of the Arts on the night of the ball in his high officer's collar, winged epaulettes and white gloves, as crowds of Seville tobacco girls from 'Carmen', Dniepr mermaids from 'Rusalka', and crusaders and soldiers from Mussorgsky's *Khovanshchina* poured in. The hall was filled with flowers from the Tauride Orangery and the Botanical Gardens, and one wall was covered with a huge painting of World Capital, in top hat and hornrimmed spectacles, his huge belly pierced by a red bayonet, surrounded by European bankers gnashing their teeth.

The violins were tuned, buckets of precious pink and yellow ice-cream were delivered, and the Eliseevs' old servant Nikifor dragged in a sledge with a basket of theatrical props. Then Larisa appeared, in the flounced white 'Columbine' dress decorated with painted crimson cherries, her loose hair tied back with a violet ribbon. The orchestra struck up the 'Blue Danube', and they waltzed round the hall. Minutes later, the Mariinsky's manager arrived, and they waltzed straight out, ran downstairs, rushed by cab to the costume department, and returned to the House of the Arts to find the manager still on the phone to the theatre, unable to believe the dress was in its place.[18]

Her next writing assignment later in October was in the Latvian capital Riga, where she was sent by *Izvestiya* to cover the negotiations between officials from the Polish government and the Commissariat of Foreign Affairs for an armistice in the war with Poland.

By then she was ill and exhausted, and in desperate need of a rest. When Nikulin visited her the night before she left, he found her barely conscious from another malaria attack, 'lying on the sofa like a wax statue, with a fever of over 104. We all thought Larisa Mikhailovna was dying, and we watched with amazement as she prepared for the journey next morning, still very pale and weak'.

Riga had been occupied for the past eighteen months by a bitterly divided German-British government, and was a city still at war. In her first article for *Izvestiya*, 'Travel Notes', she described the outskirts ploughed into a welter of mud by German artillery, and inside the city, 'the gutted factories, bare of machines, the silent ruins of the workers' quarters, the jails filled with starving Red prisoners, through whose barred windows a dim light falls on the waiting

---

18   Rozhdestvensky, 'The Youth of our Days', LRRC, pp. 26–31.

faces and the hands of the clocks, which have stopped at the only date in all time – the unshakeable 25th of October'.[19]

The Russians stayed in the same hotel and formed a tightknit group, in daily contact with Lenin in the Kremlin. She was the only Soviet journalist reporting on the talks, and on 12 October she witnessed the signing of the Treaty of Riga, ratified the following March, which re-drew Russia's borders to give parts of Western Ukraine and Belorussia to Poland.

Japanese troops would remain in Siberia and Mongolia until the following summer. But the end of the war with Poland effectively meant the end of the Civil War, and the Armistice was celebrated with a round of parties, at which she met Pilsudski's legionaries, 'reeling from the "Miracle of the Vistula,"' and the British and German diplomats who had travelled to Riga from London and Berlin. It was her first encounter with the capitalist world since the Revolution, and she stored away her impressions to use the following year, when she would meet their counterparts in Asia.

In a letter to Nikulin, she described dancing the Mazurka with the Soviet military attaché Captain Egorov, 'driving the Warsaw countesses and English wives green with envy'. The head of the Soviet delegation, Trotsky's close friend the diplomat Adolf Joffe, had brought his fourteen-year-old daughter Nadezhda with him to Riga, who remembered her as a wonderful storyteller, with a racy sense of humour. 'She called things by their real names, and whenever she came to the most interesting parts, my very proper father would send me out "for cigarettes"'.[20]

A week after the Armistice was signed, she celebrated the third anniversary of the Bolshevik Revolution in her *Izvestiya* article 'The 25th of October in Riga'. 'Every day the car of the Soviet Embassy drives through Riga's streets with its red flag flying, sticking out its tongue at the White town. Today, the whole of Riga is filled with red flags, blowing in the October wind'. She went on to describe visiting a filthy barn filled with a hundred starving Red Army prisoners, guarded by British and German officers, and an underground dungeon where another two hundred lay piled on top of each other, barely alive.

This was the background to her article 'The Bushy Tail is Falling Off', published in the same issue of *Izvestiya*, about Riga's Constituent Assembly, in which the Allies had placed all their hopes. She attended several sessions of this 'real, or nearly real, petit-bourgeois parliament', in its two-storey building near the railway station, and she reported on its deliberations with all the tra-

---

19 'Putevye zametki' (Travel Notes), *Izvestiya*, 12 November, 1920.
20 Nadezhda Joffe, *Back in Time*, 1995, p. 71.

ditional ingredients of Russian satire – grotesque humour, character assassination, animal metaphors, and allusion to fable. Here is her political journalism at its caustic overblown best:

> Ministers with portfolios bulging with incredible bribes deliver them to the podium with the solemnity of priests offering the communion wafer. Passing through the honoured speakers are a mass of military men, in uniforms cobbled together from the armies of Germany, Britain, France and America. And mingling with the spurs, daggers and cummerbunds are Riga ladies, kind, gracious and patriotic ...
> To anyone who has lived through the October Revolution, it all seems so achingly funny. The British Parliament, which our native constitutionalists cannot mention without tears, has centuries of tradition behind it, and a dizzying magnificence ... This handful of bankers, speculators and rich peasants, their waistcoats stretched tightly over their fat ministerial bellies, sincerely believe they are the Law and the Government. This paradise of power, dripping onto the bald heads from the gilded ceilings, is greedily absorbed into every fibre of Riga's new 'parliament' as it plays out its role on history's bloody stage ...
> Riga's Constituent Assembly, a collection of newspaper articles stuck together with spittle, covered with the tin roof of prejudice and the lightning-rod of compromise, is the harbinger of tomorrow's Storm. And throughout the whole of Europe, these semi-corpses have suddenly assumed a sinister new form: in a paroxysm of shame, they have discovered that beneath the folds of their frock coats, their bushy parliamentary tails are falling off. Charlatans and faith-healers have appeared, and in the great centres of culture they are trying to save the tail. Universities and laboratories argue and dream of miracles. The 1914 war didn't help, nor did Versailles. The tail is losing its bushiness. Even the tail of the brilliant Lloyd George is said to be in a bad way since he read the latest Soviet communiqué and realised it was no longer obeying him. Riga doesn't know yet. What will happen when it does ...?[21]

After two weeks in Riga, she returned to Petrograd. But in November she was sent back by *Izvestiya* to cover the next round of the talks, and on the train to Riga, she met the young English communist Andrew Rothstein.

---

21   '25 Oktyabrya v Rige' (25 October in Riga), and 'Kak otvalivaetsya pushistyi khvost' (The Bushy Tail Is Falling Off), *Izvestiya*, 14 November, 1920. (Both articles read in Andrew Rothstein's original manuscripts).

His father, the Russian revolutionary Fyodor Rothstein, had fled to England in 1890 to escape arrest, and had been Lenin's chief representative in London for the next thirty years, where Andrew had been born and raised. In November 1917, at the age of nineteen, he joined the Hands Off Russia! campaign, and a month later he enlisted in the British Army, to mobilise resistance to the war on Russia. In February 1919, as a corporal in the 13th Yorkshire Batallion, he was active in the mutiny of ten thousand soldiers at the Folkestone Transit Camp, who refused to leave for the British-occupied port of Arkhangelsk. The British consul in Arkhangelsk, Douglas Young, was opposed to the Intervention, and his outspoken letters to the Foreign Office, banned from publication at the time by war censorship, are the subject of the first of Rothstein's books on Anglo-Soviet relations, *When Britain Invaded Russia. The Consul Who Rebelled*. Rothstein was in contact with soldiers active in over fifty mutinies at army camps across the country that year, also unreported in the press, recorded in his book *Soldiers' Strikes of 1919*.[22]

In March 1920, a delegation from the Labour Party and the Trades Union Congress returned from a visit to Russia, and circulated their reports on the Intervention to every party and union branch in the country. In May, dockers in London refused to load the *ss Jolly George* with weapons bound for Poland. A month later, delegates to the Labour Party conference voted overwhelmingly for joint action with the unions against British military operations in Russia – 'with the unreserved use of our political and industrial power'.

Labour gained hundreds of new members from the Hands Off Russia! campaign, and lost hundreds more to the new Moscow-backed Communist Party of Great Britain, whose founding conference in August Rothstein attended as a delegate. His father was on the Executive, a journalist of great brilliance for the British socialist press, in regular contact with Lenin, who had played a major role in establishing the Party and recruiting members, and a week after the conference he was deported from Britain back to Russia.

After leaving the army, Andrew had won a London County Council scholarship to study history at Oxford University, where he had organised a student communist group, and his father used his Moscow contacts to arrange summer holiday jobs for him and his friends at the Commissariat of Foreign Affairs. That winter, he was travelling back from Moscow after another trip to see his father, and as the train crawled west through the snow-covered plains towards

---

22   Rothstein, *When Britain Invaded Russia. The Consul Who Rebelled*, 1979. *Soldiers' Strikes of 1919*, 1980. Republished 2014.
     Rothstein's memories of Larisa are from my conversations with him, and from his article 'Schastliv, chto znal ee' (Happy I Knew Her), *LRRC*, pp. 145–52.

the Latvian border, he was told by his Soviet courier that a woman journalist on board wanted to speak to him.

He went to Larisa's compartment, and she bombarded him with questions about England – about the strike movement, the Workers' Councils of Action and the Communist Party, his experiences in the army, and the mood of his fellow students at Oxford. 'I was enchanted by the charm of her language, her beauty, and her passionate commitment to Communism', he wrote. 'Although it's true that everyone in Russia, from factory girls to Comintern bosses, was interested in England, never before had I been questioned by someone so cultured and well-informed. She seemed to me to be from another world, one I hadn't known before'.

At the Latvian border station of Sebezh, Latvia's former Prime Minister and future fascist dictator, Karlis Ulmanis, was waiting to leave for Moscow as his country's first Ambassador to Soviet Russia. But he refused to travel on the train provided for him, demanding to use theirs instead, which held them up for several days until another could be brought from the depths of Russia for them.

Rothstein had had nothing to eat on the journey but some unripe apples he had bought at Moscow's Kamenny Most market, costing three million rubles a pound, and Larisa initiated him and his courier into the secrets of Latvia's private restaurants, where they dined on sumptuous roast chicken and potatoes, and she had them roaring with laughter at her stories about Ulmanis, the Latvian rail authorities, and Riga's diplomatic scene.

In Riga she attended the next round of the negotiations, and she and Rothstein would meet over dinner in the evenings at their hotel. She told him about fighting in Kazan, Astrakhan and Persia, and as 'a fraternal service to the British Communist Party', she agreed to write an article about the Red Fleet for the new monthly *Communist Review*, of which he was editor.

After sending back her reports to *Izvestiya*, she could take a week off work with him and relax. They went to the cinema, and to Latvia's National Opera for a performance of Tchaikovsky's 'Queen of Spades' in Latvian, and she dragged him round Riga's narrow medieval streets on shopping trips for hats – 'grotesque things, in the German style', he wrote. 'Don't come to England in those, you'll discredit the cause!' he told her.

She was waving at him from the docks as his ship left for London, and on his return he learnt that he had been sent down from Oxford – discovering years later from his former tutor at Balliol College that this had been on the personal instructions of the University Chancellor, Lord Curzon, who called him 'a very dangerous Communist, who must not be allowed to stay'.

The following May, Rothstein's translation of Larisa's article 'Heroic Sailors of the Russian Revolution' was published in the first issue of the *Communist Review*, and five years later he wrote of their time together in Riga:

Although Larisa was only three years older than me, it is hard even now to realise the depth of revolutionary experience that separated us. Yet I always felt she was a true comrade, as enthralled by my accounts of the Hands Off Russia! campaign and the soldiers' mutinies I was involved in, as I was by her stories of her raids on White-occupied territory, and her father's work on the first Soviet Constituition ...

And if I didn't fall head over heels in love with her, it wasn't because I wasn't dazzled by her brilliant mind, her beauty, and the music of her voice, but because she seemed to me, a young revolutionary, the true ideal of an 'older sister', who one could have heated arguments with, and criticise her taste in hats, and promise to send her her favourite perfume from London (Houbigant's *Rose France*) – but from whom one could learn constantly from her unswerving decisiveness, courage and devotion to the business of Communism.

She returned to Petrograd in December, rested and ready for work. That winter, with the Civil War finally over, hopes suppressed by the fighting were surfacing at mass meetings across the country about every aspect of life in the new Russia. At *Zhenotdel* meetings, women were discussing workplace discrimination, and such previously unmentionable subjects as abortion and prostitution. And in the factories, workers were debating their role in the new economy, specifically their relationship with the Party and the trade unions.

Lenin saw the unions as 'schools of Communism', which should have autonomy and the right to strike, but whose role was to 'educate workers on the lines laid down by the Party'. Several anti-Leninist Party platforms emerged on the issue. Trotsky saw the unions' work as largely redundant in the workers' state, and called for them to be 'shaken up' and integrated into the state machinery. The former Left Communist Nikolai Bukharin dreamed of their disappearance 'under full communism'. Alexandra Kollontai, director of the *Zhenotdel*, spoke for the only platform firmly based in the factories, the Workers' Opposition, which denounced the capitalist management techniques being reintroduced into industry, and called for production to be controlled by the workers, represented by the unions.

Lenin rounded on all of them. Trotsky's platform was 'a sorry excuse for a programme', based on the 'fantasy' that the workers' state already existed in Russia. Bukharin's was 'half-baked and theoretically spurious'. The Workers' Opposition was 'a syndicalist menace and a disgrace'.

'Larisa attached herself to an anti-Leninist platform in the union debate', according to her secretary Kirillov (presumably he meant Trotsky's), and in December he travelled with her and Raskolnikov to Moscow for the packed conference at the Bolshoi Theatre, where party, soviet and union members had the chance to air their views on the subject. But although they had seats close to the stage in the orchestra pit, with a good view of all the speakers, Kirillov reported her expressing no preference for any of them.[23]

Raskolnikov supported Trotsky's platform, but according to his biographer 'this was no longer so much from conviction, as from sympathy with the man he had seconded in the Civil War'.

By then he was ill and exhausted, and deeply depressed by the deteriorating situation at Kronstadt, where his men's rage at their officers' privileges was at breaking point. The sailors of 1905 and 1917 and the Civil War, in whom the Revolution had such strong roots, were deserting the Party in their thousands, and he had repeatedly begged Trotsky to intervene, and was in despair that so little effort was made to negotiate with them. Hero of the Kronstadt Republic and of countless campaigns on the Volga, loved and admired by his men, he was now blamed for allowing their anger to go unchecked.

At a conference of the Baltic Fleet in January, three thousand sailors passed a vote of no-confidence in their commanding officers, and he immediately cabled Trotsky at the Kremlin asking to be relieved of his post as Fleet Commander. He then moved out of the Admiralty with Larisa, and they left Petrograd for Moscow, where he collapsed with pneumonia.

Many in the Party felt he was being unfairly blamed for the crisis, and he had a loyal ally in his old Civil War comrade Mikhail Kalinin, now President of the Party Executive, the post he would hold until his death in 1946 – promoted, according to Victor Serge, for 'his keen nose for the state of public opinion, and his splendid peasant face'.

Kalinin had learned his management skills as director of the *Red October* train, touring the Urals battlefronts with his wife and chief strategist and administrator Ekaterina Ivanovna, and their teams of fighters, Soviet and foreign journalists, literacy teachers, film-makers and actors. And his peasant origins made him ideally qualified to run the Party's new Sowing Committees, set up at the end of the Civil War to boost agricultural production, and deal with the food crisis in the cities.

The collectivisation of the farms, delayed by the Civil War, had now begun in earnest, with the requisitioning of the war economy replaced by a fixed grain tax, and peasants officially owning the land, but working with the government to fulfil state grain requirements. There was major resistance to collectivisation, and harvests had fallen drastically. Dispossessed landowners and wealthy

---

23   Mikhail Kirillov, 'A Generous Heart', LRRC, pp. 132–6.

peasants, the *kulaks*, were storing grain, killing cattle, and leaving crops rotting in the fields, and local party activists were being drafted into the new committees to supervise the spring sowing, persuade or force the *kulaks* to open their barns, and arrest the leaders of the resistance.

In February, the Kalinins were travelling south on the *Red October* to set up the first committees in the Northern Caucasus, and they arranged for Raskolnikov and Larisa to join them as far as the Black Sea port of Novorossiisk, then to take a month's holiday in the nearby resort of Sochi.

In a letter home from the train, Larisa described nursing him on the long journey south, as he lay semi-conscious on his berth. But as they travelled into the sun, he began to recover. And at Novorossiisk, where he had supervised the scuttling of the fleet after the Revolution, the sailors had organised a hero's welcome for him, with speeches, songs and brass bands.

From there they sailed by naval launch to Sochi, where local party workers drove them though its narrow streets, filled with Red sailors, to the Europa Hotel, which housed the visiting naval élite.

Staying in the next room to theirs, sharing a balcony with them overlooking the sea, were the Black Sea Fleet commander Andrei Klimenko and his wife Olga Nesterovych, chair of the Sochi *Zhenotdel*. Nesterovych had first met them at the Mocow trade union conference that winter. 'Now I saw something new to learn from them', she wrote. 'These people know how to live, I thought. They're living with us, but it's as if they're not there, like perfect neighbours in a communal flat'.[24]

A squadron of British warships was clearly visible on the horizon, to deter people in neighbouring Georgia from rising up against their Menshevik government, and Sochi was blacked out at nights. And as Raskolnikov was still too weak to socialise, Larisa took food up to him from the canteen, and Nesterovych would meet her in the meal queue. She said she had been starved of women's company at the front, and Nesterovych told her about her *Zhenotdel* work in Sochi, and the women's conference she had attended recently in the nearby town of Tuapse, and her work in Moscow with Kollontai.

She invited her to her room, and they discussed *Zhenotdel* politics and poetry. 'A volume of Molière's plays lay open on her desk – I was a barbarian, I'd never heard of him! – and she gave it to me as my "ship of happiness, to help orientate me in the world of literature", as well as some printed material on the trade union question, "so I wouldn't have to rely on my memory"'.

---

24   Olga Nesterovych, 'Korablik schastiya' (The Ship of Happiness), *LRRC*, pp. 152–162.

Raskolnikov was there, but stayed in the background and didn't join their discussions. There was a great deal of sympathy for him in the Navy, Nesterovych wrote. 'It was understood he wouldn't be returning to the Fleet, and would be appointed to a diplomatic post abroad'. The hero of Kronstadt was now a frail invalid, still nominally Larisa's boss, but fearful and unsure of himself with her, and Nesterovych saw him taking out his misery and anger on her. 'She spoke often about her parents and brother, who she loved very much and wanted always to be with her, and there were several angry words from F.F. about this. Generally though he was solemn and aloof with her. Undoubtedly he felt crushed by the power of her personality'.

The two women joined Sochi's first sowing committee, and made several trips to the surrounding villages together. The forests seethed with bandits, robbing people at gunpoint, Nesterovych wrote, and several party workers had been ambushed and killed. 'For extra safety we walked down the roads in groups of five, and the chair of the Sochi party would bring his non-Party wife along, as a "protective tank"'. Larisa strode confidently in front of them, which produced much grumbling at the back. 'I saw it differently. I saw her lightning-fast reactions. While others were still weighing up the risks, she would already have thought them through, and if necessary taken charge'.

Once arrived in a village, they would sit with the peasants to discuss the sowing, and listen to their complaints of drought, failed harvests and broken machinery. 'In these noisy discussions, in which everyone spoke at once, she tried to get them to speak one at a time, and to answer all their questions. For them she was like a city schoolteacher, someone from another world. But it would be wrong to think the peasants hated intellectuals. If they saw a real person there, feeling and suffering for them, they not only respected them, they loved them tenderly'.

23 February was Red Army Day, and a day of meetings and demonstrations. As there were few experienced public speakers in the Sochi party, Nesterovych asked her to address meetings with her, which were held in the town's cinemas and shopping arcades, as the day was wet. 'Some people can write but not speak, some can speak but not write. Larisa Mikhailovna could do both', she wrote. 'From listening to her one could learn the Russian language, rich, powerful and expressive'.

On that day, the crisis at Kronstadt came to a head. In the weeks she and Raskolnikov had been away, acute food shortages in Petrograd had produced a series of angry strikes that spread to Moscow, and had been violently broken up by the army. Food supplies were rushed in to Petrograd, and a certain amount of foraging was authorised. But the strikes continued, and on 23 February, sailors at Kronstadt mutinied for a 'Third Revolution' – demanding increased rations, an end to official propaganda, freedom of speech, political amnesty for arrested sailors, and new elections to the Petrograd Soviet. Next day, a state of siege was declared in the city.

Victor Serge described having to balance his sympathy with the sailors' programme with pragmatism. Kronstadt was vital to the defence of Petrograd if the armies of the West were to invade Russia again, as few doubted they would, and with the working class decimated by war, this mutiny by the Bolsheviks' formerly most loyal supporters threatened them with an isolation and defeat too terrible to contemplate. Raskolnikov suffered the added anguish of being blamed for the catastrophe, and that it was his boss and comrade Trotsky who had ordered the sailors to surrender, or be 'shot like partridges'.[25]

Two weeks later, on the 8th of March, International Women's Day, the momentous Tenth Party Congress opened in the Kremlin. Over the next four days of distraught and often angry discussions, proceedings were regularly interrupted by the departure of party and army delegates to fight the Kronstadt rebels on the ice, and by reports of their progress – over five hundred sailors killed, and hundreds more wounded and left to drown.

Almost lost in the tragedy were discussions of the New Economic Policy, the NEP, designed to rebuild Russia's shattered economy after the Civil War, and replace the economy of War Communism with a strategy 'to increase at all costs the quantity of output'.

To induce the West to lift its Blockade, Lenin proposed a series of major concessions to capitalism, and the restoration of a significant amount of private enterprise. Instead of the all-out collectivisation of agriculture, peasants were to be free to sell grain surplus to state requirements on the open market, and the old capitalist system of workers' efficiency bonuses, fines and layoffs were to be reintroduced into industry, with increased powers for the managers trained under the old regime.

The Workers' Opposition, speaking now for the powerful Metalworkers' Union, and for thousands of workers in the Moscow region, the Caucasus and Ukraine, denounced the NEP in its programme as a betrayal of the Revolution. Allowing capitalists to pocket the profits from the workers' state was a cruel insult to the ideals and sacrifices of those who had brought the Party to power, they said, and they warned of the vast new bureaucratic management structure the policy would create. The Opposition's leaders were accused of trying to 'split the Party', and were threatened with expulsion, and the Congress ended with a resolution permanently banning all Party factions.

---

25   Serge, *Memoirs of a Revolutionary*, 1963, p. 129.

Raskolnikov's holiday had restored him to health, and Larisa returned to Moscow with him a week after the Congress ended, to a mood of huge sadness and confusion. Like Serge, she must have supported the demands of the sailors she loved and knew so well. But she did not do so publicly, and it was only later that she openly expressed her criticisms of the new course. For now she remained a loyal Party member, rallying people to the Bolsheviks and against their enemies.

CHAPTER 12

Afghanistan

Raskolnikov's comrades in the Fleet had correctly assumed he would be moved to a diplomatic post abroad after Kronstadt. He was the first of several troublesome high-ranking Party members to be sent out of Russia over the next ten years as 'red ambassadors', and on his return to Moscow in March, he was appointed to head the new Soviet diplomatic mission in Afghanistan.

He had the revolutionary credentials to represent Soviet power abroad, and a distinguished Civil War record in Persia and Central Asia. His brother-in-law Igor had been in Kabul for eighteen months with the first members of the mission, and had established friendly relations with the reforming King Amanullah and his family. And as leader of the new progressive Afghanistan, committed to the cause of women's equality, Amanullah had insisted Raskolnikov bring his wife.

Larisa was clearly seen as a major asset to the mission, with her poise and charm and foreign languages and connections, and they spent the next month being briefed together for their new post at the Commissariat of Foreign Affairs. They were given a crash course on the history and politics of Afghanistan, and they read books on Buddhist and Muslim culture, and a Russian translation of the Koran. They had classes in basic Farsi with the Commissariat's interpreters (the Commissariat had just published the first Farsi-Russian dictionary), and they were instructed in diplomatic protocol and the goals of the mission by the Commissar, the aristocratic Georgy Chicherin, a former tsarist ambassador.

Russia's vast mixture of races, cultures and religions made tact and compromise the key to Bolshevik diplomacy at home and abroad, particularly in Muslim Asia. The image of Soviet Russia must be promoted extremely sensitively in Afghanistan, Chicherin said, through social contacts at the Palace, and they were to 'avoid at all costs the fatal mistake of trying to implant communism in the country, and provoking Britain into another war'.

Landlocked by the mountain ranges of the Himalayas, the Pamirs and the Hindu Kush, ruled by the great civilisations of India, ancient Greece and Persia, with its vast empires and ruined cities, its history of wars and conquerors and invaders, from Tamerlane and the Moghuls to Alexander the Great, Afghanistan was at the heart of Soviet relations with the British in Asia, and their empire in India – 'the noblest trophy of British genius, the most splendid appanage of the Imperial Crown', in the words of the former British Viceroy Lord Curzon.

Between 1839 and 1880, Britain had fought two bloody wars in Afghanistan from its base in India, for its 'forward policy' to defend its empire against Russian expansion across Central Asia. By 1879, the tsarist army had occupied the towns of Tashkent, Samarkand and Bukhara, on the silk route from Persia to India, and work had started on the new Trans-Caspian Railway, to transport the oil, cotton and sugar of the East back to Russia.

When Curzon arrived in Delhi as Viceroy in 1899, at the height of the 'Great Game', the line had already reached the Afghan border. To block Russia's further advance east, and secure India's strategically vital frontier with Afghanistan (now the Pakistan-Afghan border), Curzon ordered the annexation of the lands south of the Khyber Pass, to create India's new North-West Frontier Province – 'our unalterable badge of Sovereignty in the Eastern Hemisphere' – with its capital in Peshawar, and Afghanistan's tribal mountain areas serving as a 'defensive buffer zone' against further Russian encroachment. The British army set up a line of garrisons along the North-West Frontier, supported by the RAF, and anti-British flare-ups continued on the Frontier until the British left India in 1947, and the region was absorbed into the new state of Pakistan.

Generations of feudal Afghan Emirs had been bought by successive British governments, which guaranteed to protect Afghanistan from Russian aggression, and claimed the right to control its foreign policy, in exchange for gifts to the court. The last Emir, Amanullah's father, the anti-Russian Habibullah Khan, had used his British money to bring the telephone to Kabul, improve its water supply and introduce a few reforms. Afghanistan's first hospital and a new British-owned factory appeared among the domes and minarets of old Kabul, and Habibullah had three palaces built for his thirty wives – many more than allowed by Islamic law, who his clerics were forced to declare as concubines or ladies of the harem.

Mounting anger with Habibullah and his grovelling to the British triggered a new national liberation struggle in Afghanistan. Inspired by the liberation struggles in Turkey and India, Persia and Russia, intellectuals of the Young Afghan Movement demanded an end to Afghanistan's status as a British 'protectorate', and rapprochement with Russia. They were supported by the first and most important of Habibullah's wives, the astute and ambitious Queen Ulya Hazrat, by powerful sections of the army, and by Ulya Hazrat's son Amanullah, who was in contact with Kemal Ataturk in Turkey, and with Lenin and the Bolsheviks in Russia.

A week after coming to power, the Bolshevik government issued its decree to Russia's fifteen million Muslims:

> To all you whose mosques and prayer-houses have been destroyed, whose customs and practices have been trampled on by the tsars, know that your

beliefs, your national and cultural institutions are henceforth declared free and inviolable, and that your rights, like those of all people in Russia, are now under the protection of the mighty Revolution.

To make amends for centuries of tsarist destruction and oppression, new mosques were to be built, and desecrated texts and monuments restored. Muslims were given preference in Party and government jobs, and a parallel education system was established in the *madrasas*, with parallel Sharia courts (excluding stoning and the cutting off of hands).

The Soviet government was simultaneously appealing to the two hundred million Muslims throughout the world to rise up against imperialist, mainly British, rule. Soviet foreign policy was always a balancing-act between internationalising the Revolution and seeking peaceful coexistence, and the Bolsheviks adopted the same two-track diplomacy in Afghanistan, renouncing all claims to the country after 1917, and declaring their support for its neutrality, while supporting its independence struggle against the British through trade and government-to-government relations.

On 20 February 1919, as riots and strikes exploded across India against Britain's proposed new internment laws, Britain's Afghan ally Habibullah was stabbed to death in his tent on a hunting trip. He was succeeded by his son Amanullah, who declared *jihad* on Britain, proclaiming his country's independence and its first Constitution, passed in its final form in 1923 – outlawing bonded labour and torture, limiting the use of the death penalty, promising improved healthcare, transport and technology and a free press, a secular education for the entire population, and equal rights for women. (A year later, women would be given the right to choose their husbands, something previously decided exclusively by male family members).

On 20 April, a week after 2,500 unarmed Indian nationalists were massacred by British forces in Amritsar in the Punjab, Amanullah wrote to Lenin: 'In the name of Allah, most powerful and compassionate, we declare that Russia has earned the gratitude of the whole world by raising the standard of Bolshevism, declaring the principles of liberty and equal relations for all humanity'. Lenin replied: 'Soviet Russia promises to repair the injustices done to Afghanistan by former governments of tsars, and to pursue with the Afghan people the joint struggle against the most rapacious imperialist state in the world, Great Britain'.

A month later, to bring Afghanistan back to obedience, the British army launched bombing raids on Kabul and Jalalabad, fifty miles from the North-West Frontier. Three thousand Afghans and two thousand Indian and British soldiers died in Britain's Third Afghan War, known by Afghans as their War of Independence, before a ceasefire was agreed in August, in talks between the

Afghan, British and Soviet governments in Kabul, Rawalpindi and Moscow. Igor Reisner was closely involved with Chicherin in the Moscow talks, joining his team who met the Afghan diplomat Walid Khan in the Kremlin in September to discuss the terms of a new cooperation treaty. And that month he left for Kabul with the new Soviet mission, headed by the former tsarist ambassador Yakov Suritz.

In February 1921, Chicherin and the Afghan Foreign Minister Mahmud Tarzi met in Moscow to sign the Soviet-Afghan Friendship Treaty. Ambassadors were to be exchanged there and in Kabul, Soviet consulates were to be opened in Afghanistan's western districts, away from the anti-British tribal areas in the south and east, and Russia was to lay telegraph lines from the border town of Kushka through Herat and Kandahar to Kabul, in exchange for 'financial and technical assistance'.

In April, Afghanistan's first ambassador to Russia, Ghulam Khan, arrived in Moscow, and Raskolnikov was officially appointed Moscow's first ambassador to Kabul. This made Afghanistan the first country in the world to establish full diplomatic relations with Soviet Russia, and the Soviet government the first to recognise the new independent Afghanistan. And although Amanullah would soon sign similar treaties with Persia, Turkey and Egypt, it was his first major treaty with a great power.

Amanullah was no Soviet puppet, Igor stressed in his dispatches from Kabul. His alliance with the Bolsheviks suited his ambitions to play Russia and Britain off against each other as 'Supreme Protector of all Muslims', and strengthened his hand against British-backed opponents of his reforms in the army and clergy. But the Soviet presence in Kabul brought the Bolshevik government enormous new prestige in Asia. 'Also in our favour are the power of the border armies, and the hatred of the entire population for the British', Igor wrote.[1]

Having gambled on the Bolsheviks being too weakened by the Civil War to be a serious threat in Afghanistan, the British government was then forced to change tack. In January 1921, a small delegation of 'trustworthy representatives' was sent to Kabul, headed by Sir Henry Dobbs, a senior official in the Indian administration, to regain Britain's influence with Amanullah, and advise London on the Soviet menace. Raskolnikov and Larisa were to gather information about British activities in Kabul, and report back to the Commissariat and the Comintern, and Larisa was to use her espionage and diplomatic skills to gain access to the women in Amanullah's harem.

---

1 Harish Kapur, *Soviet Russia and Asia, 1917–1927*, 1967, pp. 233–6. Igor's dispatches were published in his book *Afghanistan*, Moscow, 1929.

Traditionally, the Emirs' wives and mothers, and the wives and mothers of their grand viziers and favourites, formed a tight-knit circle at the Palace, bound by family and political loyalties. But Amanullah had broken with centuries of tradition, and had only one wife, Queen Soraya, the daughter of his Foreign Minister Mahmud Tarzi.

Soraya had studied modern languages in Syria, and was his Minister of Education, a member of his *Loya Jerga*, or Grand Council, and the moving force behind most of his reforms, an ardent campaigner for women's rights, and against polygamy, child marriage and the veil. With his sister Kobra, she had established the Organisation for Women's Protection, which encouraged them to voice their complaints and fight for their equality, and she had opened a girls' school in the Palace harem, the first in Afghanistan, attended by her two eldest daughters. She bore Amanullah ten children, and she was the new face of Afghanistan's women, known as the most powerful woman in the Muslim world, who appeared at his side at all national events, unveiled and in Western dress, riding on horseback in his parades and hunting parties, visiting the tents of soldiers wounded by the British. Also managing the fate of the country from her confinement in the harem was Amanullah's mother, Ulya Hazrat, with her dreams of a new Afghan Caliphate in Asia, believed by most to have had his father murdered to engineer his succession – described by a contemporary as 'a woman of ungovernable passions, wilful, domineering and capricious, who killed with her own hands three of her slave girls who became pregnant through intercourse with Habibullah'. Larisa was assigned the delicate task of gaining the trust of both queens and their retinues, and convincing them of the Bolsheviks' friendly intentions in Kabul.

Before leaving, she spent three days with Raskolnikov in Petrograd and Kronstadt, saying goodbye to old friends. Rozhdestvensky walked with her around Petrograd's islands, reminiscing about their student days and the Poetry Circle, dreaming of India. Then he travelled back to Moscow with them for the big party their friends and families threw for them the night before they left at the House of the Arts, where he remembered Mayakovsky begging them not to go, convinced that they would be arrested as soon as they left Russia.

Next morning, 16 April, crowds gathered at the Kazan Station to see them off on the first part of their journey on the Trans-Caspian Railway to the Afghan border. With them were the first twenty members of the mission (more would be collected on the way) – cypher-clerks, wireless operators, Farsi-speaking translators, an accountant, a cook, and a doctor, Doctor Derwitz, an Austrian former prisoner of war.

Mandelstam's wife reported that he had applied to join the mission, and Larisa had supported his application, but Raskolnikov had rejected the 'little poet' in favour of Nikulin, who was to open the new Soviet consulate in Herat. Misha Kirillov was going as Larisa's secretary, and Raskolnikov had picked seven Volga and Baltic Fleet sailors as guards – Cossack cavalryman Ermoshenko, former boatswain in the Volga Flotilla, and gunners Sinitsyn, Khramolov and Kharitonov, Astafev, Zentik and Valery Zhdanov, a broad-shouldered Ukrainian, said by Nikulin to take a new 'wife' at every station they stopped at.

Keeping them in order was their commander, Semyon Lepetenko, former Chief of Staff of the Volga Fleet, who had fought with Raskolnikov and Larisa at Svyazhsk. Also travelling with them was Nikulin's Civil War comrade the film director Semyon Naletny, with his camera team from the *Kino-Pravda* newsreel collective. Naletny had met Nikulin in the Urals, shooting his first frontline films with Dziga Vertov on the *Red October* train, and his crew would be making newsreels of the mission in Kabul to take back and show in Russia.

The first main stop on the Trans-Caspian line, two thousand miles southeast of Moscow, was Tashkent, a major centre of Soviet power in Asia, capital of the new Autonomous Soviet Republic of Uzbekistan. From Tashkent, they travelled two hundred miles east to Bukhara, capital of the new Soviet Republic of Turkestan.

The old Emirate of Bukhara, a former protectorate of the Tsarist Empire, had had a Soviet government since November 1917, and Igor's dispatches had emphasised its vital importance to the Bolsheviks in their complicated relations with Afghanistan and Britain. Amanullah had given the deposed Emir asylum in Kabul, and the British were supplying Bukhara's anti-Bolshevik guerilla fighters, the *Basmachi*, with troops and weapons to overthrow its Soviet government. Lenin had enlisted General Enver Pasha, exiled leader of the Young Turks, to fight the *Basmachi*, but Enver had gone over to the British, and was mobilising them into a formidable force to establish a new anti-Bolshevik Islamic state in the East.

Bukhara was a hotbed of international intrigue when the mission arrived, but Larisa's writer's eye was more drawn to its wild medieval beauty than to its plots and spies. Nikulin recalled her striking up a warm friendship with a woman who claimed to be working for the Bolsheviks, enthusiastically recommending her as the mission's cook, then discovering she was an agent of the exiled Emir.

They spent a week in Bukhara, and she wandered round the town, recording her impressions in her diaries. These diaries would be the material for her first sketches from Afghanistan, for *Pravda* and the journal *Red Virgin Soil*, later the first chapters of her book *Afghanistan*, a riotous lyrical account of the journey from Moscow to Kabul, of wild landscapes and new cultures and languages, and the sights, sounds and colours of the East:

> How much sun and healing warmth the desert spreads. Tashkent, glowing like a dark emerald in the sands, and finally medieval Bukhara. Its cool covered bazaars stretch for miles. Pigeons warble in the roofs, dripping water from a golden midday shower. Old men with the beards of prophets sit at the doorways to the stalls, in their white turbans and dazzling silk robes, smelling the damp roses and counting their money. Little donkeys run past laden with reeds, fresh clover and veiled women. One of our officers rides through the crowd in his tall cavalry helmet, conqueror of Jerusalem, Paladin of the Red Star.

She visited the former Emir's palace, and was allowed into his harem, where she met his little slave girls he had left behind when he fled from the Bolsheviks:

> The gardens are a paradise of peacocks, vines, roses, pools, swans, tents, buzzing bees. Women sit under the trees on carpets, drinking tea and eating spicy sweets in a silence that mutes the streams and makes the trees stop growing. The smells are so powerful you long to close your eyes, lie on the burning flagstones of the courtyard, and become lighter than the swallows flying round the carved wooden balustrades of the buildings ...
> Doors lead off the courtyard to a row of small white rooms, and in each of these rooms lives a child-woman of thirteen or fourteen, bewitching and corrupted, slender as the grapevine. Their long hair is braided into hundreds of tiny plaits, and their little toenails are painted bright crimson, and they run barefoot across the carpet in their red and yellow *shalwars*, lowering their eyes and covering their smiles with their hands ... I think we liked each other a lot.

From Bukhara, the mission travelled east on the Trans-Caspian Railway to the ruined oasis city of Merv, on the edge of the Karakum desert, an ancient centre of Buddhist, Muslim, Manichean and Christian cultures, known in the eleventh century as 'Mother of the World', since 1884 a garrison of the Russian army.

> Smoke drifts across the emptiness from the flat earth to the flat sky. The moon casts its light over hundreds of miles of silence – roads laid waste by Tamerlane, deserts that never sleep. It's impossible to read here. Even the bawdy tales of the Empress Elizabeth and her lovers and diplomats pale in the vastness. There can be no history here, the study of the dead, only a handful of sand, mixed with sunlight and salt.

From Merv, a branch-line of the railway took them another two hundred miles east to its last stop in Russia, the border town of Kushka.

Six years after occupying Merv, tsarist forces had seized Kushka from Afghanistan, digging a large white cross in the sands to mark the new Russian frontier, and the southernmost point of the Empire. Since then it had been a place of exile for arrested tsarist officers, and a major centre of smuggling and sheep rustling. In a letter home, Larisa described 'Red Army soldiers who haven't seen an unveiled woman for years, peacefully washing their underwear in the river, waging an endless war with the peasants who hop across the border every night to steal each others' fat-tailed sheep – the main stumbling block to our policies in the East'.[2]

Waiting to join them in Kushka[3] were sixty Afghan and Russian interpreters, secretaries and telegraphists, and twenty armed Afghan guards, who were to escort them on the six-hundred-mile journey to Kabul across the perilous rocky mountain paths of the Hindu Kush, the capital's only link with the frontier. A hundred and fifty horses, camels, mules and donkeys had been assembled to carry them all and their luggage, and it took even the best riders a fortnight to reach Kabul. Since most of the Russians had never been on a horse before, it would take them over six weeks, riding all day under the blazing sun.

Nikulin's book *14 Months in Afghanistan* opens with a quote from a long piece of doggerel Larisa wrote on the way, 'Ba Amoni Khodio' ('the Lord Keep you Safe'), about Soviet diplomacy's first stumbling steps in Asia:

> Our troubles started at Kushka,
> When a crowd of Russians,
> Without saddles or cushions,
> Climbed on a pack of wild horses ...[4]

Nikulin wrote unforgettably about the journey. His old horse was on its last legs, and died soon after they set off, and next day he saw its skin slung over his guard's saddle. The book-keeper struggled with his bucking stallion to keep

---

2 A selection of her letters to her family on the journey and from Afghanistan was published in 1963 in the journal *Novy Mir* (New World). Unless indicated, all letters quoted in this chapter are from there.
3 Kushka is now known by its Turkmen name, Serhetabad, or 'the Junction' in frontier slang, and is the main route for the trafficking of heroin from Afghanistan into Europe.
4 Nikulin, *14 mesyatsev v Afganistane* (14 Months in Afghanistan), Moscow, 1923, republished in *People and Travels*, republished in *People and Travels*, pp. 333–44.

hold of his precious money box, and poor gunner Zentik was struck with dysentery after cheerfully drinking water from a stream, and could barely stay in his saddle.

Travelling at the back of the caravan behind the line of pack-horses, in a lavishly decorated ceremonial litter, or *takhtaran*, were the mission's twenty women typists and interpreters. Larisa rode at the front with the 'band of devils', the five Afghan guards Lepetenko had appointed to ride a mile ahead as scouts.

Lepetenko rode up and down the line, without hat or sunglasses, teaching himself Farsi from the Commissariat's new dictionary, urging the riders on, and the sailor Kharitonov played his accordion to keep their spirits up:

> He takes it from his knapsack, and we set off at a trot along a flat stretch of the mountain path, whooping, whistling, singing. Suddenly, against the rocks and mountains, three hundred miles from India, a mullah appears, on his way back from Mecca perhaps, sitting grandly on his fat stallion counting his beads. Riding behind him on a donkey is his thin servant, leading his pack-horse, loaded with cooking equipment and a tent. Then horse and rider freeze, and the servant almost falls off his donkey – before them on a prancing horse is a woman in men's boots and trousers, wearing a helmet with the Red Star, singing at the top of her voice ...

Nikulin described Larisa plunging into the journey with a death-defying recklessness – 'swimming in the icy mountain rivers and drinking from streams, despite the doctor's warnings, and the parasites in her blood. How many times in the mountains, where the snow doesn't melt even in summer, you would say to her "Why swallow snow? Why drink from puddles?" But she would just shrug her shoulders and laugh'.

The sailors Khramolov and Zhdanov were stricken with malaria after swimming in mosquito-infested pools. Larisa, Kirillov and Nikulin also suffered attacks on the journey, and next day she would be back in the saddle, he wrote, weak but determined.

He described the devastating symptoms of the disease, in those days before antibiotics:

> For months the microbes live peacefully in the spleen, until one fine day they strike suddenly, without warning, in the saddle, when you have to travel on without stopping. The sudden sickness of will and reason, the dry lips, the face twisted with bitterness, heavy with a leaden yellow shadow. Rocks, animals, people spin round. You try to take your pulse,

but your hand drops to your side. Your body is like stone. Then the fever starts – thirty-nine, forty, forty-one degrees ...

Fifty miles east of Kushka, the caravan made its theatrical entrance into the medieval citadel of Herat, where he was to return in the autumn to open the new consulate. 'Thousands turned out to greet us', he wrote, 'veiled women and their children, men in turbans and *shalwars*, standing on the roads, the flat roofs of the buildings, the mud walls of the gardens'.

The governor of Herat, 'a portly fellow in a grey checked service jacket, crackling jodhpurs and orange leggings', threw a banquet for them, and 'against the howl of the jackals', Nikulin conversed through interpreters with their hosts – committing his first diplomatic blunder when he mentioned he had read the Koran in Russian, and was told the Koran was a miraculous revelation and untranslatable.

When they left, the governor presented Raskolnikov with a large ram, his gift to the Emir, to be eaten on arrival, and Larisa wrote touchingly of his mournful journey with them to Kabul, in a special cage on the back of a pack-horse, 'knowing the hopelessness of his situation, and refusing to eat'.

From Herat they rode to Obey, with its hot springs, and to Daulat Yar and Sar-e-Chashma, and at nights they stayed in the hot windowless clay cells of the *rabats*, old Timurid fortresses built in inaccessible spots in the cliffs, turned into caravanserais for travellers, and there she would record the days in her diaries:

> Our first riders reach the next mountain pass. A wild magnificent picture. Then the path plunges down to another plateau. The sun moves slowly across the boundless depths of a shady ravine, overhung with jagged crags glinting with micre, malachite and marble, vast columns towering over the emptiness, rising to the sky like palaces, defying dizziness from their eagle heights. Their indescribable splendour and disarray have not changed since the beginning of time, waiting in this workshop at the edge of the world for the creative act to be completed ...

She wrote of the Afghan guards who led them over the mountains, and looked after them in the *rabats* – 'fierce horseman by day, who at nights throw off their guns and uniforms and become obliging servants from *The Thousand and One Nights*, bringing us plates and glasses and salt-cellars, which they themselves don't use of course, foisted on them by this alien culture that has eaten into their customs and behaviour'.

Riding on a donkey behind the women at the back of the caravan was the Indian water-boy – 'the lowest person in the *rabat*, who no one *salaams*, neither the guards who bring us our tea, nor the collectors of the dung, which people burn on their fires in winter'. At the front was the Emir's ram, with the twenty servants attending to him – 'grinding his barley, polishing the bells on his collar, clearing his dung, trembling for his health, knowing if any harm comes to him they will be flogged to within an inch of their lives'.

> As *Safir Sahibs*, ambassadors, any kind of work in the normal sense of the word is considered demeaning for us, with the exception of writing, and my diaries inspire the same respect as the marble headstones on the holy graves that fall onto the roads from time to time, decorated with horsetails and wild goats' horns and indecipherable inscriptions.

In the sands outside Herat, her imagination was fired by a ruined Moghul palace:

> Its ramparts and high outer walls have collapsed into piles of bricks, but its cool interior hall is still intact, with its wide alcoves and comfortable seats where food was eaten. In the delicate tracery of the ceilings, now open to the wild pigeons, are the narrow openings for the fires. Once the spicy smells of roast meat wafted out, fragrant with saffron, and the clink of weapons and dishes, and Saadi's melancholy songs of war. At the wave of a yellow hennaed hand, hundreds of white-turbaned servants hurried in, with water for ablutions and carpets for love games and prayers, and the sturdy Khazars guarding the doors of the harem quailed at the peals of laughter inside ...

She wrote of the unveiled peasant women they passed working in the mountains, 'freed from the laws imposed by jealous Mohammed on his beautiful Aisha:'

> Water in these dry sandy places is more precious than life, and women work with uncovered faces, their strong arms burnt by the sun, sharing with their brothers and husbands the heavy labour of deepening and clearing the irrigation ditches, resting with them in the fragrant rushes lining these life-giving streams – dark-haired and graceful, with their ancient Greek profiles, molded from Tanagra clay.

And she wrote of quiet times, when the travellers rested with their horses at cool oases, or with nomads' families in their tented settlements on the rocks:

Children of extraordinary beauty, women liberated from their honourable purdah by toil and poverty, who bring the weary riders pitchers of water and fermented mare's milk. Graceful as women from the Bible, free as all outcasts, they give birth to their babies in the dust, nursing them beside smoking fires on sheepskins whose sour smell repels the insects.

By the second week of June, the mission had reached the ancient Buddhist kingdom of Bamiyan, in the beautiful remote Bamiyan Valley, with its two giant Buddhas carved in the cliffs, known by Afghans as the 'Light Shining Through the Universe' and the 'Queen Mother'. They stayed there a week, exploring the Buddhas, and in her essay 'Bamiyan', she speculated about who had built them:

> Aryans, spreading across Afghanistan to India, Persia and the Caucasus? A highly civilised tribe certainly, whose gods remained human, whose frescoes cover the dark walls with their unfading colours, passing from the great caves of the gods into the smaller ones where the Afghans make their homes – joyful, bright-eyed figures with a radiant glow over their heads. If the people who lived here thousands of years ago resembled their gods, they were tall and graceful, with narrow golden faces and oblong eyes, like the images of their meditating Buddhas, with their mournful goodness and wisdom ... One of the world's most ancient cultures was born here, which after passing through all the phases of its existence, was put to the sword by the invading Moghul armies.[5]

It was harvest time when they reached the fertile Kabul Valley in July. 'The path became a metalled track', Nikulin wrote, 'and an official from the Afghan Ministry of Foreign Affairs, in a pith-helmet and tussore suit, rode up on a bicycle to welcome us. Then three riders appeared in the distance, two in European civilian dress, the other in red cavalry britches and a cowboy hat'.

These were Igor, Suritz and their Afghan bodyguard, who escorted the caravan into Kabul. Fourteen weeks after leaving Moscow, their journey was over, and the slaughtered ram was served to them at a banquet at the Palace.

---

5   'Bamiyan', *SW*, pp. 452–60. The essay, published in *Pravda*, is missing from *Afghanistan*; presumably by then her references to the Islamic conquest of Buddhism were considered undiplomatic and unsuitable for publication. In 1221, Bamiyan was sacked by the armies of Genghis Khan, but the Buddhas were spared. In the seventeenth and eighteenth centuries, the Mughal emperor Aurangazeb and the Persian King Nader Afshat made several unsuccessful attempts to destroy them, as an insult to Islam, and in 1847 Afghanistan's King Abdur Rahman accidentally shot off the nose of the larger one in battle. In 1998, Taliban forces occupying the town announced plans to demolish the Buddhas. They backed down in the face of international outrage, but three years later, they tanked and dynamited them to rubble.

By then gunner Zentik was barely alive, reduced to skin and bones by what the doctor diagnosed as Asiatic cholera. Nikulin remembered Larisa defying the doctor's warnings and nursing him to the end, with his two closest friends. And when he burnt himself out, groaning in agony, she organised his funeral in the hills above Kabul, watched at a distance by a crowd of Afghans curious to see how the Russians buried their dead. Nikulin had a postcard of the gravestone she helped to design, carved with a hammer and sickle, and the words 'Here lies brave Zentik, laid to rest in the sand'.

For the next two years, her home with Raskolnikov and the eighty members of the mission would be the Soviet diplomatic residence in the suburb of Qala i Fata, a vast mansion set in extensive grounds beside the Kabul River – 'built for the late King Habibullah, in his favourite gothic Anglo-Indian colonial style', Nikulin wrote, 'with our kind fat old Afghan guard dozing at the gates with his Persian cat on his knee'.

In the two-week handover period before Igor and Suritz left for Moscow, they briefed the mission on their contacts, and the new staff took up their posts. Lepetenko replaced Igor as First Secretary, and Ermoshenko replaced Lepetenko as the sailors' commander. Second Secretary was Vladimir Kukel, a former officer in the Volga Flotilla, who had served under Raskolnikov at Kronstadt and Novorossiisk, and had fought with him in Persia. Also living in the Embassy were Naletny and his film crew, and Igor's English interpreter friend 'Miss Mary', who was staying in Kabul to work with Larisa after he left.

Unfortunately all we know of her friendship with this interesting woman is from a couple of references to her in letters home. But we learn something of her later, during the Second World War (although not her full name), when she was working as a high-level interpreter for the British government's Arctic Convoy Scheme, delivering essential supplies to the Soviet Union at the ports of Arkhangelsk and Murmansk, responsible for organising the details of many of the perilous journeys there. Members of a Soviet team sailing to Murmansk asked her about her life when she escorted them on the train from London to their ship in Glasgow, and she told them she was from a wealthy St Petersburg family who had emigrated to London after the Revolution. Bilingual in Russian and English, a passionate reader and socialist and supporter of the Bolsheviks, she had returned to Russia in the summer of 1919, at the age of nineteen, to work as an interpreter at the Commissariat of Foreign Affairs in Moscow. There she became good friends with Igor, and that autumn she left with him for Kabul.[6]

---

6 *'Dipkurery'. Ocherki o pervykh sovietiskikh diplomaticheskikh kurerakh* (Sketches of the First Soviet Diplomatic Couriers), Moscow, 1973, p. 96.

Nikulin recalled Doctor Derwitz, 'Doctor Sahib', a devotee of the Muller exercise regime, doing his lunges and sit-ups every morning in his underwear in the gardens. The sailors staged gymnastics displays and wrestling matches, and their commander Ermoshenko, respected even by the Afghans for his horsemanship, organised contests of riding skills with their Afghan guards. 'Penguin Island' Larisa called this strange new Soviet collective on the Kabul river, flying the red hammer and sickle flag. (Anatole France's novel about his community of clever penguins was very popular in Russia after the Revolution).

The British government had given Suritz and Igor permission to cross India on their journey back to Russia, and in the first week of August, Larisa and Raskolnikov rode with them as far as the Afghan-Indian border at the Khyber Pass. A week later, Naletny and his crew filmed Raskolnikov presenting his letters of accreditation to Amanullah at the Palace, in the presence of the British Minister Sir Henry Dobbs – 'a colonial bully, with a whip in his hand, hated by all Afghanistan', she wrote home. 'But how well Fedya conducted himself, very smart!'

Despite Igor's dispatches, the Russians can have had little idea of what to expect in Kabul. Until Afghanistan became part of the international postal system seven years later, all mail was delivered across the mountains on packhorses, and they had entered a society without radio or air communication with the outside world.

Letters and newspapers from Russia were brought by teams of mounted couriers employed by the Commissariat of Foreign Affairs, who travelled with diplomatic passports as members of the diplomatic corps, and were trained at the Commissariat in fighting and survival fighting skills. Hold-ups, robberies and murders were frequent. Of the twelve thousand who had volunteered since 1918 for their dangerous journeys across Russia and Europe, China, India and America with their diplomatic bags, two thousand had been killed by counterrevolutionaries, bandits and foreign agents.[7]

Even the English papers *The Pioneer* and *Civil and Military* reached Kabul a month late, and mail from Russia took up to four months to arrive. When the Embassy first made telegraph contact with Moscow in August, it was like 'a message in a bottle', Nikulin wrote.

It was from the Afghan newspapers that they learned of the famine in Russia, a result of prolonged droughts, and the economic devastation of the war and Intervention and Blockade. An estimated five million peasants, mainly in the Volga region, died of starvation, or from the cholera and typhus epidemics that wiped out those already weakened by hunger. Soviet Russia received food

---

7   *Sketches of the First Soviet Diplomatic Couriers*, 1973, pp. 49–60.

aid for the first time from the West, through Gorky's All-Russia Famine Relief Committee, and the Russians paid half their wages to Gorky's Committee and to their families. 'I'll send you more as soon as I've cleared my debts', Larisa wrote to her parents, and the first diplomatic caravan from Kabul left with a cargo of grain donated by Amanullah.

The famine was virtually unreported in the Anglo-Indian press, to avoid the inevitable comparisons being drawn with the famines in India and Afghanistan. But sections of the Afghan press hostile to Amanullah and the Bolsheviks claimed the tragedy was God's punishment, and portrayed the Russians in Kabul as devils in human form. Permission was needed from the Ministry of Foreign Affairs to leave the Embassy compound, and constant police surveillance ruled out meeting people informally in the mosques and bazaars or in their homes. And despite Amanullah's strictures against the veil and Soraya's example, Larisa's life was even more circumscribed than Raskolnikov's, and visiting Kabul unescorted was out of the question.

She and Miss Mary organised cultural and musical events at the Embassy, and noisy 'Admiralty parties', at which the sailors would reminisce about the front. The sailor Sinitsyn played his violin, and Kharitonov his accordion, and Nikulin reported visiting Afghan dignitaries' horror at seeing the Ambassador's wife singing and dancing with the men.

She practised her Farsi with the guards, tended the Embassy's menagerie of goats and chickens, fed the monkeys and parrots in the gardens, acquired a Persian kitten, and hung portraits of her family in the drawing-room, promising them to make good her absence with letters.

Having missed out on university in 1917, Igor had enrolled for a degree in Oriental studies at Moscow's Red Army Military Academy. But he evidently found it hard to adjust to student life and hated being back, and in a letter to him she referred to arguments between them before he left, and her tears of shame and remorse.

Raskolnikov's famous moodiness and abrasiveness and his strained relations with her family is likely to have made the handover period with Igor fraught with tension, and a big part of her role in Kabul was clearly to be a calming influence on him. Before they left Russia, their marriage had seemed close to breaking point. Her friend Olga Nesterovych had seen his resentment of her, and her success as a writer must have been hard for him to bear. But his diplomatic duties left him time for his own writing and hobbies. Suritz and Igor had left the Embassy with a good library, well supplied with Marxist literature and books on Afghan and Indian history and politics, and they both wrote there. He started work on a new book, *A History of Russian Thought*, and he studied the history of Afghanistan through its coins, of which he soon had a large collection.

After the years of fighting and the trauma of Kronstadt, they must have longed for some peace and stability in their lives, and those first months in Kabul seem to have been some of the happiest in their marriage. 'I live in his love which has become true love here, under the sacred sky', she wrote to her parents, in a letter signed 'Your Fantastic Ambassadors'.

At the front, they had been commander and commissar. Now they were His Excellency and his wife, and she took her new role very seriously. With strict instructions from Chicherin to avoid politics, she hosted banquets at the Embassy for the Turkish and Persian ambassadors, Fakhri Pasha and Etela-ol-Molk, and held tea-parties for their wives. She and Raskolnikov attended banquets and grand audiences at the Palace, and played tennis with Soraya and Amanullah, with whom they spoke in French or English (most of the mission had a smattering of both languages). Amanullah presented her with a thoroughbred Arab stallion she named 'Falcon', and she would escape from her confinement in the Embassy to go for long horse rides with the Queen in the mountains above Kabul, standing in her stirrups to gaze at the distant frontier with India.

She sent back detailed reports to the Comintern of their discussions, and of information she picked at the Palace from junior British officials. 'I can imagine their joy at my descriptions of the flowers, clouds, sunrises and sunsets and the humming-birds in the Palace gardens, without which, as you know, an old Bolshevik like me can't describe either the Revolution or the reaction to it', she wrote to her family with her first reports, delivered by couriers to Moscow, asking them to forward them all to the Comintern, and all but those marked 'Secret' to *Pravda* and *Izvestiya*.

While she waited for her first invitation to the Palace harem, she joined Raskolnikov in all his official engagements, visiting Afghanistan's new military academy with him, its first hospital and its first factory, *Machine Khan*, a British-owned woollen mill, whose workers she called 'the greatest conspirators in the dusty Kabul valley'.

In Afghanistan, as in Europe before the industrial revolution, wool was still mainly woven on small upright looms in people's homes. She described how *Machine Khan's* new British power-looms were transforming this cottage industry into the mass production of the factory system, turning Afghanistan's traditional craftsmen into mill-hands:

> The cruel conditions of factory life, with its interminably long working day, are turning the living artist, with his skills and traditions, into a human machine ... The shuttle on his loom flies back and forth, while his foot works the pedal that adjusts the yarn to make new patterns ... And

the sign on his loom, like a magical greeting from the kingdom of exploitation, where labour is taking on the power of capital, says 'MANCHESTER'. 'MANCHESTER' means don't despair, we'll win, we're your brothers, we support you! And the proletarian rage is like a miracle, maturing like wine in the stuffy air.

It was only through writing that she could express her true feelings about Amanullah, suppressed by polite diplomacy. 'He is burdened by guards, and drowning in corruption, and he shares his mother's lust for power', she wrote home. 'And apart from the law, he has his youth and astuteness going for him, and his undoubted talents – and his prejudices, which see all women, even the cleverest, as animals, squabbling and making alliances in the privileged henhouse of the harem'.

In *Afghanistan*, she cast a satirical eye at his reforms since coming to power:

> First he banned the turban and the *shalwar kameez* from the Palace, and his forty-stone dandies are now unrecognisable in their scratchy camelhair suits made from the rough homespun fabric produced at *Machine Khan*, mixed with sheep dung. Then having introduced his country to jodhpurs and morning coats, he turned his attention to its ignorance ... His main weapons against the hated European colonisers are to be culture and progress – you can't fight Krupps and Winchesters with scimitars and medieval superstitions. His backward kingdom must be literate and trained in the sciences, and a certain amount of Western technical expertise.

At his Military Academy, she saw 'little boys turned removed from their families to be educated, and beaten, beaten, beaten:'

> Everything in these small despotic countries is ruled by the stick. It beats the ears of the elephants bearing their loads of logs. It beats the soldiers, drenched in sweat in their camelhair uniforms. During festivals, it makes gardens spring up overnight on the bare earth, decked with flags, rugs and lanterns. And with the stick, Amanullah Khan wants to turn his impoverished country in twenty-four hours into a genuine modern state, like a small Japan, with an army and education system to match.

In early September, Nikulin rode back to Herat to open the new consulate, before the snow made the mountain paths impassable, and the Russians in Kabul felt more cut off than ever. 'We've heard nothing from Russia or the Fleet',

Raskolnikov cabled him on the journey. 'Please let us know if you hear anything as you get closer to the border'.

Soon after he left, the first Italian mission arrived in Kabul. She held a banquet at the Embassy to welcome the new consul, Marquis Paterno, and his family and staff, and she became good friends with his press attaché, Giorgio Scarpa, who gave her Italian lessons and discussed poetry with her. '*Très raffiné*, with the same *façon de parler* as at Great Gunpowder Street', she wrote home, 'who hates bourgeois politics and etiquette, and loves noisy workers' meetings and Karl Marx and arguments in smoke-filled rooms, all mixed with a d'Annunzian nationalism and cynicism'.

In late September, she reported to her family that she had received her first invitation to the Palace harem, for a grand audience with the formidable Queen Ulya Hazrat and her retinue – 'curious for their first sight of this Russian woman, silently holding important political discussions behind their impregnable *chadors*'. 'Ulya Hazrat rules only the harem now, and is part of the country's history, and the differences between the old and new queens are evident at every step'.

She became an honoured guest of the two queens, and she saw the clash of cultures between them at Soraya's girls' school in the harem, the first in Afghanistan, where she was invited to attend examination day:

> Hovering over the fresh childish faces are the puffy hairless masks of the eunochs, scurrying unceremoniously among the rustling female skirts, bringing a whiff of the bedroom to the classroom ... Lumbering through the crowd like fat kind elephants are the elderly nannies, with the blue stars of recently emancipated slaves from India, Turkey and Arabia tattooed on their wrinkled foreheads, visible through their transparent veils ... With them are the aging concubines, faded but still beautiful, who have spent their lives serving the tormenting god of desire, picking up all the nuances of passion like the brilliant colours from the carpets ... Now, instead of learning the secrets of a glance or smile, the art of dancing with two silver bells tied to their waists, girls are being taught to solve arithmetic problems with sultanas and rice, and they angrily shake their bells and rustle their silk skirts like dead leaves.

By the autumn she had written much of *Afghanistan*, provisionally titled *In the East*. In a long letter to her friend Andrew Rothstein in London, who was keen to translate the work into English (although nothing came of it), she wrote:

> You'll find Kabul's harem, its factory and hospital, its preachers and bribetakers, its festivals and heroes, and much more besides, for you know my

weakness for aestheticism, and I want its pages to smell not just of big grey politics, but of the scent of the flowering almond trees and the bright aromas of the bazaar. I'm afraid my impressionistic language won't be easy to translate, and unfortunately much of it can't be published in Russia or abroad until I get back ...

Afghanistan is a magnificent barbarian. Beside Persia and India it's a parvenu, a narrow-eyed high-cheekboned driver, whose historic role has been to lead Great Babur's horses from the Khyber Pass to the outskirts of Kabul ... Now it's the buffer-zone between British India and Russia. With British and Russian loans, it's building a more progressive administration, new schools and a new army – all welded to the Emirate under the slogan 'Afghanistan, Great Power of the East'.[8]

As in all her books, there is virtually nothing in *Afghanistan* about her personal life, and she saved the details for her family at home. In a letter to her mother, she described a banquet in the harem, sitting barefoot on the carpet next to Ulya Hazrat, who offered her her own plate as a mark of her respect. Then some musicians played wild mournful music on the Afghan harmonium and *rabab*, and she joined the women as they danced and threw off their veils and passed the hashish pipe round, and taught her to play simple rhythms on the drums. 'Afterwards I stood on the balcony with Ulya Hazrat, contemplating the courtyard cooling in the sunset, with its roses, lanterns and splashing fountains. Lightning flashed in the distant mountains, and I cursed the British in broken Farsi, and the old queen poured me a thimbleful of sweet tea, and promised not to receive the "evil English ladies"'.

This letter was delivered personally to her mother by the sailor Sinitsyn, when he returned to Moscow, and she questioned him closely about her, and worried she was 'drowning in sticky pink jam'. 'I hope this corrupting life with its court intrigues doesn't kill your spirit', her father wrote to her. 'The death of your spirit would be worse for me than your actual death'.

It seems an extraordinary thing for a father to say. But in her reply, she called his letter 'harsh but loving':

> There must always be times of retreat – I swear to you this 'hashish of the soul' is just a reaction to the marathon years at the front ...
> My last letters to you were written in a mood of despair, for the lost days and years, the incomplete and indescribable ... But despite everything, whatever I'm feeling, I try to keep up with you by reading 'proper books' every day, and I'm writing a lot ...

---

8   The letter was shown to the author by Rothstein.

Afghans had been smoking and eating hashish for centuries, for its mind-altering highs, and there is a hallucinatory intensity to much of her writing from Afghanistan. But her observations of life in the harem are always set sharply against the life beyond the Palace walls, and the women in Kabul she could never see or meet,

> hidden from the world behind their heavy *chadors*, falling from their heads to the tips of their loose backless slippers, which further impede their blind gait. Their shadows are everywhere – in the colourful bazaar crowds, riding with their children on donkeys at the back of the caravans, their faces hidden even from the babies at their breasts, as if they were held by ghosts ... When we pass a group of them, they step aside and follow us with long concealed looks. What are they thinking? Do they judge us? Do they envy us? Passing riders splash them with mud, and a car scatters the camels and catches one of their *chadors* in its wheels. She is thrown crumpled and groaning to the ground. Half-dead or concussed, it's all the same, she is just a woman.

She saw the veil as a symbol of women's oppression, a result of Afghanistan's feudal poverty and ninety-eight percent illiteracy, all of which she blamed on the British, who needed a docile uneducated workforce cut off from the rest of the world, to serve their imperial interests.

She wrote too of women's historic role in Afghanistan's liberation struggles against the British. Afghanistan's national heroine, eighteen-year-old Malalai, who led the victorious battles for Kandahar in the Second Afghan War, was seen rallying her troops by tearing off her veil and using it as a banner. Women in the tribal mountainous areas, on the frontiers with India, had been fighting with men for a century to defend their settlements against the British, and she celebrated the strength and beauty of the unveiled tribeswomen who passed through Kabul with their caravans – 'princesses in their colourful rags, with their quick light step and golden skin, which has never known the *chador*, who fight in the mountains with double-barrelled rifles'.

> People's uprisings in these isolated places, cut off from the rest of the country by a military cordon and a never-ending series of border wars, with no hope of final victory, and no help from outside, have been the first major challenge to the most powerful army in the world ... When their caravans pass through Kabul's Great Bazaar with their gleaming weapons, people step aside for them as for conquering heroes, and the mullahs busy themselves with their prayers, averting their lustful gaze from these wives' and mothers' burning eyes.

She was savagely funny about the British in Kabul, 'with their white helmets and their disdainful smiles, cutting their faces like the notches on their bullets, and their staggering contempt for these people of an inferior race'. And she wrote with a blistering humour of Afghanistan's *corps diplomatique* – 'the Hoffmanesque mirage of international diplomacy, putting down roots in this remote outpost of British India:'

> The steps of its dance were worked out over a century ago at the Congress of Vienna. It's of no importance whether they take place in Honolulu or Afghanistan, with the Nyam-Nyams or the Papuans, international diplomacy exists in and of itself, regardless of time and place. Somewhere on a patch of hallowed extra-territorial land – on a waxed floor, or a circle of earth around a campfire of cannibals – two augurers in their respective religions come together and establish official relations. They make visits, bow and retire. They hold soirees, leave visiting cards, change from lounge suits into morning suits, and from morning suits into tails, before drowning in an expanse of white flannel, topped by a colonial solar topee, dazzling the natives with the whiteness of their dress shirts and the sharpness of their 'London creases'.

And now the Bolsheviks were key players in this game, 'and decent men are expected to sit at the same table with these monsters, and no international conference can take place without them:'

> In the legal and cultural framework of their diplomacy, the Soviet government occupies a position similar to some four-legged Ostrogoth, creeping under his barbarian's shield to the throne of the Holy Roman Empire, to crown himself Caesar with his knotted horse's bridle ...
>
> Yet here again, diplomatic etiquette comes to the rescue, and it turns out it's not a Bolshevik's hand they're shaking, but that of a distinguished ministerial envoy. And if the bearer of this rank isn't a complete orang-utan, and doesn't blow his nose on the tablecloth, they can forget our criminal Revolution, and honour in us the blessed memories of our tsarist forebears ...
>
> The Ambassador is the disembodied spirit of a diplomatic dynasty that still survives, *quand même*. Once the Tsar, always the Tsar. He has simply jumped out of the pit in which the Romanov family is buried. His metaphysical being lives on ...

More subjects of comedy were the Western capitalists who visited Kabul with their business plans, and she told the story of Californian mining engineer Washington B. Vanderlip Jr., who arrived in the autumn of 1922. Vanderlip had first tried his luck two years earlier in Moscow, where he had passed himself off as banking tycoon Frank A. Vanderlip, and was referred to in the Soviet press as 'Billionaire Vanderlip', and Lenin agreed to meet him, believing he had the ear of President Wilson, and could persuade him to offer the Soviet government diplomatic recognition and loans. He was exposed as a fraud after he left, and she used the mix-up to brilliantly surreal effect:

> Billionaire Vanderlip, speculator in red, yellow and white souls, courteous as a Quaker missionary, with the eyes of a steppe horse-thief, sits with the genius of the Revolution, laying before Ilich his gold-embossed documents signed by kings and princes, and the barons of his coal, cotton, oil and armaments trusts, offering to trade with him for the untapped wildernesses of Siberia and Arkhangelsk, the sturgeon of the Caspian, the oil, coal and precious resources of the vast expanses of Russia ... And in those places where the red is pink, and the Revolution doesn't threaten his bourgeois purgatory so much, for a little of the workers' and peasants' sweat, so coveted by his sunny loud-mouthed Dollar ...

His meeting with Lenin came to nothing and produced no trade deal, and he did no better in Kabul:

> Elsewhere in Asia, Vanderlip was used to doing his business quickly and efficiently ... But the Afghans wanted none of it, and haggled for hours over their impassable mountains and worthless deserts, their filth, ignorance and nakedness ...
> At the Ministry of Foreign Affairs, he was entertained with a hookah and slices of sweet Kabul melon and some feathery verses celebrating the health of their precious American friend, and his mirage shimmered in a thousand places. He tried to work his mighty levers, but to no avail, the hospitality and hookah smoke were unassailable. As soon as he discussed a contract, the Ministry vanished in a puff of pleasantries. For hours his cunning logic beat the empty smiling air, battling with these meek fantoms like an absurd Don Quixote. And his watch showed that he had wasted a whole day, and his train, having waited at the border for him for a minute and eighteen seconds, had already left ...

On 18 October 1921, Amanullah signed the Anglo-Afghan Treaty with Britain, under which Afghanistan was free to 'determine its internal and external affairs, once its government has shown itself sincerely anxious to regain its friendship with Great Britain'. In a major snub to the British, Amanullah ordered Afghanistan's Independence Day celebrations to be held a week later, on the 25th, the fourth anniversary of the Bolshevik Revolution, and Larisa saw his relations with Russia and Britain played out on streets of Kabul:

> Crowds filled the town – Indian moneylenders in their yellow turbans, Bukhara merchants in their silk gowns, pale Western officials in their black tailcoats, bloated Palace satraps with angry faces, demoted now to mere hangers-on at Amanullah's court, and the mountain warriors, with their guns and dark woollen cloaks, who brought their own wild heroic spirit to the day, leaving the cowering bazaar crowds with a foretaste of a completely new kind of social relations, shot through with the hot bright light of equality.

Amanullah invited the tribespeople to dance before his family and members of the Soviet and British missions, and Naletny's crew were there on the platform to film them:

> Chanting spells, they lunge high in the air, like hunters pursuing their prey, then writhe on the ground like dying warriors, their chests torn open by the same British bullets used to hunt insurgents and big game in the Punjab ...
> This isn't just some traditional tribal dance, passed on from generation to generation. They are dancing their battles with the British, real living soldiers in their dusty khaki and white helmets – what happened yesterday in the Khyber Valley, and could happen tomorrow at the fortress of Michni Point ...
> The dance ends, and their best singer brandishes his rifle – a British rifle, captured in their last battle with the enemy. 'The English took our land, but we'll drive them off our fields!' he chants. 'But not all Europeans are damned *ferengi!* There are the Bolsheviks, who are with the Muslims!'
> They all know about the Bolsheviks. They sing songs about them at the edge of the world, on the borders with India ... Thousands of mocking eyes are on the British attachés on the platform, who applaud ironically and hide behind their programmes ...

It was in early November that news reached Kabul of Blok's death in Petrograd three months earlier, according to his autopsy, of malnutrition and heart failure. He was just forty-one.

By then his health had broken down. His arrest and the attacks on his works had left him increasingly unable to write, and he had abandoned his hopes for the new society he had dreamed of. He spent his last months whoring and drinking, tormented by hallucinations and fits of mania and despair, crying out against the new literary apparatus and its stifling bureaucracy – 'I'm suffocating, suffocating, suffocating! We'll all suffocate!' His memorial speech in February on the anniversary of Pushkin's death was seen as a rehearsal of his own – 'It wasn't d'Anthes's bullet that killed him, it was the lack of air, his life had lost its meaning'. He died on 7 August, and was buried three days later at the Smolensk Cemetery, where an Orthodox choir sang a choral arrangement of Akhmatova's 'Funeral Lament on the Death of the Poet' at his grave.

Victor Shklovsky called his funeral 'the last spectacle of an epoch not destined for a future in the new Soviet state'. According to Trotsky, Blok had outlived his time: 'Blok belonged entirely to pre-October literature. He overcame this, and joined the Revolution. But his impulses, for tempestuous mysticism or for revolution, were all rooted in the old Russia'.

For Larisa, Blok was the guardian of everything that was precious in the old culture as it made way for the new, who had worked with the Bolsheviks from the first days of the Revolution, and had then seen his writing belittled and pushed aside. Her views were evidently still considered controversial in the 1960s, when her *Selected Works* were published, as her tribute to him is missing from 'In Petersburg', the last chapter of *The Front*: 'For three years, in the desert of the spirit of the struggling new Russia, was there any voice more powerful in the deadly siege to bless and crown our great people's sufferings, defeats and victories than the voice of Alexander Blok?'

In a long letter to Anna Akhmatova in Petrograd, she wrote, 'Dearest most tender poet, Blok's spiritual sister, we need your poetry now more than ever, whose entire purpose and justification is to make water spring from the bare rocks ... For one line of yours, people would give a year of their wretched lives ... The trees and mountains and streams here beg you in the language that is yours and theirs to write. Your sincerely affectionate friend, Larisa Raskolnikova'.[9]

Akhmatova is unlikely to have replied to this, and her flowery language would not have pleased her. 'I taught them how to speak, but not how to be quiet', she complained of the countless women she inspired to be poets.

---

9   *SW*, pp. 518–19.

Homesick and grieving for Blok, Larisa pored over old copies of *Pravda* and *Izvestiya* for news, none of it good. The Civil War had officially ended with the Treaty of Riga, and the NEP's concessions to capitalism had finally led to the West lifting its economic Blockade. But the country was still desperately poor, surrounded by hostile states, crippled by internal sabotage. That summer, the German High Command had announced plans to mobilise the armies of Europe under its leadership in another war of intervention, and businessmen in the entrepreneurial Russia of the NEP were in contact with exiled capitalists dispossessed by the Revolution, who were openly calling for a new war on the economic front. 'We look back at our factories. They are waiting for us, calling to us, we will return to them', former millionaire Moscow factory-owner Pavel Ryabushinsky told a conference of Moscow bankers and industrialists in Paris.

After the battles to drive General Yudenich's White armies from Petrograd in 1919, the city's Party boss, Grigory Zinoviev, had given the *Cheka* drastically increased powers against suspected enemy agents. Merely a sympathetic attitude to the Whites became grounds of execution, and a new 'Literary Sub-Department' of the *Cheka* was set up, run by Zinoviev's protege the young *Chekist* and literature lover Yakov Agranov, to take on Petrograd's intellectuals. 'Seventy percent of the intelligentsia have one foot in the enemy camp, and we have to burn that foot off', Agranov said, and one of his first victims in 1919 had been Blok.

In the summer of 1921, as Petrograd filled with feverish rumours of plots and spies and a new invasion, more former tsarist officers had been arrested, along with hundreds more writers and intellectuals, including Gumilyov.

His poetry had always been filled with images of his violent death, and many felt he had written his epitaph with his last collection, *Pillar of Fire*, widely considered to be his finest, in which he expressed his desire 'not to die in my bed, surrounded by my doctor and lawyer, but to go out in a last blaze of glory'. Victor Serge saw him as a disaster waiting to happen. He recalled meeting him on the streets of Petrograd in 1919, during the celebrations for the second anniversary of the Revolution, 'dressed as an "Englishman", refusing to join the dancing as "it wouldn't be English"', crossing himself ostentatiously outside every church he passed, telling Serge he had a 'gentleman's agreement' with the regime. 'They can't touch me, I'm too famous!' he said.[10]

After the Kronstadt rising, he had written several political leaflets for a group of the sailors' supporters at Petrograd University, led by the distinguished

---

10 Volkov, *St Petersburg. A Cultural History* (trans. Antonina Bouis), 1995, pp. 229–34. Serge, *Memoirs of a Revolutionary*, 1972, p. 103.

geographer Professor Vladimir Tagantsev. In June, Tagantsev was arrested by the *Cheka* as the leader of the 'Petrograd Fighting Organisation', which was allegedly plotting to overthrow the Bolsheviks and restore the monarchy in Russia, backed by huge sums from the West. Tagantsev's interrogators promised him none of his co-conspirators would be shot if he gave their names, and on 3 August, four days before the death of Blok, Gumilyov was one of eight hundred members of the 'Fighting Organisation' to be arrested and jailed. News of his execution, on 24 August, reached Kabul in late November.

Although he claimed not to take the charges seriously, his choice of prison reading material, Homer's *Iliad* and the Bible, suggests he anticipated a long sentence. Larisa's parents wrote to her of their shock and disbelief when they learnt of the arrests, assuming at first they must have been a mistake, like the arrest of Blok. But by the time they joined the large delegation of Moscow's intellectuals and writers and members of the Academy of Sciences who visited the Kremlin to demand the prisoners' release, and Gorky had intervened personally for them with Lenin, and Lenin had ordered them to be pardoned, the death warrants for Tagantsev and his wife, Gumilyov and fifty-eight others had already been signed. Agranov was chief prosecutor at their trial.

Next morning they were taken from jail to the Kovalevsky forest outside Petrograd, and were executed by firing squad. On the wall of Gumilyov's cell he had written, 'Lord forgive me my sins. I am leaving on my last journey. N. Gumilyov'. He was said to have died like a Russian officer, smiling, with a cigarette in his mouth.

The poet Olga Forsh recalled the mood in the city that day:

> A silence such as you find only at high noon on the steppes ... Notices of the sentences, already carried out, were pasted on all the lamp-posts, with the poet's name. No crowds, no explanations, no one asked for explanations. Sometimes someone joined those clustered motionless round a notice, then moved away, and remained standing there. On the streets, squares and avenues, people turned to stone. A stone city.[11]

The executions produced a wave of revulsion against the Bolsheviks, and a series of angry demonstrations across Russia and abroad. 'Gumilyov was alien to me, but there was no need to kill him', Shklovsky said. Larisa's mother wrote to her of 'the hideous rotten features of Petrograd's Party and *Cheka* bosses', and of her guilt that she had initially failed to take the charges ser-

---

11   Olga Forsh, *Sumashedshii korabl* (Ship of Lunatics), Leningrad, 1930, p. 157.

iously. She told her she had visited Gumilyov's widow Anna Engelhardt in Petrograd, and had found her living in great distress and poverty with their three-year-old daughter, Lena, 'unwanted by anyone', and Larisa wrote back agreeing to return to Russia to help look after her. 'Yes, of course we must take the little girl in, and I'll come back'. (A relative stepped in as she was preparing to leave).

Several of Gumilyov's old friends, among them the former Acmeist and patriot Sergei Gorodetsky, wrote grovellingly of him as a dangerous counterrevolutionary, and his biographer Shubinsky believes there was indeed such a conspiracy, and that his leaflets for the group were more than just beautiful writing. According to Victor Serge, 'During the Kronstadt revolt, his friends at the University believed the regime was about to fall, and he thought to assist in this. The "conspiracy" went no further than that'. Like Serge, Larisa had never seen his politics as anything more than incoherent flag-waving, it was for his poetry she had loved him. To her friend the Italian press attaché Giorgio Scarpa, now back in Rome, she sent her Italian translation of his 'Ode to d'Annunzio', written in the spring of 1915, before the start of their affair. 'It was by one of our greatest Russian poets, Nikolai Gumilyov, who has just died in Petrograd', she told him. 'Unfortunately he understood nothing of politics and was a monarchist, who volunteered for the front in 1914, and called himself a "Parnassian".[12]

To her mother, she wrote, 'If I'd seen that bastard Hafiz before he died, I'd have forgiven him everything, and told him the truth – that I've never loved anyone so painfully, with such a desire to die for him'.

Her mother's next letter came with the latest issue of the Symbolists' *Journal of a Dreamer*, edited by Andrei Bely, containing Akhmatova's poem 'Fear', mourning the old St Petersburg, 'in which we buried Blok, but couldn't bury Gumilyov'.

> Fear fingers all things in the darkness,
> Leads moonlight to the axe.
> There's an ominous knock behind the wall,
> A ghost, a thief, a rat ...

The journal was also serialising Bely's *Crimes of Nikolai Letaev*, the second part of his autobiographical novel about living in a Russia he no longer recognised, and it inspired her to return to her own autobiographical novel *Requiem*, with a new title now, *Rudin*, and a new understanding of its Hamlet-like hero.

---

12   *SW*, p. 520.

Winter in Kabul was bitterly cold, with plummeting temperatures and freezing blankets of snow. Diplomatic life shut down, and she buried herself in her story of love and loss, and the narrator's doomed affair with the poet who prophesies her love for the East.

She worked on the novel until February, when the first draft was ready for couriers to deliver to her parents. But their response to it three months later was painfully cool. 'Why didn't even the first chapters, which seemed to me quite successful, merit justified sentence? Was it really so hateful?' she wrote to them.

She had clearly betrayed too many family secrets – her father's suffering at the hands of Burtsev, her affair with Gumilyov, and her mother's relationship with Vladimir Svyatlovsky, backer of the original *Rudin*. Perhaps they really were lovers, as the novel claimed. But she was surely writing of herself and Gumilyov when she described their last night together in his flat:

> Napoleon gazes indifferently at the two shadows clinging to each other in the darkness. They embrace for a long time, until their passion finally rises to its eternally youthful height, then disappears under the ground, trembling to its roots ...

Her mother must have been horrified. She had barely even changed the names, and it would have been obvious to anyone who knew them who they were. And whatever her relationship had been with Svyatlovsky, and despite his complicated financial arrangements with her father over *Rudin*, the three had remained good friends. Unlike his employer Duke Leuchtenberg, who had immediately emigrated after October, Svyatlovsky had stayed to work with the Bolsheviks, teaching at Petrograd University, publishing articles on economics and literary criticism and three books, two on the history of Russia's trade union movement, the other on the Utopian tradition in the Russian novel, in which he called the Bolshevik Revolution 'the first Utopia in the history of the world'.

She was evidently persuaded by her parents to drop the work, which was never finished or published in her lifetime. The surviving fragments, published in 1983 in the magazine *Literary Heritage*, with other unpublished Soviet works from the 1920s, don't seem to work that well as fiction. She had an extraordinary story to tell, but others wrote about her so much better. Despite many touching insights into her life before the Revolution, she was too close to her heroine to write convincingly of her, too knowing and quick to explain, and perhaps she accepted that *Rudin* was more successful as therapy than as art.

She dutifully carried out her diplomatic work and sent off her Comintern reports, clearly in a state of shocked grief for Gumilyov. In a letter to her mother, she described suffering deep bouts of depression – 'which seem to get worse as time goes on, when I furl my sails and sail down a silent stream of passive contemplation and dead time'.

In another, she hinted at growing strains in her relationship with Raskolnikov:

> He sits in his study conjuring with his books, with his big dictionary on his knees, which have become rather plump recently, and he is happy. Here are the roots of his Party, his law, his revolutionary shield, his holy of holies, built from his years in prison and the underground – titles of illegal pamphlets, the names of those who have died or have become great. But I am not part of this world, it's not mine … There is no war between us, and never will be …

She so rarely criticised Raskolnikov, or spoke of her suffering and struggles with him. As ambassadors, they had to present a united front to the world, and keep their arguments private, behind closed doors. But in his published letters to her later, he referred to several periods in their marriage when their rows ended with her demanding a divorce, and perhaps this was one of them.

It was only after she left Afghanistan that she could confide to a friend that he had abused and humiliated and beaten her. She told her of his insane sexual jealousy and violent rages, and how things had taken a diabolical turn in Kabul when he reported her to Moscow for conducting her intelligence work with the British 'naked, at their quarters, covered only in a fur coat', and she had been reprimanded for 'behaviour unbecoming to a Party member'.[13]

It is a chilling insight into his deranged mind, and her life with him in Kabul. In Russia he had been a broken man, hated by his sailors at Kronstadt, and hating her for being the strong one in the marriage. In Afghanistan he was in charge, with an Embassy to run, and a difficult wife to manage. Perhaps the horrors of the front had turned violence into an addiction. Perhaps like his namesake in *Crime and Punishment*, he was remorseful and promised to change. And shockingly, the Party chose to believe his insane fantasies of her naked assignations in a town full of veiled women, when she wasn't even allowed out of the Embassy on her own. But at least at home in Russia she could theoretically have had him arrested for domestic abuse. Thousands of miles away, trapped with him in the stifling conventions of diplomatic life, she was unable to plead her case, or risk the scandal of leaving him.

---

13   From the memoirs of Elisabeth Poretsky, *Our Own People*, 1969, p. 56.

'Nature gave Larisa everything, brains, beauty and courage, but one can say she wasn't happy in her personal life', Nikulin wrote. His books *14 Months in Afghanistan* and *People and Travels* are filled with his memories of her, and of their frequent quarrels and reconciliations – the last, 'over some trifle', shortly before he left for Herat. 'She didn't create illusions', he wrote. 'She spoke her mind to people as soon as she met them, and looked deep into their souls, and many flinched at her directness'.

But for all her directness and their closeness and quarrels, Nikulin confessed she remained an enigma to him, and Gorky complained that he failed to bring her to life in her books – 'So often you begin to write of Larisa, but she remains elusive'.

Nikulin almost certainly knew nothing of the two miscarriages she suffered in Kabul. We know of them from her cousin Ekaterina Sheremeteva, who mentioned them briefly in her conversations with Przhiborovskaya, and from Raskolnikov's published letters to her after she left Kabul. Unfortunately though only his side of the correspondence is published, so we learn more about his feelings than hers. He wrote of her insistence that no one but her close family and doctors must be told she was pregnant, and of the strain this had put on their marriage, and he passionately defended himself against her accusations that he had mistreated her, even that he had been responsible for her second miscarriage – 'You write of our baby as if I were his murderer'.[14]

Miscarriages are also commonly caused by malaria, and by its antidote, quinine. And although she was generally healthy and symptom-free in Kabul, Sheremeteva reported that her doctors had ordered complete bed rest if she was to save her pregnancies, which would have clearly been impossible. Eight of Queen Soraya's ten children had survived infancy, and like Soraya, she would have had the best medical care available in Afghanistan. But with some of the highest infant and maternal mortality rates in the world, she had evidently taken the difficult decision during her second pregnancy to risk the dangerous journey back to Russia to give birth.

A quarter of babies born in tsarist Russia had died before their first year, and mothers and babies were a major priority of the Commissariat of Health and Kollontai's Commissariat of Social Welfare. But the infant mortality rate barely changed in the first years of the Revolution. The new health system, stretched to breaking point by the Civil War, staffed mainly by volunteers, had to focus its resources on a mass vaccination programme against the cholera

---

14   Przhiborovskaya 2008, p. 290; Raskolnikov, *O vremeni i o sebe. Vospominaniya, pisma, dokumenty* (About Myself and My Times. Memoirs, Letters, Documents), Leningrad, 1989.

and typhus epidemics ravaging the population, and a propaganda campaign to educate people about hygiene. 'Either Socialism will defeat the lice, or the lice will defeat Socialism', Lenin said.

Pregnancy and childbirth were managed with a similar emphasis on hygiene, and in 1920 Russia became the first country in the world to legalise abortion, to save women from the dirty illegal operations in which four percent had died, and thousands suffered serious health complications. Abortion was never an easy option for women. It was a difficult and painful procedure, performed without anaesthetic, to be endured stoically, like miscarriages. In Kollontai's *Love of Worker Bees* stories, about women's lives in the 1920s, her sexually liberated young heroine bravely pays the price for her freedom, complaining only that the operation makes her take time off her Party work.[15]

Larisa's heartbreak must have been compounded by her isolation in Kabul. Even her secretary Misha Kirillov, who had worked closely with her since the first months of the Revolution, wrote affectionately of her, but from a respectful distance, as his employer.

Kirillov described her loyalty and devotion to the Embassy staff, and how she always supported their applications to go home, however much she hated losing them. She had seen his theatrical talents in his dramatic productions with the sailors in Astrakhan, and she encouraged him to return to Moscow to pursue a career on the stage, using her father's contacts at the Meyerhold Theatre to find him work at its actors' studio, while continuing to pay his wages.

They corresponded regularly after he left, and he especially treasured her letter, 'full of friendly concern about my path as artist', in which she expressed her reservations about Meyerhold's 'biomechanical' acting method, which trained actors to call up emotions through specific learned movements and gestures:

> I didn't like your last letter – please don't be angry Misha – for its complacency ... It's no good when you try to fit life through the eye of a needle. If you dream one minute of the fame of Garrick, and the next of suicide, I'll tell you you're looking for a form, and that it's right in front of you, flashing past and leaving just hints of 'how it must be done', according to the orders of your sacred craft ...
>
> I love Meyerhold and his crowd, but be careful – they're very 'oriental' in their innovations. They trust the body, which is good, but they distrust the genius of words, which is bad. It's a kind of theatrical egotism, which

---

15   Kollontai, *Love of Worker Bees*, published in Russia in 1923, and in the author's translation in 1977.

puts the director's vision above the writer's. They see speech and language like a good Voltairian sees the soul – they don't believe in that nonsense, and they don't trust the actor's brain either.

But unless the brain develops the sensitivity to study the complex workings of the soul, then I assure you Misha, the body won't discover the necessary nuances for the gymnastics of emotions, the fencing of ideas, which actors must *know*, like a botanist knows flowers. You can't act only with your head – but you can't act without it either. Someone who hasn't thought deeply about life can't act tragedy, just as someone who has never loved can't act love. For heavens sake keep your balance. Don't let your soul be crushed by the masters of formal, physical art. Spirit, spirit, spirit – it's only through spirit that you will discover full, whole, human acting.[16]

In March 1922, Britain and Afghanistan finally established full diplomatic relations. Sardar Abdul Hadi Khan was received at the Court of St James's as its first Ambassador to London, and Amanullah prepared to welcome Britain's first Ambassador to Kabul, Sir Francis Humphrys, a first-class cricketer and old India hand, former Deputy Foreign Minister in the Indian Government, and commander with the British Expeditionary Force in the Caucasus. A magnificent new Embassy was being built for him, at the insistence of Lord Curzon, who believed 'His Majesty's representative in Afghanistan must be the best housed man in Asia', and he arrived at the end of March, with his large staff of military and press attachés.

Whatever the state of Larisa's marriage, abandoning Raskolnikov in his tense encounters with this powerful new British presence in Kabul was clearly unthinkable. In a letter home, she described attending Humphrys' accreditation ceremony with him at the Palace: 'We see the swinging pendulum between the Entente and Soviet Russia in the way the British aristocrat, the polite murderer, with his mean contempt for people, sweetly shakes Fedya's hand and fawns to his wife. A sea of blood is shed for this diplomatic flirtation, this half-recognition of what will happen between us – between the cancer eating the heart of India, and us, who must sooner or later tear it out'.

A month later, an international conference opened in the Italian city of Genoa, attended by representatives of thirty-four European countries and fifty Soviet delegates, to deal with the pariah states of Russia and Germany, and settle the 'Russian question', at which the British and French set out their terms for the diplomatic recognition of the Soviet government: abolishing virtually

---

16   Mikhail Kirillov, 'A Generous Heart', *LRRC*, p. 134.

all of its socialist legislation, and allowing foreigners to be tried in special courts outside Soviet jurisdiction, repaying all tsarist debts, and paying eighteen billion dollars' compensation to foreign investers whose property had been nationalised – against the fifty billion Russia was claiming in damages for the Intervention.

Speaking for the Soviet delegation on the first day of the Conference, Foreign Commissar Chicherin caused great anger by calling for 'the representation of the colonial people in the British and French empires', and for international disarmament and peaceful coexistence – 'the socialist and capitalist property systems must cooperate economically, on the basis of full and complete recognition'. He then repeated this message at packed factory meetings in Genoa, and in behind the scenes discussions with the head of the German delegation, Foreign Minister Walther Rathenau.

Militarily and economically crucified by Versailles, the Weimar government was being forced to seek rapprochement with the Bolsheviks, and six days into the conference, on 16 April, Rathenau and Chicherin met in the nearby town of Rapallo, to sign a treaty normalising trade and diplomatic relations between the two countries. Germany accepted the nationalisation of German businesses in Russia, and Russia agreed to provide Germany with vital raw materials in exchange for German manufactured goods, and both sides agreed to cancel all debts and territorial claims since Brest-Litovsk, and to 'cooperate in the spirit of good will in meeting the economic needs of our nations'.

Two months after the Treaty was signed, the Jewish Rathenau, formerly a wealthy industrialist, was assassinated by a fascist terror group in Berlin, accused of being part of an international cabal of Jewish financiers and Bolsheviks plotting to rule the world with the 'Social Democrat Versailles traitors'. The British government claimed Germany had signed a secret clause in this 'Slavic Teutonic alliance', undertaking to provide Russia with arms and ammunition to attack Britain, and Ambassador Humphrys demanded that Amanullah expel Raskolnikov from Kabul.

For Larisa to leave him now would have created a major diplomatic incident, with major repercussions for both of them in Russia. Stories were going round Moscow of their decadent life of luxury in Kabul, and her father wrote to warn her of the criticisms she would face when she got back: 'My poor little Soviet aristocrat, nothing can erase your natural gifts and beauty, and your services to the Party. But the pretext will be very simple – the unproletarian life of the Afghan court, and your lack of contact with the working masses'.

Her family's letters to her that spring were subdued and depressed. Her mother had been ill, and Igor described his studies at the Military Academy as 'torture'. And their father, whose politics had been hated by his colleagues before the Revolution, and were never 'Soviet' enough afterwards, had clashed with the new Commissar of Justice, Pyotr Stuchka, over the use of Soviet courts to prosecute political dissidents. He had published several articles in *Pravda* warning of the excessive power being concentrated in the Party, and in January he had resigned from the Commissariat to focus on his theatre work. Then to explain his resignation, the Commissariat rehashed Burtsev's slander that he had been an agent of the tsarist secret police. The Meyerhold Theatre too was in trouble, after its repertoire spectacularly crashed with its controversial production of Alexander Sukhovo-Kobylin's play 'The Death of Tarelkin', a macabre picture of official cruelty and corruption in pre-revolutionary Russia.

In April 1922, Stalin had been appointed Party General Secretary, the post he would hold until his death. A month later, Lenin suffered his first stroke from the terrorists' bullets in his body, and he temporarily retired from politics. 'Lenin's absence is felt everywhere', Larisa's mother wrote to her.

At the Tenth Party Congress the previous year, he had entrusted Stalin, Trotsky and the head of the *Cheka*, Felix Dzerzhinsky, with the task of sanctioning the Workers' Opposition. But like Trotsky and others, he was soon expressing his alarm at the dramatic extension of Stalin's powers, transmitting propaganda downwards and curbing opposition, using the new Party machine that was taking shape to build his phenomenal power base.

Crucially, Stalin was the coordinating link between the Party Central Committee and its new Control Commission, established to weed out timeservers and careerists, which over the next fifteen years would sprout thousands of 'purge commissions' throughout the country, and expulsion would mean certain arrest. 'The purge has already begun', Larisa's father wrote to her.

Desperate to see her family, she persuaded Raskolnikov to invite Igor to return to Kabul as First Secretary, and bring their parents with him. 'I long for the sun to give back to you what you lost in the cold terrible winter of Papa's Party work and Mama's loneliness', she wrote, promising them there would be a car to drive them from the border, and no risk of malaria if they came in the autumn.

But nothing came of the plan. 'You'll never know how many tears I weep for you', she wrote to her mother. 'My one grief you know and I needn't repeat, I miss you. If only we could see each other for just a few days, we could tear the cobwebs from our eyes, which can't see clearly through the sadness and distance and the soothing consolation of words'. 'I dream of you every night', she wrote to Igor. 'Last night I dreamt we were children, and I was holding your hand at the opera. I never stop hoping you'll come. Who knows, is it impossible?'

Perhaps Raskolnikov had changed his mind about inviting them, and evidently there were more of his stormy jealous scenes that summer. In June, the Reisners' multi-talented friend Sergei Kolbasev, naval commander, poet, linguist and pioneering jazz enthusiast, arrived in Kabul as the Embassy's new translator, but he had to leave a week later, after Raskolnikov called his poetry 'Gumilyov filth', and accused him of sleeping with his wife.[17]

Raskolnikov was known to dislike her more 'feminine' writing, and her essays on Afghanistan's women were clearly not as appreciated by her male comrades as they should have been. But one person she knew would want to read them was Alexandra Kollontai.

As director of the *Zhenotdel*, Kollontai had developed an impressive education programme for women in the eastern Soviet republics. She campaigned to involve women in their emancipation, setting up delegates' assemblies in the factories and villages to fight sexual exploitation and for equal pay. She worked with the different commissariats on issues concerning their health and working conditions, supervised the publication of eighteen women's magazines and newspapers, and established a commission to get prostitutes off the streets and find them jobs. But in January 1922, her tenure at the Zhenotdel had come to an end. Threatened with expulsion from the Party for her leading role in the Workers' Opposition, she had been appointed instead, like Raskolnikov, to a diplomatic position abroad.

She was being briefed in Moscow that summer for her new post as Ambassador to Norway, when Kirillov returned with Larisa's essays 'Learning in the Harem' and 'The Covered Woman and her Child', which she asked her to publish through the Women's Section of the Comintern, of which she was still Secretary.

> My work and family boss F.F. makes me take innumerable copies of my reports, and send them to innumerable departments of the Comintern. But the only person who might be interested in these sketches of Afghanistan's women is you ...
> We live under the constant scrutiny of hordes of spies, cut off from Afghan society and public opinion, due to the fact that the former is scared stiff of its feudal Emir, and daren't meet foreigners without special permission from the police and the Ministry of Foreign Affairs. And

---

17 Kolbasev played a leading role in the Soviet jazz scene, and featured as 'Captain Kolbasev' in the popular 1983 film 'Jazzmen', about young performers and enthusiasts in Moscow in the 1920s. He described his experiences in Kabul with Raskolnikov in a letter to his friend the poet Nikolai Tikhonov, published online in 2018.

the latter – i.e. public opinion – doesn't exist, and has been replaced by the sword, the bazaar and the army, with its military flimflam and cheap bicycles …

As for the rest, it's the *nature morte* of the women's half of the court, who have accepted me thanks to my 'un-Soviet' nose and manners – so the education my parents gave me *did* come in useful after all![18]

Raskolnikov's extraordinary allegations against her must have severely compromised her relations with the Party, and made her wish she hadn't been so keen to replace Kollontai in his affections. But despite her father's fears for her in Russia, she had a firm supporter in the Embassy's press attaché, Alexander Minlos, who arranged for *Pravda* to publish her first two essays from Afghanistan, 'Diary' and 'From the Journey', and for *Red Virgin Soil* to publish her seventh 'Letter from the Front', 'July 1919' – 'to Lev Davydovich Trotsky'.

Recently published in Moscow are five letters she and Raskolnikov wrote to Trotsky from Kabul in 1922, evidently part of a longer correspondence between them (they refer to several others), with his to them unfortunately missing.[19]

In a long letter signed by both of them in April, 'to our dear friend Lev Davydovich, from our Soviet monastery in Kabul', they shared comradely memories of the front – of the victories at Svyazhsk and Kazan, 'where by a miracle you escaped death', and of his return to Moscow after the gunshots fired at Lenin. Raskolnikov then asked him, as Chair of the Revolutionary Military Soviet, to speak for him at the Commissariat of Foreign Affairs about his unanswered cables urgently requesting clarity in his instructions: 'It's one thing then it's another. First I'm to promise Afghans the moon, then it's the two-finger treatment'.

A few days later, Raskolnikov asked for his comments on four new pieces of writing he sent him, with 'communist greetings to dear Lev Davydovich' – three Civil War sketches, and his essay 'On the Eve of October', later all chapters in his books *Stories of a Flotilla Commander*, and *Kronstadt and Petersburg in 1917*.

In a long letter to him from Larisa in June, she thanked him for writing to them, 'lost in the baking oven of Kabul, with its melancholy sunset hours, when the mullahs from all the surrounding villages cry out to their god … I hate to complain, Fedya desperately needed a break. But a year of this would turn

---

18 *SW*, pp. 528–9.
19 The letters, dated 27 April, 2 May, 13 June, 5 July and 7 September 1922, from the archives of the Revolutionary Military Soviet of the Republic, were published in 2003 in the journal *Historical Archives*, with extensive commentaries, and republished online in 2019.

even Lensky[20] into a suicidal misanthropist. So if you hear anyone speak of Raskolnikov's comfortable life in Afghanistan, enjoying the same leisurely pursuits as his British counterparts, waiting for the fruits of his diplomacy, bitter and sweet, to fall in his lap – then please Lev Davydovich, dear Lev Davydovich, put them right!'

In July, Raskolnikov wrote to Trotsky in a mood of deep despair, about the insurmountable difficulties of his work 'in this oppressive Islamic state, with its primitive political ideology, which sees swindling and treachery as the highest form of diplomacy. And when we make clear to them with our Bolshevik directness that we can see their cards, it makes absolutely no difference ... Sometimes the only way to impose order is with a powerful fist on the table. But within days, some new betrayal will have been dreamt up'. He ended by asking Trotsky for news of the Fleet. 'I long to know its fate. But in the house of the hanged man, people don't mention the rope'.

Larisa lightened the tone in her letter in September, telling him the Embassy had just been watching the Moscow newsreel of the Red Army May Day parade on Red Square – 'laughing with joy and pride at the sight of you, the Square, and the red flags of the Republic, blowing over Afghanistan and reaching out to India'. That summer, she wrote to her family that she had started work on a long article for *Pravda* on the British in India, and was reading Marx and Engels in the Embassy library – their *First War of Indian Independence*, and the third volume of *Capital*, for its analysis of advanced capitalism. 'My mental machine hasn't completely rusted yet – although there's no comparison with Goga's of course! – and as soon as I'm home I'll get it working properly again'.

In August, she and Raskolnikov were invited by Amanullah to escape Kabul's burning heat at his summer palace in Paghman, on the outskirts of town, and she wrote home that they were wandering around its lake and cool tropical gardens, 'holding professional discussions under the apricot trees'. But their holiday was cut short by news from Bukhara, where Enver Pasha and his *basmachi* had launched their assault on its Soviet government – 'reviving Amanullah's dreams of a Central Asian Confederation, and Britain's of a new war against Russia'.

She vividly described the weeks that followed in her letters home. Enver was killed after a week of bloody fighting, 'finally laying to rest the secret lusts of the "Supreme Independent", and Fedya and I felt the familiar blissful shiver up our spines as the spiked helmets and furled flags of the Red Army appeared over the dead sands'.

---

20 Lensky is the naive young romantic poet in Pushkin's *Evgeny Onegin*.

A complete breakdown in Soviet-Afghan relations followed, and days of angry silence from the Palace. Anti-Bolshevik fighters from Bukhara flooded into Kabul, and the British Embassy increased its pressure on Amanullah to expel the Russians. Raskolnikov was ostracised by the Turkish Ambassador, Fakhri Pasha, who 'under the influence of stinking White Guard information', demanded that 'the Bolsheviks withdraw their damned Red Army from Bukhara, and stop oppressing good Muslims'. Relations with Fakhri Pasha were further strained by an unfortunate incident with his cat, which 'married' Larisa's Persian kitten, then killed it. She arranged for its body to be delivered to the Turkish Embassy with full diplomatic honours, and Raskolnikov received a note from the Palace accusing him of killing kittens, 'sacred animals'.

Over the next weeks of arguments and misunderstandings, Amanullah was driven deeper into intrigues between Britain and Russia. An avalanche of British gold landed in his lap, and the Soviet Embassy's radio was confiscated, forcing the mission to rely on old information from couriers from Moscow. Raskolnikov paid frequent visits to the Palace and the Ministry of Foreign Affairs, pressing for guarantees and trying to restore calm, and much tactful diplomacy was needed as more British cash poured in, and the Embassy's radio was returned, then confiscated again.

But by September the Russians were back in favour, after Larisa warned Soraya of rumours she had heard from her British contacts of an assassination plot against Amanullah by senior officers in the army, backed by the British. 'This morning the distraught Emir arrived in the harem, saying he had heard a "big English bird in a bush" telling people in town he was dead. Soraya threw herself at me sobbing, and we kissed, and I dropped a diplomatic tear on her peach pink shoulder'. As a token of his gratitude, Amanullah gave her his plumed cavalry cap to wear while out riding with the Queen – 'and I took the opportunity to curse the British, and all in all it was "big politics!"'

Relations were soon restored with Fakhri Pasha, who invited her to host a banquet in his honour at the Turkish Embassy, at which he presented her with a gold embroidered cloak for her father – 'as worn by Oriental despots, which you can wear to the "Purge Commission" of our Party's revolutionary fighting family', she told him.

To placate the British, Afghanistan's Independence Day celebrations were held that year in late September, a month before the Bolshevik Revolution, not in Kabul, but at Amanullah's palace at Paghman. Crowds poured into the gardens, and Raskolnikov, Larisa and Miss Mary, their Afghan guard and driver and Naletny and his crew joined the royal family and Humphrys and his officials on the platform – watching 'Amanullah's fighting rams and jumping elephants, and his grandees' friendly wrestling matches'.

But on the fourth day, when the Emir appeared dressed not in his uniform, but barefoot in sandals, in an austere grey turban and cotton tunic crossed with a rifle, as worn by the border tribes, it was clear that this marked the start of a deeply mystical, national part of the celebrations.

Standing behind him were his armed Waziri and Afridi tribal chiefs ..., and at the sight of them, the British Ambassador felt suddenly indisposed, and roared off in his Rolls-Royce, pursued by their derisive bugles. Then the dance began ...

Fighting fraternities, they circle like mighty falcons, their gleaming black locks flying over the battlefield. Their swords, stained with the blood of countless wounds, guard and punish, calling enemy after enemy from the earth – the currently thriving Sir Francis Humphrys and Sir Henry Dobbs, and countless nameless British troops in Afghanistan's deserts and mountains, the Pamirs and Himalayas ... "Burn! Burn!" roars the music, and in the thunder of victory, the Emir gallops off with his smoke-blackened face, crying '*Salaam bad isteqlal-i-Afganistan!*' ('Independence to Afghanistan!')

Amanullah invited the Russians to spend the next day with him and his family at Paghman, where Naletny filmed him and Raskolnikov walking in the gardens together, and on the drive back to Kabul, they suffered a near fatal car accident. 'We shot through a thick brass cable stretched across the road, which would have sliced off our heads if we'd been standing up, as I'd wanted to (luckily Fedya wouldn't hear of it)'. She, Miss Mary and Naletny were sitting at the back and were uninjured, but Raskolnikov and the guard and driver all suffered cuts and concussions, 'and my little one is in bed now with a big bandage on his head'.

They were told later that workers connecting the cable to the Palace, out of their minds with hunger on a fast-day, had abandoned it without attaching it properly – 'in other words, exactly the conditions in which people lose their heads'. But as the British stepped up their pressure on Amanullah to expel the Russians, Raskolnikov was in no doubt it had been an assassination attempt.

To keep relations open with the Palace, she hosted a banquet at the Embassy for Walid Khan, who had headed Afghanistan's first diplomatic delegation to Moscow three years earlier. The mission's telegraphists had just that morning been allowed back to their exchange, and to bring some drama to the event, she asked them to construct two cardboard battery-operated model radio stations, flying the Soviet and Afghan flags, which were placed on the dinner table with leads running to her plate. At the banquet she switched them on to communicate greetings to the Emir and curses to the British, to electrifying effect, and she repeated the performance at a women-only banquet she held for Soraya and Ulya Hazrat and their entourages.

'Now everyone has left, and I'm sitting with Miss Marychka as she translates the Russian newspapers into English, watched by the bats and mice, and sweet silly Naletny is playing Mozart on the piano *café chanson* style', she wrote home.

At the end of September, Naletny and his crew left Kabul with their precious cans of newsreels (now stored in Moscow's State Archive of Documentary Film). A few letters and telegrams arrived from the Baltic and Caspian Fleets, but the sailors were depressed and homesick, and their commander Ermoshenko spent his time gossiping and playing cards. Couriers returning to Russia rarely returned, and Larisa told her mother she longed to join them:

> I've seen the East, the camels, the Middle Ages, the wild harem, the dances of the tribes, the storms of blossoms and storms of snow, and the experiences will be with me as long as I live, and I'll never regret them. What was bad was very bad – life without you has been a drought. But darling Mother, I've come out of it all not with the bourgeois the spic-and-span ethics of the *Leusen-Allee*, but as a true revolutionary.

In October 1922, Mussolini's fascist legions marched on Rome, to save Italy from communism, and her *Pravda* article on the British in India turned into her essay 'Fascists In Asia', later the final chapter of *Afghanistan*.

She starts by identifying the origins of the new doctrine of fascism in the gangster politics of colonialism, and Britain's history of plunder and aggression in India:

> The body of India is infested with white leeches. Every so often, its people struggle desperately to tear the bloated suckers from their sides, but death squads, armoured cars and artillery pour along the newly built roads to crush them ... At the officers' club, the shriek of the foxtrot drowns out the planes roaring across to shower death on the tribespeople's settlements. Over the next week, the Anglo-Indian press will denounce the natives' savagery. Illustrated supplements of *The Pioneer* and *The Englishman* will publish portraits of the respectable white-flannelled planter hacked to death with his pink-cheeked family, and will honour the heroes who killed the insurgents besieging the *zemindar's* verandah, where his family had taken refuge behind a barricade of chaises longues laid out for their after-dinner rest. Engineers will repair the bridges and telegraph lines, and the law will hang any criminals who weren't caught on the blown-up railway tracks ...

She then shows the human face of fascism in Asia – 'the young entrepreneurs from Italy and Germany and the other less successful European powers, nipping at Britain's feet, grabbing every morsel of brown flesh from its devouring jaws'.

> They know they have no chance in India, but now these new opportunities are opening up in terrible Afghanistan, so feared by the British ... Lack of funds makes them resourceful, and their aristocratic titles give them a brazen insolence ... What belongs to others is theirs, and no legal or parliamentary nonsense can stop them tearing the clothes off people's backs and beating the life out of them with their clean white hands, which have the strength of two well-fed animals. No wonder little Afghanistan grabs its pockets at the sight of them, and runs to count its furs hanging up to dry ...
>
> But after running an eye over the place, they realise there are no profits to be made – no ivory to exchange with the natives for alcohol, no rubies or carpets for rusty razors, glass beads or red calico. Peering disdainfully through their monocles at this hostile country not yet ripe for exploitation, they scramble over Afghanistan's inhospitable rocky landscape and the large face of the Emir, their appetites thwarted at every turn, and they are soon on their way home.

Not before visiting the Soviet Embassy, however:

> It's not pleasant having to meet them, titled fops à *la* d'Annunzio, and hulking thugs with faces like flat-irons. Seeing the red flag the red flag of the Soviet Mission in this outpost of British Asia, they are at first guarded with us, and their hackles are up ... But there is nothing hypocritical about these young men, no veneer of bourgeois respectability or shame. They don't mince their words, and they spare no one, and they don't expect to be spared themselves when they're up against the wall ...
>
> They speak of Russia with a shocking, cynical respect ... For them the rest of the world lies in an abyss of contempt, a craven herd, offering itself to the rich and powerful, and they see their meetings with us as the prelude to a war that will leave only one ruler of the world.
>
> 'I'll be happy fighting you reds at the barricades', the German Count smiles, drumming his fingers on the table, impatient to crush his only worthy opponent. And the two black Afghan servants bow and lead him through the dark gardens, running ahead of him with their lanterns, as if escorting him to the guillotine ...

In December 1922, two months after Mussolini's coup, delegates from Russia, Belorussia, Ukraine and the Central Asian republics met in the Kremlin to sign the Treaty on the Creation of the Union of Soviet Socialist Republics, the USSR, or the Soviet Union, successor to the Tsarist Empire, the world's first socialist state.

Britain's new Conservative government (described by *Pravda* as a 'second-rate government of second-rate minds') responded to this new threat to British interests in Asia by ordering the army to use the winter months in Afghanistan, when the border tribes were unable to move, to bomb their settlements, and poison their flocks, pastures and wells.

Amanullah was again torn between Britain and Russia, softened by more British cash, but knowing that after the tribespeople they would come for him. Raskolnikov sent more cables to Moscow, urgently requesting instructions, but suspected they were not being received, and Larisa told her family the Afghan police were openly reading his diplomatic mail, and that the Embassy had put up a 'wall of China' against the outside world.

By now she was desperate to go home. But when she applied to Amanullah for permission to leave, he was reluctant to guarantee her safe passage to the border, or provide her with transport. Sleepless nights followed as he prevaricated, and she wrote home of the toll the uncertainty was taking on her health, and that she was 'close to psychosis'. Then after eighteen months' remission from malaria, she came down with an attack that kept her in bed for two weeks.

Raskolnikov too had been ill that winter, and in January Amanullah invited them to escape snowbound Kabul for his palace in the warm oasis of Jalalabad, the ancient winter capital of the Afghan kings. Their car crawled across the mountain passes through fierce snowstorms, and by the time they descended in the darkness into the valley, they were exhausted and chilled to the bone. But she was enchanted by the town. To Kirillov in Moscow, she wrote:

> The air is sweet with roses and cypresses and castor-oil trees, flowering like red torches. I'm trying to spend my last days here so I remember the East for the rest of my life, and the bright carefree moments when we're happy because the fountains splash, and there's youth and beauty and everything that's sacred, creative and hopeful ... Gods lived in these gardens, and they were kind and blessed ... I can't wait to get home.[21]

---

21   Mikhail Kirillov, 'A Generous Heart', *LRRC*, p. 136.

Jalalabad had been Britain's main garrison in the First Afghan War, and was her closest experience of a colonial town, 'a showcase for England's now abandoned policies in Afghanistan, watered, blessed and manured by English gold'.

> The tips of the date palms rustling in the boundless sky, the white palaces with their fountains and gardens, the scented stocks and tea-roses in January, the mimosas filling the air with gold and honey – all represent the peaceful paradise the rest of this scrap of Asian desert could become if its ignorant citizens allowed it to be blessed by the wand of British capital.

Women were less confined there than in Kabul, and she could explore the town veilless on her own, and the fiercely anti-British mood of the people she spoke to inspired her to finish her 'Letter' on the Persian campaign. She brooded on her Kazan 'Letter', which she told her family she now very much disliked (possibly because of its first-person voice), and she tried to work on *Afghanistan*. But she needed to be back in Russia to write it, alone and undisturbed.

By then she had evidently decided her marriage to Raskolnikov was over, and in letters to her later he referred to their long agonising discussions in Jalalabad, when he begged her to change her mind and give him another chance.

Back in Kabul, she kept up her pressure on Amanullah to leave, and he finally relented when she threatened to buy an elephant to take her to the border. He received a *note verbale* from Humphrys allowing her to travel back via India, and he ordered a car to be sent for her from Peshawar. But a month later, her car had still not arrived, and it was now urgent that she leave, because she was pregnant again.

She was clearly taking a huge risk with her pregnancy in travelling back to Russia, and she can have had little idea of what to expect there.

In March 1923, Lenin had suffered his third stroke from his injuries, leaving him paralysed and unable to speak, and he had retired to his dacha outside Moscow. Although occasionally dragged out on display, he had been too ill to attend the Twelfth Party Congress that month, at which the 'triumvirate' of Stalin, Zinoviev and Zinoviev's close ally Lev Kamenev emerged to manage the succession during his last illness, and exclude Trotsky from the leadership.

The Party was in limbo when it needed to be united against the new fascist threat. And the leadership crisis was exploited by the British government in ways that would have far-reaching consequences for the Bolsheviks, and would further delay Larisa's return to Russia.

On 8 May, Foreign Secretary Lord Curzon issued Britain's sharply worded ultimatum to the Soviet Union, demanding the immediate release and generous financial compensation of all British citizens jailed in Russia as spies, and

Britain's right to intervene in Soviet domestic policy to fight religious persecution, accusing the Bolsheviks of 'stirring up propaganda against Great Britain throughout the East', and ordering them to recall their diplomats from Afghanistan and Persia.

The 'Curzon Ultimatum' was seen as a declaration of war, and was immediately followed by a build-up of British military action, with a squadron of gunboats moved from Malta to the Dardanelles, and a warship and two cruisers sent to the Arctic port of Murmansk. Amanullah was ordered to expel Raskolnikov within a week, and Humphrys withdrew his *note verbale* guaranteeing Larisa's safe passage across India, meaning she would have to return to Russia the way she had come (although by car this time), via Bukhara and Tashkent.

Thousands in London, Newcastle and Nottingham, Liverpool, Edinburgh and Dundee demonstrated with banners saying 'Don't Play with Fire Mr Curzon!' and 'Hands off the USSR!', demanding that he was sacked, and that Britain established diplomatic relations with the Soviet Union. Chicherin warned Curzon that blackmail and bullying were no way to resolve international differences, and accused him of threatening the cause of world peace.

In November 1922, seven months after the Genoa conference, another international summit had opened in the Swiss town of Lausanne, to negotiate a peace treaty with Turkey, attended by delegates from Britain, France and Turkey, fascist Italy, Japan and Soviet Russia, at which the Russians, Turkey's neighbours, were excluded by the British from all the main negotiations, and the Swiss government refused to provide them with the normal diplomatic police protection.

The conference dragged on for the next six months, with delegates unable to resolve their differences on Turkey, and the Russians still without police protection. On 10 May, two days after Curzon's Ultimatum, a former general in Denikin's White Guards working with British intelligence, who had attempted to assassinate Chicherin in Berlin, walked into the dining-room of the Russians' hotel in Lausanne and shot dead the former Soviet Ambassador to Rome, Vatslav Vorovsky, injuring his two companions.

'The revolver shots in Lausanne coincided with Mr Curzon's new diplomatic onslaught on Russia', headlines in *Pravda* declared, and at a huge protest rally in Red Square, Mayakovsky declaimed his poem 'How Curzon's Appetites Grow as the Feast Goes On' – 'Curzon fastens his blackened jaws on Chicherin, gobbling and yelling, cursing him for his strength, demanding we pay every spy a hundred thousand roubles. And we say demand all you like, Raskolnikov has raised the East from the proud British Empire, whose flags are flying downwind in tatters and fluff'.

To her family, Larisa wrote:

> Now that Britain is effectively at war with Afghanistan again, when its borders are soaked in blood, and the Emir can rely on no one but us; when all is put on the table, and working Russia can't refuse to defend the tribespeople, for a hundred years besieged and killed – if we let this moment slip, then we might as well shut up shop here … But how good it is after Genoa and Rapallo to remind the British of their weak spot in the East!

Nikulin was recalled from Herat to Moscow, and the Ambassador to Persia, Fyodor Rothstein (Andrew Rothstein's father), was recalled from Tehran, after failing to negotiate a settlement between the government and the new Communist Party of Iran. But he was replaced in Tehran by another 'red diplomat', the old Bolshevik Boris Shumyatsky. Chicherin had initially considered transferring Raskolnikov there, and Larisa was given a letter from Kabul's Persian Ambassador, Etela-ol-Molk, to deliver to his counterpart in Moscow, recommending him as 'a sincere, peace-loving man, who our country needs at the present time'. But he would serve out the remaining nine months of his term in Kabul, and was merely instructed by Chicherin to tone down his anti-British activities.

Britain's attempt to isolate Russia diplomatically and create an anti-Soviet bloc in the West failed to win international support. According to the son of a Moscow comrade of Raskolnikov's, the journalist Sergei Schulz, writing six years after the end of the Soviet Union, Curzon's gamble served only to expose the capitalist powers' conflicts of interests in Asia and Russia: '"Let us kill, burn and rob in the East. Expel Raskolnikov, or it's war!" Yet even without Raskolnikov, the great Soviet Republic would have survived, to inspire the world against the imperialist plunderers'.[22]

Larisa's car finally arrived in Kabul on 15 May, and next day the Afghan Foreign Minister cabled the Governor of Kandahar informing him of 'the departure of F.F. Raskolnikov, L.M. Reisner and A.A. Baratov from the Embassy'. Three days later, Raskolnikov left her in Kandahar, and she set off on the journey back to Russia, three and a half months pregnant, with a mass of diaries, notes and rough drafts waiting to be turned into a book.

22 Schultz, *Dom isskusstv* (House of the Arts), St Petersburg, 1997, p. 129.

CHAPTER 13

The New Culture

The third person in the car, Arshak Baratov, with his diplomatic bag, was the nineteen-year-old Embassy courier and interpreter Larisa had picked as her bodyguard on the journey from Kandahar to Tashkent. Baratov had made many dangerous postal journeys across Central Asia since he arrived with the mission in Kabul, and he was later interviewed about them in a book of memoirs of the first Soviet '*dipkurery*'. 'You had to see like a hawk, blink and you were dead', he said.[1]

An Armenian, from a poor workers' family in Azerbaijan, he had joined the Party in 1918, at the age of fifteen, and had fought for the next two years with the Red Army in Azerbaijan and Turkestan. Multilingual from birth in Armenian, Azerbaijani, Turkish and Russian, he picked up some Farsi and Arabic at the front, and his exceptional language skills and his bravery had earned him promotion to the Embassy's staff. After weeks of rigorous training at the Commissariat of Foreign Affairs, he joined the mission's caravan at Kushka, and he became friends with Larisa on the ride to Kabul. He remembered her reading the poetry of Lermontov and Schiller to him when they rode together, and her saddlebags stuffed with books.

His instructions from Raskolnikov were to deliver her to Tashkent 'without a scratch', and he recalled barely sleeping on the drive from Kandahar, keeping one eye on his precious diplomatic bag, the other on her, as she sat up late at nights in the *rabats* working on 'Fascists In Asia'. They celebrated his twentieth birthday together in Tashkent, then he saw her onto the train to Moscow, and travelled on to Bukhara with his mail.

Nikulin had returned to Moscow a month earlier, and he joined the crowds who gathered at the Kazan Station to welcome her home, and take her to a party at the House of Soviets. He remembered her emotional reunion with her parents and Igor, and her tears of joy to be back.

Her pregnancy had miraculously survived the journey, and she had a mass of friends to catch up with and writing to do. But it was a different Moscow she returned to. The executions in Petrograd had left their legacy of anger and sadness, and Nadezhda Mandelstam wrote that she was convinced she could have helped to stop them if she had been in Russia. 'Larisa kept coming

---

1 *Sketches of the First Soviet Diplomatic Couriers*, 1973, p. 129.

back again and again to the subject of Gumilyov, and her guilt that she hadn't saved him'.[2]

She had left Russia hungry and impoverished, still in the grip of War Communism, and in the years she had been away, the New Economic Policy had produced astonishing results. Hundreds of state-run businesses had been returned to private ownership, and the defeated bourgeoisie was back. Factories were working again, and speculation had virtually vanished, and anti-Bolshevik emigre and internal emigre writers in Russia were welcoming the policy in their privately funded journals as a return to capitalism.

Workers were calling the NEP the 'New Exploitation of the Proletariat', and she can have found little to like in the new bright 'American' Moscow, with its privately run shops, bars and casinos and commercial sex, where prostitutes huddled outside shops piled with foreign goods, and the new 'Nepmen' and 'red businessmen' trotted past on their horses. This was the world of Kollontai's best-selling stories *Love of Worker Bees*, published that year, which she would almost certainly have read, whose heroines lost so many of the freedoms they had won in the Revolution.

Women suffered most under the new economy, with its layoffs and pay cuts. Despite the Bolsheviks' progressive labour legislation, and the introduction of equal pay, women remained the least skilled and lowest-paid workers in Russia, and they were the first to lose their jobs. State nurseries, canteens and laundries had failed to keep pace with women's employment, and owners of the new private enterprises were reluctant to invest in them, and thousands were forced by unemployment and nursery closures back into the home, or onto the streets.

When recommending the policy to the Party two years earlier, Lenin had called it a temporary retreat – a step back to take a step forward. 'NEP Russia will be socialist Russia!' But Lenin was now slowly dying from his injuries, and Larisa must have found an extraordinary amount of confusion among her comrades about what was socialist about this strange mixed economy, in which the Party called on workers to donate a day's wages each month to an unemployment fund.

'Scope had to be given to the business initiative of the peasants to obtain the raw materials for industry, if only not to die of hunger', Radek wrote. 'Larisa understands this, as we all do. But in her heart, she longs for a heroic breakthrough to the new social order, with arms in hand, and in the summer of 1923 she is uneasy'.

---

2   Nadezhda Mandelstam, *Hope Against Hope*, 1971, p. 109.

The Bolsheviks had declared on coming to power that they had to earn the right to rule from the workers, Russia's new ruling class. Believing that only they were qualified to assess the new policy correctly, she applied to the Moscow party for a teaching job in a factory, and worked on a course of lectures she planned to give there on the history of Russia's strike movement. She told Nikulin she was immersed in the underground literature of 1905, and re-reading Lenin's strike leaflets with a new appreciation of his style. 'The key is his simplicity. It's as if he's having a conversation with people, and they like that'.

She evidently managed to conceal her pregnancy from everyone but her close family. Although past the most dangerous twelve-week mark, she was still at high risk of another miscarriage, and we can only speculate about how she saw her life as a mother, and whether she was still determined to leave Raskolnikov. She was due to give birth in late November, two months before he returned to Moscow, and it is quite likely she was planning to raise the baby on her own.

Thousands of women in Russia, widowed, abandoned or by choice, were bringing up children without men, and single mothers received generous state benefits. Soviet family policy reflected the contradictions of the NEP, encouraging women to give birth after the Civil War, to prevent a demographic catastrophe, while privatising many childcare provisions, with the inevitable cuts and closures. But soviets in flats and factories were fighting to save their nurseries and kindergartens, and opening new ones, and single mothers were making their own communal childcare arrangements.

Kollontai had dreamed of the communal homes of the future, in which childcare and housework would be collectivised, and by the mid–1920s there were over five hundred communes in Moscow, financed by the Soviet, with housing committees elected to manage budgets and allocate domestic tasks, and occupants paying part of their wages into a communal fund. Several model communes opened in the capital for single mothers, with creches, daycare centres, and medical committees responsible for supervising children's health. Most communes however fell far short of Kollontai's communal dreams. Many were just cramped squalid rooms in workers' barracks, separated by curtains, or dormitories in student hostels. Unlike the student communes' free-living fun-loving image, overcrowding and lack of privacy meant men and women generally slept separately, and sex was banned. The emphasis was on comradeship and equality, with money, possessions and clothes held in common. 'Overcoats, shoes and underclothes are at the disposal equally of all communards', declared a group of students from Moscow State University. 'Should it turn out that one prefers to wear his own coat or underwear, this would be seen as a backslide into darkest capitalism, a residue of bourgeois ideology'.[3]

Most of Moscow's communal living spaces were overcrowded ramshackle arrangements like the House of Soviets, in buildings inherited from the old regime, where strangers had been thrown together to share their lives in the first months of the Revolution. Limited kitchen and bathroom space led to endless arguments, but people had to learn to rely on each other, share housework and care for each other's children. Children were seen as the commune's children, to be raised at the general cost, and this collective approach to childcare was at the heart of Kollontai's vision of the more open and generous family life possible under socialism.

Against the advantages of raising a child at the House of Soviets was the Reisners' cramped flat, three small rooms for four people, lavishly appointed but basic, still without gas or geyser to heat the water. Since her six months' rent-free luxury at the Admiralty, the NEP had abolished free accommodation for Party workers, and many smaller municipalised buildings had been returned to their old owners, who had doubled the rents. The Reisners now paid a small monthly rent to the Moscow Soviet, and although the rationing of War Communism had officially ended with the NEP, they were still on the basic 'labour' rations of half a pound of bread a day.

But despite the hunger and discomfort and the exhaustion of early pregnancy, she clearly thrived on the freedom of her life in Moscow. New people had moved into the building, camping in boxrooms and corridors, families with children, workers and students, and she made friends with a young poet and actress called Galina Serebryakova, living in a small room in the basement, whose mother was a well-known concert pianist, and they organised recitals for her in the grand reception hall, now a popular venue for lectures and concerts. She picked up her teaching work at the *rabfaks*, went to writers' meetings and poetry readings, and worked on her factory lectures and *Afghanistan*.

On her Moscow residence permit, she was still registered as married, and couriers had been delivering Raskolnikov's letters from Kabul since she returned. According to their mutual friend the young poet Varlam Shalamov, he wrote hundreds of them to her – 'I never wrote so much in my life', Raskolnikov told him. Excerpts from twenty-five of these letters were published in a 1989 edition of his autobiographical writings, *About Myself and My Times*, filled with passionate expressions of love for her, clearly with the wilder passages edited

---

3   See Lynne Attwood on Soviet housing policy, 1917 to 1991, *Gender and Housing in Soviet Russia. Private Life in the Public Sphere*, 2012.

out. Her letters to him though are unfortunately missing, so unless he was quoting her words back to her, we can only guess what they said. Perhaps she told him to destroy them, fearing they revealed too much and could be used against him in Kabul. Perhaps he destroyed them because he disliked what she wrote.[4]

In his first letter, he thanked her for some coins she had sent him from Herat on her journey back, several of them very valuable. 'Little did you know, silly girl, you were holding in your hands a coin of Alexander of Macedonia! I embrace you passionately, your devoted Fedya'. In another, he told her he reminded himself of her by watching Naletny's newsreels at the Embassy every evening. 'I am very, very sad without you. My love for you is as strong as ever'. Later, he wrote that at a banquet he held for the 'dear Paternos', before they left for Rome, Paterno had raised his glass to the Russians, for welcoming the Italians to Kabul with flowers – 'but sadly, our most precious flower is not with us'. In another long letter, he reminded her of all the reading and writing they had done in Kabul, and of the writers they both loved. 'I'm devouring slim volumes of poetry like oysters. There have been so many good poems in the last two years, one is worth everything by Kipling. Of Gumilyov's posthumous poetry, I like best his "Invitation to a Journey". Shklovsky's memoirs *Sentimental Journey* and *Revolution and the Front* are excellent too'.

It was an interesting choice of writers – her executed former lover, whose poetry he had called 'filth', and Shklovsky, whose *Sentimental Journey* was written abroad, and had been poorly received in Russia.

In an extraordinary and inexplicable about-turn, Gumilyov's *Pillar of Fire* collection had been published three months after his execution, together with new editions of several of his works. Shklovsky had left Russia in 1922, sickened by the executions, and had settled in Berlin with the poets Pasternak and Andrei Bely, where he and Bely both wrote their memoirs of the Revolution. But they were all homesick for Russia, and a year later Gorky arranged for them to return to Moscow, where the three would live for the rest of their lives. Shklovsky became one of Russia's most prolific and influential writers of the 1920s and 30s, publishing biographies and works of literary criticism and writing screenplays. Bely dedicated himself to promoting Soviet culture, and his works were republished in popular mass editions. Pasternak wrote some of his most beautiful works between 1922 and 1924, described by one critic as the 'crown jewels of Russian literature' – his poetry cycle *Themes and Variations*, his love poems *My Sister Life*, and his short story collection *Aerial Ways*.

---

4 Varlam Shalamov, *Vospominaniya* (Memoirs), Moscow, 2011, p. 156. Raskolnikov, *About Myself and My Times*, 1989, pp. 170–95.

Gumilyov had been one of the first of the emigre writers to return. Count Alexei Tolstoy had left Moscow for Paris after the Revolution, vowing to 'put out the eyes of Lenin and Trotsky if they fall into my hands', but he had returned in the spring of 1923 to a hero's welcome. Many writers spent long periods in Germany, just a train ride from the Russian border, and the only foreign country to which Soviet citizens could get visas. Osip Mandelstam stayed in Moscow, but published his second poetry cycle, *Tristia*, in 1922 in Berlin. Some writers settled in Berlin permanently. Others virtually commuted between Russia and Germany, making it hard to know if they were emigres or not.

Yet despite the chaos and poverty and the predicted death of literature, the years after the Civil War saw an extraordinary flowering of new writing in Russia. In 1922, the new Censorship Board, *Glavlit*, had been established under the Commissariat of Education, to clamp down on the more overtly counterrevolutionary works produced by the new private publishing houses of the NEP. But censorship was still virtually non-existent, and the 1920s were a time of huge freedom for writers. A mass of new literary groups and alignments published their journals and manifestos, battling for the purpose and meaning of literature in the new Russia, and Larisa went to an endless round of meetings in Moscow's cafés and workers' and writers' clubs.

The Futurists' journal LEF (Left Front of Art) published the works of Mayakovsky, Shklovsky, Isaac Babel and Eisenstein, and called on writers to join the fight against illiteracy, poverty and ignorance. Mayakovsky became a poet-agitator for the Revolution, travelling the country reading his poems to vast audiences of workers in sports stadiums and factories. 'In my work I'm consciously becoming a newspaper man', he said.

Members of *Proletkult*, workers and intellectuals, saw the new proletarian culture as a 'vehicle for building the socialist society in the spirit of comradely collective labour'. Generously funded by the Commissariat of Education, *Proletkult* had sent writers, film crews and drama collectives to the Civil War fronts, and by 1923 was a mass movement, with a membership of over half a million, which claimed to be the 'leading cultural class organisation of the proletariat', on a level with the Party.

Proletkult sponsored and financed over thirty publications, via the Commissariat of Education, including the *Komsomol* journal *Young Guard*, which published songs, poems and articles from the factories, garrisons and villages, and declared itself 'inseparable from the worker peasant masses'. Closely identified with *Proletkult* were the proletarian poet Demyan Bedny, Vsevolod Ivanov, of the proletarian 'Cosmists', Alexei Gastev, of the 'Smithy' group, the peasant poet Nikolai Klyuev, and Sergei Esenin, of the 'Imaginist' group.

Esenin's application to join the Party in 1918 had been rejected, on the grounds that he was 'totally alien to discipline', and he was a noisy presence in Moscow's avant garde café scene, playing the accordion in his peasant cap and blouse, acting the 'hooligan poet' in the style of Mayakovsky, with his drunken brawls and frequent spells in jail. This was the comic opera peasant Esenin of the city, experimenting with 'images', from the sublime to the grotesque. There was also the authentic Esenin, the poet of the villages, the cornfields and the open steppes, who Gorky called 'Russia's greatest lyrical poet since Pushkin'.

Gumilyov's posthumous works had been published three months before *Glavlit* was established, and were still in print and discussed at meetings. And despite widespread condemnation of Akhmatova's poetry after his execution, in 1922 she had brought out her *Anno Domini* collection, her haunting account of staying in her beloved St Petersburg to share its fate after her friends emigrated.

'I'm so grateful to her', Larisa wrote to Rozhdestvensky in Petrograd, after reading her 'Everything is Plundered' cycle:

> She has put into her work all my contradictions from which there seemed no escape ... Her poems delight and disturb me, like returning to a long abandoned house, at once loved and hated. The floors are littered with the pages of good books, scattered sheets of old letters, comfortable beautiful things, and the special smell of a cultured elegant life run wild ... She has opened up old wounds with pain and tears, and has closed them forever ...[5]

There was the high art of Akhmatova, and the sentimental mass-produced poetry of the NEP – 'written for the *nouveaux riches*, smelling of lavender-bags', Larisa told Rozhdestvensky.

The most popular works produced by the new commercial publishing houses were Western-style adventure and 'red detective' novels, about brave revolutionaries defeating capitalist plots. Nikulin followed his *14 Months in Afghanistan* with a series of Civil War dramas and political thrillers, including *Not By Accident*, *Ataman Drunkenness*, *Diplomatic Mystery*, and *Secrets of the Safe*, all of them later made into successful films with his screenplays. The bestseller of 1923 was *Mess Mend, or A Yankee in Petrograd*, by Marietta Shaginyan, who wrote under the name 'Jim Dollar', about a group of Russian ex-aristocrats and Western capitalists who plot to assassinate Lenin and the Soviet govern-

---

5   *SW*, p. 549.

ment, and are foiled by members of a secret American workers' organisation. This too was later turned into a popular film, inspired by the images on the cover, a photomontage of scenes from the story by the artist Alexander Rodchenko.

The film industry took off in the years of the NEP. Closed studios reopened, many reprivatised, and hundreds of new cinemas were built, even in the remote provinces, and were invariably packed. By 1923 there were eight-nine cinemas in Moscow and seventy in Petrograd, where the seventeen-year-old Conservatoire student Dmitry Shostakovich was getting his training as a composer, working to support his family as a movie pianist. The main features always opened with newsreels, and audiences across Russia and Central Asia were watching Naletny's films of Larisa and Raskolnikov with Amanullah in Kabul, and Afghanistan's dancing tribespeople.

Almost half the films shown in the 1920s were American. Russia's favourite Hollywood stars of the silent screen were Douglas Fairbanks and Mary Pickford, closely followed by Charlie Chaplin, Buster Keaton and Harold Lloyd, and the huge profits from their pictures subsidised the first Soviet films.

Einsenstein's first full-length feature, 'Glumov's Diary', opened in Moscow in 1923, produced by the *Proletkult* First Workers' Theatre, where he and Meyerhold had both worked after the Revolution. Most of the new Soviet films were fast-moving American-inspired action comedies and adventure stories with a revolutionary message, like 'Mess Mend'. The hits of 1924 were Lev Kuleshov's 'The Extraordinary Adventures of Mr West in the Land of the Bolsheviks', and Yakov Protozanov's masterpiece 'Aelita Queen of Mars'. In the first, a Harold Lloyd-style parody of an American Western, full of car chases, cops and robbers and circus acrobatics, the bumbling Texan Mr West arrives in Moscow with his cowboy sidekick on a mission to civilise the Bolsheviks, and is kidnapped by a criminal capitalist gang. He is then rescued by sturdy Bolshevik soldiers, and the film ends with Mr West hanging Lenin's portrait in his office. In 'Aelita', from Alexei Tolstoy's science fiction classic of the same name, the hero and his friend blast off into space in a homemade rocket to organise a socialist revolution on Mars. The action is set in a fantastic Martian landscape, with a cast of thousands dressed in spectacular Futuristic costumes. The earthlings meet the workers, toiling in underground slave labour camps, living in bunkers next to their machines, then are taken to the 'Tower of Radiant Energy', to meet Mars's cruel ruler and his bride Aelita, where the hero and Aelita fall in love, and together proclaim the new 'Martian Union of Soviet Socialist Republics'.

The Hollywood sensation of 1925 was the swashbuckling 'Thief of Bagdhad', starring the athletic Douglas Fairbanks, battling terrifying monsters, climbing a magic rope, and flying on a magic carpet. Asked in a writers' questionnaire that year where she would like to live, Larisa wrote 'Nowhere, on a magic carpet'.

The Revolution was dissolving the boundaries between literature and film, and the old literary hierarchy that had put poetry and fiction above journalism. Her writings from the front pioneered a new kind of literary political journalism, in which writers were creators of life, directly involved in events and reporting back.

Her old friend Mikhail Koltsov, now on the editorial board of *Pravda*, a favourite of Trotsky's and Lenin's, loved by millions in Russia for his satirical essays lampooning capitalists, bureaucrats and NEP black marketeers, with many admirers abroad, had started his stellar career as a journalist reporting from the Civil War battlefields, and he wrote of the lasting influence of her 'Letters' on his writing, with their combination of hard reportage and personal reflection – and 'her sharp bright images, ticking like little clocks, bursting with poetry'.[6]

In her frontline classes, she had encouraged the sailors to turn their experiences into poetry and fiction, and the Civil War produced a new generation of novelists, most of them young workers and peasants who had never written before, dashing down their stories between battles, often delivering the manuscripts straight from the front in their army uniforms, writing with a rough eye-witness power and poetry that spoke to millions of readers.

Many of these works too were later turned into popular films, rarely watched now in Russia, where the books are being thrown out of the libraries. In the West, the new fiction of the Revolution is virtually unknown, and is conventionally dismissed as crude propaganda for the masses written by uneducated workers, socialist realist potboilers, with one-dimensional characters and unbelievable plots.

Socialist realism had its origins in the great romantic humanist tradition of Tolstoy and Gorky. As the first and greatest of the socialist realists, Gorky believed writers should stay as close as possible to the reality of people's lives in the Revolution, exploring the hopes and passions and inner struggles of those making the new society with a minimum of moralising analysis or political commentary. In the words of the Civil War novelist Alexander Fadeev, 'Ideas should be conveyed through their living bearers, in their mutual relations, in the flaws and contradictions of their characters, in their flesh and blood'.

Fadeev's novel *The Surge* became a Soviet classic, a touching account of his experiences fighting with a group of Red partisans in the Far East, bat-

---

6 Mikhail Koltsov, 'Milyi sputnik' (Dear Companion), *LRRC*, pp. 113–16.

tling to win the hearts and minds of the peasants in the remote villages. Vsevolod Ivanov's novels *Partisans* and *Armoured Train* are vivid accounts of his years fighting as a young partisan in Siberia. *The Iron Flood*, by Alexander Serafimovich, recounts an incident when his ragged band of volunteers in Ukraine led peasants from a village encircled by Yudenich's Cossacks in a desperate escape across the steppe, and avoided death by joining up with a unit of the Red Army, and submitting to its iron discipline. Konstantin Fedin, who fought the Czechs on the Volga, delivers an uncompromising message against fraternising with the enemy in his *Cities and Years*, about a spineless intellectual who fails to find his place in the Revolution, betrays his lover, and helps a counter-revolutionary escape Soviet justice.

Women's liberation comes to the countryside in the story 'Maria the Bolshevik', by the peasant teacher Alexander Neverov, whose heroine learns to read, sets up a *Zhenotdel* in her village, and leaves her family and husband to fight at the front. The Futurist poet Boris Lavrenyov, who fought as a commander of an armoured train in Central Asia, modelled the heroine of his best-selling novel *The Forty-First* on a young woman partisan and sharp-shooter he met in Turkestan. She has seen hundreds of her comrades die, and has never missed her target, and misses for the first time with her forty-first, a White officer. She becomes his guard, and marches him in a convoy of prisoners across the desert to the Aral Sea, and they end up living on an island together and falling in love. But he soon reveals his bourgeois attitude to women by trying to possess her. And when he tricks her and tries to escape, she is forced to shoot him, finally fulfilling her orders.

The most popular of the Civil War novels, the inspiration for countless poems and plays and a blockbuster film, was Dmitry Furmanov's *Chapaev*, published in 1923, a thrilling adventure story and documentary portrait of the charismatic Urals Cossack commander Vasily Chapaev, whose Political Commissar Furmanov had been in the battles with Kolchak. Three years later, Isaac Babel published his masterpiece of war journalism, his *Red Cavalry* stories, drawn from his diaries of fighting as a Jewish intellectual with the First Cavalry Army in the war with Poland.

After the Civil War, there were novels about workers' experiences of returning from the front to rebuild their shattered family lives and wrecked factories. The first and finest of the 'industrial novels', published in 1925, was *Cement*, by Fyodor Gladkov, who had fought with the Red Army in the Crimea, the poignant tale of a soldier who comes home to find his cement factory in ruins, and his wife hardened by suffering. 'Everything's all mixed up now, love will have to be arranged differently', she tells him, and he must mobilise his comrades to get their factory going, and fight to win her back. In an essay in the arts magazine

October, the literary critic Zhores Elsberg showed interestingly how the novel was influenced by Larisa's language and imagery – 'with her poetry of everyday life, and her enormous genuine optimism'.[7]

She went to the meetings of all the different literary groups, and joined their discussions, encouraging and criticising the new writers, as she had as editor of *Rudin*. But she was never a follower of programmes or platforms, or the schematic formulations of *Proletkult* or the Futurists. She was closest in spirit to the writers published in *Red Virgin Soil*, which had brought out several of her 'Letters from the Front' and her first pieces from Afghanistan.

Three hundred pages long, bold and poetic as its title, *Red Virgin Soil* had been launched the previous summer, with the personal backing of Gorky, Lenin and Lenin's wife Nadezhda Krupskaya, modelled ambitiously on the 'thick' literary journals of the nineteenth century, to keep the great traditions of Russian literature alive in the commercial culture of the NEP, and show that highbrow writing could still move and excite people. *Red Virgin Soil* was now the largest selling literary publication in Russia, with an enthusiastic readership in the new intelligentsia, in the army, the *rabfaks* and the *Komsomol*. Gorky himself, father of Soviet literature, had been living abroad for the last eight months, and his successor in Russia was widely seen as the journal's chief editor, the Marxist literary critic Alexander Voronsky, who became good friends with Larisa.

Under Voronsky's editorship, *Red Virgin Soil* encouraged new talents, and published original works by some of Russia's finest writers, communist and non-communist, including six complete novels. There were essays by Lunacharsky on art and the theatre, translations of Marcel Proust and the philosophers Henri Bergson and Rabindranath Tagore, articles on economic theory by Bukharin and the late Rosa Luxemburg, essays on international politics in the 'From Abroad' section, edited by Radek, and a large popular science section, edited by Gorky's science editor on *Chronicle*, the biologist Professor Timiryazev.

The journal was consistently attacked by *Proletkult* hardliners for publishing non-communist writers, and Lunacharsky was increasingly distancing himself from its members' more rabid pronouncements on art and literature. 'In the name of tomorrow, we will burn Raphael, destroy museums, trample the flowers of art!' the *Proletkult* poet Vladimir Kirillov said in 1917. Arguments between writers were often leading to abuse and mudslinging, and in the sum-

---

7 Elsberg's essay, published in 1927, 'Sravneniya i metafory kak klassovaya, obrazovaya otsenka obiecta pisaniya' (Similes and Metaphors. A Class-based Assessment of Literary Imagery), was republished online in 2018 by the University of Lausanne.

mer of 1920, the Party had issued a statement in *Pravda* serving notice against *Proletkult* or any other literary group claiming the right to proletarian orthodoxy.

Lunacharsky, Bukharin and Trotsky all endorsed the principle of literary diversity. Disputes between writers were not to be 'won' by one side or another, Bukharin wrote, there must be room for discussion and differences; the clash between communist and non-communist values was a 'valuable molecular process', which would produce the new proletarian culture of the future. Trotsky spoke out sharply against literature being used for propaganda purposes. Poetry and fiction were not suited to being didactic, he argued, and he coined the term 'fellow-travellers' for writers like the Serapion Brothers, who were sympathetic to the Bolsheviks, but wanted to produce high quality work free from Party scrutiny. (The group included Shklovsky and the novelists Boris Pilnyak and Marietta Shaginyan – several women were members). Trotsky wrote especially warmly of Pilnyak's truthful observations of village life in his sensationally successful novel *Naked Year*, published in 1922 in *Red Virgin Soil*, about the mystical 'elemental' revolution in the villages, based on his travels around the Moscow countryside after October in search of food.

Larisa was a Party writer, who gave her full support to the new proletarian literature of the Revolution, and her works were filled with 'Party spirit'. But like the fellow-travellers, she often exposed the gaps between slogans and reality in her writing.

Government policies in the 1920s were focused on transforming the country's largely agrarian economy into one to rival that of the West. 'Communism will be Soviet power plus the electrification of the whole country', Lenin said, and the Futurists wrote hymns to the new age of machines, speed and electricity. 'We must snatch God's thunderbolts from him!' Mayakovsky wrote in his play *Mystery Bouffe*, staged by Meyerhold in 1918 to celebrate the first anniversary of the Revolution.

In 1920, the State Commission for the Electrification of Russia, GOELRO, had been established, to bring 'enlightenment' to the masses, and in the spring of 1923, the All-Russian Exhibition of Agriculture and Light Industry had opened in the capital, to showcase GOELRO's achievements. Covering the sixty-acre site of the Neskuchny Park in central Moscow were a hundred and ninety pavilions from all over Russia, designed by some of the country's finest architects and artists, displaying tractors, farm and factory machinery, a wind-turbine, even a working hydroelectric power station. Larisa was commissioned by *Izvestiya* to report on the exhibition, and she joined the thousands who flocked to see 'this miracle of technology and progress, this dazzling vision of Russia's tomorrow, the Russia of yesterday's Red Army rations, destroyed towns, dead factories and deserted ports, dreaming of electricity'. But she was less interested in the machines and technology than in 'the millions of workers who have built this island of wealth and power, whose lives have barely recovered from the inhuman sacrifices of Revolution, war and toil, who know that this banner of the USSR fluttering in the sky represents only a thousandth part of the creative energy in its iron body'.

Within a decade, all written works would be required to carry the *Glavlit* stamp, forcing journalists to cover up problematic issues and bend the truth. Yet even under the relaxed censorship of 1923, her article apparently failed to project the correct image of Soviet power to the world, and it was published only forty years later, in the magazine *Literary Russia*, almost as a period piece, when the huge gothic Stalinist pavilions of the Exhibition of Economic Achievements were already a permanent fixture in Moscow.[8]

Most of the new writers' groups had their headquarters in the former home of the millionaire industrialist Savva Morozov, near the House of Soviets on Vozdvizhenka Street. The *Komsomol* and the *Proletkult*-sponsored October group published their journals *Young Guard* and *On Guard* there, and she regularly attended their meetings in its chandeliered oak-panelled hall.

She must have been an incongruous figure at these gatherings of soldiers, workers, rabfak students and *Komsomol* members, many still in their teens, most of them men. The nineteen-year-old poet and playwright Mark Kolosov, editor of *Young Guard*, described the young writers showing their disdain for bourgeois culture by tramping mud into the hall and throwing their cigarette ends on the floor, while she sat at her seat by the window, with a bulging briefcase on her knee, frowning and smiling and scribbling notes. The fashion then for women Party members was factory workers' overalls, or a version of the Civil War uniform of leather jacket, boots and cap, and she didn't look the part, he wrote, in her smart suits and blouses.

The *Komsomol* journalist Lev Sosnovsky was dazzled by this legendary commissar and journalist, and described her as modest and unassuming in the discussions, praising and criticising the Young Guardists, and defending them against the On Guardists. But like others, he distrusted her bourgeois appearance and fancy prose style. For Sosnovsky, her Afghanistan writings were her 'third test': 'Wasn't this young woman being drawn towards exoticism? Wasn't she turning her face from our workaday prose and Russian greyness? Weren't her articles and essays merely her private escape into foreign lands and peoples and "beautiful writing?"'[9]

---

8 *Literaturnaya Rossiya* (Literary Russia), 1965, no. 5.
9 Mark Kolosov, 'Larisa Reisner i *Molodaya Gvardia*' (Larisa Reisner and *Young Guard*), LRRC, pp. 169–75. Lev Sosnovsky, *People of Our Time*, 1927, pp. 95–6.

But by then she had turned against them herself, and was more interested in the new writers being published in *Red Virgin Soil*. That summer the talk of Moscow was its publication of Yury Libedinsky's novel *A Week*, based on his experiences in the Civil War as a Political Commissar in the Urals, a frank and controversial account, full of lyricism and psychological complexity, of the dilemmas facing the Bolshevik soviet in a village of peasants murderously hostile to the Revolution.

Libedinsky first met Larisa in July, in the writers' village of Kuntsevo outside Moscow, where he was on holiday with his wife and children, and the Reisners had rented the next dacha. She came round the afternoon they arrived, he wrote, 'and as she entered our wicket gate in her simple cotton dress and straw hat, followed by her mother, who was carrying a little dog, we were entranced by her delicacy and beauty, like a classical goddess or Nordic Valkyrie, and I felt it would be an extraordinary joy to talk to her'. They talked for hours, and she hotly defended *A Week* and *Red Virgin Soil* against the attacks of *Proletkult* and the *On Guardists*. 'And when I ventured to say I found parts of her Afghan pieces overwritten, she agreed and thumped the table. "That's all behind me now, I'm going to write differently from now on, more simply!"'[10]

In Moscow, Libedinsky introduced her to Dmitry Furmanov, author of *Chapaev*, and their fellow activists in the Moscow Association of Proletarian Writers (*MAPP*), who held their meetings in the Vozdvizhenka Street building. And that August, the different groups all buried their differences to welcome three young Ukrainian worker poets, Mikhail Golodny, Ivan Yasny and Mikhail Svetlov, who had arrived in the capital to study at its Art *rabfak*.

They read their works at a meeting chaired by *Young Guard*'s editor Mark Kolosov and the editor of *On Guard*, the poet Alexander Bezymensky, who recalled her making for her usual seat by the window as the hall filled with workers and poetry lovers. Then the Ukrainians read their poems, which were warmly applauded, especially Golodny's discussion with his machine, which was about to be replaced:

> She tells me her secret pain,
> And in my heart I understand
> My iron sister's sorrow.

After they finished, Larisa led Bezymensky discreetly aside, and asked him to carry out some 'battle orders', which some might find amusing, but were in fact very serious. To her annoyance, he burst out laughing when he heard what they were.

---

10   Libedinsky, *Sovremenniki (Contemporaries)*, Moscow, 1958, pp. 42–4.

At the party the next evening for the poets, she arrived early, her briefcase more bulging than ever, and asked Bezymensky to find an empty room in the building where she could meet the three in private. 'They arrived, and she said, "Comrade poets, your poems are wonderful, but your clothes aren't smart enough!" Then opening her briefcase, she took out three pairs of new trousers and two pairs of shoes. "Accept these as a gift, I'll be mortally offended if you refuse. I'm sure you know what real comradeship is, in big things and small. Don't worry, I've something to discuss with Comrade Sasha while you make yourselves presentable"'.

Bezymensky ended his story with three observations:
1. The poets did not reject the clothes.
2. My assignment from Larisa Mikhailovna had been to discover their shoe sizes.
3. She couldn't find shoes big enough to fit Svetlov's feet.[11]

By the end of August, she could evidently no longer conceal her pregnancy, and Raskolnikov wrote to thank her for finally allowing him to tell people in Kabul. 'I think of you always. My love for you is boundless'.

Then in the first week of September, she was in hospital for a week with unspecified complications. But before her cable reached him in Kabul, the Afghan government was informed that she had died. 'I couldn't think why everyone was greeting me with such tragic faces, and they weren't asking about you', he wrote to her. 'Five interpreters were rushed in, and the diplomatic corps met to decide how to break the news to me. You can imagine the panic. Our darling *marchese* was in floods of tears. But by the time it was all cleared up, *tout le monde* decided you would live a long long time. I miss you desperately'.

His letter arrived a week after she was rushed to hospital with her third miscarriage. Scarce medical resources meant that miscarriages had to be managed without pain relief, and late miscarriages are particularly dangerous and devastating, physically and emotionally, and apparently she knew the baby was a boy. But in her cable to Raskolnikov she insisted that no one in Kabul must be told. 'My stomach churns when people ask "How is Madame?"' he wrote to her, 'and following your policy of pretending everything is fine, I say, "Thank you, she is well, I look forward to being a father soon"'.

It is hard to see why she felt the need to keep up this pretence. But she must have had to accept that illness, constant travelling and her impermanent living conditions had wrecked her chances to have a child. And with nothing now to keep them together, she wrote to tell him she had filed for divorce.

---

11   Alexander Bezymensky, 'Vot chto okazalas v portfele' (What Was in the Briefcase), *LRRC*, pp. 176–9.

It was clearly a long anguished letter, filled with grief and anger, and their friend Varlam Shalamov felt deeply sorry for the rejected Raskolnikov. 'He went out of his mind', he wrote, 'rushing around Kabul, forgetting diplomatic etiquette, weeping in meetings'.

In his reply, to 'my darling, my only Larunechka', he defended himself against her accusations of his 'cruelty and coldness', and begged her to give him another chance – 'if not for my sake, then for the sake my poor ageing mother':

> People can't always account for themselves when they're together all the time. Things said in the heat of the moment shouldn't be taken seriously ...
>
> You write of our baby as though I was his murderer. Neither of us was to blame, Mouse. As you said, it's a miracle he survived the terrible journey back to Russia ...
>
> I'm putting it down in black and white, so that there's no misunderstanding, I never wanted a divorce, and I don't want one now. In Kabul and Jalalabad, I said only that we should think about it, and that a separation would be a test of our feelings. And what it has shown me is that we're not simply chance travellers, but true husband and wife ...
>
> I know there are men far cleverer than me, but you'll never find one so passionately devoted to you, who loves you so deeply after five years of marriage ... Our love will be as it was when I get back.

He went on to hope that his letter would reach her directly, 'without unwanted readers', from either the Afghan or Soviet authorities.

> There's no question the Party trusts me completely, but several of your letters to me have been crudely opened. According to the law of course, diplomatic mail mustn't be opened. But there are criminals who abuse their power to satisfy their curiosity, and this grieves me, and makes me hold back from expressing my most intimate feelings. I've begun to distrust even my closest comrades who take these letters back to my divine wife.

A week later, he wrote to tell her he had suffered what the doctor had diagnosed as the symptoms of poisoning, and the Afghan cook had been sacked. 'Please don't mention it to anyone though, and please don't worry about me, it's just a storm in a teacup. For me such things are mere episodes in the sea of life. Remember how calm I was when there was the attempt on our lives at Paghman?'

This was followed by a letter from the Embassy accountant, Vladimir Bazhenov: 'F.F. is better thank god, but he can't sleep or eat, and he speaks of you twenty times a day. He keeps saying "Is Larisa Mikhailovna thinking of me?" Otherwise all is well here. Don't forget us. Your faithful servant, Bazhenov'.

She waited until he was fully recovered to send him the divorce papers, and in his reply to her 'fateful document', he thanked her for 'the sensitive way you considered my feelings:'

> For the benefit of the outside world, we're parting by mutual agreement, although we both know you're discarding me like an old shoe ... So many times you said you wanted a divorce, and our love would reach new heights of happiness – after I left prison in England, in Astrakhan, Baku, Anzali. How can you forget the golden threads forged in the Civil War that still connect us?
>
> You write of the 'flabby stagnation' of life in Kabul, which was particularly hard for people like us with sensitive natures. But was it really so bad? Didn't we prove in those difficult hothouse years that we could be partners for the rest of our lives? Decide as you wish darling, I don't want to force myself on you. But please meet me off the train when I get back. It would be too painful to give the divorce papers to anyone else.

Perhaps he was still hoping she would have a dramatic change of heart and they would be reconciled at the station. But by then she was already planning her next journey without him.

For the past nine months, headlines in the Soviet press had been reporting on the mass strikes sweeping Germany, which seemed to be bringing the country close to another revolution, and in October she applied to Radek, Secretary of the Comintern, for a post in Berlin.

'She needed to escape from her unresolved doubts about Russia, and breathe the air of revolution again', Radek wrote.

> Her application pleased me greatly. Just as the German working class could get no clear idea of what was going on in Russia, workers in Russia saw the proletarian struggle in Germany in oversimplified, schematic terms. I knew that Larisa, better than anyone else, could make the link between the two proletarian armies. For she wasn't simply a contemplative artist, she was a fighting artist, who saw the struggle from inside, and could convey its dynamics.

CHAPTER 14

Berlin and Hamburg

Germany's new alliance with Soviet Russia had produced a major international crisis. In January 1923, nine months after the Treaty of Rapallo was signed, normalising trade and diplomatic relations between the two countries, seventy thousand French and Belgian troops marched into Germany to seize its unpaid war reparations ordered by Versailles, occupying the mines and factories in the Ruhr Valley, the centre of Germany's coalmining and steel industries, and throwing out the German managers.

Backed by industrialists with assets in the Ruhr, and by its new Soviet allies, the government declared a policy of 'passive resistance', ordering workers to refuse to produce goods for the invaders, guaranteeing to subsidise the strikes with state funds. As paper money was issued desperately to the strikers, inflation soared, firms went bankrupt, and the Mark collapsed. The occupying forces brought their own workers to the Ruhr to replace the strikers, and introduced the death penalty for sabotage. Paramilitary groups sprang up, assassinating the hated occupiers, commandeering trains and blowing up railway lines, and the new Nazi Party capitalised on the anger and instability by blaming Jews, foreigners and communists for bringing the German people to their knees.

In September, the new pro-French Chancellor Gustav Stresemann (Radek called him the 'German Kerensky') ended the policy of passive resistance, and imposed a state of emergency. The government guaranteed to pay France and Belgium their war reparations, and strikers were ordered back to work to keep industry and transport going for the foreign managers, who pocketed the profits.

That autumn, as the fate of the Weimar Republic hung in the balance, the Comintern had to give guidance to Germany's small new Communist Party. Radek urged caution. As the Comintern's leading authority on the country that was to spearhead revolutions across the capitalist world, who had helped to establish the Party in 1918, he saw little prospect for revolution in Germany until communists had drastically increased their numbers. He had lived through the Party's near suicide in 1918, and he had been deeply affected by the senseless martyrdom of Luxemburg and Liebknecht, and he feared the Comintern had failed to learn the lessons of the premature *putsch*.

In his Comintern reports, he described the Ruhr occupation as the start of a new bitter phase of the class struggle in Germany. 'Finance capitalism will inevitably degenerate into fascism when its rule is threatened', he wrote in the

German communist paper *Red Flag* that summer. Unlike the cautious liberal Social Democrats in government, the fascists were drawing the masses into politics, he wrote, the demobilised soldiers and unemployed workers who had left the party in disgust after 1914, and were seeing the Nazis as the solution to the injustices in their lives. He argued that the Communist Party must work with the widest possible range of political organisations, even the Social Democrats, to build a powerful united offensive against fascism, and that communists would gain strength and numbers in the process.

He had first made the case for a united front anti-fascist strategy in Germany at the Comintern's Second Congress in 1920, to which he had unilaterally invited members of Germany's alternative Hamburg Communist Workers' Party, and Lenin spoke of 'Radek's vile spirit of intrigue', and called for him to be expelled from the Executive. But he soon regretted this. 'Radek predicted how it would all turn out in Germany', he said. 'At the time I was very angry with him, and accused him of defeatism, but in all the main arguments he was correct'.

Trotsky would publish his groundbreaking works on the anti-fascist struggle in the 1930s. Victor Serge saw Radek as virtually alone in the Comintern in the 1920s in acknowledging the fascist threat (he evidently hadn't read Larisa's 'Fascists In Asia'). According to Serge, communists in Russia and Germany 'tended to see the Weimar government and the National Socialists representing two varieties of fascism, and the rise of Hitler and Mussolini as a piece of reactionary buffoonery that would soon die away and open the path to revolution'.

Even as the Fourth Congress of the Comintern opened in October 1922, three days after Mussolini's coup, Zinoviev was using his authority as Chair to argue that fascism represented the 'death agony of capitalism', and exposed the 'fake democracy of the social democratic parties'. It was only as the Congress drew to a close that Radek brought some sanity to proceedings, and delegates voted for his united front resolution.

In the Comintern's debates on the German crisis the following autumn, he again called for a realistic assessment of the Communist Party's forces. Zinoviev argued that with the necessary determination, communists could use the social collapse to lead a showdown between workers and state, setting off uprisings across Germany which would spread to the rest of the world. Hugely outvoted by Zinoviev and the majority, Radek agreed against his better judgement to back an uprising in early November in Dresden, capital of 'Red Saxony', where socialists and communists held the balance of power in the state parliament. This would be the base from which to arm Dresden's sixty thousand workers reported to be ready to fight.

Since Larisa was bilingual in the language and could pass for German, she was the ideal choice for him to send to Germany, and he appointed her to work illegally in Berlin, as a liaison officer between its Comintern agents and Dresden's communists. He provided her with a false German passport, in the name of a Magdalina Unschlicht, who was leaving Moscow to work as a secretary in Berlin, and he gave her a crash course in the techniques of underground work. But he saw her main asset as her pen, and he arranged with *Pravda*, *Izvestiya* and *Red Paper* for her to report back on events as they unfolded.

In the second week of October, she left Moscow with him by train for Dresden, where the Comintern agent Solomon Dridzo (known by his Comintern name A. Lozovsky) found her so focused on guarding her cover as to be unreachable, and he had to smuggle a message to her through Radek: 'Why do you give us no masonic sign of your existence? In view of your future activities in Berlin, I need to see you urgently. Please phone me or visit. Greetings to the Star of Afghanistan, who suddenly appeared in the grey sky of the Comintern, and has just as suddenly vanished'.[1]

On 21 October, she left Radek in Dresden and set off on her own for Berlin, arriving soon after General Muller's troops surrounded Dresden's parliament building and deposed the socialist government. As Radek had predicted, workers lacked the power or numbers to rally a general strike, and the insurrection had to be aborted. Three days later, in a last desperate show of resistance, fourteen hundred workers and communists in Hamburg, Germany's second largest city, the largest port in Europe, occupied twenty-six police stations, and seized their weapons.

For two days and nights, they battled with the armed soldiers and police of the *Reichswehr*. In the poor working-class districts of Barmbeck and Schiffbeck, where communists had major support, residents brought food to the insurgents, built barricades, and demonstrated with banners saying 'Long Live Soviet Germany!' 'Long Live the World Revolution!' But they were hopelessly outnumbered. As in Dresden, Radek's calls for a general strike in the city were rejected, and within twenty-four hours, over a hundred fighters had been killed, with thousands more injured and arrested.

On 25 October, the sixth anniversary of the Bolshevik Revolution, Radek had no choice but to approve the Communist Party's decision to retreat. A day later, he joined Larisa in Berlin.

She was living there under her Magdalina Unschlicht alias, lodging with a worker's family she became very close to, whose granddaughter she would take out to play in the Tiergarten. It was a bitterly cold winter, and life in inflation-ravaged Berlin was desperately hard, and much had changed in the

---

1 *SW*, p. 548.

city since she had lived there as a child. But she immediately felt at home there. To her parents she wrote:

> My darlings, of course I'm alive and well. I'm eating into this country, which feels so familiar to me when people sing the *Internationale*, or I visit our old street in Zehlendorf ... Send letters to M. Unschlicht. Remember, no one must know who I am, or I'm done for. Have no fears about me, I feel wonderful.[2]

She begged Radek to send her to Hamburg, to report on people's lives after the uprising, she wrote. 'But my "boss" has ordered me to stay in Berlin and not touch my pen for a week, and to study everything that's dead and alive in the country'.

She spent hours in the library of the Soviet diplomatic legation at Unter Den Linden, 'devouring Luxemburg, Mehring, Kautsky, and all the best that's been written about Germany', and she worked with Radek smuggling Soviet funds into Hamburg, via the communist leader Ernst Thälmann, who with thousands of others had gone into hiding in the city. She attended sessions of the Reichstag, and she went to meetings of the ruling Social Democratic Party, and to Communist Party meetings in the poor suburbs, and she spoke to the new army of the starving unemployed on the streets, reporting back to Berlin's Russian Comintern agents, who 'lived in a tight-knit group', Radek wrote, 'with little opportunity to meet the masses'.

> Larisa lived the life of the masses, who were as close to her as the workers in Petersburg or the sailors of the Baltic Fleet ... She sat in hospitals packed with exhausted working women, she stood in the dole queues and food queues, meeting crowds of the unemployed, trying to buy a bit of bread for millions of Marks ...

Unlike Radek's frequently unflattering judgements of his comrades, his love and admiration for her are evident in everything he wrote about her, and what had started as a working relationship quickly deepened into a romantic one.

Radek was one of the most popular and erudite of the Bolsheviks, a lifelong rebel and non-conformist, a member of the first Bolshevik government, and the Party's most brilliant journalist, author of hundreds of articles for the international socialist press on Russian and European politics, art and literature,

---

2 *SW*, p. 551.

written in Russian, Czech, German, French, English, and his native Polish – although according to Victor Serge, 'Radek spoke only one language, his own, the accent he used to express himself in all the others being so incredibly bad'.

He was born Karol Sobelson, in 1885, to a family of middle-class Polish-speaking Jews in the town of Lemburg,[3] a hundred miles south of Lublin, in the area of Galicia then under Austro-Hungarian rule. His father died when he was four, and he and his older sister were raised by their mother, who worked to support them as a primary-school teacher. He adopted his name Radek at his Kraków boarding-school when he was thirteen, from the working-class hero of the Polish novel *The Labours of Sisyphus*, who fights with his friends to resist the Russification of his school. Three years later, he was expelled for leading a student occupation, and he studied at home for his law exams to Kraków University. There he discovered the works of Marx, and he neglected his law studies to concentrate on his Marxist studies and his journalism, and his campaigning work with Kraków's bakers, hatters and construction workers.

In 1902 he joined the Polish Social Democratic Party, and in 1904 he fled Poland for Switzerland to escape arrest. He lived for the next year first with Lenin and his associates in the Swiss capital, Berne, then in Zurich, a popular destination for exiled revolutionaries, where he discovered Trotsky's writings on permanent revolution, and the works of Rosa Luxemburg.

Luxemburg had written her doctoral thesis at Zurich University seven years earlier, and her writings on imperialism and the mass strike would be a lifelong inspiration to him. Luxemburg later developed a deep dislike for him, and accused him of embezzling Polish party funds, warning her German comrades, 'Radek belongs to the whore category. Anything can happen with him around, it's best to keep him at a distance'. But for several years they had a friendly correspondence, and when strikes and riots broke out in Poland in 1905, she provided him with a false passport to travel to Warsaw.

He spoke at demonstrations and factory meetings there against the occupying Russian forces, and published articles in the underground Polish press, and in April 1906 he was arrested, with Luxemburg and her lover Leo Jogiches. After six months in Warsaw's Pawiak Jail, he left Poland for Austria, and for the next years he was based there and in Germany, living usually in dire poverty, mak-

---

3 After 1918, Lemburg became part of the new Polish Republic, and was named Lwów. In 1939, the town became part of the Soviet Union, and was named Lvov. In 1941, Lvov was occupied by the Nazis, and became Lemburg again. In 1944, Lemburg was liberated by the Red Army, and reverted to Lvov. Since the end of the Soviet era, Lvov has been part of the new independent state of Ukraine, known by its Ukrainian name Lviv.

ing frequent trips to Scandinavia, France and Switzerland, speaking at anti-war and anti-conscription meetings, agitating for mass strikes and revolution.

In Berlin, he was part of the lively crowd of revolutionaries Larisa had described meeting as a child at the Liebknechts. And he was in Berlin in August 1914, at the outbreak of war, where he worked underground with Liebknecht and Luxemburg and the small anti-war minority in the Social Democratic Party. A month later, he was deported from Germany and returned to neutral Switzerland, where he rejoined Lenin and the Bolsheviks in Berne, mobilising opposition to the war.

He was one of hundreds of exiled revolutionaries who joined the Bolsheviks in the July Days of 1917, and his knowledge of Germany made him invaluable to the new government when he returned to Petrograd in October. He was appointed to a key post at the Commissariat of Foreign Affairs, in charge of frontline propaganda and fraternisation work with German troops, and in January 1918, he joined Trotsky's negotiating team at Brest-Litovsk. There he distributed anti-war leaflets to German soldiers under the noses of their officers, while simultaneously acting as a semi-official liaison agent between the Bolsheviks and the German High Command, leading to rumours that he was negotiating secret deals with Germany – despite his enormous German police files describing him as 'a most dangerous individual, who will stop at nothing to destroy Germany'.

At the Seventh Party Congress in March, he spoke for the Left Communists, who opposed Lenin and the majority in rejecting Germany's predatory peace terms. But with all hopes still pinned on revolution in Germany, he was still irreplaceable, despite his oppositionist views, and in October he was appointed Vice Commissar of Foreign Affairs.

Two months later, as Germany was swept with strikes and demonstrations, he was sent on a clandestine mission to Berlin to help establish the new German Communist Party, which was to lead the strikes and turn them into a revolution against the state. Better placed than anyone in Russia to assess events correctly, he compared the situation in Berlin to the July Days in Petrograd, and believed like Luxemburg that workers were not ready for a revolution. And he was proved right when thousands of communists and fighters were thrown in jail.

He was arrested in February 1919, after a month on the run, two weeks after the murders of Luxemburg and Liebknecht, and was jailed in Berlin's Moabit Prison, where Luxemburg's lover Jogiches was shot soon after he arrived, and he was lucky not to be shot himself.

At the Eighth Party Congress in Moscow in March, he was elected *in absentia* to its Central Committee, and he described being visited in his cell by Berlin's government and business leaders, who saw him as a valuable source of information about the Bolsheviks, and entertaining them in his 'political salon'. He was released in January 1920, and on his return to Moscow, he was appointed Secretary of the Comintern.

Trotsky and others close to him described him as a sparkling companion, side-splittingly funny, often at his own expense, a master of political invective, and a brilliant mimic, intellectually insatiable, and a baffling mix of contradictions – romantic, sensitive and ruthless, selfless and self-aggrandising, idealistic and opportunistic.

Victor Serge saw him, with Lenin, Trotsky and Bukharin, as 'the brains of the Revolution, who spoke the same Marxist language, who understood each other so well, by the merest hints, that they seemed to think collectively'. The British spy-diplomat Robert Bruce Lockhart, who had been interrogated by him in the Kremlin in 1918 as a suspect in the attempted assassination of Lenin, portrayed him as 'a grotesque figure, a Jew, whose real name is Sobelsohn, who looks like a cross between a professor and a bandit'. His predecessor as Comintern Secretary, Angelica Balabanova, who had worked with him and Zinoviev, but had since broken with the Bolsheviks and left Russia, found him 'a strange mixture of amorality and cynicism, and a spontaneous appreciation for ideas, books, music and people. Today he would prove that events on various fronts had to be so and so. Tomorrow, when the opposite had occurred, he would attempt to prove it couldn't have been otherwise'.

Trotsky considered him 'indisputably one of the finest Marxist journalists in the world, with an encyclopaedic knowledge of international socialist affairs, and an ability to react with exceptional speed to new phenomena and tendencies. But Radek's strengths as a journalist are also his weakness, and he exaggerates and goes too far. He measures in miles when he should be measuring in inches, and invariably finds himself either to the left or to the right of the correct line'.[4]

In 1921, two and a half years after Germany's failed revolution, he had opposed the Comintern's new 'theory of the offensive', which called on German communists to rouse workers to a series of armed actions that would fatally damage capitalism. Yet when strikes broke out in Berlin that year, he appealed

---

4 Details of Radek's life in the *Granat Encyclopaedia*, op. cit.; Lerner, *The Last Internationalist*, 1970, and 'The Unperson in Soviet Historiography,' *South Atlantic Quarterly*, no. 4, 1966. Haupt and Marie (eds.), *Makers of the Russian Revolution*, 1974, pp. 361–5.; Victor Serge, *Memoirs of a Revolutionary*, 1972, p. 135.; Robert Bruce Lockhart wrote of his failed attempt to bring down the Soviet government in 1918 in *Memoirs of a Secret Agent*, 1932.; Balabanova, *My Life as a Rebel*, 1938, p. 246.; Trotsky, *Contre le Courant (Against the Current)*, Paris, 10 June, 1929.

for them to escalate, then saw their disastrous consequences played out on Berlin's streets in the 'March madness' of another failed revolution.

As the Comintern's chief adviser on Germany, he was then blamed by his boss Zinoviev for the Dresden and Hamburg debacles, despite having argued from the start that the Comintern's strategy was based on a vast miscalculation of the German army and working class. He loathed and despised Zinoviev, and the feelings were mutual. In October 1917, Zinoviev and his close ally Kamenev had voted against Lenin and the majority in opposing the seizure of power, and as Chair now of both the Petrograd Soviet and the Comintern, he was passing himself off as Lenin's heir. Radek and his German comrades saw him as a disaster for the Comintern, out of his depth in international politics, switching policies at will, banging the table, bullying foreign communists and blaming others for his mistakes, mainly Radek.

As one of Trotsky's closest comrades, Radek also took many of the attacks on him in the power struggles that consumed the Party during Lenin's last illness. Trotsky's humiliating defeat of Stalin at Tsaritsyn over the political and military leadership of the Civil War had been the start of his long campaign against him and his allies, and Radek's exchanges with Stalin and his second in command, Voroshilov, were famously rude and insulting. Arriving with Trotsky at the Twelfth Party Congress in April 1923, he was greeted by Voroshilov with the words 'Here comes the tail of the lion!' (Trotsky's name Lev means 'Lion'), to which he replied 'I'd rather be the lion's tail than Stalin's arse!'

That summer, when most of the Party leaders were identifying the successes of the Revolution with the dying Lenin, Radek paid tribute to Trotsky in his *Pravda* article 'Trotsky, Outstanding Organiser of Victory'. And in October he was a founding member of the new Left Opposition group, formed to support him against Stalin.

Before he met Larisa, he had been living in Moscow with his wife Rosa, a doctor, and his beloved four-year-old daughter Sonya, born while he was in jail in Berlin. He didn't believe in sexual faithfulness – for men. He expected women, particularly educated women like his wife, to be monogamous, and Rosa Radek appears to have remained in the background, frequently discarded for other women.

His wildly indiscreet love life was much discussed in international Marxist circles, and his affairs were numerous and very painful for her, but they had never lasted. 'With Larisa it was different', wrote his German Comintern colleague Rosa Levine-Meyer, who met them together that autumn in Berlin. 'He had vowed never to break up his marriage. But the brakes he had put on his relationships with other women didn't work this time, Larisa proved too strong.

She was young, beautiful, ambitious and highly talented ... He made one concession to his wife, that he wouldn't "leave" her and the family home. But it didn't help'.[5]

He was living in the Comintern safe house in Berlin rented by the Polish communist writer and anthropologist Elisabeth Poretsky, and Larisa moved in there to live with him. 'She stayed with us rather than at a hotel, as she had a false German passport', Poretsky wrote. 'She had spent one night at a hotel, where the manager told her, "Madame, if you want people to think you're German, don't smile so much. German women don't smile like that, only Russian ones". That was the reaction of all men to her, she was stunningly attractive'.[6]

Censorship was banned in Weimar Germany, with the exception of fascist 'hate speech', and in the midst of poverty, inflation and unemployment, she was discovering another Berlin with Radek – of Marxist philosophy and Freudian psychoanalysis, Dadaism, Cubism and Expressionist film, Thomas Mann and the Bauhaus, agitprop theatre, and cross-dressing cabarets.

Berlin was a magnet for freethinkers, bohemians and revolutionaries, and home to a large community of Russian writers, Soviet and emigre, who met for parties, political meetings and poetry readings and political meetings at the Café Landgraf on Nollendorfplatz, known as the 'House of the Arts', after the one in Petrograd. The Soviet writer Ilya Ehrenburg, who lived in Berlin between 1921 and 1922, and was on the organising committee, called the Café a 'Noah's Ark, where the Clean could meet the Unclean peacefully'. Mayakovsky and Esenin read their poems with the anti-soviet emigre poets Marian Tvetaeva and Vladimir Nabokov (Pasternak, Shklovsky and Bely had all left Russia by then), and Lunacharsky, Bukharin and Victor Serge arrived from Moscow to speak at meetings.

A young Russian Comintern telegraph operator staying with Larisa and Radek in Poretsky's house, Abram Zusskind, who spoke to Przhiborovskaya in the 1960s, remembered parties there where Radek was always the centre of attention, and would have Larisa in tears of laughter with his stories. They both loved to dance, and the 'dazzling beauty' the French communist Elsa Triolet, friend and translator of Mayakovsky, taught them the Argentinian Tango. 'It was immediately obvious that these were two people who had just met and were deeply in love', Zusskind said.[7]

---

5   Rosa Levine-Meyer, *Inside German Communism* (ed. and trans. Zane Mairowitz), 1977, p. 104.
6   Elisabeth Poretsky, *Our Own People*, 1969, p. 56. Poretsky wrote vividly of life in Weimar Berlin. But her memoirs are chiefly a haunting account of her life in the 1930s with her husband the Polish communist Ignace Reiss, killed in the purges.
7   Przhiborovskaya 2008, pp. 427–8.

People described them as an extraordinary looking couple, Larisa with her St Petersburg charm and elegance, Radek several inches shorter, with his thick tortoiseshell spectacles, sprouting beard and messy mop of hair covered in a worker's cap, dashing round Berlin with his pockets stuffed with books and leaflets. 'Esmeralda and Quasimodo', his American biographer Warren Lerner unkindly calls them. In photographs of him as a young student and aspiring lawyer, he is clean-shaven in a suit, with slicked back hair. 'He then adopted the dishevelled bohemian style popular with revolutionaries, and simply overdid it', Lerner writes.

Nikulin reported her mother's horror when she learnt of her affair with this dreadful man in decadent Berlin, when they hadn't even divorced their respective partners; she hadn't approved of Raskolnikov either, but at least he was unmarried. Rosa Levine-Meyer claimed she took him on the rebound from Raskolnikov – 'her real target being the inaccessible Trotsky'.

There is nothing in Larisa's published writings about her relationships with either Raskolnikov or Trotsky to support this piece of Comintern gossip. But she wrote at length to her mother about Radek:

> I can't tell you what this man has done for me. I've never worked so closely with anyone, or studied so deeply people's experience of socialism, which I'm still so shamefully ignorant about, despite all my superficial reading ... He gives me the freedom to work, and he has stirred the creative strings in my lazy bitter soul so the Party can have the best of it ...
>
> Karl is a Freudian, like Papa, so they'll have plenty to talk about ... Darling Mother, I just hope Pa's personal unhappiness, however justified, doesn't stop him seeing the tragic but principled core of our lives now ...[8]

They shared the same reckless energy and wanderlust, the same love of German poetry, the same satirical brilliance as writers, the same sense of the absurd. He encouraged and often directed her reading, with books on Russian and international politics and economics, and he was genuinely and generously appreciative of her work, and left her alone to write.

Now that she was free of Raskolnikov, she could finally speak of the abuse she had suffered from him. She found a friend and confidante in Poretsky, and told her about the time in Kabul he reported her to the Party for conducting her intelligence work with the British 'naked, at their quarters, covered only in

---

8   This and the following three letters in *sw*, pp. 552 and 554–6.

a fur coat'. 'She said he was insanely jealous and terribly violent', Poretsky wrote, 'and she showed me the vicious scar he had made on her back with his riding crop'.[9]

To her mother, she wrote of him in a remorseful restrained tone. 'Please don't be angry with me. I feel sorry for F.F. with all my heart, but it doesn't change anything'.

Despite the police 'Wanted' posters with Radek's picture displayed throughout Berlin, offering ten thousand Marks for his capture, he made little effort to disguise his instantly recognisable appearance, and the risk of arrest was clearly a thrilling ingredient of their affair. Zusskind remembered Larisa abandoning her 'Magdalina' cover to go for daily horserides in the Tiergarten, where she made friends with all the stableboys – 'who thought she was Scandinavian, and were all in love with her. I was just a boy myself then, and was in love with her too. So was Bukharin, who cursed Radek as unworthy of her'.

Had she opted for the conventional female route to power through powerful men, as Levine-Meyer insinuated, she would not have chosen Radek, whose status then in the Party and Comintern was not high, and there was clearly something deeply protective and maternal about her feelings for him. She supported him in his difficult relations with Zinoviev, and she would be his ally in all his future clashes with the Comintern Executive.

According to the journalist Sergei Schulz, who met him in Berlin then, 'Hamburg and Dresden ate him up'. Many in Germany believed the Russians had never been serious about wanting a revolution, and thousands of desperate workers who had put their faith in the communists were now suffering a new round of pay cuts and layoffs, and the abolition of the eight-hour day. The Nazis were then able to gain major new support by whipping up anger against the 'November criminals' – the Jews and Bolsheviks. Armed fascist units, precursors of Hitler's SS, were already appearing on the streets, and the Nazis would almost double their vote in the coming year's elections.

On 8 November, the day after the sixth anniversary of the Bolshevik Revolution, Hitler and the Nazi leaders Himmler, Marshal Goering and General Ludendorff, former Quartermaster of the Kaiser's General Staff, addressed a thousand swastikaed Stormtroopers and crowds of their supporters outside the Bavarian parliament building in Munich, then broke inside, ordering deputies at gunpoint to march Mussolini-style on Berlin, to seize the Reichstag and save Germany from Bolshevism. Armed police quickly arrived and shot eighteen dead, and hundreds were arrested for treason. Hitler was sentenced to five years in

---

9 Poretsky 1990, p. 57.

Bavaria's Landsberg Fortress (commuted to eleven months), where he wrote *Mein Kampf*, the blueprint for the Third Reich. This was the background to all Larisa's Comintern reports, which she later turned into her book of essays *Berlin, October 1923*.

Despite the official ban on Nazi hate speech, Hitler's 'beer-hall *putsch*' produced a new race hysteria in the mainstream press, which blamed workers' suffering and unemployment on Germany's poorest most vulnerable citizens, Russia's Jewish immigrants who had fled the tsarist pogroms, accusing them of stealing gentiles' jobs and homes. Armed fascist gangs stormed through Berlin's Jewish Scheinenviertel quarter, killing over a dozen Jews, setting fire to synagogues and smashing shops, and the Communist Party led the resistance with large anti-Nazi demonstrations. Larisa described marching with thousands in an illegal rally organised by communists in the working-class Lustgarten district, which was violently broken up by the police – 'where Berlin's proletariat demonstrated to General von Seeckt and his armoured cars the visible existence of the "banned" German party'.

She was savagely critical of all-powerful Social Democrats' abject failure to provide any leadership in the crisis. She described a meeting she went to the day after the Nazi *putsch*, in the working-class Kreuzberg district, where a small apathetic audience listened to two-hour patriotic speeches from the 'party's law-abiding fake socialists, Mensheviks and bureaucrats', followed by a children's choir singing folk-songs. 'Not one word to workers on how to defend themselves, no fighting slogans, no worked out plan of defence'.

Amidst these upheavals, she received a cable from *Izvestiya* proposing to send her as its special correspondent to China, where mass strikes and riots were taking on the character of a civil war. But she was too busy to leave Germany, and in the second week of November, Radek sent her with Zusskind to Hamburg.

She visited the poor workers' districts where the first barricades of the rising had gone up, and the industrial barracks of Barmbeck and Schiffbeck, with their chemical factories and manufacturing plants, and Hamm, where communists had seized five police stations. 'After the sluggishness of Berlin, there's something solid, strong and vital here', she wrote to Radek three days after arriving. 'At first it was hard to get past workers' distrust. But as soon as they accepted me as their comrade, I was able to learn their great simple tragic experiences'.

And from the ruins of the uprising, she wrote the essays that became her book *Hamburg at the Barricades*, telling its story through the lives of its heroes and heroines – 'the hope of the new Germany'.

'Defeat didn't break her in Hamburg', Radek wrote. 'She saw the fire under the ashes, and how defeat raises new fighters for future battles'

She lived with the wives of freedom fighters, and sought out the fugitives in their hideouts. She attended Socialist Party meetings and court hearings, where summary justice was delivered to the fighters. She disappeared into workers' homes and slept on filthy beds, picking up a mass of impressions and lice (poverty is the same everywhere). And in the factories, she questioned workers and managers tirelessly and purposefully, and in a few minutes she could get from any of them, man or machine, whatever she needed.

'Liebe, Liebe, Leri! I see you and think of you every minute', he wrote (interestingly, using Gumilyov's name for her). He sent her books to read, and she immersed herself in the works of the communist historian Heinrich Laufenburg, President of the Hamburg Workers' and Soldiers' Soviet in 1918, who left a vivid account of its role in the revolution.

To her family in Moscow she wrote:

> I'm mending my sails, whistling like an old sailor over his maps. I'm being forced to think and read, I've never worked so hard in my life. At first my brain creaked, but it's getting easier ... Sometimes I despair at these skyscraper events, but if I don't enter the great revolutionary storm, I'll become stagnant and shallow. There's so much to learn, I'm almost grateful for this brief respite history has offered.

Within a week, she had posted her first two essays back to her family, 'Hamburg, Free City' and 'Barmbeck in Struggle' (later the first two chapters of *Hamburg at the Barricades*), asking them to forward them to *Izvestiya* under the name 'Revera'.

Her next two letters home were delivered by Hans Kippenberger, leader of the Communist Party's military organisation, the *M-Apparat*, who was seeking asylum in Moscow. To Igor, now a lecturer at Moscow University's Oriental Studies Institute, she passed on an unspecified task from the Comintern's Eastern Section – 'it would be a tragedy if your experiences in Asia were wasted'. To her mother, she wrote:

> Darling Mother, I haven't lived so purely since 1918, or thought or studied so much in such complete unbroken solitude. The snow falls on my soul, and I'm like a tree in winter ...
>
> I long to see you and Russia again. What joy that the Soviet Union exists. Worlds collapse, and classes settle their centuries-old scores. If only you could see the breakdown of a whole nation here ... In my writing I try

to start from the main thing, the stinking bourgeoisie, which smothers and leeches off the proletariat. A genius of this rage is the artist George Grosz,[10] but there's something almost abnormal about his disgust ... I spit on them, and try not to fill my mouth with carrion.

At the end of November, she left Hamburg for Berlin. A week later she returned with Radek to Moscow, where she worked on her Hamburg writings, studying trial records, corresponding with those still there, checking her material with them and with the exiled Kippenberger, who was writing his own account of the rising. (9)

The first complete edition of *Hamburg at the Barricades* was published in December in German, by the socialist *Neuer Deutscher Verlag* in Berlin, 'to introduce German readers to the best writing from Russia'. The first chapters of the book appeared in Russian in early January 1924, in the journal *Life*, titled 'Sketches of Contemporary Germany, by Special Correspondent Revera'. Two weeks later, *Hamburg* was published in its complete form in Russia, with *Berlin, October 1923*, by the Comintern's International Aid Organisation, MOPR, *Hamburg* evokes the 'smell' of revolution, the smashed barricades, the buildings pockmarked with bullets, and captures the energy and speed of the modern city in its joyful pile-up of images – 'lying on the shores of the North Sea, waterproof as a pilot's oilskin, stinking like a sailor's pipe', its language 'soaked in the sea, like some rare creature of the deep, salty as cod, ripe and juicy as Dutch cheese, rude, smelly and cheerful as English vodka'.

The book opens with the city's topography: the bourgeois villas overlooking the Elbe, with their gardens and tennis-courts; the factories, shipyards, oil refineries and chemical plants clustered round the harbour (all flattened by British carpet bombing in the Second World War); the unemployed workers besieging the docks in search of work; the bars, pawnshops and brothels of the St Pauli red-light district; the canals 'filled with industrial waste, like inky vomit'. And 'like a carnival in this oily black Venice', 'the armies of workers pumped in and out through a tunnel under the river, whose elephantine lifts raise and lower this human flood to and from the concrete exits. Out of this forge came the Hamburg rising'.

---

10 Published in A. Neuberg, *Der bewaffnete Ausstand, 1928*, translated by Quinton Hoare as *Armed Insurrection*, 1977. ('Neuberg' was the collective pseudonym for Kippenberger and the Comintern agents Mikhail Tukhachevsky, O. Pyatnitsky and the Vietnamese revolutionary leader Ho Chi Minh).
  George Grosz (1898–1959), savage caricaturist of bourgeois life in Weimar Germany].

She then moves to the sequence of events: 'Regular pitched battles continued all through Tuesday. The first heavy police assaults started at eleven in the morning, around Barmbeck's von Essen police station, and along the barricades on both sides of the railway embankment. Detachments of snipers ran along the tracks, picking off the fighters from above, and quickly seized back the police station'.

Hamburg's workers fought with unbelievable courage, she wrote:

> But by Wednesday, with no news of insurrections elsewhere in Germany, the leaders were compelled to sound the retreat. Not because the rising had been smashed, but what was the point of continuing the struggle in isolation, flaring up in the midst of the general collapse ...?
>
> The first courier bringing the order to retreat was knocked off his feet with a terrible punch – so unjustly received – and working Hamburg clutched its jaw and was blinded with grief.

She was writing with a sense of her historic responsibility to save the rising from the 'distortions of those who would suppress documents to cast its hated memory into oblivion, and dismiss it as a communist *putsch*'. She identified from the start the differences between a *putsch* – 'which has no past or future, only total victory, or an equally total and futile defeat' – and a revolution, 'with its rich pre-history, whose future lies in the memories of those who survive, which to be successful must be guided by a strong, flexible, battle-ready party, able to spring back when ruthlessly attacked'. And she brought the rising to life in her portraits of its fighters – 'a wonderful blend of courage, alcohol, revolutionary ardour, and the last hopelessly fallen sinner'.

For security reasons she disguised their names, and she was even less specific with names in the book's German edition, using only 'X', or 'a comrade'.

There was impetuous 'Comrade K', of the Hamburg Soviet, 'a pub brawler and tyrant, who constructed the amazing network of barricades at Barmbeck, and died defending them'. There was 'Kb' (Kippenberger), and 'U' (Hugo Urbahns), and 'sober incorruptible "T" (Thälmann), setting up his radio equipment in a park under the open sky, grasping the reigns of the insurrection in his iron hands'. The 'fearless delightful curly-haired giant Roth', a construction worker at Hamm, and the beautiful Elfrieda, a worker at Schiffbeck's chemical factory, 'who refused to be anyone's wife, conquered whoever she chose, made love for as long as there were no lies in the loving, then proudly returned her captive to his freedom'. Many saw the character she identified most with as Hamburg's carpenter and artist, another 'K' – 'an epicurean and real Renaissance man, with his frothing unstoppable love of life and pleasure and warm tangible beauty, who believes that the process of life will one day become the most great and beautiful thing'.

'The Hamburg rising was the crucible of the most advanced and active detachments of the German proletariat', she wrote, and she blamed its lack of support elsewhere in Germany on the 'treachery and sham democracy' of the all-powerful Social Democratic Party, 'whose avoidance of decisive action has entered the bloodstream of the workers' movement'.

Berlin, October 1923 opens with 'In the Reichstag', a satirical *tour d'horizon* of the 'parliamentary fauna' of the Weimar Republic – 'idols of the stock exchange of political corruption, swarming round the venerated jackboots of an old soldier'. 'Scattered over the red carpets of the Reichstag are a multitude of deadbeats and played-out hands. Everything is from the past – yesterday's men, members of the old ministries thrown into paroxysms of self-loathing, belching statesmen whose tailcoats are stained with an indelible filth, a gallery of crumpled, beaten, disgraced physiognomies, who have learned to endure the hatred of those they have betrayed'.

In 'Workers' Children', she wrote of soaring infant mortality in Berlin, of 'unemployed families living on 60,000 million Marks a week, when bread cost 80,000 million the day before yesterday'. Of 'seven-month-old babies who look like old men, with infected sores and swollen bellies', and their desperate mothers – 'in the winter of 1923, the pregnant wife of an unemployed worker is already a corpse'. Of starving tram-drivers, and strong men fainting on the streets, and 'the hunger that haunts even the magnificent empty counters at the Wertheim department store, where the shopgirls sell themselves for a few pfennigs'.

In '9 November in a Working Class District', she reported on the Social Democrats' meeting the day after Hitler's *putsch* – 'a requiem for the 1918 revolution, and for the party's betrayal of those whose interests it had pledged itself to defend'. And in 'A Prosperous Workers' Family', she showed how quickly those no longer facing extreme hunger learnt to find the suffering of others bearable, 'grateful for "their" loaf of bread and "their" lump of margarine'. She wrote of Social Democrats' strategy to stifle and neutralise workers' healthy class anger, and accused them of normalising fascism, colluding with the bourgeois press to brainwash people to 'accept the unnatural as natural' – the same embattled double-think mentality explored in the novels of her contemporaries Joseph Roth and Thomas Mann.

Hamburg at the Barricades and *Berlin, October 1923* are unforgettable portraits of workers' lives in Weimar Germany a decade before the Nazis took power. At the books' Moscow launch party at the House of the Press, the novelist Yury Libedinsky said, 'We want to write like that or not at all!' The literary critic Zhores Elsberg wrote of the 'double optics' of her German writings – 'her style is the style of European aestheticism reflected by the Revolution. She sees Renaissance Italy and eighteenth-century France peering into the present'. Vera Inber saw *Hamburg* as a turning point in her work, and praised the new simplicity of her prose: 'She writes with incredible accessibility for those untrained in scientific truths, yet without mindless popularisation. She has the ability to bring distance near with one apt image, and a whole book could be written about her similes and metaphors'.

According to Inber, every writer had their favourite and often repeated image, and in Larisa's writings from the front this had been swans – 'symbols of death and rebirth, the aesthetic vessels into which she tried to pour new wine'. 'In *Hamburg*, she goes to places where there is nothing beautiful, and her images no longer have to carry that burden. For the first time she finally abandons aestheticism for its own sake, and describes the subterranean depths she can no longer deny, and they no longer frighten her'.

For the journalist Lev Sosnovsky, the books were her 'fourth and final test:'

> It was impossible now to ignore her, because there was simply no better journalist amongst us. Had each of our party organisations that had undergone their great revolutionary experiences possessed her pen, her sense of colour and her sharp eye, we could have achieved ten or a hundred times more. If added to our Bolshevik temperament were her education and her European experience – which didn't pass without trace – we could have worked miracles.[11]

Raskolnikov's diplomatic work in Kabul had been rewarded by Amanullah with the exceptional honour of a royal medal, and he returned to Moscow in the second week of January. She met him off the train, as he had asked her to, and he handed the divorce papers back to her unsigned, insisting they meet first and talk. She refused and left, and he immediately wrote to her begging her to change her mind. 'Precious little bird flown from the nest, I need desperately to see you tomorrow. Our stormy meeting at the station, inevitable after all our months apart, broke the programme of our discussions, and we have so much to discuss. I promise I'll control myself better next time, and won't upset my little one and "drag her into the ditch", as you put it'.[12]

---

11   Libedinsky, *Contemporaries*, 1958, p. 97. Zhores Elsberg, 'Comparisons and Metaphors,' 1927; Inber, 1966, pp. 279–81; Sosnovsky, *People of Our Time*, 1927, p. 97.
12   Raskolnikov, *About Myself and My Times*, 1989, p. 196.

A week later, on 21 January, their problems receded into the background when Lenin suffered his fourth and final stroke, at the age of fifty-four, and Russia was plunged into mourning.

His coffin, draped in black and red flags and a faded banner from the Paris Commune, was escorted on the train from his dacha to Moscow by Bukharin, Zinoviev and Kamenev. It was an exceptionally cold winter, forty degrees below zero, and the train moved slowly along the icy tracks, lined with thousands of mourning workers. His coffin was carried through the capital to the House of Unions on Okhotny Ryad, where his family spent four hours alone with him. Then at seven in the evening the doors opened, and the crowds poured in, to scenes of huge emotion and grief. Hundreds fainted as they filed past his open coffin, and had to be carried out on stretchers, and the poet Demyan Bedny was too anguished to write about him until several weeks later.

Larisa visited the House of Unions several times with her *Izvestiya* press pass. In her obituary 'Tomorrow We Must Live, Today We Grieve', she wrote of Lenin's greatness and his suffering – 'He could have died six years ago from the bullets fired at him, buried in the earth like Rosa and Liebknecht and the millions who gave their lives for the Revolution'. And she ended with a solemn invocation of the Russian Motherland, 'a warrior standing over his coffin, conscious of her great power, weeping and bowing her head to her sword, which her worker's hands will never drop'.[13]

As Party Secretary, Stalin was in charge of organising the state funeral on Red Square, attended by millions of mourners from across the country, and he then took Lenin's place as leader of the Communist Party and the Soviet state.

The Revolution had survived under Lenin's pragmatic and sometimes brutal leadership, something even he had called a miracle, and there were high hopes in the West that without him the communist experiment would collapse. Within a week, the European General Staff in Paris were drawing up plans for a new intervention, and a group of industrialists in London, led by legendary string-puller and fervent anti-Bolshevik Sir Henry Deterding, Director of Royal Dutch Oil, a personal friend of Hitler's and major financial donor to the Nazis, declared themselves owners of the oil of the Caucasus.[14]

A directive from the Kremlin ordered soviets to deal ruthlessly with the Revolution's enemies, and dozens of suspected foreign agents were arrested and shot, and within weeks, plans for a new invasion had been dropped in

---

13   'Zavtra nado zhit – sevodnya gore' (Tomorrow We Must Live – Today We Mourn), *Izvestiya*, 27 January, 1924. *SW*, p. 491.
14   Glyn Roberts, *The Most Powerful Man in the World. The Life of Sir Henry Deterding*, 1938, p. 436.

favour of diplomacy. Lenin had long predicted that the capitalist governments would sooner or later be forced by the post-war economic crisis to trade with the Bolsheviks, and the first to establish diplomatic relations with the Soviet government, on 2 February, was Ramsay MacDonald's Labour government in Britain, followed by those of Norway, fascist Italy, Sweden, Switzerland and Denmark.

Petrograd was renamed Leningrad, and at factory and soviet meetings across the country and in thousands of obituaries, people were called on to express their sorrow for Lenin through solidarity. But with no one of his stature to steer the Party through this new diplomatic minefield, solidarity among his heirs crumbled, and the Central Committee split into warring factions.

In 1918, Lenin had declared that October had proved Trotsky's theory of international revolution to be correct. According to Stalin, two failed revolutions in Germany and a civil war that had put a deadly strain on Russia's resources proved otherwise, and he advanced his 'socialism in one country' thesis, arguing that the Party's priority now must be to defend the Soviet Union against foreign aggression, and declare war on its internal enemies.

Before the Thirteenth Party Congress opened in May, Lenin's widow Nadezhda Krupskaya circulated to a stunned Central Committee his 'Testament', written a year before his death, in which he called for Stalin to be removed. But he was saved by Zinoviev, who declared that circumstances had fortunately proved Lenin wrong, then mobilised with Stalin and Kamenev against the Left Opposition to prevent Trotsky from succeeding to the leadership.

Radek had returned from Germany in disgrace, and was denounced at the Congress as a 'petit bourgeois rightist', for arguing that the time for revolution in Germany was temporarily over, and was voted off the Party Central Committee for his 'past mistakes'. At the Fifth Congress of the Comintern a month later, he was openly derided by Zinoviev, who blamed him and the incompetence of the German Communist Party for Germany's failed revolutions. Trotsky spoke out against this scapegoating of Radek and German communists for the Comintern's mistakes, and Radek again paid extravagant tribute to Trotsky's military and organisational genius, and was removed from the Executive and was replaced by Stalin. Stalin then consolidated his position in the Comintern by changing its common language from German, which he did not speak, to Russian, and by then Trotsky and Radek were already on their way out.

Radek published non-controversial articles on foreign politics while he planned his next move. 'He was fortunate to have his beloved trusted Larisa at his side, whose love helped him face the humiliation of his disgrace', writes his biographer. But she did not attend the congress that presided over his expulsion. Instead she reported for *Pravda* on the conference of the Communist Women's International that followed it, and its campaigns against fascism and for women's reproductive rights.[15]

Raskolnikov was still refusing to sign the divorce papers, and she was still refusing his repeated requests to meet. But it would have been hard to avoid him that spring. On his return to Moscow he had been appointed Director of the Comintern's Eastern Section, working under the name 'Petrov'. But he was bored by international politics, and was more interested in the politics of literature, and he seemed to be everywhere – working with Lunacharsky at *Gosizdat*, editor-in-chief of the *Moscow Worker* publishing house, and on the editorial boards of both *On Guard* and *Red Virgin Soil*. He was also working on his own writing. He had followed his recently published *History of Russian Thought* and *Tales of Sub-Lieutenant Ilin* with a new book of memoirs, *Kronstadt and Petrograd in 1917*, and he was working on his first screenplay, an adaptation of Tolstoy's novel *Resurrection*.

The *On Guardists*, claiming to act under the direction of the Party, had consistently attacked *Red Virgin Soil*'s policy of publishing non-communist writers, and many readers cancelled their subscriptions after Raskolnikov's appointment, seeing it as part of an attempt to turn the journal into a Party mouthpiece. Its founding editor, Gorky, wrote witheringly from his new home in Italy of Raskolnikov's literary talents, calling him 'an ungifted, uneducated kid'. According to Radek, 'The *On Guardists* had broken so much glass by then that the broad circles of the Party, which had so far paid little attention to literature, were finally forced to do so'.

In Trotsky's pamphlet *Literature and Revolution*, published that year, he called for strict discipline for Party members, and freedom outside it for the arts to flourish – 'the domain of art is not one the Party is called upon to command'. While Russia was in the painful transition to the new classless society, he wrote, the proletariat must be free to experiment and create the culture best suited to its needs, and he denounced the proletarian pieties of *Proletkult*, and its bullying of fellow-travellers.[16]

Gorky, the most distinguished of the fellow-travellers, the most published writer of the Soviet era, would live abroad for the next nine years. Pasternak had decided against life in exile after his year in Berlin, and never officially identified with any of the literary groups, but he was close to Boris Pilnyak and the fellow-travelling Serapions. That spring Larisa and Radek would join Pilnyak

---

15   'Na mezhdunarodnoi konferentsii kommunistok' (The International Conference of Communist Women), *Pravda*, 15 July, 1924. sw, p. 579.
16   Trotsky, *Literature and Revolution* (trans. Rose Strunsky), 2005.

and Pasternak and Pasternak's wife, the painter Evgenia Lurie, for concerts at the House of Soviets and trips to the theatre. They all loved Moscow's new State Yiddish Theatre, and Alexander Tairov's Kamerny Theatre, with its German Expressionist-style comedies and melodramas. Over a dozen new Yiddish theatres had opened since the Revolution, generously funded by the state, and Moscow's was considered one of the finest theatres in the country. Pasternak and Radek were friends with its distinguished leading actor and artistic director, Shlomo Vovsi, and Larisa was a passionate admirer of the Tairov's leading actress and co-founder, Alisa Koonen, famous for her great tragic performances in Racine's *Phaedra* and Oscar Wilde's *Salomé*. The literary critic Marc Slonim remembered 'jamming into the frozen theatre with the starving haggard audience' for the Tairov's production of 'Salomé' in the winter of 1918, and Koonen's 'fiery aggressive' heroine.[17] Larisa's English friend Andrew Rothstein, who was in Moscow in the spring of 1924, told the author it was common knowledge that Radek had left his wife for her, and he assumed they were living together, as when he visited Radek at his flat in the Kremlin, he apologised that she was out at a meeting, and 'couldn't pour tea'.

In contrast with this homely scene, is the extraordinary picture of her conjured up by her contemporary the Red Army commander Alexander Boyarchikov, active with Radek in the Trotskyist Left Opposition, who later survived many years in the camps. In Boyarchikov's recently published memoirs, she is a scheming sex maniac and demented stalker of Trotsky, 'with whom she was insanely in love'. She slept with all the Party leaders as a way of getting close to him – 'flitting from lover to lover in the manner of Alexandra Kollontai's worker bees' – but he resisted her. Marrying Raskolnikov had been part of this strategy, but she was then separated from him in Kabul, where she compromised Raskolnikov by having an affair with a 'local prince' (does Boyarchikov mean King Amanullah?), and she was recalled to Moscow and threatened with expulsion from the Party. There she continued to pursue Trotsky by 'making a play for Radek'. 'She then used her lover to pass on to him an extraordinary, even indecent, proposal – she wanted to have a baby with him, to produce offspring that would harmoniously combine the beauty of the mother with the mental genius of the father'. After many jealous scenes, Radek finally agreed to put her request to Trotsky, who 'let him down gently: "Calm down Karl, tell your beloved I refuse to father her child"'. All this nonsense, including the 'local prince' story, is repeated as fact by British historian Robert Service in his 2009 biography of Trotsky.[18]

---

17 Slonim, *Russian Theatre from the Empire to the Soviets*, 1963, p. 249.
18 Boyarchikov, *Vospominaniya* (Memoirs), Moscow, 2003, pp. 149–50; Service, *Trotsky*, 2009, pp. 341–2.

Whether or not she moved in with Radek, she continued her independent life in Moscow, going to meetings, teaching at the *rabfaks*, catching up with old friends and making new ones. And it was then that Lydia Seifullina came into her life.

Seifullina was one of the most popular and talented of the writers of the Revolution, author of four best-selling novels and over forty novellas and short stories. Her characters were Russia's downtrodden and oppressed, overcoming hardships to become full members of society, and she brought them unforgettably to life, complex, passionate, suffering and human. She was read by millions, and Lenin had spoken warmly of her works before his death. But she never joined the Party, and all her life she identified herself as a fellow-traveller.[19]

She was born in 1889, in a village in the Urals, close to the Siberian border, the eldest of three sisters. Their mother was a semi-literate Russian peasant, who died of tuberculosis when she was five, and they were raised by their father, a Muslim Tatar who had converted to Christianity, and had been ordained as an Orthodox priest. She was educated at a school for the daughters of poor priests, and left at the age of fifteen to earn her living. For the next three years she worked as a village literacy teacher, then she joined a touring theatre company as an actress, performing in over twenty different roles in productions across Russia, from tsarist Poland and Ukraine to the Caucasus. After six years on the stage, she returned to the Urals, travelling around the remote mountain villages, with their populations of Bashkirs, Mordvinians, Kazakhs and Old Believers, setting up literacy classes and the Urals' first children's theatre, organising libraries and reading groups. 'It was life that made me a writer', she said.

When war broke out in 1914, she helped illiterate peasant women to write letters to their loved ones at the front, and she became known as the 'women's defender'. 'It was life that made me a writer', she said, and these women were the subjects of her first short stories, published in the local Urals press.

After the Revolution, she worked for the Bolsheviks' *Likbez* literacy programme, teaching peasants in a village outside Moscow, and in her diaries she described her first encounter with Mayakovsky that winter, walking the twenty miles to the capital with her team of young teachers to hear him read his poems – 'his face alive with his talent, the fire of his soul'.

In 1918 she returned to the Urals, with her husband the journalist and publisher Valerian Pravdukhin, where they worked in the new self-governing

---

19   Details of Seifullina's life in A. Yanovsky, *Lydia Seifullina. Literarny kriticheskii biograficheskii ocherk* (Lydia Seifullina, A Literary Biographical Study), Moscow, 1972.

homes for orphans and street children, the *besprizorniki*, whose lives were to be turned round through kindness and respect, education and hard work. Both were exceptional teachers and organisers, and in 1920 they set up the first children's agricultural colony in the Urals, on beautiful Lake Turgoyak, which existed until the end of the USSR, with a board outside celebrating her work with the children.

That year they moved to Moscow, where she studied for a teaching diploma, and in 1921 they left for the Siberian capital Nikolaevsk (now Novosibirsk), and it was there that her writing took off.

Her literary career would be shaped and defined by *Red Virgin Soil*. In her diaries she described its impact on her Nikolaevsk writers' group when the first issues reached Siberia, and she became an editor of the first of the 'thick' Soviet journals it inspired, *Siberian Flames*. Her first novel, *Four Chapters*, appeared in the first issue in 1921, a warm and truthful account of peasants' lives in a Siberian village during the Revolution. But it was her second novel, *The Lawbreakers*, published a year later, that catapulted her to fame.

She described dashing it down in a week, 'with joy in my heart', the story of fourteen-year-old Grisha, an orphan she had known at the Turgoyak home, who had been begging and stealing on the streets, seeing crime as the only way to survive, until he was offered a job as a youth leader at the home, and he realised he could make a better life for the children in his care. Grisha is lovable and human, and the children's language is rough, witty and colourful, and the novel's optimistic heartwarming message made it instantly popular.

She followed *The Lawbreakers* with her novel *The Mulch*, published in the next issue of *Siberian Flames*, a raw and powerful account of the upheavals during the Civil War in a remote Siberian village encircled by the Whites. In a 1923 poll of peasants' reading habits, she was voted their favourite author, and that winter she was invited by Alexander Voronsky to join the editorial board of *Red Virgin Soil*.

She arrived in Moscow in January 1924, two days after Lenin's funeral, and wrote her 'Peasant Tale About Lenin' for *Red Virgin Soil* 'before his coffin was closed'. The work was inspired by legends she had heard about Lenin in Siberia, 'where Old Believers proclaimed whole pages of the Bible by heart, to attack him or prove the holy truth of his message', and was based on a story told to her by an old Siberian peasant woman – about 'Tsar Mikolasha, and a person of unknown rank going by the name of Lenin, who ground him and his generals to ashes, and took his people away from war'.

She was now working on what would be the most popular and controversial of her novels, *Virineya*, based on the life of a beautiful orphaned girl she had met in Siberia, a Bolshevik factory worker, whose dreams of getting an education and serving the Revolution come to a tragic end when she sleeps with two men outside wedlock.

Photographs of Seifullina show a small bright expressive face, full of humour and energy. She and Pravdukhin kept open house for Moscow's writers, who would crowd into their small hospitable flat on Basmannaya Street to read their works. 'Tiny, dark, brainy, sharp-tongued, ready to scratch your eyes out in an argument, she won all our hearts', wrote the literary critic and *Gosizdat* editor Kornei Chukovsky.

The poet and *Izvestiya* journalist Nikolai Smirnov recalled Victor Shklovsky 'sonorously declaiming his famous aphorisms', and 'stout Olga Forsh, who looked like a schoolmistress, reading in her manly baritone from her new poetry collection'. Isaac Babel read his stories about Jewish ghetto life in his native Odessa, and his gangster hero Benny Krik. The nature poet Mikhail Prishvin, 'in hunting boots and belted peasant shirt, a new manuscript dangling from his pocket', read his sketches of his travels around Russia and Europe. A young Siberian peasant friend of Seifullina's 'nervously read her poems about her Bashkir mares', and a chain-smoking Seifullina read drafts of *Virineya*, 'while her red setter Taiga passed silently between the guests, laying her bronze head on our knees'.

Larisa would drop in after meetings, Smirnov wrote, and Seifullina would instantly recognise her ring and rush to open the door. 'Bursting in in her worn brown leather coat, her wonderful face slightly flushed, her eyes glowing with happiness, she would talk of books or the meeting she had just been to, announcing she was tired and hungry, but unable to sit still or touch her food, jumping from the armchair to the sofa, from the sofa to the bookshelf, throwing herself at Taiga, rushing to Seifullina's desk to pore over her latest writing'.[20]

They were ardent admirers each other's work, and it was the start of a deep and passionate friendship between them that would last until Larisa's death.

There was a new intensity to women's friendships then. Russia had lost almost a fifth of its male population in the war and Civil War, and throughout the 1920s, when women significantly outnumbered men, they made new living arrangements, and experimented with new kinds of family life. Same-sex marriages were allowed by law, and close friends became lovers. 1917 had released a whole spectrum of new feelings and ways of writing about them, and the two women's feelings for each other came close to worship.

In an essay on Larisa, Seifullina wrote:

---

20   Smirnov, *Lydia Seifullina v vospominaniyakh* (Lydia Seifullina Remembered), Moscow, 1961.

> The power of her literary imagination could glorify the significance of a picture, a book or a play. At the dress rehearsal of a play that moved her, you would see this woman, who so rarely cried, her face wet with tears. Yet later, when a more dispassionate assessment was required, she would be straightforward and even sharp in her judgements ...
>
> She was never afraid to search, and she tirelessly expanded her reading. And after patiently absorbing some specialist work, she would smile her astonishing smile, in which a secret light seemed to burn, and say 'That should produce something tasty!' This meant some new literary work, enriched with all the fullness of her emotions.[21]

In April 1924, her reworked and edited 'Letters from the Front' were finally published by *Red Virgin Soil* as *The Front*, connecting the separate episodes of the 'Letters' to make a complete picture of the campaign from Kazan to the Caspian:

> For two years, twenty thousand Kronstadt and Baltic sailors and their Flotilla of warships, tugs and armoured barges sailed thousands of miles, from the Baltic Sea to the Persian border. In those years, they went through the fire, ate bread with straw, rotted with fever on dirty beds in lice-ridden hospitals, and fought with old artillery and aeroplanes that fell to bits from bad fuel. And in the end they defeated the enemy, three times stronger than they were ...

The Front is an extraordinary work of memory and imagination, hurtling along at breakneck speed, conveying the energy and rhythm of events in dizzying torrents of words, passages of lyrical beauty punctuated by staccato telegraphic cut to the bone accounts of battles, defeats and victories, capturing the mass dynamics of the Revolution through its vast cast of characters. Many she mentions by name, others are anonymous. To some she devotes several pages, to others just a few lines. But all are taken from life, and embody all the drama and heroism of the Civil War.

She was writing for future generations, to keep the collective memory of the struggle alive, and she dedicated the book to her *rabfak* students – 'our future statesmen and judges, scientists, writers and professors, who in a few short years must not only assimilate the old bourgeois culture, but shape its most valuable features into new ideological forms'.

---

21 Lydia Seifullina, 'Larisa Reisner', *Leningrad Pravda*, 9 February, 1927; republished in Seifullina 1969, vol. 4, p. 159.

She wrote of the *rabfaks*' distrust of words and emotions – 'because actions speak so much louder' – and her preface is both a polemic against the 'crude soulless beauty of the *Apollo* poets', and a manifesto for a new language:

> You children of the proletariat are brave principled people, who have fearlessly rejected the mystical consolations of bourgeois art and aesthetics. Say the word 'Beauty' at the *rabfaks*, and they'll jeer. 'Creativity' and 'Feelings', and they'll bang the desks and leave. That's natural. If we reject such things now as just 'bourgeois sentimentality', it's because they were beaten out of us in the hungry typhus-ridden years of the Civil War.
>
> But beware of falling into the bourgeois trap that tries to deny the truth of those years ... Our refined Apollo aesthetes and literature-lovers, repelled by the Revolution in its naked glory, hold their noses at such vulgar words as 'heroism', 'brotherhood' and 'self-sacrifice'. But what if we have experienced these beautiful terrible things? Don't we need to find a new way to describe them, to see beyond the blood and filth, to defeat the native cowardice of our human flesh so easily torn by any rusty nail?
>
> Let the *rabfaks* curse the book. Let heretical words like 'they loved', 'they died beautifully' stick in their throats. But let them read how it was from Kazan to Anzali, about the victories and defeats on the Volga, the Kama and the Caspian, in the years of the Great Russian Revolution.

The Front has been compared to the American communist John Reed's eyewitness account of the Revolution, *Ten Days That Shook the World*. Reed too wrote as a passionate supporter of the Bolsheviks, with no pretence at 'objectivity', and he too wrote himself out of the picture. But while Reed's writing is orderly, understated and restrained, hers is a riot of impressions, full of poetry and dazzling shifts of mood, from lyrical joy to tragedy and comedy.

After discussing her 'Letters' with her students she had drastically pruned them for the book version, often cutting whole pages. Vera Inber praised her 'writer's cool, which she wears like a gas-mask'. 'She writes with a diamond-sharp pen, while others are scribbling with pencil on an envelope'. Inber also felt she could have cut more. 'Her metaphors are sometimes thick on the page, piled on top of each other like two riders in the saddle', and in these clashing images Inber saw 'the clash between the new and the old Larisa, and against the Petersburg aesthete in her soul'.[22]

---

22   Inber 1966, pp. 276–7.

The Front came in for more serious criticisms from writers who saw her style as too poetic and impressionistic to convey the reality of workers' lives in the Revolution, and believed her class disqualified her from describing events from the proper political perspective. The journalist Vladimir Polyansky, writing in the *Proletkult* paper *Press and Revolution*, 'in the name of worker peasant Russia', found 'the author's purely intellectual psychology dull and incomprehensible', and accused her of 'emasculating the Russian language'. 'Although as for the book's ideology, it is communist, and could not be otherwise'.[23]

According to Seifullina she was deeply hurt by these criticisms, but characteristically defiant. 'Some accuse her of overloading her writing with beautiful images, like precious stones', Seifullina wrote, 'but the depth and richness of her language is inspired by her insatiable literary appetite for life, which makes her describe it in ever more festive words'.

Trotsky is known to have considered *The Front*, with Isaac Babel's *Red Cavalry Stories*, the most outstanding works of the Civil War. *Pravda*, *Izvestiya* and the magazines *The Bookseller* and *Red Fleet* all praised the brilliance of the writing, and called the book a masterpiece. '*The Front* is exceptional for its psychological insight into those who fought for three years from the Baltic to the Persian border, and for its analysis of the ideas for which they went through the fire', Igor Ilinsky wrote in *Pravda*. 'Anyone who wants to understand this exceptional epoch, and how people made the Revolution, and how the Revolution made them, must read this captivating work', wrote Nikolai Smirnov in *Izvestiya*.[24]

She gave her first copy of the book to Raskolnikov, who wrote to thank 'the woman I will always think of as my wife for her beautiful poem to our love under fire', and finally signed the divorce papers.[25]

A week after it was published, she was invited by *Izvestiya* to join its permanent staff, as one of its special correspondents (*spetskors*), and she wrote back with her conditions: 'I need to spend at least five months travelling round the Union, I insist on that. Travel notes and sketches of people are what I'm good at, I'm totally unsuited to any kind of office work'.[26]

A month later she was off on her travels again, to the industrial heartlands of the Soviet Union, in the Urals and Eastern Ukraine, reporting for *Izvestiya* on workers' lives in the new conditions of the NEP. 'Being a person with an immediate grasp of reality, she needed more than simply reading and discussions', Radek wrote. 'She had to find out what was happening in the depths of the masses, who in the final count dictate the course of history'.

---

23   Polyansky's article quoted in Naumova's Introduction to sw, p. 31.
24   *Pravda* and *Izvestiya* articles quoted by Naumova, sw, p. 32.
25   Raskolnikov, *About Myself and My Times*, 1989, p. 263.
26   Letter to *Izvestiya* in sw, p. 468.

CHAPTER 15

Across Workers' Russia

In May 1924, she set off on thousand-mile journey east on the Trans-Siberian Railway to the Urals. She had first travelled on the railway as a young child, seven years after construction started, when it took her family into exile in Siberia. By the time the work was completed in 1919, it was the longest line in the world, stretching five thousand miles east, from Moscow to Vladivostok on the Sea of Japan, with hundreds of new stations and branch-lines connecting the towns and villages of Central Russia to the Urals and Siberia, and in a letter home from the journey, she described the train packed with workers and peasants and their families, leaving to find work and make new lives in the East.

On the boundaries between Asia and Europe, with its vast mineral resources, the Urals had been the most industrially developed area of the Tsarist Empire since the reign of Catherine the Great in the eighteenth century, when over two hundred new factories were built and new mines opened. Serfs were rounded up from the villages to work in them, and between 1762 and 1769, serfs at sixty-four factories rioted against their inhuman working conditions, and were driven back to work by the army. In 1773, a hundred thousand factory and peasant serfs and former soldiers across a vast area of the Urals rallied to the Cossack Emelian Pugachev, to fight poverty and injustice, seizing weapons from the army, occupying the town of Kazan. A year later, ten thousand rebels were killed in the battles for Tsaritsyn, and by 1775 the rising had been crushed. Pugachev was driven by cart in chains to Moscow to be publicly beheaded, and his village was burnt to the ground. Thousands were sentenced to hard labour for life in the mines and factories, including many barely involved in the rising, and mining and factory settlements were turned into penal colonies, which in 1925 became labour camps for Russia's next arrested revolutionaries, the Decembrists. The camps were then used for successive generations of tsarist political prisoners, and in the 1930s they were were remodelled and expanded as the main operating base of the *gulag*.[1]

The more industrially developed Southern Urals had produced most of the iron and steel for Russia's new railways in the 1860s, and by 1905 was Europe's

---

1 Paul Dukes, *A History of the Urals: Russia's Crucible From Early Empire to the Post-Soviet Era*, 2015.

main exporter of iron. Russia's first factory soviets had sprung up there that year, and Bolshevik soviets were elected to power in 1917. Seventy thousand in the Urals joined the Red Army to drive out Kolchak's armies, and workers then returned from the fighting to rescue the wrecked mines and factories.[2]

Russia's impoverished predominantly rural peasant economy was to be transformed at top speed into a major industrial power, with the defence capabilities to withstand the next attack from the West. During the first two Five Year Plans, between 1928 and 1937, with their arrests and repressions and mighty achievements, agriculture was to be rapidly collectivised, and industrial output drastically increased. Five million answered the call of the 'Man of Steel' to build the vast new engineering, chemical and metallurgical plants in the Southern Urals, and Stalin's model city, Magnitogorsk, with its giant steel-mills, the largest in the world.[3]

Larisa was travelling to the still barely developed Northern Urals, populated by Muslim Tatars, Bashkirs and Kalmyks and Pagan Udmurts – 'where instead of digging iron and mining coal, people pick raspberries and cut down the graceful pine trees to build homes'. Only a fraction of the region's resources were being exploited then, in the little towns around the Urals capital Ekaterinburg, the first stop on her journey.

Two hundred miles from the Western Siberian Plain, Ekaterinburg had been founded by Peter the Great in the name of his wife, the first Empress Catherine, to showcase his industrialisation programme for Russia. Russia's first iron-smelting plant had been built there in 1724, and over the next century new foundries, factories and mines opened in the city, with their ready supply of cheap serf labour. By the early twentieth century, Ekaterinburg was the centre of operations for dozens of mainly foreign-owned companies with mining and factory interests in the Urals and Siberia, including the British-owned Siberian Lena Goldfields Company, in which the Tsar's family had major investments, known for its exceptionally cruel treatment of its workers. Larisa and her father had joined the large angry demonstration in St Petersburg in the spring of 1912, after two hundred and seventy miners were shot dead by the army for striking against their brutal working conditions, setting off solidarity strikes and riots across Russia.

Nine months after the Revolution, Ekaterinburg became the last refuge of the Tsar, shot with his family and servants by local *Cheka* agents, to show that the Red Terror would be merciless with its enemies. A week later, Kolchak's

---

2 D. Lisovsky, *Oktyabr na yuzhnem Urale. Borba za istanovlenie sovetskoi vlasti 1917–1918* (October in the Southern Urals. The Battle for Soviet Power), Chelyabinsk, 1957.
3 See John Scott, *Behind the Urals. An American Worker in Russia's City of Steel*, 1942.

Cossack forces entered the city with the Czech legions, and executed or tortured to death over twenty-five thousand of its citizens, ending the Czechs' alliance with Kolchak.

After the Whites were finally driven out by the Red Army in the spring of 1919, Trotsky had stayed there for a month, restoring order in what he called 'one of the most economically important areas of Russia', and the city was now a stronghold of Bolshevik power in the Urals. Ekaterinburg was also one of the first honouring the tsars to be renamed after the Revolution, and was now Sverdlovsk, in memory of the late much loved Party Secretary Yakov Sverdlov, a native of the Urals.[4]

Leaving the grime and politics of the city, she travelled on a branch line of the Trans-Siberian Railway four hundred miles south, through dense forested *taiga*, to the ancient iron-mining town and former prison colony of Bilimbay (now Belebey). She then spent the next three months travelling around the nearby mining and factory towns and settlements, with their primitive pits and foundries, and their portraits of Lenin and Party slogans on the walls – 'Workers of Russia, Boost Production Tenfold!' 'Comrades, Roll Up Your Sleeves and Work!'

She stayed in the metal-working towns of Lysva, Revda and Shaytanka, and visited the Nadezhdinsky Metallurgy Plant, 'Pride of the Northern Urals'. She explored the coalmines at Kyzyl, and the platinum mines at Kytlym, high in the Urals mountains, and she joined workers in their shifts, living with their families as she had in Germany, writing the essays and articles for *Izvestiya* that later became her book *Coal Iron and Living People*.

'She spends days in railway carriages, in carts, on horseback', Radek wrote.

> She goes down the pits, she sees the working masses engaged in production, descending half-naked to the mines, drenched in sweat at a blast furnace, cursing their low wages, while the best of them are stoutly convinced their torments and forced labour are the sacrifices that have to be made in the fight to build socialism ... She goes to meetings of factory boards, shop committees and trade unions, and she talks, hours, daily, with workers, feeling a way through the gloom, lending an ear close to life.

She was the first journalist to report on workers' lives in this epoch in Russia, as they built the foundations for the new Soviet economy, and she saw the same

---

4   Sverdlovsk became Ekaterinburg again in September 1991, three months before the official end of the USSR.

sacrifices and heroism as in the Civil War – 'the same workers' class solidarity, which nothing the world throws at them can shake'. Her *Izvestiya 'spetskor'* uniform, of leather jacket, boots and cap, was a version of her commissar's uniform, and her writing was filled with the language and memories of the front. Fifty miles south of Bilimbay was the Volga town of Samara, captured in July 1918 by the Czechs, then two months later by the Red Army. Further north were Kazan and Svyazhsk, and dozens of other towns and villages the Flotilla had fought for in the Civil War. Thousands had gone straight back to work after the fighting, and she wrote of the broken machinery, the failure and suffering, and 'workers' superhuman sacrifices, labouring to drag Soviet industry out of poverty, all on the rations of 1920, which will one day be displayed in museums – a pound and three-quarters of flour per family a day, a pound of sugar a month, a quarter of a pound of meat, a twentieth of fat and vegetables, and four cigarettes'.

Yet four years later, output was already back to its pre-war levels, and had often outstripped them, she wrote. 'Clearly this is due not to any technical improvements, but to workers' incredible heroism and endurance, fighting to save Russia from economic ruin'.

In the Bilimbay mine, she joined miners crawling on their knees along dripping airless tunnels lit with primitive kerosine lamps, propped up by rotten wood. 'For centuries, prisoners were sentenced here to long years of hard labour for the gravest of crimes ... Yet when our government wanted to close the mine, the miners refused outright, and even voted to go without electricity to keep costs down'.

At the mighty Nadezhdinsky Plant, she explored its 'cranes and furnaces and smoking chimneys and narrow-gauge railway-tracks, with the shriek and roar of machines in unknown workshops, raging like madmen trying to break down the walls', where 'the only sound audible through the din, as quiet as the squeak of a mouse under a giant's feet, is the foreman's whistle, worker's signal of discipline, calling them from the bench where they have collapsed exhausted, to come back and help'.

At the Shaytanka steelworks, workers operating its great rolling-mills were 'ruled by the supreme punishment:'

> Delay means death. Clumsiness means death. Iron has no colour at 800 degrees, just the colour of death. Yet their mastery of the metal gives an extraordinary lightness to their movements. All have their job to do, and they are confident and unhurried, with perfect timing, throwing the blazing half-ton strips in the machines as easily as throwing a lazy dog in the river in summer.

At Kyzyl, she spent days in the mine, the largest working coalmine in the Northern Urals, from whose six massive shafts miners produced over ten million tons of coal a year – 'with its capital, "Lenin," its squares surrounded by glistening three-foot deep walls of fuel, its centres and highways, its outskirts and country tracks, its wagons with bells like electric trams, pulled by short-sighted ponies, stumbling into the eternal night'.

The mine's decrepit machines were powered by the region's first hydroelectric station, the 'magnificent grey palace' of *Kyzylstroi*, which would later seem so small. Three hundred workers died in its construction, digging a seven-hundred-foot concrete channel to divert the water from the river Kosva – 'exceptionally hard work, started in 1922, virtually without machines or protective clothing, and finished two years later, not only phenomenally quickly, but to a high standard, on the pay and rations of 1922, and in Kyzyl's harsh climate, where ninety percent of babies are still born with symptoms of tuberculosis'.

She had written *The Front* for her *rabfak* students. *Coal Iron and Living People* was written for the workers in the mines and factories. The Revolution had lifted millions out of dire poverty, and she wrote of the free education, housing and healthcare, the vastly improved working conditions, increased wages and better food. 'The Revolution has become part of workers' lives, like the miner's portrait of Lenin on the arch of one of Kyzyl's deepest horizontals. Only a few of the older ones are left now to keep memories of the old regime alive, with its gallows and shootings and mass funerals. For most, the recent past has dropped forever from their consciousness, and no longer has any reality'.

She met workers who had found their way to books and politics and the Party, and she joined the recruitment drive for the 'Lenin Enrolment', which doubled the Party's membership between 1923 and 1925 to over a million. 'Comrade Reisner, please don't doubt my commitment', Ivan Buinov of the Bilimbay miners' union wrote on his application form. 'I am the son of a worker, and I volunteered with the Red Army, and every moment our workers' government survives is precious to me'.

She described the same spirit of revolutionary optimism at the Party meetings she went to. But she saw her job as a journalist as not to glorify the Party, but to record conscientiously what workers were saying. Most of these meetings were organised by the workers themselves, she wrote, 'without a single senior official involved, often in direct opposition to their inert bureaucratic will'. And mixed with their hopes and dreams for the new society, she saw their deep anger with the Party bureaucrats and highly paid 'specialists' and capitalist-style managers of the NEP, and their scandalous neglect of their basic needs.

Russia's heavy industry, mines, mineral resources and railways, nationalised two months after the Revolution, remained state-controlled under the

NEP. Smaller enterprises were grouped together on a commercial profit-making basis, as semi-autonomous Industrial Trusts, and economic competition led to pay cuts, layoffs and deteriorating working conditions. The first law after the Revolution, the Labour Law of November 1917, had cut the working day to eight hours, which was then reduced to six, and the all-powerful Trusts now wanted to bring back the eight-hour day for six hours' pay.

In the two years Stalin had been Party Secretary, he had packed posts with his supporters, creating a vast new bureaucratic elite that already exceeded tsarist levels, and for these new Party bureaucrats and the manager bureaucrats of the NEP, hitting industrial targets took priority over workers' health and happiness.

Workers also bore the main burden of the financial instability of the NEP's recent currency reforms, introduced to tackle the hyperinflation of War Communism, and bring the rouble closer to the currencies of the Soviet Union's hoped-for new capitalist trading partners. She met those who were paid late, or even not at all. She met miners at the end of their strength, suffering from 'miners' asthma' and 'black spit' (as lung cancer and pneumoconiosis were known then). She wrote of the painful reality of the new Soviet health system, starved of funds and strangled by red tape. She wrote of the empty shelves in the shops, and of the housing crisis, the perennial curse of the Soviet system, and she stayed with workers in their squalid slums and tenements:

> It's a scandal that we still house people in these disgusting places we inherited from the old companies, with their broken windows blocked with rags and sheets of metal, their sewage and age-old filth seeping through the walls ... This shocking neglect of workers' living conditions can only partly and with difficulty be explained by our lack of resources ... If we don't put the same energy into solving this crisis as we did with the food crisis in 1918, their tuberculosis-infected slums will continue to be hotbeds of counterrevolutionary agitation, right under the noses of the *Cheka*.

'Those who want to see the achievements of our Great October Revolution should visit our factories and mines not only in the peaceful times, but on the days marked on workers' calendars by flare-ups and disputes', she wrote. 'Their labours and sacrifices give them the right to make the widest criticisms. And the sharper these criticisms are, the closer to production and its needs, the more clearly we will see the face of the new post-revolutionary Russia'.

In the Bilimbay mine, she joined a group of miners 'at the bottom of their wet grave', discussing the Trust's proposed new hours:

A young miner speaks, his voice breaking like an empty bucket dropped down a shaft on an unwound chain. 'Forget it, we can't do eight, we're done in! The sons of bitches promised us vodka! At least give us cigarettes!'

'What can they do?' another says. 'There was the Blockade, and now the English won't give us loans'. And the extraordinary paleness of the man, speaking of the fate of the world in the silence of the seventy-metre shaft, his pickaxe in his hand, clouds of icy sweat steaming from his shoulders, gives his words a special seriousness, filled with a consciousness of our Party's responsibilities in carrying out its programme, in whose name workers endure their punishing labour.

'We're not doing eight, you write that!' workers at Revda's sheet-metal shop tell her. Then their union leader Maslyannikov speaks. 'Tall, severe, incorruptible, hero of the Civil War, Comrade Maslyannikov summarises everything that can be said in defence of the present in the name of the future. Soviet power must survive, that is the starting point, these are the terms under which everything must be discussed. Each hammer blow, each strike of the axe, is made in the hope of the speediest possible advance to a more just, more human life. And with his speech, it seems the hours are voted through'.

Her *Izvestiya* wages book showed her salary to be a hundred roubles and fifty kopecks a month, three times that of the most highly skilled worker. Women and newly 'workerised' peasants were generally the least skilled, on the lowest pay rate of twenty-two roubles a month, and she reported little or no resistance to the new pay deal in their workshops.

Working in the fumes and din of one of the Nadezhdinsky Plant's rolling shops were a team of elderly peasants from the same village in the south, evacuated after the Revolution when the old masters left – 'thrown onto the proletarian street like old men thrown out by their families after losing at cards'. 'They have given not one worker to the Party in the Lenin Enrolment, they have silently boycotted it.'

> Comrade Legotkin fought with the Red Army for two years, before he was invalided out with typhus and sent back to his machine. Pinned to his thin chest, as bent and crooked as a Chinese worker's knee, is his badge of the Red Banner, awarded to him for taking five White officers prisoner while he was out on patrol. He was in the Party too once, before it lost him in the typhus-infected trains, where he lost his memory, his residence permit and his name ... And now his fellow peasants stand like a wall between him and the Party, which has no time to notice this man who has fallen overboard, no time to reach out and pull him up.

Women made up almost half the workforce in the 1920s, and she wrote of their atrocious working conditions, and men's reluctance to take their complaints seriously. '"The girls are moaning again!" they say'.

The 1917 Labour Law had banned women from heavy work in the mines and factories, and introduced maternity benefits and equal pay. But as Kollontai had correctly predicted, war, poverty and male chauvinism meant that much of this early progressive legislation would remain on paper. Thousands of women had fought with the Red Army in the Civil War, and some thirty thousand joined the Party in the Lenin Enrolment. Millions would be mobilised into industry in the Five Year Plans, and they would play a heroic role in the defeat of Hitler. Seven years after the Revolution, eighty percent of women's work was still classified as unskilled, and they were the first under the NEP to lose their jobs. And despite Lenin's eloquent words at the 1918 Women's Congress against domestic drudgery, a survey in 1924 showed that they spent an average of five hours a day on housework.

Hidden from view behind the main foundry at Revda was a small brickworks, where the workers were exclusively women, most of them widows, who had lost partners in the war or the Civil War, struggling to support themselves and their children – 'working in temperatures that hover between those in a greenhouse, where the soft young bricks are germinated, and a roasting hot kitchen, where they are baked. And every part of their work, from start to finish, which no man would touch, is injurious to human health'. One had lost both her two sons fighting with the Red Army, and three had new-born babies at home, and almost all had joined the Party in the Lenin Enrolment. 'Nobody likes the place', she wrote, 'neither the Factory Committee nor the directors or specialists. Its messy manual labour brings down the tone of the factory, and outsiders rarely visit'.

At the Lysva factory, women working in the enamelling shop 'stand for hours in burning puddles, breathing in the foul air. The body fills with a burning exhaustion, and you long to lay your head on the nearest workbench. Anything to sleep!'

> Beyond a certain point, sensitivity to pain is numbed. Life must look very different through a fog of fumes that produce nosebleeds, nausea, dizziness and severe chest pains. All of this, so unbearable to begin with, soon becomes constant and familiar, and reduces the will to fight. Take pity on these workshops in the factories of the future! They must be the first to be opened to the light, they need the sunniest windows, the freshest air!

In July she left the factories and mines around Bilimbay, and made the long journey by train and on horseback to the platinum mines at Kytlym, in the summits of the Urals mountains.

Buried in the swamplands around Kytlym, just below the eternal snowline, were the world's largest deposits of 'white gold', the most precious of the metals. Deep underground mining would start only in the 1930s. In the 1920s, the platinum was still mined from open pits, and she described the devastating environmental impact of the process:

> Massive excavators are dragged across the remote *taiga* and erected in hollows in the mountains, surrounded by millions of tons of mud and bare rocks ... Thousands of kilowatts are thrown at the swamps, freezing cold in winter, plagued by mosquitoes in summer. Machines blast the landscape night and day, moving mountains to produce a few ounces of the metal ... The whole valley is turned into a graveyard for the sake of these fragments humanity considers valuable for some reason. Forget its notional value, and it's a picture of insane waste and destruction.

She visited the pits, with their floating platforms and diggers:

> Wide grey shovels dip in and out of the water like steel frogs, somersaulting under the surface, floating up with their mouths full of mud. Each scoopful is deposited in the sluice-box in the machine's entrails, then moved to a perforated cylinder, where it is given a cold shower to hose away the gravel and impurities. Then the larger rocks are hauled to the surface on a narrow mechanical belt, scattering lumps of granite, and the remaining sludge is moved to the wash-plant above the mine, where it is sieved into special trays for its final rinsing.

She was fascinated by the labour process, and her journalist's notebooks in her archives are meticulous records of new machines and factories, with statistical tables and diagrams and columns of data. But the Revolution's greatest resource was its people, and her notebooks 'Living Portraits' are filled with sketches of the workers who would make up her vast cast of characters in *Coal Iron and Living People*.

Her crowd scenes live in the memory. The stokers at the Bilimbay foundry, 'bare-chested warriors, in their Red Army caps and felt boots'. Peasant workers at Shaytanka, 'in their baggy homespun tunics and bast shoes, made from the peasants' birch trees in the workers' forest'. Women machine-operators at Revda, 'frail-looking and tireless, in their severe kerchiefs and aprons'. The Tatar miners at Kyzyl, 'proudly carrying their sacks of coal on their shoulders like their best gowns'. The older miners, in their 'tall boots, peaked leather caps and black shirts buttoned to the neck, the uniform of the industrial Urals in the Civil War'. And the shifting population of miners at Kytlym, lured there by dreams of platinum:

> The peasant working to earn enough to buy a new bath or plough. The brilliant communist and intellectual, unable to support his family, who has fallen hopelessly back into the barracks. The strange workers who aren't workers, exiled political prisoners and *Chekists* sacked for their crimes, cursing Soviet power under their breath, burning their throats with cheap brick tea that tastes of urine ... All are drunk on the metal, drunk at the sight of the water flushing the gravel from the mud, blind drunk, secretly drunk, without alcohol ...

As in all her works, she cuts *montage*-style from her big set-pieces to closeups of individuals, picking them from the crowd and telling their stories.

In the wash-plant at Kytlym, she was mesmerised by the old Udmurt Guryan Malstev at work on his rinsing-tray:

> Only Guryan can see the metal hidden in the mud, chasing the silver mouse under the water with his quick sensitive hands, like two little white cats ... The whole workshop trembles as the communist controller scoops it into his ladle and dries it by the fire. But Guryan watches with the detached look of a gambler whose luck ran out long ago ...
>
> His life hasn't been easy. He lost his family when his village burnt down in a forest fire, and afterwards he set off alone across the Urals to pan for platinum ... Then in 1917, he was seized with the longing to search for something better, and the old hunter returned home to gamble everything on one last find. And what he found were people like him, crawling around in the mud, and he stopped searching ... The Revolution had cured him of his platinum lust, and he went to work on a Soviet digger.

At Bilimbay, she was shown round the foundry by the foreman and 'master of the boilers and ovens' Alexei Kashin, 'a small man with the most good-natured face, loved by all for his friendliness, and a true "specialist," who helped build his furnaces thirty-five years ago, nursed them through their brief childhoods, and has spent three-quarters of his life with them'.

At the Revda brickworks, she met the forewoman and 'women's defender', 'popular rosy-cheeked Comrade Natasha'. At the Lysva factory, she met Anna

Balkova, union organiser in the stamping workshop – 'a tiny woman who all the women love and trust, who wears her headscarf knotted to one side, like a wise hare with one ear up, who lives on nothing but dry bread dipped in slops of coffee, and flourishes like summer ... A truly new kind of woman, who lost her family in the years of hunger, typhus and Kolchak, and cheerfully bears on her shoulders her great work for the factory, enduring the hardships, making life easier for others'.

In Kyzyl, she met the Civil War heroes who had returned from fighting at one front after another to build the new power-station and restore the mine. 'Underground Kyzyl has no seasons, no day or night', she wrote, 'just labour, broken up into three shifts, each sending a ton of coal to the surface'.

The foreman in one of its deepest most dangerous pits, the young communist Mikhail Matveich, when asked what made him join the Party in the Lenin Enrolment, said, 'It was to show the foreign capitalists we count for something!'

> And all the pegs on which a worker's life is measured – the wretched housing, the wet shoes and low pay – paled into insignificance. If the mine is throw its extra half-million tons of coal onto the market, and cut the price by twelve kopecks a ton, and if Kyzyl's party organisation is to grow stronger in the process, it will be thanks entirely to those like Comrade Matveich, who have kept their faith in communism, despite the exhaustion and the disillusionment and the shortcomings of the transitional period.

The elderly Tatar Tatarinkov, foreman at the 'Lenin' pit, wasn't so keen on the Party or the Revolution:

> A tall distinguished figure in an old-fashioned peaked cap, his long thin body squeezed through a tight leather belt, like a napkin through a napkin-ring, Comrade Tatarinkov has propped up Kyzyl's drifts and faces for twenty-seven years, and he knows and respects every seam ... Of all the laws and decrees passed by the Revolution, it seems only one has reached these elders of the mine, making the miners its sole legal owners, and however much they grumbled and tried to avoid politics, this transfer of ownership was passed. And now the new owners with full rights hover anxiously over their successors, initiating the younger generation into their fine old trade.

In one of Kyzyl's darkest tunnels, she met 'the remarkable Comrade Derevnin', 'an underground fanatic, who hates sunlight and fresh air:'

Nothing would induce Derevnin to abandon the mine for the shadows of a summer morning, creeping over the soft green fields. Even in the Epiphany frosts, when workers above grip their rifles in their frozen hands, the coalfaces are as hot as at harvest time, and he throws off his shirt and reaps the black crops ...

The Revolution called him up to the surface, and he fought with the Reds then with the Whites, and found them both equally alien ... Riding the trains, out on patrol, lying in hospital, at his political education classes – run first by his communist teacher, then by a dashing speech-maker from the Whites' propaganda unit – he dreamed of Kyzyl's welcoming shafts ...

Working in the tunnel below, 'through a silent *taiga* of coal, connected to the drift above by a low winding gallery', was the miner Mindulaev – 'as black as if the gloom had closed door after door behind him. And never in my life have I met anyone blacker and more exhausted or more joyful'.

Woken by the Revolution, Comrade Mindulaev was released to the surface to fight with the Red Army. He loved his new freedom, and became addicted to the sun, and married a woman from the race of the pale earth-dwellers ... But his Party duties called him back to the mine, where despite working to the limits of his strength, from seven in the morning until six at night, he earns a pittance. Yet every word of Mindulaev's is measured. He stamps out every irritable remark like a cigarette end to avoid a fire. Greedy for the joys of life, good-natured and long-suffering, passionate about his work, he is driven by the iron discipline and self-sacrifice that made him abandon the sun for his airless cell.

She wrote of the slums and hovels where Kyzyl's workers snatched some sleep between their shifts – 'living piled on top of each other like the proletariat throughout the entire Urals, if not the whole of industrial Russia, eating, sleeping and choking on filth'. And she speculated on what might be built there in the future to replace them. 'What if in the place of Kyzyl's wretched little field hospital, on whose bunks over three hundred workers died building *Kyzylstroi*, their sacrifices were rewarded with a new Palace of Labour, where they could take a break from work, enjoy some culture and entertainment, and do some studying?'

In looking beyond the poverty and suffering to the better world workers were fighting for, she described following Gorky's advice to writers after the Revolution, to juxtapose scenes of their lives with episodes from the past, and set these against an imagined 'unknown third' – the limitless possibilities of the future.

She used this technique particularly successfully in her Revda essay – parallel narratives moving back and forth in time between the era of serfdom, when the foundry was built by the aristocratic Demidov family, one of the wealthiest in Europe, related to the tsars, the post-Emancipation years under its new owners, Russia's ruthless self-made millionaires and first merchant capitalists, and the revolutionary struggles of her lifetime.

The story opens in 1774, when the last units of Pugachev's serf rising were crushed at Revda, and ends with their descendants, Revda's future, the stokers working in the foundry:

> Bent double, stripped to the waist, their faces hidden behind the visors of their helmets, they hurl pig-iron and quarter-ton logs of wood into the furnaces, dodging the sparks streaking to the floor to sniff their ragged bast shoes ... Poverty forces us to keep these barbaric long-obsolete work practices, but they are connected to each other like the cables carrying the electricity. Each keeps a keen eye on the other, resting and smoking in the brief breaks in their labours, noticing everything between two drags of tobacco, and at the critical moment, never a second too soon or too late, sharing the weight, beating back the fire.

Her report from Kytlym is another skilful blend of the past and the present, tales of capitalist greed, NEP corruption and sabotage, and workers' heroism.

The story begins in the 1820s, when the first British and French prospectors arrived in Kytlym to buy concessions to the platinum:

> By 1905, wild *troikas* were galloping across the *taiga* with their spoils, totalling millions of roubles ... Profits peaked in the years before the 1914 War. It was for platinum that the imperialists fought this war, which we are now having to pay for all over again. It was for platinum's millions and billions that Kolchak marched his Cossacks across the Urals to Kytlym in the winter of 1918, armed to the teeth by Britain and France, littering the ground with corpses, urged on by imperious cables from London and Paris over the wires of his field-telegraph, looped from tree to tree – 'Dammit Admiral, what are we paying you for!'

She met Kytlym's partisans who had survived the desperate battles in the freezing snow to drive out Kolchak's forces. And she lived with the family of the mines' director, Sergeev, a former partisan, one of several hundred tsarist political prisoners sentenced to hard labour in the mines, who had stayed on after the Revolution to work with Kytlym's native Bashkirs, Tatars and Udmurts.

She met Party members who 'protect themselves from the platinum fever by devouring Lenin, like quinine for malaria, reading him late at night after the long working day, under the weak electric lights of the remote Urals'. And she rode on horseback with the communist head of Kytlym's militia on a tour of inspection of the surrounding villages – 'our American Wild West' – where mining rights had been sold to private prospectors, mainly wealthy peasants.

The most successful of these new 'mining Nepmen', the peasant Pichugin, 'with his sharp wolf's ears and cunning eyes', 'speaks lovingly of his family, who from generation to generation will live comfortably on their wretched embezzled platinum inheritance, like bedbugs on a wall ... Then smiling craftily, he lifts his shining eyes to the portrait of Lenin in the corner, where the icons used to be, removes his cap and crosses himself'.

> Meanwhile Kytlym's partisans, who almost starved to death in 1918, and suffer from rheumatic fever and tuberculosis from their work on the diggers, must rot in their fetid slums, which produce more counterrevolutionary propaganda than the Whites could dream of ...
>
> If someone manages to lift their head in their nine-foot cell, and in the voice of someone who has been stranded on a desert island for years, says they want to join the Party – 'All the young ones are joining, you can't stay behind!' – it means the Revolution has pulled a truly great human being from the mud.

Within a decade, the little towns and settlements she visited would be new factory cities, producing unheard-of quantities of steel and coal, and *Kyzylstroi* would be supplying vast areas of the the Northern Urals with power. She was writing of the first heroes and heroines of Soviet labour, building socialism with superhuman energy and optimism on the eve of the 1930s, when the heavy industry of the Urals would be switched to producing arms, and thousands would be arrested for failing to fulfil their impossible labour targets.

Hitler had written in *Mein Kampf* of *Lebensraum* – 'living space' in the East for the German people – and his assault on the Soviet Union was a foregone conclusion when he took power in 1933. The Urals was not occupied during the three-year Nazi occupation, and was on the front line of the resistance. Seven hundred factories were packed into flatcars and evacuated east from Central Russia, with two million workers and their families, and thousands of new arms factories were built, with their portraits of Stalin and slogans 'Death to the Fascist Invaders!' 'All for the Front!' After the Nazis were driven out in 1944, when

Soviet industry returned to civilian production, and occupied European Russia and Ukraine were in ruins, productivity in the Urals had increased dramatically, with a stronger industrial base than before.

Kytlym's platinum mines and other non-essential industry had closed, to free up workers for the war effort, and miners returned to work after the war under strict military conditions, with the platinum surrounded by an army camp. Two new underground mines were built, and by the 1960s output had outstripped its pre-war levels.

In the new Russia, Kytlym's platinum is back in capitalist hands. Mining rights have been sold to the London-based multinational Eurasia Mining Plc., and the army camp is now the 331st Combat Management Centre – a vast heavily fortified military installation, buried deep in a disused underground mine, connected to the Russian Army's nuclear submarines and missile-launchers. Hikers in Kytlym from Ekaterinburg recently posted joke pictures on the internet of the entrance to a small underground mine, buried in snow, with the sign 'Putin's Nuclear Bunker'.

∵

In August, she travelled a thousand miles south from the Urals to the Donbas region of Eastern Ukraine, and stayed for the next month in the coalmining town Gorlovka, twenty miles from the Donbas capital Donetsk.

'It's as if the whole landscape has been redesigned with pyramids', she wrote of the view from the train, 'identical, geometrically regular slag-heaps, towering over the factory chimneys, with little wagons scuttling up them like ants, tucking their iron legs under them as they feed the tips with tons of industrial waste'.

The Donetsk Basin had been one of the main centres of heavy industry in the Russian Empire since the 1860s, producing over seventy percent of its iron and coal, and was known before the Revolution as the 'tenth Belgian province'. Ninety percent of its mines and factories had been owned by Belgian and French companies, and in 1825 the concession to the Gorlovka mine was bought by the Belgian Joint Stock Company for the South Russian Coal Industry, whose foundries in the Donbas were some of the largest and most technologically advanced in the world.[5]

Gorlovka's miners were treated better by the foreign capitalists than by the Russians, she wrote, until their profits were threatened. In December 1905, at

---

5   Orest Subtelny, *Ukraine. A History*, 1994.

the height of the industrial unrest in Ukraine, miners had led a general strike in the town. Four thousand workers surrounded the company's machine-building plant, demanding increased wages and the eight-hour day, and the army was sent in, leaving eighty with life-threatening injuries. Thirty-two of the leaders were sentenced to be executed, with hundreds more sentenced to hard labour in the mine, and miners' pay was cut to teach them a lesson.

In 1914, safety standards at the mine were scrapped in the race for quick profits. 'The Imperialist War was the age of lucrative speculation, in which the owners had no choice but to play an active part', she wrote, and in 1918, three hundred miners lost their lives in the worst methane explosion in the mine's history. 'Managers put out fantastic figures about safe air levels, and the miners, for whom unemployment and the sack were a cruel reality, believed them ... It was only two years later that the victims could be brought up and buried by the new Russia, born while the lethal fumes were dispersing at the bottom of the shaft'.

Some of the bloodiest battles of the Civil War had been fought in Ukraine, for its fertile agricultural lands in the west, and its mines and factories and precious natural resources in the east. 'Without the Donbas, the construction of socialism would be just a piece of wishful thinking', Lenin said after the Revolution.

Between the summer of 1919 and the spring of 1920, the entire region had been overrun by the British-backed armies of Denikin, Wrangel and Kolchak, the German-backed 'White Wolves' of the Cossack Hetmans Shkuro and Kaledin, the 50,000-strong 'black armies' of Nestor Makhno's Free Anarchist Republic of Ukraine, and the forces of the Ukrainian nationalist Symon Petlyura, responsible with Denikin for the slaughter of over a hundred thousand Jewish, Russian and Polish men, women and children.

In towns under White occupation the old managers returned, and it was a war to the death for profits and class revenge. Workers suffered savage exploitation and starvation wages, and retaliated with wildcat strikes. Denikin ordered one in every ten strikers to be publicly hanged, and the White Terror was matched by the ferocity of the resistance, led by the Cossack Revolutionary Committee in Donetsk. On Kollontai's frontline speaking tour of the Donbas in 1919, she reported travelling through villages burnt to the ground by Denikin's armies, and to Gorlovka and other mining communities around Donetsk, 'where workers' lives are one long hellish underground struggle, and where the true power of the resistance is to be found'.

Gorlovka's miners finally took control of the mine in 1920, after throwing out the Belgians and fighting off the Whites. By then most of Ukraine was under the control of the Red Army, and in 1922 Ukraine became the largest of the republics of the new Soviet Union, Russia's main ally and trading partner – until the breakup of the Soviet Union in 1991, when Ukraine became an independent state for the first time in its history.

Larisa was in the Donbas at the start of the Stalin 'personality cult'. Donetsk was now 'Stalino', the first of eight major cities he would name after himself over the next decade, including Stalingrad, and the Donbas, like the Urals, would be on the front line of his Second Five Year Plan.[6] The Stakhanovite movement was born there, named after the miner Alexei Stakhanov in the Donbas town of Kadievka, who in 1935 produced an amazing 102 tons of coal in his six-hour shift, fourteen times his quota. Three years earlier, *Pravda* had reported the Gorlovka miner Nikita Izotov producing an even more amazing 122 tons in his shift. Izotov had arrived in Gorlovka from Russia after the Civil War as head of a work brigade to restore the mine, and he had introduced new mining methods, based on a scientific study of the seams – methods taught at over a dozen new Izotov Mining Schools across Ukraine in the 1930s, and used by miners there and in Russia to this day.

Gorlovka in the 1920s was a lively, ethnically mixed town of Ukrainians, Poles, Tatars and Russians. Most then, as now, were of Russian origin, and the main languages spoken were Russian and the mixed Ukrainian Russian dialect known as *surzhyk*.

Russians had been arriving to work in the mine since the 1860s, when coal was first discovered in the Donbas. The rapid development of Russian industry in the 1890s had brought new waves of settlers to the town, and the mine's director, Ivan Korobkin, whose family Larisa stayed with, was one of hundreds who arrived after the 1905 revolution – 'a big polar-bear of a man, who worked his way up from delivery boy to lamp-carrier, pony-driver, faceworker, Red Guard and Bolshevik fighter, and finally Red director'.

> When miners returned to work after the fighting ended, all the equipment was wrecked, the ventilation and water system had collapsed, and coal dust and firedamp [*methane*] flew through the tunnels like moths through an empty house, leaking through cracks in the seams and gathering in the coal pockets like rainwater in a bucket, threatening to give a more terrible force to even the smallest explosion than the glorious explosion of 1917 ...
>
> Every day they risked being blown up, or drowning in the underground water. After two hours' work, they would be knocked off their feet by hunger. But Korobkin fought for every lamp-screw, every inch of reinforced cable, somehow getting supplies from the front, often doing the work

---

6   Donetsk returned to its old name in 1961, eight years after Stalin's death.

himself ... And finally the turning point came, and Gorlovka has now more than doubled its annual output of coal.

She joined miners on their shifts in the deep diagonal pits, some of the deepest and most dangerous in the Donbas, if not the world, 'with their massive walls and ceilings of coal, three-hundred feet wide in places'. She met those who had worked in the mine all their lives, and had defended it against the Whites. She met communists 'intoxicated by the underground, who left to fight at one front after another, until the fighting finally ended and they returned, their longing for the mine undiminished by their years defending the Great Revolution'. She met miners who had not joined the Party in the Lenin Enrolment – 'and if you saw where I live, you'd know why', one told her. And she saw them all competing for the most difficult jobs at the most perilous faces.

In the 'Mazurka' pit, a narrow cleft propped up by wooden struts, 'fantastic figures, barely visible through the fumes of their underground slum, hang from thin crossbeams above bottomless open pits, hacking the coal, hurling it down to the wagons that carry it to the lift'. At the 'Magpie' seam, 'miners straddle narrow girders, attacking the coal from above. The same thundering avalanches of coal pouring down the chutes, the same dust and lack of air, the same laboured breathing and soul-soothing curses, the same steady tapping of the metal woodpeckers hollowing out the rocks'.

Perched on a ledge are three miners 'as different from each other as you could imagine – in other words, as different as people are everywhere'. The former soldier from St Petersburg's elite tsarist Preobrazhensky Regiment, 'striking the coal with grand sweeping gestures, as if taking the salute on St Petersburg's Palace Square', 'who wears his Soviet citizenship like a badge of honour, his talisman against misfortune'. The old communist who had fought to defend the mine against Shkuro's Cossack Cavalry, and was jailed for two weeks, 'sitting in his drawers', waiting to be shot. The dreamy provincial schoolboy, 'stirred by the spirit of adventure to join the Red Guards then the Russian Communist Party, whose punishing work in the mine has turned into a man'.

Working below them, Gorlovka's 'master of all trades', faceworker Gondar, 'lowers himself onto a foothold, spreads his chest against the wall, and hanging upside-down, hacks at a new seam ... Then he timbers up the cleared spots before they fall on miners' heads, hammering a stake into the open jaws of the coal and slipping in a tie-brace, as neatly as a tram conductor slipping her thick timetables in her bag'.

All four have their own way of holding their axe in their shifts, their own way of being alone with their thoughts. Yet whatever the differences in their ages, classes and political backgrounds, all would agree unquestioningly on two things. The first is their elemental, blood connection to the workers' state. The second, and at the heart of their grievances, is that the masses who defended the mine with their rifles in the hungry years of the Civil War, littering it with their corpses, achieving what the economists and 'specialists' thought was impossible, have the right now to expect the Party to pay the same detailed scrupulous attention to their needs and living conditions as they pay to the needs of the mine.

Gorlovka's housing crisis was so desperate that many lacked even their own bunk to sleep on after their shifts. An emergency building programme was being carried out, and she inspected the new homes going up, 'with their shining silver roofs of fireproof Urals asbestos, and their own front doors and stoves and shelves, where miners can dry their wet clothes'. 'But although Donbas coal is hungry for homes, the State Building Committee unfortunately hates to spend money, and only twenty are being built, for a population of twenty thousand'.

She wrote of the unbreathable air in the mine, and the miners' usual chest infections, and of the town's barely functioning medical services. The hospital was desperately poor, with beds only for the most seriously ill. The rest were sent home to be seen at the clinic, or returned to work.

> The bottomless earth gives up its tons of coal, hooters signal the beginnings and ends of the shifts, miners come and go, and the victorious march of labour steps over the heads of its fallen fighters ... After years of heroic struggle against hunger and exhaustion, working until their last breath to get the great mines of the Donbas back on their feet, they are left to die alone and neglected.

Coal Iron and Living People is the darkest of her books, and her reports from Ukraine are the darkest of its chapters, written in the buildup to the Five Year Plans, less than a decade before the Great Famine, known in Ukraine as the 'Holodomor'.

The government was completely unprepared to deal with the catastrophic droughts that hit the agricultural areas of the Soviet Union between 1932 and 1933, at the height of the collectivisation drive. Seven million deaths from hunger and epidemics were recorded (the same number, it was noted, as those who died in America's Great Depression), and the greatest suffering was in Ukraine, Russia's 'granary', with records showing that almost two million peasants starved to death.

Hundreds of thousands of tons of food aid were rushed to the villages, but famine relief efforts were beset by incompetence, bureaucracy and mass embezzlement. Local officials cashed in by stealing food supplies and selling them to weathy farmers and private traders and speculators, who sold them on the black market at vastly inflated prices, leading to more untold hunger and suffering.

In many countries abroad, the famine is presented as engineered and weaponised by Stalin, to punish Ukraine's peasants for resisting collectivisation, in his 'genocidal war' against the Ukrainian people. Recorded deaths in Ukraine are contested with wildly higher figures, given as anything from three to fourteen million, with more insults to the dead in the terrible photographs of starving Ukrainian peasants published in the West, most of them taken of the peasants in the 1921 famine on the Volga.

News from Ukraine was first brought to Britain by freelance journalist Gareth Jones, whose mission was to tell the world about their suffering under Stalin's murderous collectivisation policies – the mass requisitioning of grain, the countryside littered with corpses, the cannibalism. His reports have now been given sensational new life in the 'troublingly relevant' 2019 Hollywood blockbuster biopic 'Mr Jones', 'the most important true story you will ever see', about his travels around the villages, staying with the peasants and starving with them in their huts. At one point in the film, Jones is shown personally eating 'the boy Kolya', not realising it is human flesh.

In a letter to the *Sunday Times*, his great nephew attacked the film's 'multiple fictions' – 'he saw no dead bodies and no requisitioning, and he witnessed no cannibalism, let alone took part in it'. Judging from his diaries, he never left Kharkov, and his reports were based almost entirely on conversations with unnamed sources. Nothing in the film of his two visits to Nazi Germany in 1933, at the beginning and end of his trip to Soviet Ukraine, where he reported on Hitler's swearing in as Chancellor – 'inspired by a great national force' – flew with the Fuhrer and his staff as a member of his press team on his private plane, 'the fastest most powerful three-motored aeroplane in Germany', attended his rallies, and was entertained by his 'amusing and likeable' Minister of Propaganda Dr Goebbels, 'with his remarkably appealing personality, and keen brain and sense of humour'.

During the Nazis' three-year occupation of Ukraine, many who had suffered under Stalin saw Hitler as their saviour, and some quarter of a million joined fascist battalions, or worked as concentration camp guards. Over five million joined the Red Army to drive them out, or fought in well supplied Soviet partisan units, sabotaging Nazi communications lines, blowing up garrisons, releasing prisoners from the camps.

Thirteen million died in Ukraine under Nazi rule, proportionately more losses than were suffered by any other country in the Second World War. 'I am not the slightest concerned if ten thousand of these females die digging an anti-tank ditch for us', Hitler said, and the Nazi *Untermensch* doctrine was spelt out in a mass of directives to the occupying forces. Virtually the entire Jewish population of two million was exterminated, and atrocities against Jews started in the first days of the occupation. 'We are the Master Race', said Hitler's *gauleiter* in Kiev, General Koch. 'The lowliest German worker is racially and biologically more valuable than the population here'.

The industry of the Donbas was vital for the Nazi occupation of Soviet Russia and the post-war expansion of the Reich, and men, women and young children were rounded up to work as slave labourers for the *Wehrmacht*, or 'exported' to Germany to be used in the Krupp and Junkers arms factories. By the end of the 1930s, Gorlovka had recovered from the poverty of the Civil War to become a thriving industrial and cultural centre, with thirteen mines, nine factories, two hundred schools, kindergartens and hospitals, and forty Palaces of Culture and public libraries. Under Nazi occupation, the city was surrounded by a concentration camp, and the bodies of fourteen thousand workers, tortured and shot by the Gestapo, were thrown down a disused mine shaft.

By the autumn of 1944, the last of the occupying armies had been driven out of Ukraine, with instructions from Himmler in Berlin to 'leave not a single person, head of livestock or measure of grain. The enemy must find a completely burned and devastated land'. Half a million Soviet troops were drafted into the wrecked depopulated towns and villages to join the reconstruction work, restoring water and electricity supplies, reopening schools and hospitals, and thirty thousand Party officials arrived from Moscow to arrest collaborators, hoarders and speculators, and impose harsh new quotas on the collective farms.

The next decades saw a mass labour migration from all over the Soviet Union to Ukraine's industrial areas, mainly to the Donbas. When Ukraine gained its independence in 1991, a fifth of the population, eight and a half million, were of Russian origin, seven million living in the Crimea and the Donbas. In a survey two years earlier, sixty percent polled in the predominantly Russian-speaking Donbas had identified as patriotic Ukrainians, in favour of Independence, providing the language was protected and ties with Russia weren't lost. After Independence, Russian place names across Ukraine changed to their Ukrainian ones, and Kiev became officially Kyiv. Russian-speaking Gorlovka is now Horlivka, and has been on the front line of the Kyiv government's war against Russian 'terrorists' in the Donbas.[7]

---

7 Richard Sakwa, *Frontline Ukraine. Crisis in the Borderlands*, 2015; Stephen Cohen, *War with Russia. From Putin and Ukraine to Trump and Russiagate*, 2008.

The process of 'de-communising' and detaching Ukraine from Russia began under the third president after Independence, Nato-backed Victor Yushchenko, swept to power in 2005 by the mass demonstrations of the 'Orange Revolution', for EU membership and against state corruption and the oligarchs. Yushchenko packed his government with his business associates and members of several far-right nationalist organisations, who called for Russians and Jews to be expelled from Ukraine, and the Russian language banned. Anti-Semitic posters and portraits of Ukraine's Nazi war criminals appeared in schools, offices and government buildings. Synagogues and Holocaust memorials were burnt and desecrated with Nazi hate slogans. Russians and Jews were called 'filth' and 'scum' in parliament, and attacked on the streets.

Yushchenko and his fascists were increasingly loathed, and their criminal business activities were exposed in the press. His successor in the 2010 presidential elections, pro-Russian Victor Yanukovych, became mired even deeper in corruption scandals, accused of raiding state funds to support his lavish lifestyle. His rejection in November 2013 of another punishing IMF loan in favour of a Russian bailout produced more mass protests across Ukraine, with pro-EU campaigners and anti-corruption activists joined now by armed balaklavaed fascist fighters with Nazi banners. Over four hundred protesters and police were killed or critically injured in Kyiv's 'Euromaidan' demonstrations that winter, and Ukraine seemed close to the brink of civil war.

It was at the height of the violence that the late US Senator John McCain made the first of several 'business trips' to Kyiv, to pick members of the new government to replace Yanukovych. His favourite for Prime Minister was his friend Oleh Tyahnybok, leader of the neo-Nazi All-Ukrainian Freedom Union, advised by the Josef Goebbels think-tank in Kyiv, with its ethnic cleansing programme for Ukraine's Russian areas – 'exterminating Russian Jew terrorists' and 'liberating Ukraine from the Moscow Jew mafia', arresting Russian speakers and members of the Communist Party, sending 'unreliable elements' to concentration camps. 'Tyahnybok inspires the world! We bring Peace, we bring Freedom!' McCain told a rally of twenty thousand of his supporters in Kyiv in December.

President Obama's State Department preferred the slightly less disreputable Hitler-saluting ('I was only waving') Arseniy Yatsenyuk – 'Yats is the guy!' – leader of the fascist neo-liberal alliance the All-Ukrainian People's Front Party.

On 21 February 2014, heavily armed Nazi stormtroopers surged to the front of the assault on Yanukovych's estate outside Kyiv, and he fled for his life. Next day, the Ukrainian parliament voted to impeach him. The White House called it a great day for Ukraine. The Kremlin called the overthrow of an unpopular but elected president an illegal coup, and moved forces to annexe the Crimea, also in violation of international law, to secure Russia's access to its Black Sea Fleet.

The EU imposed drastic economic sanctions on Russia. US Secretary of State Hillary Clinton called the leader of the country that had lost twenty-seven million of its citizens to the Nazis the new Hitler, and compared Putin's 'Crimean landgrab' to the Nazi annexation of Poland and Czechoslovakia. For Nato's Allied Commander in Europe, General Breedlove, the Crimean crisis was the green light to stockpile more weapons in Poland for his 'Russian Blitzkrieg' scenario, involving ground forces on Russia's southern and western borders, and war games in the Black Sea. Ex-Prime Minister billionaire gas magnate Yulia Tymoshenko, leader of the Orange Revolution against the oligarchs, recently released from a three-year jail sentence for abuse of her office, called in the Ukrainian parliament for 'the nuclear incineration of the eight million Russians remaining on our territory'.[8]

In April, Kyiv's acting president announced the start of its 'counter-terror operation in the East'. Thousands of anti-Maidan protestors demonstrated across the Donbas with banners saying 'Fascism Will Not Pass!', occupying government buildings and broadcasting stations, taking control of border crossings and transport, demanding a referendum on its future. Donetsk was the centre of the resistance, and in May, the Cossack Revolutionary Committee of the Civil War was resurrected as the Russian-backed Donetsk People's Republic. On the 11th, in elections organised by the DPR and Moscow, voters braved clashes with the army to vote for the Donbas to return to its pre-Independence status, as part of the Russian Federation. Twelve days later, the first government in post-war Europe to offer cabinet seats to neo-Nazis was installed in Kyiv, under billionaire chocolatier and funeral king President Petro Poroshenko, oligarch of oligarchs, owner of three car-plants, a shipyard, and Ukraine's main TV news station. His Ministers of Defence, Education and Agriculture and Procurator General were all members of Tyahnybok's Freedom Union. Deputy Secretary of National Security, overseeing the armed forces, was Dmytro Yarosh, leader of the Right Sector, whose armed Nazi gangs had been at the centre of the Euromaidan violence. 'Yats' was Prime Minister – until forced to resign two months later over a string of bribery and corruption allegations. Senator McCain was offered an 'advisory post'. The US State Department was reported to be 'monitoring events closely'.

---

8   Hillary Clinton, *Hard Choices*, 2014; Noam Chomsky, 'The Politics of Red Lines. Putin's Takeover of Crimea Scares US Leaders Because it Challenges American Global Dominance', 2014.

Next day, DPR fighters from Donetsk and Horlivka occupied Donetsk International Airport, symbol of Kyiv's vastly superior air power. The next eight months of bloody battles for the airport have been compared to Stalingrad, and the surrounding towns and villages were pounded by Ukrainian heavy artillery in a campaign of escalating brutality.

In July, rocket attacks on Horlivka's central police-station, occupied by armed anti-government rebels, left six dead, and fifty with life-threatening injuries. In August, the main hospital was bombed, killing seven patients and narrowly missing the maternity home. In September, the Russian Orthodox Church of the Annunciation was burnt to the ground by artillery fire, and the Orthodox Cathedral of the Epiphany was bombed while the Sunday Eucharist was being read, killing six worshippers. In October, bombs fell half a mile from the Stirol chemical plant, threatening ecological catastrophe. In January 2015, 50-kilogram shells were dropped on the city for forty-eight hours, hitting the bus station, four schools and a kindergarten, killing and injuring over fifty people, including ten children. In June, sixteen were killed in an artillery attack on the railway station. In July, ten were killed in a fifteen-hour bombing raid that hit the power-plant and put it out of action.

Human Rights Watch has called on the International Criminal Court in the Hague to charge Kyiv with war crimes for its cluster bombing of civilians. A British Doctors Without Borders surgeon working with local doctors in Horlivka reported in the *Guardian* in February 2015 that his hospital was running out of water, power, food and drugs, and he was performing at least one amputation a day – 'people go out shopping, and an hour later they're without their legs'. At the height of the bombing, OSCE monitors reported heartbreaking scenes from the hell of the Donbas, of people living in Soviet-era shelters, under economic blockade from Kyiv, without gas, electricity, running water or medical supplies, dependent on convoys of food aid from Russia.

Direct Russian intervention in the war started in August 2014, with the shelling of Ukrainian positions from the Russian border, and hundreds of casualties were reported. The next months saw a steady buildup of Russian troops, tanks, artillery and anti-aircraft weapons in the Donbas, and local DPR units were brought under the overall control of the Russian military. Ukrainians suffered savage reprisals in areas held by the DPR – 'a totalitarian North Korean style statelet', according to the *Al-Jazeera* news channel. Ukrainian media outlets were blocked, members of international press and medical aid agencies, including the Red Cross, were expelled, and Human Rights Watch and other human rights organisations were flooded with reports of DPR lawlessness and brutality, of revenge killings and kidnappings and arbitrary arrests and torture, of units running amok raping and looting, requisitioning public transport, throwing people out of their homes, beating up gays, journalists and foreigners.

For the highly disciplined and well-funded forces of the Nazi Azov Battalion, fighting with the Ukrainian army in the Donbas with their Nazi banners, who played a key role in the 2014 encirclement of Donetsk and the capture of seven DPR checkpoints, the war was a war of extermination against Ukraine's Russians and Jews: 'At this critical moment, the historic mission of our Nation is to lead the White Races of the world in a final crusade for their survival – a crusade against the Semite-led *Untermenschen*'.[9]

Fascists patrolled the streets of Kyiv and the corridors of power. Russian journalists and critics of the regime were arrested, and had their names and addresses and those of their families posted on Poroshenko's 'Truthteller' website. Russian TV stations and social media sites were blocked, Russian books and films were banned, and the school history books were rewritten by the new Institute of National Remembrance, teaching children to honour the 'patriots who fought our hated enemies in the East for a greater Ukraine, stretching from the Caucasus to the Carpathian Mountains'.

Civil War nationalist and mass murderer Symon Petlyura, assassinated in 1926 by the only survivor of one of his pogroms, has been posthumously named Hero of Ukraine, and a minute's silence is held in Kyiv on the anniversary of his death. Nazi war criminal and *Ubermensch* Stepan Bandera, whose army slaughtered, tortured and mutilated over fifty thousand Jews, Poles and Russians, including new-born babies, is celebrated in Kyiv on his birthday with mass torchlit rallies of armed Sieg Heiling Nazis, chanting his slogan 'Jews Out!' Streets across Ukraine have been named after him, including central Kyiv's Moscow Avenue, and there are Bandera beer-mugs, teeshirts and children's story books. 'We're all Banderites now!' a fourteen-year-old schoolgirl said in recent a TV interview.

US taxpayers have so far paid the Kyiv regime over \$50 billion for 'security assistance' – \$250 million from the Trump government in 2019 for weapons, logistics and reconnaissance, \$50 million more than in 2018. So much for Trump being a Putin puppet. The IMF's loans for austerity package has brought rocketing unemployment, slashed wages and benefits, runaway inflation and out of control oligarchs. The Israeli government was also quick to do business

---

9 Political scientist Ivan Katchanovski, of Ottawa University's Human Rights Program, gives clear detailed accounts of the Russian intervention, DPR crimes, and the role of the far right in the fighting, in his 2014 paper 'East or West? Regional Political Divisions in Ukraine since the Orange Revolution and the "Euromaidan"', and 'The Separatist Conflict in Donbas. A Violent Break-Up of Ukraine?' https://academia.edu/9092818, 2018.

with Kyiv's Holocaust-deniers, with a Free Trade Agreement allowing Israeli companies to run large parts of Ukraine's health, science and technology sectors.

Poroshenko's closeness to Israel was cited by his political enemies as evidence that he was Jewish himself, which he hotly denied, and there was fierce opposition to his appointment in 2016 of his Jewish friend and business partner Volodymyr Groysman as his new Prime Minister. But Groysman was soon forced to distance himself from the President, after his large-scale financial fraud in the defence sector and vast secret offshore business investments were exposed in WikiLeaks' Panama Papers.

Poroshenko's slogans 'Army, Language and Faith' and 'It's Putin or Me' proved unpopular in the April 2019 elections, and voters voted overwhelmingly for the unifying message of TV comedian Volodymyr Zelenskyi, a Russian-speaking Jew, who called for talks with the Kremlin to end the war in the Donbas. Zelenskyi is pro-Nato, the EU and the IMF, and is said to be modelling his new acting role on Presidents Bolsonaro and Macron of Brazil and France, and Israeli President Netanyahu – 'one of the greatest statesmen of our time'.

Kyiv's Bandera Avenue is now Moscow Avenue again, and Zelenskyi has been weakly critical of the Bandera cult: 'I know people see him as a great guy and a modern day hero, and that's cool, he fought for the freedom of Ukraine, but I don't think it's right to name so many streets after him'.

In November 2019, the film 'Mr Jones' opened in Kyiv (part funded by Ukraine's State Film Agency), and was celebrated by the Institute of National Remembrance with an exhibition in honour of its hero – 'who risked his life to tell the world the truth about Russia's Holodomor Genocide in Ukraine'. The following month, Zelenskyi had his first face to face meeting with Putin at the start of talks in Paris for a ceasefire in the Donbas.

Meanwhile the war grinds ruinously on, with daily injuries from landmines, and regular shelling raids on Donetsk and the frontline towns. Vast profits were to be made from the Donbas in Ukraine's privatisation programme of the 1990s, and oligarchs fighting for their billions have been running the mines illegally. In two decades of cost-cutting and neglect, eighty thousand miners have lost their lives in floods, fires and explosions, and most of Horlivka's pits are now too bomb-damaged to operate. Factories, school and offices have closed, and there is no work, and families with children have left.

Washington's undeclared proxy war with Russia to put another Zelenskyi or Poroshenko in the Kremlin has been catastrophic for the Ukrainian people, pitting swastikaed fascist fighters against ultra Russian nationalists, threatening the world with untold new dangers, ramping up tensions between its two nuclear-armed superpowers, bringing them into open confrontation.

Larisa had seen the wreckage of human society in Germany that produced the Nazis' insane dreams of world domination and race extermination. In Afghanistan, she had met young fascists impatient for Hitler's inevitable war with the Soviet Union – 'a war that will leave only one ruler of the world'. She was writing from Ukraine and the Urals in the bloody aftermath of the Petlyuras and Kolchaks, as workers geared up for the next attack from the West. She wrote of their miracles of courage and endurance, fighting to defend the Revolution against its enemies, building a new society to inspire the world. And she wrote of the human cost, the suffering and injustices, and the ways the Party was failing those who had fought for it and brought it to power.

Coal Iron and Living People is a resolutely direct warm-hearted denunciation of official incompetence, corruption and bureaucracy, and a celebration of the new Soviet life, and she captures both with a quick intuitive sympathy, and an inexhaustible faith in workers' creativity and class solidarity.

Her report from Gorlovka ends as the whole town packs into the *Komsomol* building to discuss the new family life of the Revolution. The *Komsomol's* brass band plays a speeded-up wedding march version of the *Internationale*, and a young communist delivers a passionate speech against marriage – 'we should be free to love and be happy after our long hours of labour, without having to turn every experience into a life sentence!' 'But what about families and children?' some women in the audience protest.

> And isn't this all part of our new life? The glorious long-legged *Komsomol*, not knowing what to do with his hot blood in the long days of summer. The shy young woman who has defied her family to join the Party. The old miner discussing his marriage problems with our smart clever *Komsomol* leader Comrade Shishov. He is having trouble divorcing his wife, the old man says, as they have so many things in suitcases he doesn't know whose is what, and Shishov goes into the details with him, and questions him about his sheepskin coat, and quietly draws him to the Party ...
>
> Questions of great importance were discussed at the meeting, about love and marriage and our responsibilities to each other in the new society, as we square off the hard brick of the old life with our collective tomorrow ...
>
> Gorlovka's beaten, defeated pre-revolutionary face is gone, and in the shadow of the mine, where there was once drunken animal poverty, are its workers' clubs and meetings, the *Komsomol* and its brass band, the wagon-drivers whistling at the girls, the old miners' songs and the *Internationale* ... Peace and struggle, light and shade – all the strength and creativity of this little town in the fourth year of Soviet victory.

CHAPTER 16

Seifullina and Alyosha

She left Gorlovka in September, and on the journey back to Moscow she spent three weeks in the industrial city of Ekaterinoslav (present day Dnipro), now a major centre of Bolshevik power in Ukraine.

Formerly in the Jewish Pale of Settlement, Ekaterinoslav had been on the front line of the Jewish resistance movement before the Revolution. Jews made up almost half the population, and had suffered some of the worst of the tsars' pogroms of the 1880s and 1890s, when anti-Semitic gangs stormed through the city, killing men, women and children, setting fire to synagogues, wrecking homes and shops. Self-defence groups sprang up, and in the pogroms that swept Ukraine in 1905, the Black Hundreds were driven off the streets by armed paramilitary units of Ekaterinoslav's new Jewish Socialist Workers' Party.

The city's first workers' soviets were formed in the strikes and riots of 1905, and its Bolshevik Soviet was elected to power in December 1917, defended by Red Guards. The following February, Denikin's forces entered Ekaterinoslav and overthrew the Soviet, and control of the city over the next eighteen months changed often week by week – from the armies of Germany and Austro-Hungary, to the 'black anarchist' armies of Nestor Makhno, from Denikin again, to the nationalist forces of Symon Petlyura, who brought the pogroms back to Ekaterinoslav, and was responsible with Denikin for the slaughter of over fifteen hundred of its Jews.

The Whites were driven out by the Red Army in the summer of 1919, and the reconstruction work could begin. Wrecked schools, hospitals and factories reopened, and plans were already being drawn up for the massive V.I. Lenin Hydroelectric Power Station, Dneprostroi, to be built on the River Dnepr, the largest in Europe. But behind Soviet victory were countless personal tragedies. Over five thousand had died in the fighting, families had been torn apart, and the streets were filled with orphans and homeless abandoned children, the *besprizorniki* Lydia Seifullina wrote about in her novels and stories.

By 1924, there were an estimated seven million of these children across the Soviet Union, desperate and often armed, begging and prostituting themselves for food. The Bolsheviks had ruled out individual adoption and fostering in their 1917 Family Code, for fear that people would be forced by poverty to use children as unpaid labour. Instead, a nationwide network of self-governing state children's homes was to be set up, where they would be cared for, educated and rehabilitated. 'There must be no wretched children who belong to no one. All children are the children of the state', Lenin's sister Anna Elizarova said at a conference after the Revolution to discuss the *besprizorniki*.

Several model children's homes opened in the 1920s, inspired by the educationist Anton Makarenko's pioneering children's colonies in Ukraine. There was the Rosa Luxemburg children's commune outside Moscow, the Turgoyak agricultural colony Seifullina helped establish in the Urals, the setting for her novel *The Lawbreakers*, and the G.B. Chicherin Children's Home, on the Chicherin family's former estate in Tambov, which exists to this day. But in the first months of the Revolution, resources had been inadequate to the crisis. Children were periodically rounded up and packed off to hellish orphanages, which had barely improved since tsarist days, and government policy soon changed, to promoting private fostering and adoption as the best short-term solution. Kollontai's slogan 'Be a mother not only to your own child but to all children!' appeared on posters throughout the country, with images of the red-headscarfed Party worker tramping round the towns and villages with a rifle on her shoulder, visiting women in their homes, taking their children in if they were unable to provide for them.

Possibly Larisa had considered fostering a child since her last miscarriage. Her parents had fostered Vadim and adopted Lev, and such arrangements had been common between socialists before the Revolution. Gorky had adopted the elder brother of the late Party Secretary, Yakov Sverdlov. Bukharin's future wife, Anna Larina, was the daughter of jailed revolutionaries adopted as a baby by Lenin's close friend and colleague Yury Larin and his wife. The fourteen-year-old cabin boy on the *Summer Tide*, Alexander, 'Buttercup', was the much loved son of Lev Kamenev and his wife, Trotsky's sister Olga Davydovna, who had adopted him as a baby when his parents were arrested. After October, he had sat in on Central Committee meetings with Kamenev, and organised the other children in the Kremlin into a military league of young communists, the prototype for the *Komsomol*, and in the summer of 1918, he volunteered with the Red Navy, and left with Raskolnikov for Svyazhsk.

Caring for orphans was seen as part of women's work during the Civil War, and commissars' wives became 'Party aunts'. Lunacharsky and his first wife, the novelist Anna Malinovskaya, adopted a son. Voroshilov and his wife Ekaterina Davydovna, unable to have children of their own, adopted three boys and two girls. The Kalinins had three children together, and adopted two. Stalin's second wife, Nadezhda Alliluyeva, had two children with him, was stepmother of his son Yakov from his first marriage (who he treated as brutally as he treated her), and was foster-mother of the infant son of his friend Artyom Sergeev, killed in 1921 in a train crash. Stalin accused Trotsky's supporters of derailing the train, and his foster-son (also named Artyom) became his favourite child. He was twenty when the Nazis invaded the Soviet Union, and he immediately volunteered for the front, fighting in the battles for Moscow, Kursk and Stalingrad, and serving in the army for the rest of his life, remaining devoted to Stalin's memory until his death in 2008.[1]

In Ekaterinoslav Larisa met Vera Inber, who was travelling around her native Ukraine, writing articles about the *besprizorniki* and their families, and Inber introduced her to a small twelve-year-old boy called Alyosha Makarov who was begging on the streets.

He later spoke about his life to Seifullina, who would write touchingly about him, in his own words, in her story 'Alyosha'. One of seven children of a Bolshevik factory worker killed fighting the Whites, he had been sent to a wretched orphanage in the nearby town of Pavlograd, when his mother became unable to feed them all on her wages as a cleaner. He had escaped with his dog, stowing away on the train back to Ekaterinoslav, where he joined his two elder brothers on the streets. And when Inber told his mother 'a comrade from Moscow' was in town, she saw her as her only hope.

He told Seifullina about the day he was called home to meet her – 'sunburnt, in a white dress'. '"This is Larisa Mikhailovna," Mother said, and I couldn't say her name, and called her "Boris." She asked me what I was interested in, and I said I liked music. Then someone upstairs started playing a violin, and she held my arm and we stood there listening'.

She took him and his younger sister to town and bought them ice-creams, then to the cinema and the Hippodrome, for an evening of eating and dancing. And when she visited him and his mother again next day, and asked if he would like to live with her in Moscow, he eagerly agreed.[2]

She returned with him in October, minus his dog, and he settled into his new life with the Reisners at the House of Soviets. 'Thank you for your kindness to my Lyolya', his mother wrote to her. 'Can you write to me once in a while about how he's getting on and if he's behaving himself? Listen to Larisa Mikhailovna, darling, she can give you a better life'.

She moved another bed into her room for him, fed him up, took him to a clinic for his ringworm and rickets, found him a good school and helped him with his homework, arranged piano lessons for him, and taught him to skate at the Petrovka ice-rink, where she bought them both season tickets. All this she paid for with her own money. Despite generous benefits for single mothers, fosterers whose hearts were melted by these traumatised children, missing their mothers and hardened by their lives on the streets, received minimal

---

1 Larissa Vasileva, *Kremlin Wives*, 1994, pp. 47, 59–61.
2 'Alyosha' was republished in Seifullina's *Prostye rasskazy* (Simple Stories), Moscow, 1928.

assistance from the state, and she now had to support both of them with her journalism. But somehow she organised her work around him, turning more of her travel notes into articles and essays for *Izvestiya* and *Red Virgin Soil*, and expanding them into her book *Coal Iron and Living People*.

After her five months apart from Radek, they were sharing their lives and their work again, and as before, he guided her reading, giving her a mass of material on the economics and history of the Urals and Ukraine, and leaving her alone to write. 'I won't pretend she liked balance-sheets or statistics, but she had a real taste for economics', he wrote. 'After ploughing through several tedious textbooks, she would beg me for something on petroleum or cereal crops to get her teeth into, and relax over Delaisi's book on oil trusts, or Norris's epic work on wheat. But she never saw economics and history as goals in themselves. For her they were a way of investigating the relations between people, and what they lived and breathed for'.

Before delivering her articles for publication, she would post the handwritten drafts to workers she had met for their comments, and her correspondence with them fills a large file in her archives. To the Kyzyl miner Fillip Lokotsky, she described the historical accounts of the Urals' trusts and enterprises she was reading as 'more exciting than a novel – a record of the bosses' desperate struggles for workers' labour power, their every working hour, their right to life, and the dizzying prospects of their future'. Several workers wrote to thank her for helping their families. The Gorlovka communist Ivan Kochin reported that there had been 'a swift retreat from religion at home' since she left, and his wife had let him throw out the icons, 'and is beginning to see faith in God as something completely unnecessary'.[3]

A week after she returned to Moscow, on 18 October, she joined the thousands of writers from across the Soviet Union who gathered in the great hall of the House of the Press for Mayakovsky's first reading of his epic three thousand-line poem 'Vladimir Ilich Lenin':

> Time speed on, spread Lenin's slogans!
> Not for us to drown in tears,
> There's no one more alive than Lenin in the world,
> Our strength, our wisdom,
> Surest of our weapons,
> Who grasped the earth whole, all in one go,
> Saw what lay hidden in time ...

---

3 Letters quoted in Naumova's Introduction to *Coal Iron and Living People*, sw, pp. 563, 565.

Mayakovsky had known and worked with Lenin since the first days of the Revolution, and had been in the Smolny with him the night the Bolsheviks took power. 'Volodya considered Lenin's struggle for the shining ideals of communism the meaning of his own life, and with his death, he lost a dear close friend', his elder sister said.

The poem was the last of his four-poem Lenin cycle, beginning with 'Vladimir Ilich!', published in 1920, to celebrate his fiffieth birthday – 'I wouldn't be a poet if I didn't sing it, star in the five-pointed sky, mighty arch of the Russian Communist Party!' 'We Don't Believe It!' was his cry of pain at the official notices being posted in Moscow in 1923 on Lenin's failing health – 'The spring day darkens, the bulletin is pasted. No, It cannot be!' The following January, he was a delegate at the Eleventh Congress of Soviets where President Kalinin first broke the news of Lenin's death, and he was thrown into a deep depression. He made ten visits to his coffin at the House of Unions, and published his '*Komsomol* Song' in the *Komsomol* journal *Young Guard* two days after the funeral, with its repeated refrain 'Lenin lived, Lenin lives, Lenin will always live!'

The final poem, 'dedicated to the Russian Communist Party', contains elements of all three, and became the most popular of all his works in the Soviet Union. Passionate, lyrical and declamatory, it presents through countless unforgettable images a panoramic view of life in Soviet Russia, and the life of its leader, showing him not as an idol, 'garlanded in tinsel', but as struggling, suffering and human, setting his life and legacy against the history of capitalism: 'The manager, fat beast, flips his abacus, cries "Crisis!", and pins up his list saying "Fired"'. 'Marx catches the pilferers of surplus value with their spoils'. Lenin, 'genius of practice, architect of victory, leads the nation from books to battlefields'.

His reading ended with storms of applause, and a twenty-minute standing ovation. Three days later, Mayakovsky repeated the performance to ecstatic crowds in the Red Hall of the headquarters of the Communist Party, and he went on to read the poem at meetings across the country, and on his travels the following year in Europe, Cuba, Mexico and the United States. 'Workers' response has been heartening, reassuring me it's needed', he told friends. 'Never in my life have I wanted to be understood so much as in this work, it's probably the most serious thing I've written'.

A seventeen-year-old Moscow factory worker and aspiring journalist, Alexei Gudimov, who was at that first reading at the House of the Press, called the poem 'wild, joyful and beautiful', and he described meeting Larisa at the noisy party afterwards. She questioned him closely about his work at the factory and his writing, and encouraged him to pursue his dream of being a journalist, reminding him of Chekhov's words that writers' job was to ask questions, not answer them – 'and if you get impatient, take Chekhov's advice and strap yourself to the chair! If you can't listen patiently for eight to ten hours before you write your twenty lines, forget being a journalist!'

A few days later, Gudimov joined her and her friends at a skating party at the Petrovka ice-rink, where she practised the Dutch Waltz with her skating partner, Anatoly Gulb, 'in a cherry-coloured skating dress, edged with grey caracul'. '"We'll definitely win the national dance championships next year, and with luck the Moscow ones this year too!" Gulb said. And when they changed partners, she asked me to dance with her'.

> We stood with linked arms as the musicians warmed themselves at the brazier in the corner. Then the band struck up, and we pushed off on the insides of our blades, gliding forward side by side, driven on by the music, building up speed, tilting in the long arcs of the dance step. She moved so lightly her skates barely seemed to touch the ice, and ended with a graceful upright spin, lifting her arms like a bird taking flight.
>
> Then the Snow Queen vanished with her friends. But one stayed, and we skated round arm in arm together. 'Never forget today, you've just skated with the great journalist Larisa Reisner!' he said. And I never have.[4]

There were more trips to concerts and the theatre with Radek, the Pasternaks and Pilnyak, and Alyosha became part of her circle of friends who met for sociable evenings at Lydia Seifullina's flat. In Seifullina's story 'Alyosha', published a year later in *Red Virgin Soil*, she portrayed him as a lively clever affectionate little boy, much loved by the Reisners, an avid reader and talented pianist, who built a radio in the room he shared with Larisa, and made friends with all the dogs in the House of Soviets.

That March, Seifullina's novel *Virineya* had been published in *Red Virgin Soil* to celebrate International Women's Day, to storms of controversy. *Izvestiya* compared her portrayal of the suffering female soul to Flaubert's *Madame Bovary*, and the novelist Dmitry Furmanov described 'weeping over the death of Virineya as for a loved one'. *Communist Woman*, paper of the *Zhenotdel*, called *Virineya* 'decadent and immoral'. Neither Seifullina's spirited Bolshevik heroine nor her superstitious illiterate peasant women in her novel *The Mulch* conformed to the positive image of the new Soviet woman the paper wished to see depicted, and both works were attacked for their rough peasant language, and scenes of male brutality and rape – although as Catriona Kelly points out in

---

4 *O partiinoi i sovetskoi pechati: sbornik dokumentov* (Collection of Documents on the Soviet and Party Press), Moscow, 1954, pp. 315–16.

her book on Russian women writers, the same criticisms were not made of the powerful themes of violent sex in the works of Blok, Babel or Mikhail Bulgakov (or for that matter Gumilyov).[5]

Seifullina exposed this double standard, and Larisa fiercely defended her work against *Communist Woman*'s one-dimensional picture of women, which bore so little relation to the reality of their lives. She knew the women she was writing about, and she wrote in their language. She knew their painful struggles to throw off their old subservience and assert themselves, and her works were loved by workers and intellectuals, and by thousands who had barely opened a book before.

The campaign to eradicate illiteracy completely by the year 1923 had proved over-ambitious. But Russia now had a new literate proletariat and peasantry, and the media were flourishing. Bukharin was editor-in-chief of *Pravda*, and *Izvestiya* had become a byword for bold investigative journalism under its distinguished new editor the old Bolshevik Ivan Skvortsov-Stepanov, Commissar of Finance in the first Bolshevik government. Hundreds of new magazines and newspapers were published in the fifteen republics of the Soviet Union, in some fifty-six languages, and 'worker and peasant correspondents' from the factories and villages, the *rabkors* and *selkors*, were trained to write for them. Radio was coming into people's homes, with a network of three hundred transmitters across the country, and a year later, the Russian Press Agency ROSTA would be replaced by the Telegraph Agency of the USSR, *TASS*, under the supervision of the Commissariat of Foreign Affairs, which recruited journalists, coordinated stories, and managed the reporting of foreign news. By the Second World War, *TASS* was one of the four largest news agencies in the world, along with Reuters, Associated Press and Agence France-Presse, with thousands of bureaux and journalists in Russia and abroad. Head of its London office for thirty years was Larisa's friend London's ROSTA's correspondent Andrew Rothstein, writing under the name 'C.M. Roebuck'. *TASS* has survived the end of the Soviet Union, and is still state-run, rebranded as the 'Russian News Agency *"TASS"*'.

The poet and *Izvestiya* journalist Nikolai Smirnov remembered Larisa hurrying into the paper's offices with the drafts of her articles, her skates slung over her shoulders, throwing her scarf off and tidying her hair, shaking hands with Skvortsov-Stepanov and his deputy, Boris Volin, dictating her copy to a typist, then dashing off to the ice-rink.

The *Izvestiya rabkor* Georgy Ryklin described people crowding round 'our talented Larisa, loved by all the staff'. The paper had recently given its new *rab-*

---

5 Catriona Kelly, *A History of Russian Women's Writing*, 1994, p. 240.

kors some friendly advice, to 'write not with a pencil but with a pen'. Her advice to Ryklin was to 'write not with a pencil or a pen, but from the heart', and to be bolder in his criticisms of official corruption, bigotry and red tape. She suggested any number of articles he could write on this theme, and showed him a letter she had received from a nurse named Lydia Shaburina she had met in the Urals, who had served on a Red Amy medical train in the Civil War.

For 26 rubles 20 kopecks a month, nurse Shaburina was expected to:
1. Vaccinate children and adults
2. Do night duty
3. Receive visitors politely
4. Not get pregnant.

Giving him the letter and some other material, she sent him off to write his article. Next day he came back with his first draft, which ended:

> You can be fruitful and multiply in education and agriculture, but not here, for it makes people late for work. Today the nurse is pregnant, tomorrow it's the doctor, next day it's me, and who'll be left?
>
> But nurse Shaburina disobeyed her orders. She did her vaccinations, was punctual for night duty, and received visitors politely. But she got pregnant, so she got the sack.

She approved his ending, and said, 'Now you must write the rest with more anger, so it never happens again!'[6]

In December 1924, *Coal Iron and Living People* was published by the State Publishing House, a montage of scenes from her travels, interweaving workers' stories with episodes from history, from the era of serfdom and the birth of capitalism, to the revolutionary struggles of her lifetime. The writing had all her old wit and bravura, but had been stripped down to a simpler more idiomatic style, and a raw naturalism often reminiscent of Zola's *Germinal*, building a picture of their lives that was epic and intimate, tragic and inspiring.

Coal Iron and Living People shone a light on a world that was completely unfamiliar to many of her readers, and although eleven-year-olds no longer worked fourteen-hour days in the mines, as in tsarist Russia or Zola's France, many of the working conditions she was describing seemed barely to have changed since the nineteenth century. Vera Inber, although praising her paint-

---

6   Smirnov, 'Pamyati Larisy Reisner' (Memories of Larissa Reisner), *New World*, 1926. Republished as 'Neotrazimyi obraz' (An Irresistible Image), LRRC, pp. 137–44. Ryklin, *Esli pamyat ne izmenyaet* (*If My Memory Doesn't Deceive Me*), Moscow, 1968, pp. 70–3. Story republished as 'Ne karandashom i ne perom' (Not with a Pencil or a Pen), LRRC, pp. 165–7.

erly eye for detail and ear for dialogue, found it a grim and depressing read – 'as if her shoulders were weighed down by her heavy miner's cape, and she was robbed of her strength by the harsh sunless underground ugliness of the mines'.[7]

Reviews in *Pravda* and *Izvestiya* called the book a *tour de force* of Soviet journalism, gripping and atmospheric, filled with pathos and poetry. 'Nothing in our literature now is more truthful, accurate or direct', wrote the *Proletkult* journalist Vladimir Polyansky, who seven months earlier had attacked *The Front* as 'dull and incomprehensible'. The poet Maria Shkapskaya saw her as a consummate stylist, who could make even statistics poetic, while insisting on the importance of facts and figures and scrupulous research – 'you have to be able to count not only the stars in the sky, but the kopecks in the government's pocket' – and she was inspired to set off on her own travels across Russia, from Bukhara to Murmansk, writing sketches of the people she met.[8]

Despite *Proletkult's* praise for the work, her writing was still attacked by proletarian hardliners as too refined and poetic to be accessible to the masses. And her critics gained a powerful new supporter in the poet Demyan Bedny, who spoke at a Moscow writers' conference in January 1925 to attack *The Front* as 'tortuous, pretentious and affected'.

Bedny's unspoken target though was clearly Trotsky, and her glowing praise for him in *The Front*. Chair of the St Petersburg and Petrograd Soviets, creator of the Red Army, hero of the Civil War, Trotsky was respected even for the policies that made him unpopular – labour conscription, his call for the trade unions to be tied to the state, his crushing of the Kronstadt rising. His handling of Stalin in the 1918 Tsaritsyn crisis had increased his authority as the leader capable of taking the harsh measures needed if the Revolution was to survive, and Stalin's public humiliation at his hands had been the start of his six-year campaign to remove him as War Commissar, accusing him of plotting a 'Bonapartist coup' against the Party. Bedny was speaking just two days after Trotsky suffered his first major defeat, and was forced to resign from the Commissariat.

Bedny was the most popular poet of the Revolution, admired even by Pasternak, who called him the 'spirit of the people'. Born into extreme peasant poverty, he had written his first poems under the name Bedny, 'Poor', during the 1905 revolution, about the ruin in the countryside, and peasants' fight for their freedom. Seven years later he joined the Bolsheviks, and published his

---
7   Vera Inber, 'Evolution of a Swan.' 1966 p. 279.
8   Polyansky and others quoted in *Periodika po literature i isskustvu za gody revolyutsii* (Periodicals on Literature and Art in the Years of the Revolution), Moscow, 1933. Shkapskaya's articles were published in her book *Sam po sebe* (For Myself), Leningrad, 1927.

poems in the Bolshevik press – sharp political attacks against the Tsar and his family and the capitalists in his Duma, which Lenin called 'witty, well-aimed and beautifully written', and quoted in his speeches.

After the Revolution, he read his poems at mass meetings in the factories – caustic attacks on priests, capitalists and enemies of the state, full of catchy rhythms and bawdy slapstick wit – and he was extraordinarily generously rewarded by the Party, with an apartment for his family in the Kremlin Palace, and his own Ford motorcar. During the Civil War, he published hundreds of agitprop songs, poster captions and verses, which he read with great success on his frequent trips to the front, travelling there in his own railway carriage, and in 1923 he was the Soviet writer to be awarded the Order of the Red Banner of Labour.

Lenin still appreciated the propaganda power of his work after the Revolution, but had told Gorky before his death he found much his writing coarse and crude – 'writers should be ahead of their readers, not behind them'. Stalin considered him a genius. Bedny shared his love of poetry with him, and lent him books from his impressive library, said to be the largest private library in Russia, and they enjoyed a long correspondence about literature, politics and the anti-Trotsky campaign, in which both referred to him in openly anti-Semitic terms. 'If I go for Shlyapnikov it's a brawl. Kick Trotsky, and it's a pogrom!' Stalin wrote.

It seems more than likely Stalin was behind Bedny's attack on Larisa, as the opening shot against her in his ongoing campaign to destroy Trotsky. But if so, it spectacularly misfired. *Pravda* derided 'Bedny's belching communist arrogance', and *Izvestiya* published dozens of letters from her admirers. '"Tortuous and affected" – that scum Demyan is just envious, he knows nothing, Larisa Mikhailovna is a tiger!' wrote the Urals miner Vladimir Lavrov.[9]

Radek continued to support Trotsky against Stalin, while privately entertaining wild hopes that the two could be reconciled at the expense of his old enemy Zinoviev. But his biographer speculates that Larisa convinced him he had already been too villified in Trotsky's name to defend him openly, and that to do so would be political suicide.[10]

She was involved in a different campaign that spring, in what she called 'Nepland'. The NEP was offering vast scope to corrupt new business schemes, from the ethically dubious to the downright criminal, and the *rabkors* and *selkors* were being attacked and intimidated for naming and shaming those who abused their power. That February, the story reached Moscow that a young

---

9   Quoted in *SW*, p. 469.
10 Warren Lerner, *Karl Radek. The Last Internationalist*, 1970, p. 132.

demobilised Red soldier and *selkor* named Grigory Lapitsky, in the new Soviet Republic of Belorussia, had had his house burnt down after he exposed a gang of criminals in his village, led by the local police-chief, who were carrying out illegal requisitions and embezzling Party funds, discrediting its authority for miles around, and Larisa was sent by *Izvestiya* to the Belorussian capital Minsk, to cover the trial of Lapitsky's persecutors.

She stayed at the Europa Hotel on Cathedral Square, leaving early each morning to support Lapitsky in court, returning in the evenings to write her reports for *Izvestiya* and the Minsk paper *Star*, entertaining crowds of villagers and journalists in her room, encouraging them to speak as witnesses for the prosecution.

Fifteen-year-old Moisei Goldberg, who wrote for the *Star*'s youth section under the Russian version of his name, Mikhail Zlatogorov, recalled the impact of her journalism on Minsk's young writers: 'We were enraptured by her reports from the court. She called herself a "defender of the poor", and her writing seethed with anger at the "parasites and bureaucrats, many of them unfortunately with Party cards, who turn the blood of the Revolution into cheap ink".[11]

Zlatogorov invited her to a meeting of his *Komsomol* writers' group, where 'Semyon Pilitovich, a gloomy lad from the tannery, growled his clumsy but powerful verses, followed by the young frontier guard Nikolai Korobkov, in his army uniform. Then it was my turn, the youngest, to read my poems, mainly about my Pioneer scarf and my *Komsomol* cell'.

She listened with keen interest, then asked them all to talk about themselves and their work. '"So what else do you write about? Girls? Love?" she said, turning to me. I was struck dumb with embarrassment. I did write such poems, but they were my shameful secret'. Then quickly changing the subject, she asked him to come to her room next evening and take her to the Jewish quarter of the city, in the Nemiga market.

Like Ekaterinoslav, Minsk had been in the Pale of Settlement, and had the fourth largest population of Jews in Russia. Since the Revolution new Jewish schools had opened, and there was a flourishing Yiddish press, and Minsk's Yiddish theatre, now the State Jewish Theatre of Belorussia, drew huge audiences. Yet most of Nemiga's Jews still lived in poverty, struggling to survive as tailors, craftsmen and small tradesmen. And when she learned that the son of a poor tailor in Nemiga, Chaim Kaplan, had hanged himself because he had no shoes to wear to school, she wanted to hear his story from his mother and write about him.

---

11   Mikhail Zlatogorov, 'Pamyatnaya vstrecha' (A Memorable Meeting), *LRRC*, pp. 124–31.

When Zlatogorov arrived at her room the next evening, it was crowded with peasants, party workers and journalists. A group of shawled village women, witnesses for the prosecution, were sitting round the samovar with her, deep in discussion, and she waved at him to wait. Then everyone left, and she set off briskly with him across Cathedral Square.

He led her out of the gentile part of the city, into the narrow streets of the market. 'And there she slowed down, listening to the shouts of the women fishmongers, peering through the doors of the synagogues, diving into little shops to buy shoelaces, hairpins and reels of cotton. I have listened to many talks over the years about the way writers work, and have read many books. But no academic analysis could give a tiny part of the unforgettable lesson of Larisa Mikhailovna's determined concerned investigation of life, in all its Rembrandt-like tones of light and shade'.

In the Kaplans' small room, crammed with beds around a long tailor's table, she sat with Chaim's mother and cried with her, then asked to see his exercise books. She brought out some roughly sewn-together scraps of newspaper covered with physics diagrams and columns of Russian declensions, then she began to talk, in Yiddish and broken Russian, of his struggle to better himself, of his love of science and gymnastics, and of the poverty that had forced him to go without textbooks or shoes.

Afterwards she walked back quietly with Zlatogorov.

> In a banal attempt to be positive, I condemned suicide as a solution to life's tragic contradictions – 'it's not *Komsomol*-like!' She reacted sharply to this, and said we shouldn't only see the bright happy side of life, and that she was ashamed of us, Chaim's comrades, for being blind to his spiritual crisis. How he had longed with all his heart for a better life, and hadn't wanted to grow up sick and consumptive, like generations of tailors before him who had worked for the rich. He wanted to study at a *rabfak* and be a sportsman, and everything old, with its roots in the Middle Ages – she swept her hand over the river, sinking into sunset – was dragging him back. 'That's what drove him to the noose. How can we condemn him for that?'

Hundreds of towns and villages across the Soviet Union with large Jewish populations who had suffered the tsars' and Whites' pogroms would be ethnically cleansed in Hitler's 'Final Solution'. When the Nazis occupied Minsk in July 1941, they massacred seventy-two thousand of its Jews, and turned Nemiga into a slave labour camp. In Ekaterinoslav, Riga and other cities Larisa visited on her travels, Jews were exterminated in their thousands, or shipped off to the gas-chambers and concentration camps in occupied Poland. Fifty thousand Jews were killed in Radek's birthplace, Lvov. Two hundred thousand were killed in Lithuania, including the entire Jewish population of her father's birthplace, the capital Vilno, the 'Jerusalem of Lithuania'. In her birthplace Lublin, the 'Jewish Oxford', three hundred and fifty thousand Jews, including forty thousand from Lublin's Jewish Podzamcze district, were slaughtered with prisoners from Germany, Austria, France and Holland at Majdanek, the 'Little Square' camp, so named because it was virtually inside the city. Even now, there are only an estimated two hundred Jews living in Lublin, most of them elderly Holocaust survivors and their relatives.

'The Revolution has abolished the forbidden boundaries of the Pale', she wrote in her *Izvestiya* article 'The Heritage of the Ghetto'. 'But until Jews can rise from its ruins and leave this stinking place, they suffer hunger, their necks are broken by endless toil, and those who cannot take the giant step forward are mown down'.[12]

Her *Izvestiya* articles 'For the Poor' and 'The Forest Dweller', about police-chief Ovsyannikov, and 'his house of lies, built like an illegal still', were used as evidence against him at the trial, which ended with jail sentences for all the accused, and afterwards she threw a party to celebrate. When Zlatogorov came to her room to say goodbye, it was so packed he could barely get through the door. Someone was telling a story to hoots of laughter, and thinking she would have no time for him, he turned to leave. But she stopped him, looked thoughtfully at him, then wrote on the back of a postcard: '21.2.1925. Dear poet, Comrade Mishka, write and rejoice in life darling, and love the Party as you do, and listen to the old women in the streets of the ghetto! Larisa Reisner'.

She made many friends in Minsk, and continued to correspond with them long after she left. Mira Samuilova from Nemiga thanked her for the shoes she sent her daughter. Lapitsky's friend the *selkor* Igor Bashnak wrote, 'Before I met you, I was an enemy of intellectuals, I didn't trust them an inch. The experience of struggle showed they despised us workers and thought they were above us. There was none of that in you. I know now that there are intellectuals who are on the side of working people'.

Her phrases for the trial's defendants – 'wreckers and parasites', 'blemishes on society', 'isolated cases' – were fresh and original when she was using them. But they would become standard clichés of the journalism of the 1930s, when writers were required to tell people what was important and what to think. The Minsk *rabkor* Andrei Yakimovich wrote to praise her 'surgical, timely' reports

---

12   'Nasledie getto' (The Heritage of the Ghetto), *Izvestiya*, 24 March, 1925. sw, pp. 436–7.

of the case. He also warned presciently that by dividing people into heroes and villains, journalists risked turning trials into witch-hunts: 'Some of those in the dock were no worse than Lapitsky. Why do you surround him with a halo of saintliness and stoicism, and write off the rest?'[13]

According to Nikolai Smirnov, her articles from Minsk produced a huge volume of letters to *Izvestiya*, many of them critical, which the editor Skvortsov-Stepanov would wave goodnaturedly around the office. One objected to her comparing the wheels of a car to 'the bobbins on which space is wound'. That was a matter of personal taste, Skvortsov-Stepanov said. More serious were the numerous complaints, many from settled gypsies, of her description in 'The Forest Dweller' of police-chief Ovsyannikov's 'thieving gypsy eyes', and she was mortified by her lapse of judgement.

Smirnov remembered crowds of journalists from the factories and villages visiting the paper to show her their stories, including Lapitsky, in his bast shoes and shepherd's felt hat, and that she always took her writing away for further work after talking to them – 'for she was very demanding of the written word, particularly her own'.

And then she crashed. She had barely rested after her exhausting five-month travels, caring for Alyosha and working to support them both, and she told Vera Inber she was at the end of her strength. 'My tropical malaria has flared up again, and I literally can't work'. Her parents persuaded her to leave Alyosha with them for a month and get medical treatment in Germany, and in April she booked herself at her own expense into a specialist tropical diseases clinic in Hamburg, asking *Izvestiya* for a three-month advance on her salary to cover the cost, promising to send back articles as soon as she felt well enough.

Inber threw a party for her the night before she left, and recalled her telling people about the illness that robbed her of so much of her strength. '"It sucks the life out of me", she said. "Each attack leaves me with a feeling of total emptiness, as if some vile animal had come and eaten all the greenery in my soul". I'll never forget that phrase about the greenery in her soul. It made me think of fresh strong leaves washed by the rain, shining in the energy of the sun'.[14]

13 Letters in sw, pp. 446–7.
14 Vera Inber 1966, p. 282.

CHAPTER 17

Germany and China

In the two years since she was last in Germany, the powerful militarist bloc in the Reichstag had moved the government drastically to the right. The new President of the Weimar Republic, elected a week before she arrived in April, was the former Chief of the Imperial High Command, Field Marshal von Hindenburg, figurehead of German victory and unity in the First World War, whose reputation had survived the military collapse of 1918 and the Kaiser's abdication.

Economic ruin had been averted with a 25 billion dollar loan from America, but the Ruhr was still under French and Belgian occupation, and managers elsewhere, desperate to save their businesses from ruin and Germany from another revolution, were punishing workers for the crisis, with cuts to their wages, pensions and unemployment pay. In this climate of anger and despair, fascism flourished. Hitler was drawing thousands to his rallies in Bavaria, and units of the Nazis' ss were providing him with armed protection, and attacking Jews, 'non-Aryans' and communists on the streets.

Writing from her Hamburg clinic to her novelist friend Yury Libedinsky in Moscow, Larisa described the other patients as 'a bunch of German, French and British crooks, bankers and arms-dealers', and told him the only one she spoke to was an Indian, who they ostracised – 'you have to stick with your own kind!'[1]

As soon as she had recovered her strength, she discharged herself to stay with her old Hamburg friends, and marched with them in a large anti-Nazi demonstration organised by the Hamburg Communist Party. Igor took time off from his teaching work in Moscow to join her there, and they left together for a week's holiday in the spa resort of Wiesbaden, the 'Nice of the North', popular for its temperate climate, its hot springs and casinos, where Dostoyevsky had become addicted to the roulette tables.

Wiesbaden was also famous for its military guests. In 1918, the city had been occupied by forces of the French army. Three years later, French and German officials had met there to sign their pact on war reparations, and five months after Larisa left, the city became the base of the British Army on the Rhine. Wiesbaden is now the German headquarters of the Computer Sciences Corporation, the largest software company in the United States, employed by the

---

1 Libedinsky, *Contemporaries*, 1958, p. 45.

CIA to coordinate its drone attacks and rendition programmes, flying prisoners back and forth to secret prisons across Eastern Europe to be tortured.

They stayed at the picturesque gothic-style Neroberg Hotel, on a forested hill above the city, accessible only by funicular railway, and enjoyed its restaurants, gardens and tennis courts. They celebrated her thirtieth birthday there, and Igor sent their parents a photograph of them relaxing in their tennis whites, and a postcard of the hotel, with a top floor window marked with the words 'L.M. stayed here, May 1925'. They took the waters and various cures in Wiesbaden, ate in cafés, and explored the ruined medieval citadel of Sonnenberg Castle. Then Igor returned to Moscow, and she left for Berlin.

A week later, she set off south for the Ruhr Valley, and spent the next month travelling around the mines and factories of the 'Arsenal of the World', under their new French and Belgian managers, writing the articles and essays for *Izvestiya*, *Pravda* and *Red Paper* that became her book *In Hindenburg's Country*.

Two years earlier, she had been in Germany as a fugitive from the law. This time she was there as a respected journalist and representative of Germany's new Soviet ally – 'interviewing bankers and businessmen in their oak-panelled boardrooms, with their own general staff and diplomatic corps and paintings of their kings on the walls', wrote the young Soviet journalist Isaac Kramov. 'Little did they suspect that the elegant young woman questioning them wouldn't be satisfied with their answers, and would go on to the factories and mines to hear from workers their heartbreaking stories of poverty and shattered hopes'.[2]

'Germany's "economic recovery," trumpeted in the press, skinned over with the thin scab of "stabilisation," is built on worker's blood and suffering', she wrote in *In Hindenburg's Country*, and her portraits of their lives are all set against Hindenburg's drive for a new war. 'The decisive factor facing us in the tremendous tasks facing us for a successful result in this war is the labour problem', Hindenburg said.

The book opens in the French-occupied city of Essen, home of the mighty Krupp steel empire, capitalism's largest business monopoly and weapons manufacturers, which had armed the victorious Prussian Army in the Franco-Prussian War, and the Imperial German Army in the First World War, and would serve the Nazi war machine throughout the entire Second World War. At the Nuremberg Trials after the war, twelve former senior Krupp directors were found guilty of crimes against humanity – for 'arming the *Wehrmacht* in

---

2   Kramov, *Literaturnye portrety* (Literary Portraits), Moscow, 1962, pp. 32–3. In 1968, Kramov published a fictional biography of Larisa, *Morning Wind*.

its plunder, enslavement and extermination in the occupied countries', and for their brutal treatment of their slave labourers from occupied Europe and the Soviet Union.

'The story of German imperialism is written in the lines of the factory buildings', she wrote In her essay 'Krupp and Essen':

> The streets, plants and coalpits are all marked with the name 'Krupp', like the teaspoons and pillowslips of some propertied family ... 'Krupp' has become a world name. Short and cast in one piece, like his steel, it boomed out first in Europe, then in Asia. 'Krupp' is uttered wherever stormclouds gather. 'Krupp' means war, and war is its customer. And now new wars are being prepared, whose horrors are still unknown to humanity – new strategies, and a new mode of death, unlike any other before.

Banned by Versailles from producing weapons, Krupp's factories were being forced to make cash-registers and false teeth. 'But the German bourgeoisie still has an inexhaustible source of wealth at its disposal – the sinewy backbones of the miners and metalworkers of the Ruhr. And the workers' tenements hugging the factories hear the iron cry out night and day like an infant in pain, and mentally adjust their hearts and watches back and forward in time to the sound of the hooters'.

In 'A Concentration Camp of Poverty', she goes from the managers' offices – 'insulated from the outside world behind glass walls, in a silence so deep even the lifts gliding past can't plumb its depths' – to the former army barracks housing Essen's unemployed, 'surviving on too little to live on, too much to die on'. Outside, 'half-naked children play in the gutters under the sentry-boxes'. Inside, she meets a destitute cobbler and his wife, and 'their barefoot bandy-legged little son, whose baby brother died last week, crawling over the gaps in the dirty floorboards, half of them chopped up for firewood'. In the next room lives a bankrupted factory manager, who has lost everything in the economic crash, 'apart from his useless Iron Cross'. Living opposite is the widowed Frau Fritzke with her two children, who she saves from starvation by working as a charwoman and a prostitute. 'And now the state, which stole their father from them in the war, and has stolen their orphans' benefits for subsidies to Krupp and Stinnes, is to steal them from their immoral mother. In a few days, a policeman will arrive to take away her plump naughty little boy and her mentally disabled twelve-year-old daughter, who has constant fits, and will place them in a Catholic orphanage'.

In 'He a Communist, She a Catholic', she writes of the sacked communist factory worker living there with his wife and children:

She is now the family breadwinner and head of the household, he is the domestic help, the nanny in trousers, who must care for the children and polish her shoes. He shouts at her, making her beg his forgiveness, and the children cry. Then he takes her to the bed and violates her with hatred, and her screams can be heard on the staircase. And afterwards he sends her out for cigarettes. Never before, even in the days of good money, has he loved her with a more jealous love than when it has to be bought.

From Essen, she travelled west to the vast coalmines of Westphalia. In 'The Ruhr Under the Ground', she wrote of the miners working for their new French bosses in infinitely more hellish conditions than in the Urals or Ukraine – 'exhausted and humiliated, many of them sleeping in the tunnels at night to avoid the sack'. And she saw their hatred of the managers matched by their contempt for their union leaders. When they asked her to thank Russian workers for sending them deliveries of grain during last year's strike – 'in our hour of need' – they told her that most had been 'gobbled up by the union'.

Back in Berlin, she took a tour around the vast Ullstein media empire, publisher of most of Germany's major newspapers, including *Berliner Zeitung*. 'Ullstein' is a vivid portrait of its headquarters in Berlin Tempelhof, a seething warren of offices, phonebooths and printshops – 'pumping out their cocaine for the masses, turning the non-party papers, to which the average German philistine has become accustomed, into mouthpieces for the most rabid reaction, condemning new generations of workers to be slaughtered in new wars'.

From Berlin, she travelled a hundred miles south to the town of Dessau, birthplace of Germany's aviation industry, home of the mighty Junkers aircraft factory, where she talked her way into its technical laboratory, and saw 'Junkers' highly skilled engineers turning Count Zeppelin's stupid sausages into new metal planes, monstrous prototypes for a new war. In this shipyard of the air, the day is not far off when the new flyers, drunk on spirits and oil, will realise what the patch of sky outside the doorway is there for, and will be rolled out to the field'.

For her last sketch, 'Milk', she joined a milkman on his rounds of Essen's poor tenements, and wrote of 'the illusion of food, the stink of a workers' boots drying by the fire. That smell is sweeter than incense, for it means they're working and won't die'.

At some point Radek joined her in Germany, provoking a furious letter from her mother: 'You swore to us you wouldn't meet him abroad until he'd settled things officially with his wife, and you've gone back on your word so easily. You call our tears and pleading "bourgeois family nonsense," but if you don't stop lying to us and yourself, these lies of yours will pursue you for the rest of your life'.[3]

Larisa later told a friend that her mother's refusal to accept her relationship with Radek was a source of deep unhappiness to her. And since he had made clear from the start that he would never divorce his wife, she must have kept this from her, to avoid more painful arguments.

She returned to Russia in late July without him, and spent the month of August with her parents at their dacha in Kuntsevo, working on *In Hindenburg's Country*. Back in Moscow, she was finally assigned the factory job she had applied for, at the Khamovniki armoured-car plant, where she gave her lectures on the Russian strike movement. She was also working closely with Radek again, and her mother evidently had to resign herself to their working relationship, if not their romantic one.

Finally forgiven his mistakes in Germany, Radek was back on the Executive of the Comintern, which was now turning its attention from Germany to its potentially powerful new allies in China. Ruled by a succession of ruthless warlords, economically exploited by the governments of Europe and Japan, China had been in an almost constant state of revolution since 1911, when mass strikes and peasant riots had toppled the last Imperial dynasty. The new Republic of China had been established, the first republic in Asia, and a Provisional Government had taken power in Nanking, headed by Sun Yat-sen, Chair of the National People's Party, the *Kuomintang*. Sun Yat-sen made contact with Bolsheviks in Russia and with Lenin in exile, and although most of the country was still divided and dominated by warlords and foreign imperialists, Lenin saw China's anti-imperialist struggles spearheading uprisings across the rest of the colonial world, threatening the entire capitalist system.

After the Bolshevik Revolution, Sun Yat-sen declared his support for the new government, and invited Soviet advisers to Nanking. They were active in the next explosion of upheavals across China, in the spring of 1919, triggered by the signing of the Versailles Treaty, which expelled German oil companies from China's oil-rich Shandong province, and replaced them with Japanese ones. In Beijing, Shanghai and Hong Kong, factory workers and students of the new 'May the 4th Movement' rioted to throw out the imperialists, and the movement's leaders would form the core of the small new Moscow-backed Communist Party of China, established two years later, which organised mass strikes in foreign-owned factories. The strikes were initially supported by the *Kuo-*

---

3   Letter in Przhiborovskaya 2008, pp. 449–50.

mintang. But its nationalist leaders became increasingly reluctant to alienate their landowning and capitalist base, and hundreds left to join the Communist Party, which by 1925 had a membership of over fifty thousand.

That July, it was announced that the new Comintern-sponsored Sun Yat-sen University for the Toilers of China was to open in Moscow, to train the country's next generation of revolutionary leaders, and Radek was appointed to the highly responsible post of Rector. He, Trotsky and Stalin were all to teach there, representing the Comntern. Despite Trotsky's removal as War Commissar, he would play a major role in the University's politics and day-to-day running, and it would be at the heart of the bitter Trotsky-Stalin dispute in the Comintern on the objectives of the international revolution.

In his writings on China, Trotsky predicted that the Chinese revolution would be the second of the great socialist revolutions after Russia to sweep across the colonial countries of the advanced capitalist world. Like Russia, he wrote, China lacked the material resources to build socialism without the support of workers in the advanced West, and unless the revolution was internationalised, it was doomed to be defeated by a hostile capitalist world.

Stalin, in his new post on the Comintern Executive, contended that it was quite possible for China to buld socialism in one country, once capitalism had had time to develop and 'accomplish its national tasks', and he compared the situation there to Russia in 1905, when workers had not been ready for a proletarian revolution, and could only aspire to a bourgeois one.

Their disagreements focused on the Comintern's relations with China's Communist Party and the *Kuomintang*, under its new anti-communist leader *Generalissimo* Chiang Kai-shek. From the start, Trotsky had opposed any alliance with Chiang Kai-shek. According to Stalin, Comintern policy should be to build up Chiang Kai-shek's prestige in working for a bourgeois democratic revolution, until circumstances allowed communists to take power in a 'quick victorious revolution', and Chiang Kai-shek and the *Kuomintang* could be swept away.

Trotsky objected to this treatment of China's communists as the Comintern's 'coolies' – 'ordered to keep the agrarian revolution in check, and abstain from arming the workers without the permission of the bourgeoisie'. Unlike Russia, which had had eight months of bourgeois rule before October, he saw China's bourgeoisie, represented by the Kuomintang, as too small for even this role, and he argued that workers and peasants would have to seize the factories and land directly, without waiting for the first capitalist stage of the revolution envisaged by Marx.

Radek shared Trotsky's assessment of the international revolution, and was equally opposed to any alliance with Chiang Kai-shek. But as Rector of the

University, he had studied conditions in China more closely than Trotsky, and believed he vastly overestimated the power of its proletariat. With capitalism barely developed, he wrote, peasants would have to lead workers in 'the class struggle against the exploiters and capitalist-backed imperialists', and until communists had gained strength and numbers, they should work with more progressive local elements of the *Kuomintang*, 'in a united front against imperialism'.

In these differing visions of the Chinese revolution, it was Stalin's that prevailed. Soviet military experts were sent to China to arm and train the forces of Chiang Kai-shek, and Chinese communists were instructed to join the *Kuomintang en bloc*, which was admitted to the Comintern as an associate member. Chiang Kai-shek was made an honorary member of the Comintern Executive, and was consulted on the setting up of the Sun Yat-sen University, and he enrolled his fifteen-year-old son, Chiang Ching-kuo, as its first student.

In the months before term started in November, Radek hired lecturers and planned courses, in consultation with Nadezhda Krupskaya, who had guided the work of the *rabfaks*, and the University was run on the same principles as the *rabfaks*, with basic literacy the only qualification required of students. Several of Radek's lecturers were Russian Sinologists, fluent in Mandarin, but the majority were Chinese. Chinese workers had been arriving in the Far East and Siberia to work as immigrant labourers since the 1860s, and some seven thousand had fought with the Red Army in the Civil War. A large Chinese detachment fought in the Urals, and in *The Front* Larisa had described meeting Chinese fighters in the Volga town of Sarapul. Hundreds went on to study at the *rabfaks* and the universities, then worked in government or teaching jobs, and the Sun Yat-sen would launch many successful academic careers.

Larisa's father was to lecture in Marxist philosophy, and Igor in Asian history and politics. She was to teach Russian literature, one of eight women lecturers Radek appointed, and she worked with him writing to six hundred workers in China, inviting them to enrol as students, setting up a hardship fund to support the poorer ones and their families.

No expense was spared to make them comfortable. The University was in an old and beautiful building on Volkhonka Street, near the Kremlin, with a hundred rooms, ten large auditoriums, and a well-stocked library. In the gardens were volleyball and basketball courts, which froze in winter to make skating rinks, and opposite were the golden domes of the Cathedral of Christ the Saviour, where students would do their morning callisthenics.

Lecturers were well paid, and the job carried great prestige, entitling them to accommodation in large comfortably furnished rooms in a building in the grounds. Radek had a room there, and Igor moved in with his second wife, the English communist Violet Lansbury, who has left a fascinating and sharply observed account of her life with him in Moscow in her best-selling memoirs *An Englishwoman in the USSR*.[4]

The youngest of the twelve children of George Lansbury, future leader of the Labour Party, founding member of the Hands Off Russia! campaign, Violet had marched with him in rallies at the age of sixteen, and joined a Workers' Council of Action, and in 1920 she joined the British Communist Party. Lansbury called the Revolution 'a new star of hope across Europe', and he made the first of his three visits to Russia that year, where he met Lenin and the other Party leaders. On his return, he arranged for her to work and learn Russian at the new Soviet Trade Mission in London, and in the summer of 1925, she left for Moscow.

She immediately joined the Party, then set off with a young 'red professor' on the Trans-Siberian Railway to the Urals, where she enrolled at the Communist University of Sverdlovsk, studying and sharing a hostel for the next two months with workers and peasants from all over the Soviet Union, grappling with her challenging programme of courses in philosophy, mathematics, European history and Marxist economics. On graduating, she was qualified to work in Russia, and her first job was as a translator and editor at Moscow's *Komsomol* Young Guard publishing house.

She described first meeting Igor at a vegetarian café in Moscow's Arbat district – 'a leisurely dining place frequented by musicians, poets, professors and followers of Tolstoy, with a fair number of cranks, in their sandals and "sensible" square-necked clothing. The men tended to wear long hair and beards, a fashion that had gone out with tsarism, and the sight of the greasy unwashed hair and dusty feet poking from dusty sandals wasn't exactly my idea of taking food in hygienic conditions'.

Radek had a table there with two men, she wrote – 'for once Radek wasn't surrounded by his usual crowd of admiring young people sitting at his feet, listening to his interpretations of world events'. The older of his companions was 'an extremely handsome well-built man in his early sixties, who looked like a professor'. The other, clearly his son, 'of slight build but muscular', came over and introduced himself, and three months later, Igor had divorced his first wife to marry her.

1925 was a good year for Reisner. The Meyerhold Theatre, where he was still a director, had confounded its critics with its dazzling production of Nikolai Erdman's satire on the NEP 'The Warrant'. Six short revolutionary plays he had

---

4   Violet Lansbury's *An Englishwoman in the USSR*, first published in London in 1940, went through three more editions in the next two years. (The actress Angela Lansbury is Violet's niece).

published in 1921, collectively titled *God and the Stock Exchange*, had entered the repertoires of several theatres in Moscow and Leningrad, and that year he published two ground-breaking and widely discussed essays on Freud, *The Individual and Social Origins of the Family*, and *Psychoanalysis and Class*.

Research in psychology flourished in the cultural revival after the Civil War. Leningrad's new Institute for the Study of the Brain, under its director Reisner's colleague Professor Bekhterev, Larisa's mentor at the Psychoneurology Institute, was conducting revolutionary research into human behaviour, and ran its own therapeutic children's nurseries and psychoanalysis clinic. Analysts were trained at the State Psychoanalytical Institute in Moscow, established in 1923, with the personal backing of Freud, the third such Institute in the world after those in Vienna and Berlin, and Reisner was one of the eight founding members of Moscow's Psychoanalytical Society, which produced a nine-volume Russian edition of Freud's works, organised courses in hospitals, universities and schools, and published articles on art, philosophy and aesthetics, and the latest discoveries in medicine and science.

Psychoanalysis was seen in the 'scientific state' as a method of interpreting human behaviour in accordance with a definable set of scientific principles. Trotsky and Radek had both discovered Freud's ideas while living in exile in Vienna, and had explored them in their writings. Reisner's essays were the first coherent Marxist account of Freudian theories of sexuality and repression as the basis of bourgeois society, and the key to the new family under socialism, and they would be hugely influential on the new generation of Soviet psychologists.[5]

1925 was also a year of anniversaries – the first anniversary of Lenin's death, the twentieth of the 1905 revolution, and the centenary of its doomed precursor, the Decembrist uprising, when officers had marched to St Petersburg's Senate Square to demand a constitution and an end to serfdom.

Eisenstein's masterpiece 'Battleship *Potemkin*', celebrating the sailors' 1905 mutiny in Odessa, had its gala premiere that December in Moscow at the Bolshoi Theatre, which was decorated as a battleship, with staff, orchestra and cast members all dressed as the ship's crew. In Leningrad, Senate Square was renamed Decembrists' Square,[6] and their burial place, Goloday Island, was named Decembrists' Island

---

[5] See Frank Brenner's 'Intrepid Thought. Psychoanalysis in the Soviet Union', World Socialist Website, June 1999, for an excellent synopsis of Reisner's ideas.

[6] Decembrists' Square became Senate Square again in 2008, seventeen years after Leningrad returned to its tsarist name St Petersburg.

Larissa had written her first poems as a schoolgirl about Pushkin's association with the rebels, and they had come alive for her when she stayed in their prison settlements in the Urals. A mass of articles and jubilee monographs on the rising were published that year, based on documents locked in the tsarist archives and released after the Revolution, and she spent weeks in the Moscow archives researching a series of essays she was commissioned to write for *Izvestiya* and *Red Virgin Soil*, studying police files and court records, reading their letters, poems and diaries.

The officers who had driven Napoleon's armies from Moscow to Paris had read Voltaire, Rousseau and Montesquieu, and returned to Russia as atheists and freethinkers, with new ideas about the fate of their country, and the serfs who had fought under them. Secret discussion groups sprang up across Russia, to plan direct action against the autocracy, and after a mutiny by the élite Semyonovsky regiment, honoured for its heroism in the Napoleonic wars, the groups coalesced into two organisations – the Northern Society in St Petersburg, and the Southern Society in Kiev. Pushkin was friends with the brilliant aristocrats, poets and officers of the Northern Society, and was part of all their discussions, and in 1820 he was banished from the capital to the Caucasus, then to the Crimea, where he wrote political poetry and his masterpiece *Evgeny Onegin*.

He was still in exile in 1825, when the Decembrists began to plot the insurrection. It was planned that on the 14th of December, officers in the capital would refuse to take the oath of allegiance to the hated new Tsar, the first Tsar Nicholas, due to accede to the throne after the death of his brother Alexander. But the plan was fatally flawed by the Societies' fundamental disagreements about their goals. Members of Kiev's Southern Society, led by the Jacobin Pavel Pestel, called for the Tsar to be assassinated and replaced with a democratic government – the 'Dictatorship of the People' – and for the landowners' estates to be redistributed among the peasants. St Petersburg's more moderate and powerful Northern Society wanted the Tsar's powers merely to be limited with an English-style constitutional monarchy, and the serfs to be emancipated without land.

Due to the general confusion and lack of leadership, hundreds of officers in the capital failed to appear on the Square on the 14th. As the first columns approached, they were met by nine thousand government troops, who shot seventy dead on the spot, and threw their bodies in the River Neva. Five of the leaders were publicly hanged, and hundreds who had been barely involved in the plot were sentenced to long terms of hard labour, often for life, in the Urals and Siberia, Kazakhstan and the Far East. Their wives were allowed to join them on condition that they left their children behind, and never returned.

That August, a selection of Larisa's writings from Afghanistan were published by the *Ogonyok* (Flame) Publishing House, as 'Asiatic Tales'. A month later, they were published in their entirety by the State Publishing House as *Afghanistan*, in a print-run of ten thousand, with the opening 'Notes From the Journey' dedicated to Ambassador Suritz, the Vanderlip chapter to Raskolnikov, and the rousing finale, 'Fascists In Asia', published separately as a pamphlet.

Afghanistan was savaged in the *Proletkult* press for its sumptuous language and 'exoticism'. 'Larisa's prose style becomes ever more lush and self-indulgent. Like an aging woman looking in the glass and seeing more wrinkles on her face, she looks into her soul and sees new cavities there', wrote an anonymous reviewer in the *Proletkult* magazine *Communist*.

Alexander Voronsky, who had published her first essays from Afghanistan in *Red Virgin Soil*, wrote:

> Each sketch resembles a tree loaded with an abundance of fruits, and as in a vast and varied garden, the eye is often dazzled by the wealth of images, the sharp and unexpected descriptions, saturated with oriental brightness and colour ... Some call her writing self-indulgent, for she has mastered the written word, and knows all its secrets. But this isn't self-indulgence, it is the generosity of one who lightly scatters handfuls of what she possesses in such abundance.

Igor Ilinsky in *Pravda* praised her as the first Soviet journalist to show the ugly human face of fascism, and for 'exposing the true state of Soviet-British relations in Afghanistan, and the inexorable hatred between the two worlds that lies beneath the ceremonies of diplomatic etiquette'. Nikolai Smirnov in *Izvestiya* saw the book as a model of political journalism: 'Afghanistan belongs with those great works that smell more of gunpowder than roses'.[7]

The Party's tensions with *Proletkult* had come to a head that year, in the making of Eisenstein's first full-length feature film, *Strike*, acted by members of the *Proletkult* Drama Collective, financed with *Proletkult* money, via the Commissariat of Education. Eisenstein had been given his start as a director by *Proletkult* in 1918, and it had financed his first film. But like Meyerhold, he had only ever given the organisation his qualified support, and *Strike*'s opening in April had been marked by their public acrimonious break.

---

7 *Press and Revolution*, 1925, no. 9. Voronsky, *Literaturnye Zapisi* (Literary Notes), Moscow, 1926, pp. 159–60; Igor Ilinsky, 'A Cut-glass Talent', LRRC, p. 123; Smirnov, 'Memories of Larisa Reisner', 1926, p. 40.

Three months later, the Party issued a statement in *Pravda* denouncing *Proletkult's* 'communist conceitedness and arrogance' and intolerance of non-communist writers. The literary journal *Novy Mir* (New World), which was closely identified with the Party, then responded with a lengthy diatribe against the 'excessive negativity' of the fellow-travellers Pilnyak, Isaac Babel and Lydia Seifullina. Gumilyov's work disappeared from print, and a secret Party decree banned Akhmatova's poetry from publication, on the grounds of her 'introverted bourgeois aesthetic and trivial female preoccupations', and she would remain unpublished in Russia for the next fifteen years.

Larisa entered the battle for the fellow-travellers in her long essay 'Against Literary Banditry', in the magazine *Journalist*. Writers' responsibility was to present an honest picture of Soviet society and its contradictions, she wrote, 'without varnish or adornment', and she defended Seifullina's truthful depictions of Siberian village life against the 'soul-daubers, who dip their critical brushes in the buckets of cheap idealism, and want to colour and sweeten the truth'.

> Those who have lived through the Revolution know the importance of these works born of 1917, incorruptible eye-witnesses to its suffering, its heroism, its poverty and magnificence ... The intelligent eyes of our idealists and romantics have looked without flinching into the flames of the furnace in which whole strata of the old culture have been burnt to ashes, and they have portrayed with great honesty the shocking, formless, incomparably beautiful face of the Revolution.[8]

Seifullina had been commissioned by Leningrad's Vakhtangov Theatre to write a stage version of her novel *Virineya*, and when she left Moscow with Pravdukhin in October to supervise rehearsals, they felt lost without each other, and exchanged long passionate letters. Excerpts from these letters (all written in the formal 'vy' form) were published in 1927, in a long sympathetic essay on Seifullina in the journal *Novy Mir*, which two years earlier had attacked the 'excessive negativity' of her work.

'Where are you, you wonderful extraordinary woman? I miss you desperately', Seifullina wrote to Larisa. 'From a Marxist viewpoint you're a monster, but as a fellow-traveller with a complex ideology, I think you're an angel, and I love you more than ever ... Please drop me a line about yourself, horrible creature.

---

8 'Protiv literaturnogo banditizma' (Against Literary Banditry), *Journalist*, no. 1, 1926. SW, pp. 503–7.

Or better still, visit us and see how we live in our four-room apartment with kitchen and all conveniences ... Greetings to Karl, I love him very much too. Yours in spirit only, for my body is here'.

In Larisa's five-page reply, scribbled on the back of some *Izvestiya* proofs, she wrote:

> Beloved Lydia Ivanovna, I'm writing to you from a sad place, like this paper. The longer you're gone, the more I miss you – your flat, your samovar, your extraordinary warmth, which I've never known before ... I swear I'll stop writing if you ever leave me again ...
>
> I sit here crying my eyes out for you, not only because I miss you, but because you belong here in Moscow. This is where people make art, and the whole spiders-web of writing which we need to breathe. Peter is a city of reflections, and you're living with a lot of stuffy soul-daubers whose time was up long ago ... Just so long as you stay healthy, and Valerian has strong fists ...
>
> Moscow must feel as remote to you there as a Samarkand bazaar, and you're being attacked here, and of course there's no justice in it. But despite all the petty rubbish being thrown at you, everything that's best in this wicked city of ours thinks of you as it should, and applauds you for writing as you please. That is the privilege of great talents like yours ...
>
> I'll write to you soon about the Pasternaks and the theatre and life in general ... You'll never know how much I love you. Your Larisa.[9]

Later that month, she took a few days off from her work with Radek to stay with Seifullina, and to meet the distinguished Leningrad historian Professor Shchegolev, known to have a mass of material on the Decembrists. Seifullina described her appearing unannounced at her flat late one night, before her letter arrived to say she was coming, telling her Shchegolev had been 'as mean as Pushkin's Miserly Knight with his material, and would need at least three more dinners to change his mind'. They discussed rehearsals of 'Virineya', and a book of essays they planned to publish together for a mass readership on Russia's best writers, communist and non-communist, for which Larisa had written a memoir of Leonid Andreev, 'My First Love', to mark the sixth anniversary of his tragic death. 'Then she spoke of Germany, and in just a few words she could describe a German working woman, and you would see her with her eyes'.

---

9 *Sochineniya Lydii Seifulliny i ee kritiki* (The Works of Lydia Seifullina and Her Critics'), *New World*, 1927, no. 10.

By the end of October, the first Chinese students were arriving in Moscow, most of them young men and women factory workers from Shanghai, Beijing and Canton, who had left in secret to avoid arrest, many without telling their families, sailing from Shanghai to the port of Vladivostok, then travelling by train the five thousand miles to Moscow. They arrived with little money and less Russian, and each was given a warm coat, shoes and boots for the cold weather, with smart suits for the women, and high-buttoned Russian peasant shirts and 'Lenin' jackets for the men. They were housed in large comfortable dormitories, and given five large meals a day (reduced to three after they objected to this waste of food when so many in Russia were hungry), and many complained to Radek of being racially abused on the streets, accused of scrounging off the workers' state.

Radek and Trotsky had both grown up with similar experiences of racism, and Trotsky was a favourite target of the Revolution's enemies. 'You're getting this for Trotsky', Jews were told in Petylura's pogroms in Ukraine. But like other Jewish members of the Bolshevik government, neither made a political issue of their Jewish origins. Trotsky's biographer Isaac Deutscher, who himself grew up in the Pale, has written powerfully of those who lived at the boundaries between so many different cultures, languages and religions, and the extraordinary breadth this gave to their vision of revolution – 'leaving the confines of the Pale to lift their gaze to the universal and the international, fighting with the persecuted and dispossessed of the world against all forms of class and racial oppression'.[10]

The University's opening ceremony was on the 7th of November, the eighth anniversary of the Revolution, and the six hundred students (including several from Japan and South East Asia, Africa and the Middle East, even America) gathered in the great hall, decorated with Chinese and Soviet flags, and portraits of Sun Yat-sen, Marx and Lenin. Radek spoke first through interpreters to welcome them, and express 'Russia's undying solidarity with the Chinese people and their anti-imperialist struggles'. Then Trotsky spoke, ending to roars of applause with the words, 'From now on, any Russian who treats a Chinese student with contempt, whether a Party member or not, is not worthy to call themselves either a communist or a Soviet citizen'.

To protect students from the risk of arrest on their return home, the Soviet press was banned from reporting on the University, and we know all this from one of the first to enrol, the Shanghai factory worker Yueh Sheng, whose wonderfully engaging book is the only full account of its activities.[11]

---

10   Isaac Deutscher, *The Non-Jewish Jew and Other Essays*, 2017.
11   Sheng, *The Sun Yat-sen University in Moscow and the Chinese Revolution. A Personal Account*, 1971.

The Sun Yat-sen published its own academic journal on Chinese politics, and the first Mandarin-Russian dictionary, but the lectures were all in Russian, and Sheng was given a crash course in the language, speed-reading Russian newspapers and works of poetry and prose. He was keen to learn quickly, and was soon attending lectures in history, Russian literature, military science, and the basic principles of Marxism, propaganda and mobilisation. He particularly enjoyed his Marxist philosophy course, where he struggled with Lenin's *State and Revolution*, but was 'captivated by the freshness of Marx's theory of Dialectical Materalism – and the fact that it was taught by a beautiful woman instructor made it even more enthralling'.

This could possibly have been Larisa, but unfortunately there is nothing about her in Sheng's book. Radek was very popular, he wrote, greeting students personally by name, inviting them into his office to discuss their studies and problems. Keeping an eye on him was his 'nanny', the unpopular young historian Pavel Mif, appointed by Stalin as Vice Rector. But most of the teachers Radek appointed were Trotsky supporters – as was Chiang Kai-shek's son, who later publicly renounced his father – and Sheng described the Sun Yat-sen as the 'cradle of the Trotskyist movement in China'.

Stalin was less involved with teaching than with his organisational work, building his famous 'twenty-eight Bolsheviks' – the communist cadres who later included Mao Tse-tung's allies in the Cultural Revolution Deng Wenyi and Ch'en Poita, and the future leader of the People's Republic of China, Deng Xiaoping. Radek accused Stalin of wanting to turn the University into the 'Soviet equivalent of a Chinese missionary school'. He and Trotsky believed in encouraging critical argument and debate, and their lectures on the Chinese and Russian revolutions were invariably packed, Sheng wrote, with students staggering out loaded with reference books and notes.

Trips to the theatre, the ballet and the cinema were laid on for them, and he remembered his two years in Moscow as a heady mix of revolutionary and sexual politics. Several of the students were married, and most were having affairs. Three babies were born, and several abortions had to be arranged, and Radek set up a kindergarten and a 'Comrades' Court', where two men were tried for the counterrevolutionary crime of wife-beating.

Larisa turned down the offer of accommodation there, and stayed with Alyosha and her parents at the House of Soviets, working on her lectures and her Decembrist essays. And her work in the Soviet archives led her to her next two books – a collection of fictional biographies of the early French, German and English socialists of the eighteenth and nineteenth centuries, and a fictional trilogy about a factory in the Urals, telling its story through five generations of workers, from Pugachev's serf fighters to the revolutionaries of her lifetime.

'She was very modest about her powers as a writer, and sometimes she took fright at the scope of her ambitions. But her writing was growing more powerful by the day', Radek wrote. 'She wanted to see everything, know everything, be part of everything', wrote Trotsky, 'and in a few short years she captured everything in her writing'.

CHAPTER 18

'How Extraordinary to Be Alive'

Throughout the 1920s, at packed meetings across the Soviet Union, people were discussing the new family life and sexual morality of the Revolution. Larisa beautifully captured the mood of the *Komsomol* meeting in Ukraine, when the whole town crowded into the building and a brass band played, and men and women, young and old, discussed love, sex, marriage and divorce, in 'our new collective tomorrow'.

In 1925, the Bolshevik Family Code was to be updated with the new Soviet Marriage Law, which had been thrown open to public debate. Kollontai flew back from Norway to speak at meetings and publish articles taking issue with the NEP spirit of the Law's main proposals: to replace state benefits for divorced or separated mothers with private alimony, and make spouses financially responsible for their partners 'in times of high unemployment' – seventy percent of Russia's unemployed being women. She rejected this unsocialist approach to the family, arguing that alimony demeaned giver and recipient alike, and that most men would be unable to pay anyway. She proposed instead that people make small monthly contributions to a General Insurance Fund, which would provide financial support for single mothers and their children, organise accommodation for those who were homeless, and increase Russia's still woefully inadequate number of day nurseries.

Her successor as director of the *Zhenotdel* accused her of being 'infected with bourgeois ideas', and claimed the scheme would 'enflame men's African passions', encouraging them to abandon wives 'who no longer pleased them', leading to more broken families and abandoned children. Even Trotsky weighed in, saying now was not the time for her 'social experiments' to replace the nuclear family, and the Law's purpose was to bring some stability to family life, and protect the 'weaker sex'.

Larisa's *Zhenotdel* friend Olga Nesterovych was in Moscow that winter, speaking in support of Kollontai in the debate, and they met again at a meeting in November. They discussed poetry and *Zhenotdel* politics, and caught up on the four years since their time together in Sochi. Afterwards, Nesterovych had enrolled for a literature degree at Leningrad University, and she was now on the editorial board of Leningrad's *Oblit* literary publishing house – 'my ship of happiness from Larisa was already full of literature and politics!' she wrote.[1]

---
1 Olga Nesterovych, 'The Ship of Happiness', LRRC, pp. 152–61.

One evening after work, she joined Larisa and a group of her friends on a trip to the town of Zagorsk, forty miles from Moscow, where Alexander Voronsky and Isaac Babel had rented a dacha. They all piled into an open car and drove off through the snow, and sat around the samovar all night with their hospitable hosts. Babel read some of his *Red Cavalry* stories, 'which Larisa praised for their heroic form, and called classics of the new Soviet fiction', and they discussed the works of Proust, whose stories *Pleasures and Days* Nesterovych had brought out in Russian translation. Then she read from a little book of memoirs she had published, *Tales about Pushkin, From the Mouth of his Friend P.I. Bartyonev*. 'Larisa was deeply moved by the author's account of Pushkin's last visit to Moscow, where he foretold his death', she wrote. '"What extraordinary premonition", she said. "It's nothing to do with superstition, it's about how people were shaped by their experiences", and she shuddered with sadness, and visions of the inevitable'.

Next morning, as they drove back along the forested roads to Moscow to start the day's work, she sat quietly at the back, while the others sang popular songs, 'Overgrown Paths', and 'A Young Cossack Walks Along the Don'. 'Then someone put Esenin's poem "Song" to music – "The best song the nightingale sings is the funeral song over my head" – and she said he had found exactly the right music for it, from the melody of the verse itself'.

Nikolai Smirnov remembered seeing her in Moscow that December, striding along the Tverskoi Boulevard to the Patriarchs' Pond skating-rink, 'wearing a coat of soft Siberian silver fur, her "Snowmaiden" skates jingling on her shoulders'.

> When she saw me she stopped and smiled, and said 'What a wonderful day!' Everything seemed magical to her – the mirror-like surface of the ice, the silver hoarfrost on the lime trees, the screech of the sledges on the sugary snow, the low mother of pearl sun gilding the statue of the thinking Pushkin. When we parted, she shook my hand firmly and hurried on. Then she looked back and said, 'How extraordinary to be alive!'[2]

Smirnov next saw her at the funeral of Esenin, in tears at his grave. Tired of poetry, women and life, Esenin had spent his last days on a drinking spree in Leningrad, before slashing his wrists in his room at the Angleterre Hotel, and writing his last poem with his blood:

---

2 Smirnov, 'Memories of Larisa Reisner', 1961.

Goodbye my friend, goodbye.
Dying is nothing new in this life,
But there's nothing new to living either ...

Next morning he was found hanging from the heating pipes. His body was brought by train to Moscow, where his family and friends gathered on 31 December to bury him at the Vagankovo Cemetery, graveyard of poets.

Two days later, Larisa's first Decembrist essay, '14 December 1825', was published in *Izvestiya*. The scene is set dramatically on Senate Square, and the officers' mood is evoked in noble restrained language. But flashes of anger keep breaking through, at this handful of aristocrats and poets cut off from the 'rabble', and their doomed battle with the autocracy. Their defeat was a tragedy, she wrote, but the rising was dead as soon as it was hatched. They had the backing of an entire Moscow regiment, and they could have won. But the soldiers marching to the Square had been ordered not to appeal to people on the streets to join them. 'The young politicians clearly understood society and its laws, and they feared above all a popular mass uprising, and this clouded their noble thoughts and deprived them of historical perspective ... And the old fox Speransky[3] mentally put his big blue censor's cross on the constitution flickering in his consciousness, and signed their death warrants with his elegant hand'.

This opening piece was followed over the next five months by psychological portraits of the Decembrists: their treasurer, Baron Shteingel, the lowly Pyotr Kakhovsky, their pawn, and the leader of the insurrection, Prince Trubestskoi.[4]

Her Shteingel piece is filled with sadness and irony. She quotes from the letters and diaries of his father, a German lieutenant in the Russian army, 'an honest servant, who longed to help rebuild Moscow after the 1813 fire, and never took bribes', but was hated as a German, and forced to serve in Siberia, 'where his dreams of a better Russia ended with his early death'.

She sees Shteingel's life as inseparable from his father's – 'as if his father had entered his soul, along with his worthless education, his military service, and his official business in the tsarist administration, all of which led him to Senate Square'. Like his father, Shteingel never took bribes, and used his position to save many innocent prisoners from exile and death. 'And he had another fatal flaw, he had to think everything through to the end. He hated Russian

---

3   Count Mikhail Speransky (1772–1839), hated chief adviser to Tsars Alexander 1 and Nicholas 1, who headed the special court of investigation into the Decembrists, and delivered their sentences.
4   '14 December 1825' and 'Prince Sergei Petrovich Trubetskoi', *Izvestiya*, 1 and 5 January, 1926. 'Baron Shteingel' and 'About Kakhovsky', *Red Virgin Soil*, June, 1926. SW, pp. 519–40.

sloppiness, and took an almost mathematical approach to the revolution – a rebel not from emotion, but from cold reason, like spring water'. Since no one could agree on what should be in their Manifesto, he wrote it himself. And in the weeks before the uprising, 'as others left or wavered, the colder and more determined he became. He was against killing the Tsar. But if it must be done, let it be done properly, as the royal family sits behind their golden screen in church, like chickens in a coop'.

After the insurrection was crushed, Shteingel was sentenced to ten years' hard labour in a Siberian coalmine, 'where as an additionally cruel punishment for this fastidious man, he was forbidden to wash', and was then sent into permanent exile in the Urals. His sentence was commuted by the new Tsar Alexander II, in his amnesty for the Decembrists in December 1855, the thirtieth anniversary of the rising, and at the age of seventy-six he returned to St Petersburg, where he was treated as a criminal. He died in 1862, a year after the Tsar's emancipation of the serfs, leaving his 'Testament' – 'Who would condemn a martyr for throwing a few words into the ocean of time, in the hope that one day his grandchildren will read them?'

Equally tragic was the fate of Kakhovsky, a minor government official from the impoverished gentry, a character straight out of Gogol, 'with a small estate in Smolensk, and a couple of hundred souls, unsuccessful in love, filled with bitterness against society'. Unlike the others, with their valets and carriages, he arrived at meetings alone and on foot, and he knew nothing about German poetry or French philosophy, and couldn't join their discussions. But they flattered him and fed him oysters and champagne. And as arguments raged over whether to kill the Tsar, he fell under the spell of the sincerest and most idealistic of the Decembrists, Pushkin's close friend the poet Kondraty Ryleev.

Ryleev made him his ally and confidant, and spoke to him of revolution and a better life in Russia, and he secretly appointed him to shoot Tsar Nicholas in the Winter Palace the day before the planned insurrection. Kakhovsky was impatient for action. But as weeks passed in indecision and frivolous talk (it was even suggested the Tsar could be 'accidentally' crushed to death by the crowds as he entered the Palace), he grew increasingly disillusioned. Forbidden by Ryleev to discuss the Society with outsiders, ask questions, or recruit new members, 'he listens to the idle chatter that cheapens the highest ideals, from which no business ever follows, and realises "they're playing with me, as they're playing with the whole of Russia, they simply want a new dictatorship of the masters. Revolutionary phrases are just *bon ton* in these circles, like the strong tea and tobacco smoke at three in the morning, and they change nothing. The servants throw open the windows to air the rooms after their meetings, and the terrible words fly out with the cigarette ends"'.

On 13 December, the day appointed for the shooting, Kakhovsky still had no instructions from Ryleev. He finally received his pistol on the 14th, and went straight to the Square and shot dead the Governor-General of St Petersburg, General Miloradovich. He was arrested on the spot, and sentenced to hang, with Ryleev, the poet Alexander Bestuzhev, the officer Muravyov-Apostol, and the firebrand of the Southern Society, Pavel Pestel.

At his trial, Kakhovsky spoke up boldly about the evils of tsarism, and it was only then that he discovered he had been betrayed by Ryleev and Bestuzhev, who had accused him of plotting to assassinate the Tsar on his own. Larisa wrote with sadness and sympathy for Ryleev, whose poetry was filled with the Decembrists' lofty ideals of patriotism and freedom, and she quoted his last poem, written on a maple leaf, while he was sitting in the Peter and Paul Fortress waiting to be hanged:

> Prison is an honour for me, not a disgrace.
> I am here for a just cause.
> How can these shackles shame me,
> When I bear them for the Fatherland?

But she was bitterly critical of his treatment of Kakhovsky. Kakhovsky had never been one of them, she wrote. Ryleev had picked him because he needed an outsider to carry out the assassination, not a true member of the Society, 'so they could keep their white trousers clean'. 'The Decembrists were the finest, most brilliant people of their day, the flower of their epoch. But no one at Kakhovsky's trial spoke of him with more icy contempt than Ryleev and Bestuzhev. A hundred years on, our faces flush with shame when we read the slippery well-turned phrases of their testimonies'.

Prince Trubetskoi was the brilliant officer appointed to lead the rising and act as interim dictator afterwards, who on the 14th failed to appear on the Square, and hid in the Austrian Embassy.

She described Trubetskoi 'feeling' the revolutionary ideas in the air, 'as he feels his heavy bearskin coat on his shoulders, and the drifting snow, and hears his galloping horses and the clash of his sword:'

> Flitting between balls and banquets, drunk on revolution, its blood flashing against the icy immensity of tsarist despotism, the prince sucks on his pipe, and sees how indifferently the blizzard extinguishes its sparks. Beautiful words fly from his mouth into the frozen night, and are lost in the darkness. And on the morning of the 14th, greyer than the walls of jail, fear speaks to him from the depths of his soul, in the voice he will hear a few hours later in the Peter and Paul Fortress.

The Decembrists' revolutionary goals had always been fundamentally alien to him, she wrote. He believed officers only had to stand in the Square and refuse to take the oath to the Tsar, and he would grant them a constitution. But he was still sentenced to seven years' hard labour in Siberia, 'having condemned his comrades to death for trusting a traitor'.

The story ends as the five are driven through the streets to be hanged, 'with boards over their prison shifts saying "Tsar Murderer". And with this glorious epitaph, they entered the history of the Russian Revolution'. The final scene is set at the old site of the gallows opposite the Kshesinskaya Palace, the Bolsheviks' military headquarters before the Revolution, from whose balcony Lenin had addressed the crowds on his return to Petrograd in 1917.

She was accused by several historians of letting her imagination run away with her about the Decembrists' personal lives, and playing with the facts. Victor Shklovsky thought the essays were the best things she ever wrote, deeply researched, full of living breathing characters, with their hopes and struggles and their complicated relations with their times. Igor Ilinsky compared her approach to history to Pushkin's poetic retelling of the Pugachev rising in his novel *The Captain's Daughter*, and praised her exceptional empathy with the Decembrists and the ideas that inspired them:

> She summons up a whole epoch, without props or powdered wigs, and she has a special spiritual affinity with the period. A hundred years ago, she would have been a Decembrist. Sixty years later, she would have joined the People's Will who killed the next Tsar. But this is more than a vivid evocation of the Decembrist rising by the hand of a brilliant artist. Although captivated by the past, she lives in the present, and sets the events of 1825 against the mighty struggles of her own lifetime.[5]

A week after her first Decembrist piece was published, *In Hindenburg's Country* was brought out by the *Pravda* publishing house in a huge print run of half a million.

Vera Inber considered it her most accomplished work, filled with poetry and big ideas and the everyday details of workers' lives:

> People, places and ideas are described by a writer who has achieved new brilliance. The characteristic beauty and refinement of her prose is transformed by a mature pen, unafraid to write well today, knowing it will be even better tomorrow ...

---

5   Igor Ilinsky, 'A Cut-glass Talent', LRRC, pp. 121–2.

In her essay on the Junkers aircraft factory, she writes of the 'rapturous moment of single combat at a height of 5,200 metres, where air dissolves in space like a diamond in water'. It doesn't matter if a diamond can really dissolve in water, that's how she sees it – transparency and hardness. And that could be a description of her writing, a stone dissolved in the fire of the Revolution.

'*In Hindenburg's Country*, like *Hamburg at the Barricades*, is the work not of an observer, but of a fighter in the world revolution', Nikolai Smirnov wrote in *Izvestiya*.

She is always drawn to broad epic themes, and the sparkling well of her talent has grown strong in the Revolution. But she is also a genius of the miniature. She sees all the heroism, sacrifice and pathos in the day-to-day work of building socialism, and she writes with a sharpened stiletto. No detail is too small, nothing is too commonplace ... We see her tirelessly perfecting her style, discarding, adding and improving, shaping each image to make it more expressive, promising new work wonderful in its clarity and simplicity ...[6]

Nikulin regretted that they hadn't seen more of each other since she returned from Afghanistan, and they caught up on a long walk around Moscow in January. He asked her about her plans for the future, and she told him about the two new historical works she had started on, and her two forthcoming trips abroad, recently announced in *Pravda*, joining a Soviet delegation in Paris for 'Franco-Soviet talks', and flying on a diplomatic mission to Tehran, and she was excited about making her first plane trip. 'Then she spoke with her old simple candour about herself, and the man she had been close to. "Ah, that *bürger Gemütlichkeit*! How strange that such a fighting revolutionary could be such a petit bourgeois in his private life! But that's all over now," she said'.[7]

Torn between his love for her and for his adored daughter, desperate not to break up his family, Radek had gone back to live with his wife. But their relationship was evidently far from over. She was still working with him at the Sun Yat-sen University, and things dragged on in an unhappy complicated way, and the stress and uncertainty took its toll on her health.

---

6   Vera Inber 1966, p. 280. Smirnov, *Memories of Larisa Reisner*, 1961, op. cit.
7   Nikulin, 'Years of Our Life', 1966, p. 91.

Radek's Comintern colleague Rosa Levine-Meyer, who had first met them together in Berlin at the start of their affair, barely recognised them when she saw them at a meeting in Moscow that winter. 'Radek was very tense and subdued, lacking his former brilliance. He was still the same matey informal man I had known before, and one of the few on whom power had left no trace. But all was clearly not well in his household, and the proud beautiful woman I had met before seemed drained of life, with tight-pressed unsmiling lips and empty eyes'.[8]

A series of increasingly severe malaria attacks robbed her of her energy and confidence and enthusiasm for life, with more and more days when she was too exhausted to work, and her parents were begging her to go abroad for more treatment. Her student friend Lydia Rosenblum was shocked by how ill she looked when she met her alone at the theatre one night. 'Her eyes barely shone, and there was none of the old spark in her face. Exhausted by her ambiguous relationship with Radek, and her family's lack of sympathy with the situation, she said she no longer believed in herself as a writer, and she had lost her way'.[9]

At the end of January, her friend Rozhdestvensky arrived in Moscow with a large delegation of Leningrad writers for the grand opening of the new Herzen House, home of the nineteenth-century philosopher Alexander Herzen, later the headquarters of numerous publishing houses and literary associations (the setting for much of Mikhail Bulgakov's novel *The Master and Margarita*).

Rozhdestvensky joined the hundreds of writers who attended the opening ceremony in the great hall, and Larisa arrived for the party afterwards. 'She lit up the hall when she appeared, and was greeted with happy exclamations and outstretched hands, and she was her usual friendly unaffected self. But she seemed distant from this boisterous rather drunk crowd, and her glass rarely touched her lips'.

Leaving her seat, she moved quietly from group to group, and when she reached Rozhdestvensky, she asked him to read his latest poems to her. 'And I thought what beautiful intelligent eyes she had, and how much youth, as if the stormy experiences of her life had barely touched the pure lines of her brow, the fine slightly ironic curve of her mouth, and her bright chestnut hair ... Yet sometimes her attentive gaze would be clouded with anxiety, or perhaps simply tiredness'.

The party went on into the small hours, and as everyone was leaving, she clasped his hand and said, 'It's too noisy in the city, I can't think. I need to rest and write in the country'.

---

8 Levine-Meyer, *Inside German Communism*, 1977, p. 104.
9 Rosenbaum in conversation with Przhiborovskaya 2008, p. 451.

The next evening she took him to her beloved Tairov Theatre, 'and her laugh rang out from the audience, infectious and joyful, as people laugh only in their youth'. But the following morning, when he phoned her about some journalistic matter, her voice was barely audible. '"I'm ill, the malaria's beating me," she said'.[10]

A few days later, she was overcome with headaches and a high fever, and her family rushed her to the Kremlin Hospital, where doctors diagnosed typhoid fever. She was thought to have been infected from a cake made with unpasteurised cream, meaning the bacteria had been in her blood for five weeks.

Her eyes became heavy, and she grew drowsy and confused and drifted into unconsciousness, broken by fits of restless energy when she would grab her pen to work on a new story. But it was never written. 'She was dying slowly, long after the illness had lost its danger and acuteness, dying from a weak heart', wrote Lydia Seifullina, who had rushed from Leningrad to be with her. 'Sometimes she lacked the strength to lift her arm. She felt flies crawling on her eyelids. She was tormented by thirst, heat and an inexplicable sadness for a life she had suddenly forgotten'.

She spent her last days surrounded by her family and friends. 'Robbed of her last strength, she drifted from life, like an ice block slowly drifting from the beloved mainland', wrote Vera Inber. 'In her relentless battle with illness, it was writing that had tied her to life, and she dropped her pen only when the dark waves of the fever carried her away forever. Then she said "Now I know the danger I'm in"'.[11]

'In her last flickerings of consciousness, she rejoiced in the sun, whose rays were sending her a last farewell', Radek wrote. 'She said how good it would be in the Crimea, where she could recover her strength and fill her weary head with new ideas. She vowed to fight to the end, and she abandoned her fight only when she lost consciousness for the last time'.

She died on 9 February, three months before her thirty-first birthday. For two days her body lay in state at the House of the Press with her family. Then her coffin was carried out, guarded by a division of soldiers from her Party cell, accompanied by a string quartet playing the Funeral March. Her seven pallbearers were Radek, Pilnyak and Isaac Babel, Boris Volin, deputy editor of *Izvestiya*, Avel Enukidze, of the Party Central Committee, Mikhail Lashevich, Commissar of War, and her comrade from Svyazhsk Ivan Smirnov.

---

10   Rozhdestvensky, 'The Youth of our Days', *LRRC*, pp. 40–1.
11   Lydia Seifullina, 'Larisa Reisner', 1969, vol. 4, p. 165. Inber 1966, p. 282.

The poet Varlam Shalamov described feeling 'purified and exalted' by his love for her. Radek collapsed, wracked with sobs, and had to be propped up by friends. Three thousand mourners joined the funeral procession to the Vagankovo Cemetery, cemetery of writers, where she was laid to rest on the Square of the Communards, and Pasternak read his 'Memories of Reisner' at her grave, 'walk in the depths of legend, heroine'.

The paper *Evening Moscow* was the first to announce her death, in a long appreciative front-page obituary, and she was mourned in over three hundred articles, letters and sketches by those who had known her at different times of her life – and many of her readers learnt only then that *'Izvestiya spetskor* Comrade Reisner' had been a woman.

The Reisners' friend the writer Vivian Itin, who had sent his poems to her years ago at *Rudin*, and had worked with Seifullina in Siberia, spoke of 'her wonderful soaring gifts, and a bottle of dirty milk'. 'She was a warrior spirit, who should have died at sea, on the steppe, in the mountains, with a rifle in her hands', wrote Alexander Voronsky. 'Neither a Volga bullet nor a lice-covered army greatcoat at Svyazhsk nor the torturer Ivanov in Kazan could kill her, and she died on a hospital bed of typhoid', Vera Inber wrote:

> Her path was not an easy one. Her extraordinary joy and beauty against the gloomy background of our everyday work often aroused censure, and many who had been through the hard school of jail and the underground questioned if it was right for so many rare qualities to be combined in one person. But with each year, and with each new book, these doubts lessened. 'She always seemed slightly strange to us', people said, 'and we know now that we misjudged her and we were wrong'.[12]

Raskolnikov was in Tashkent and missed the funeral, and cabled his condolences to her family, and there were telegrams from her comrades in Hamburg and Berlin, from King Amanullah in Kabul, from Kollontai in Oslo, and from Andrew Rothstein in London. 'I still feel the icy grip on my heart I felt when I learnt that Larisa had died, and to the end of my days I shall consider myself lucky to have known her', Rothstein wrote.

Even Akhmatova was shocked by her death. 'Esenin's I took relatively calmly, because he wanted to die. But Larisa! So healthy, so beautiful, she wanted so much to live. Who would have imagined I would outlive her. Poor thing,

---

12 A.V. Gorshenin, *Vivan Azarevich Itin*, Moscow, 2004, p. 76; Voronsky, *Literary Notes*, 1926, p. 170; Inber 1966, p. 281.

people will speak badly of her abroad for having been so quick to support Soviet power'.[13]

The Historical Department of the Red Fleet celebrated her life with an exhibition at Leningrad's Naval Military Museum, and her friends and family in Moscow held a memorial evening at the House of the Press, 'at which many spoke seriously and at length about how wrong they had been to doubt her', wrote Igor Ilinsky.

'Standing before you as we remember Larisa Mikhailovna, I must be absolutely frank', said the *Komsomol* journalist Lev Sosnovsky, who had set her 'tests' as a writer after the Revolution. 'We were unfair to her, and I was one of those who was unfair to her':

> She lived her whole life with us having to pass through a succession of barriers, at which she was silently checked. In our Party circles, which had come through the underground years frayed, ragged and unversed in the elementary conventions of civilised life, the figure of a thoroughly beautiful person, from head to foot, in appearance, words and deeds, was alien to us. We had been deceived so often by those who had come over to us, and we didn't want to risk disappointment again. So a silent, endlessly repeated trial was held on Larisa, which strangely transformed itself ...[14]

'Remembering Larisa now, I'm filled with sadness that we didn't meet more often', Rozhdestvensky wrote. 'I saw her only in the quiet times in her life, not at its most significant times, which she described in her books, and my memories of her are chiefly connected to that part of her rich and generous soul that found a place for memories of our student years'.

Nikulin remembered 'her braided hair, whose gold defied photographs, and her laugh, ringing like steel'. 'She will enter history as the beautiful model for a completely new kind of human being, someone standing at the edge of the old and the new worlds, enriched by the culture of the old, and by her loyalty and courage in the fight for the new'.

Four months after her death, *Red Virgin Soil* brought out her last two Decembrist essays, 'Baron Shteingel' and 'About Kakhovsky'. 'It's as if she's still having a conversation with us', wrote the journalist Mark Kolosov, 'about poetry, and about something much bigger, the poetry and prose of the Revolution, and the struggle for human happiness, which was the main business of this exceptional but simple woman's life'.

---

13   Akhmatova quoted in Luknitskaya 1990, p. 126.
14   Sosnovsky, *People of Our Time*, 1927, p. 98.

CHAPTER 19

Afterlife

'Don't mourn for us. The 9th of February is over, and we must bear the consequences', her mother wrote to Seifullina a week after the funeral. 'All of these I meet calmly, and if you hear I have given up the ghost, be a good friend and rejoice for me'. She died the following January, at the age of fifty-three, some said of cancer, others that it was suicide. Mikhail Andreevich died two years later, of a heart-attack.

Larisa had left fourteen-year-old Alyosha the royalties from her writings, and Violet and Igor moved into the House of Soviets to look after him – 'a task I undertook with bad grace', Violet wrote. There are only a couple of passing references to Larisa in her memoirs. The story of her married life with Igor begins really only after her death, when she was thrown into her role as his new foster-mother, and she described her difficult relationship with this lost traumatised child, and the trouble she had with his 'training'.

In Seifullina's story 'Alyosha', he refused to cry for her, playing his radio at top volume in their room, skipping school and hanging out on the streets with his friends, living by his own rules. '"She saved me because she wanted me to be happy," he said. But his dark lively little face became very sad and serious when he said, "I miss her very much, especially at night. But I'll never run away, Larisa Mikhailovna taught me how to behave"'.

He lived with Violet and Igor for the next two years, until she became pregnant with their first child, and Igor used his contacts at the University to find a room for him in a commune of science students.

Violet wrote in vivid detail of her experiences in a Soviet maternity hospital, of the kindness and gentleness and professionalism of the staff, and 'the splendid privileges and opportunities offered to mothers in the Soviet Union'. After three months' paid maternity leave, she returned to her publishing job, leaving the baby in his well-run creche, with two hours off work every day to feed him.

They named him Lev, after Igor and Larisa's adopted brother, now a submarine commander with the Soviet Navy in the Arctic. He would stay with them when he was on leave in Moscow, and Violet wrote of him with huge respect and affection, as a natural leader, generous, kind and high principled, with a passion for music, literature and art.

Igor encouraged her to continue her studies, and she enrolled in courses in Natural History at the Moscow branch of the Sverdlovsk Communist University – 'the most fascinating studying I have ever done in my life, a wonderful combination of theory and practice'. She was soon promoted to a job as a trade union administrator at Moscow's huge Trekhgorny Textile Mill, sorting out members' wages and accommodation, and in 1934 she gave birth to her second son, who they named Georgy, after her father.

Her memoirs are an unforgettable picture of life in Moscow as it geared up for the industrialisation of the 1930s, when workers from all over the Soviet Union poured into the capital to work in the factories – 'with the great slogan "There is no fortress a Bolshevik cannot take" in their hearts'.

> There were many factors that delayed improvements to people's living conditions in Soviet Russia then. Not least of which were the lies told about Russia by the rest of the world, through its media and its ruling class. Five-sixths of the world never ceased to do everything in its power to obstruct the achievements of the Revolution, most frequently against the will of ordinary progressive working men and women – putting a spoke in the wheel with their wrecking activities, destroying the fine new machinery bought from the West with the Soviet people's loans, sabotaging the government from within, through the subversive efforts of foreign diplomats, engineers and the like, in league with oppositionists in the Soviet Union, urging one government after another to make war on Russia.

She also wrote of the sickening levels of privilege and corruption she was seeing in the increasingly powerful new Party élite. And when several of her trade union comrades were arrested as 'enemies of the people', she could no longer stay in Russia. Her marriage to Igor broke down, and she fell in love with the English communist Clemens Palme-Dutt, who was working in Moscow for the Comintern. Her memoirs end in 1937, when she leaves Igor and their sons and sets off with her lover for Paris.

After looking after the boys on his own for a year, Igor married his university colleague Maria Pevzner, who became their much loved stepmother, a professor in child psychology, known throughout Europe for her pioneering work with children suffering brain trauma. Igor continued his teaching work at the University's Institute of Oriental Studies, and ran courses on the colonial countries at Moscow's prestigious Narimanov Oriental Institute, attached to the Soviet Academy of Sciences, which advised the government on its policies in India, Persia and Afghanistan.

Like his father, he was remembered by his students as a demanding teacher, ruthlessly critical of any analytical weakness in their work, and by his colleagues for his generosity in sharing his research. Marx, Engels and Lenin had written of India's anti-colonial struggles, but their sources had necessarily been limited. Through Igor's connections in Afghanistan, the Institute was able to establish contact with independence fighters there and in India, and in over fifty books, monographs and articles, he produced an encyclopaedic picture of British imperialist plunder and aggression in India. He wrote of the role of the landless peasants in India's agrarian uprisings, and of the independence activist Bal Gangadhar Tilak, 'Father of Indian unrest'. Of Bengal's Islamist Jamat ul-Mujahadeen movement, and the Sikh independence movement in the Punjab. Of Gandhi and the Indian National Congress, the British army and its hero Baden-Powell.

His book *Afghanistan*, published in 1929, was another compelling account of colonial skulduggery, the first scholarly Marxist account of the country's economy and culture and its historic importance to Soviet Russia, filled, like Larisa's *Afghanistan*, with sharp observations of Amanullah and the British.

Two years after her death, her two-volume *Collected Works* were published with Radek's Preface. The following year, filming of *Hamburg at the Barricades* began, based on her dramatic account of the daring jail escape of one of Hamburg's fighters, like Eisenstein's *Battleshp Potemkin* shot in Odessa, as a revolutionary adventure story of workers' struggle and heroism and ultimate victory.[1]

Four years later, in the first months of the Third Reich, *Hamburg* would be the first Soviet work thrown into the flames in the Nazi book burnings – followed by the works of Lenin, Gorky, Babel and Mayakovsky – 'for pursuing under the pretext of historical accuracy an entirely different aim, of giving instructions to the German Communist Party for a civil war'.

By then her writings had already disappeared from print in Russia. And as Stalin's full sadistic weight fell on her friends, comrades, fellow writers and all who challenged him, she became a posthumous 'non-person' by association, and she would remain unpublished for the next twenty-five years. 'Larisa died just in time', Osip Mandelstam said.

One of his earliest victims was the great scientist and teacher seventy-year-old Professor Bekhterev, her mentor at the Psychoneurology Institute, renowned throughout the world as the founder of modern neuroscience, who had treated the dying Lenin. In December 1927, he was about to open an international conference of psychiatrists and neuropathologists in Moscow, when

---

1 'Hamburg at the Barricades' was produced by the State Film Organisation of Ukraine, which later produced Dziga Vertov's *Man With a Movie Camera* and *Symphony of the Donbas*, and is one of 12,000 German and foreign silent and sound films stored in Berlin's film archive the Deutscher Kinemathek.

he was called to the Kremlin, to advise the leader on neurological treatment for his semi-paralysed left hand. Bekhterev's Institute of the Brain in Leningrad had been conducting ground-breaking research into the neurological connections between hand movements and speech, and was successfully helping what Bekhterev termed 'dry-handed' people to express themselves more effectively, through psychotherapy and hypnosis. Possibly he took his consultation with Stalin in this direction, and things clearly went badly. Returning late to his conference, he unwisely told colleagues he had been held up by a 'dry-armed paranoiac'. Next morning he was found dead in his hotel, having been in perfect health. His obituary in *Izvestiya* reported that he had fallen ill after a trip to the Bolshoi Theatre, where he been fed poisoned sandwiches.

Trotsky's interest in psychoanalysis did not help its cause. Moscow's Psychoanalytical Society was closed in 1930, and the Psychoanalytical Institute was reorganised under its new director, Aaron Zalkind, a former Freudian, who now argued that the importance of sex had been overemphasised in Freudian theory, and psychoanalysis had been misrepresented to condone 'debauchery and perversions' and 'undermine the vital energy citizens owed to the Soviet collective'. 'Women's lack of culture and education plays a major part in this', Zalkind wrote. 'The real political emancipation of women, the increase in their human and class consciousness, depends on the complete desexualising of our culture'.

Larisa had written in *Coal Iron and Living People* of the brutal impact of industrialisation on women. Women would provide most of the new labour in the First Five Year Plan, most of them young and unskilled, on the lowest pay rates, often barely literate, drawn into social production on a mass scale, working in the iron and steel factories, digging canals and breaking coal in the mines, catching up on their education at night in the *rabfaks*.

Education was seen as the key to Soviet victory against the West, and they were soon entering the professions, not only in such traditionally female jobs as schoolteachers, secretaries, nurses and librarians, but as doctors, engineers and university lecturers. In farms and factories they became managers and administrators, and posters showed them operating heavy machinery and driving tractors, bursting with socialist pride.

Women's departments were arbitrarily closed by local parties and scaled down their ambitions, and in 1930 the Zhenotdel was disbanded. Women were officially full and equal citizens of the USSR, its work was done.

Four years later, homosexuality was recriminalised. A letter to Stalin from a British communist asking why homosexuals who were helping to build communism were being arrested was left unanswered, with the words 'degenerate idiot' scribbled over it. Head of the NKVD during the purges of 1937–8, Nikolai Yezhov, arrested a year later, confessed among his many crimes to his 'long-standing vice of homosexuality'.

Homosexuals were driven back into the closet, abortion rights were restricted to boost the birthrate, forcing women back into dangerous illegal operations, divorce was made more difficult and expensive, unmarried couples were stigmatised, and Muslims and Jews lost many of the freedoms they had won in the Revolution.

The Bolsheviks had welcomed ethnic and religious minorities into the Party to work with them, promising them freedom of worship, and encouraging them to conduct Party business in their mother tongues. In the chaos and poverty of the Civil War, when vast areas of Central Asia were cut off from Moscow, funds to the new Muslim republics had been slashed. Money had then poured in during the NEP, and thousands of new mosques and madrasahs had been built, and were run as commercial enterprises. Larisa's father wrote of the Allah of the NEP as a 'smart capitalist', and 'the delights of paradise' as 'the public relations of God's company'.

In the 1918 Soviet Constitution, Reisner had declared 'the complete equality in law of all Soviet citizens'. The goal of Stalin's Commissariat of Nationalities was 'to ensure peaceful coexistence and cooperation between all nationalities in the Soviet republics'. When the NEP ended in 1928, at the start of the First Five Year Plan, it was Stalin who took charge of the new anti-assimilationist policies in the Muslim and Jewish areas of the Soviet Union. The Jewish Sections were wound up in 1929, and synagogues were turned into Party offices. Mosques across Central Asia were closed, and anti-Muslim activists in Uzbekistan, Azerbaijan and Turkestan arrested mullahs, burned the Koran, and ordered the forced unveiling of women, alienating Muslims from the Bolsheviks throughout the Muslim world.

Igor Reisner used his authority as the government's chief policy advisor on eastern affairs to speak out against the new policy, and its assault on the internationalist principles of the Revolution. He led a campaign at the Narimanov Institute against the new travel restrictions on Muslim students and cuts to their grants. And he published articles in the Institute's journal sharply critical of Stalin's socialism in one country view of India, which mangled Marx's writings to represent its independence struggles as serving the interests only of India's ruling class, and called Gandhi and Nehru 'conciliators and agents of the bourgeois counterrevolution, which wants to create a bloodbath with its bayonets'.

In January 1927, a week before Larisa's mother died, she had written to Radek to make her peace with him. 'I'm writing to you from my bed, Karl. I don't know if you'll understand, but I would like to shake your hand. She loved you to the end, my friend'.[2]

That summer was the start of Radek's agonising public ten-year fall from grace, and the end of the Comintern's four-year alliance with the *Kuomintang*. In April, Chiang Kai-shek's Soviet-armed *Kuomintang* forces had launched their attack on the Chinese Communist Party. Twelve thousand communists and suspected communists were executed in Shanghai, and in June the Party was expelled from the *Kuomintang*. Thousands of its leaders were arrested, including Chou En-lai and Mao Tse-tung, and an estimated three hundred thousand Party members and sympathisers were killed. 'I would rather kill a thousand innocent people than allow a single communist to live', Chiang Kai-shek said.

Broken-hearted after Larisa's death, Radek spoke out recklessly at the Sun Yat-sen University against Stalin's socialism in one country strategy in China, and in June he was sacked as Rector, and was replaced by his Stalin-appointed 'nanny', Pavel Mif. Trotskyist students were sent home, and Trotsky was expelled from the Party in November, followed by Radek a month later. Victor Serge was expelled in 1928, for attacking Comintern policy in China, and in 1933 was stripped of his Soviet citizenship and deported to the Urals, before he finally escaped to France and settled in Paris.

Although one of Trotsky's closest allies in the Civil War, Raskolnikov had been devastated by his handling of the Kronstadt crisis, and he was equally critical in private of Stalin. But he kept his distance from the Party power struggles, and never joined an opposition group, remaining involved in the complicated politics of *Red Virgin Soil*, speaking out against 'anti-proletarian culture'. He became a leading spokesman for the Russian Association of Proletarian Writers, RAPP, with its crude distorted version of socialist realism, and in 1928, he was appointed Chair of Moscow's Theatre Repertory Committee, supervising its draconian censorship policies. 'Enjoying art is one thing, managing it is another', he wrote to Gorky.

At the same time he was writing his play 'Robespierre', an open attack on Stalin, about the incorruptible leader of the French Revolution, whose reign comes to embody its cruellest features. 'Robespierre' opened in several theatres in Russia in the summer of 1930, to derisive reviews, and that autumn he 'resumed his diplomatic career', as he put it, as Soviet Ambassador to Estonia, where he married his second wife, the eighteen-year-old Estonian student and

---

2 Letter quoted in Vladimir Shalamov, *Memoirs*, 2001, p. 180.

writer Muza Kanivez. In 1933, he was appointed Ambassador to Denmark, and a year later to Bulgaria.

Literary policy under Stalin focused on consolidating writers into one big union to control production. By 1930, most literary groups had been absorbed into the infamous RAPP, with its bombastic sloganising optimism, commanding writers in the spirit of socialist competition to perform assigned tasks, sending 'shock brigades' of novelists, dramatists and poets to the factories, farms and mines to report on the achievements of the First Five Year Plan, and calling for literature to be produced on strict assembly-line principles, in step with modern industrial techniques. The humanity and optimism of Gladkov's novel *Cement* were replaced by the 'barracks collectivism' of the new industrial fiction, showing workers heroically solving the production tasks facing them, building socialism in the factories and power-stations against the background of their mighty machines.

RAPP's first targets were Alexander Voronsky and Mayakovsky. In 1930, Voronsky was sacked as editor of *Red Virgin Soil*, and Mayakovsky and the Futurists were driven into RAPP. 'Agitprop sticks in my teeth. I submit and set my heel on the throat of my song', Mayakovsky wrote in his poem 'At the Top of My Voice', three months before shooting himself in the heart. Canonised by the Revolution then cast aside, he was eulogised by Stalin after his death as the 'most talented poet of our Soviet era – indifference to his memory is a crime'.

Two years later, the zealots of RAPP were replaced by the Party functionaries of the new Soviet Writers' Union, writers' only legal professional body. Lydia Seifullina was at the meeting held on the eve of the Union's first congress in 1932, attended by Stalin, and bravely spoke up for her fellow writers. 'So Josef Vissarionovich, how's it going? First you saddle us with RAPP, now you want to muzzle us again'.

Vsevolod Vishnevsky's play about Larisa's life on the Volga, *An Optimistic Tragedy*, had its first performance that year at the Russian Theatre in Kiev. He then took it away for further work, before it opened the following year at Moscow's Tairov Theatre, with Larisa's beloved Alisa Koonen in the leading role. Vishnevsky had written his first play in 1921, for sailors at the port of Novorossiisk, where he was serving as a Political Commissar, a powerful mass eight-hour dramatic reenactment of the Kronstadt sailors' mutiny, staged on the battleships, 'dedicated to the Red Army'. He rewrote his *Optimistic Tragedy* for its Moscow production to celebrate the fifteenth anniversary of the founding of the Red Army, with much of the play's tragedy and the heroine's complexity, subtlety and humour removed, and her last ironic defiant speech to the sailors as she lies dying, and their death-defying laughter, replaced by a grandiose spectacle of lights and sound effects, with the men marching past her body to the soft music of an accordion.³

The new version of the play remained a powerful and moving portrait of her life, and became a classic of the Soviet repertoire, performed in hundreds of theatres across the country, with Koonen's Maria seen as her most outstanding role. In 1936, Vishnevsky collaborated with the composer Vladislav Agafonnikov to turn 'An Optimistic Tragedy' into an opera, and in 1963 it became a blockbuster film, named Film of the Year at the Cannes Festival, which sold forty-six million tickets in Russia.

Vishnevsky was an enthusiastic supporter of RAPP, and a leading member of the Writers' Union, as were Larisa's comrades Alexander Bezymensky and Mark Kolosov, editors of the *Proletkult* journal *On Guard* and the *Komsomol*'s *Young Guard*. *Proletkult* was dissolved into the Writers' Union in 1932. But *Young Guard* and the *Komsomol* survived until the end of communism, and Moscow's Young Guard publishing house, established in 1922, is now one of the oldest in Russia, known for its high quality literary memoirs and biographies, including Przhiborovskaya's of Larisa.

Her Decembrist writings were her swansong. Deeply researched, from material available only after the Revolution, full of empathy and imagination and finely drawn characters, they had led her to the two new works of historical fiction she had started writing before her death. Writers who followed her, poets and novelists with an interest in history, and historians with a talent for fiction, were raiding the archives to produce novels that looked back at times of social upheaval with a new Marxist understanding of the past. Printed in mass editions and read by millions, virtually untouched by censorship, the historical novels of the 1930s were described by Gorky as 'a completely new kind of literature, unseen before the Revolution'.

There were writers who published works of heroic nationalism, celebrating the lives of the legendary creators of the Russian state and Russia's great military leaders, from Alexander Nevsky and Peter the Great to General Kutuzov in the Napoleonic Wars. And there were writers like Larisa whose novels explored history through their characters' inner dramas and struggles and contradictions.

The young Leningrad history professor and Pushkin authority Yury Tynyanov published fictional biographies of the poet's Decembrist friends, and his three-volume poetic re-imagining of Pushkin's life and the genesis of his art, which included a long section on his African ancestry, and the life of his great-grandfather the Ethiopian slave Hannibal, adopted as a child by Peter the Great.

---

3 Thanks to Gabrielle Cody for her illuminating account of the play's production history in Cody, *Re Direction. A Theoretical and Practical Guide*, 2001, p. 98.

The poet Olga Forsh made her name as a novelist with her biographies of the poets of the Decembrist rising and the 1905 revolution, and her trilogy about the writer and social critic Alexander Radishchev, exiled for life in Siberia by Catherine the Great. Anatoly Vinogradov, a librarian in the French department of the Moscow archives, explored the lives of the poet Byron, the 'devil's violinist' Paganini, and the French novelist Henri Stendhal, whose adventures he followed in his novel *Three Colours of Time*, published in 1931, with an introduction by Gorky – from a burning Moscow during the retreat of Napoleon's armies, to France and Italy, where Stendhal meets Byron, members of Italy's revolutionary *carbonari*, and the Turgenev brothers, who play a major role in the story.

Vinogradov's masterpiece *The Black Consul*, published in 1933, was the dramatic story of the self-liberated slave Toussaint Louverture, leader of the world's first black insurrection, the slave uprising on France's Caribbean colonial outpost the island of St Dominique (now Haiti), which inspired a wave of slave rebellions in the British colonies and across the southern states of America. The novel opens in 1789, at the start of the French Revolution, when the slaves' French masters refuse to bring the Revolution's laws on liberty and equality to the island, and covers their fifteen-year fight for their freedom, in which Toussaint turns them into a powerful army to expel the occupiers from the island and declare its independence.

Eisenstein's film of the novel, *Black Majesty*, with Vinogradov's screenplay, has been called the greatest unmade film of the twentieth century. Eisenstein secured a contract in Hollywood with Paramount, and worked on the film there and in Moscow with Paul Robeson, himself the grandson of a slave, who was to play the hero, at a time when black people were cast in American films only as servants. But the politics proved too contentious for them to proceed. Haiti had been under US military occupation since 1915, and after repeated attempts by the American producers to dilute its anti-colonial message, the film had to be dropped. As Robeson said, 'Can you imagine a Black King being treated seriously in Hollywood?'

Seifullina had several of her plays performed at major theatres in the 1930s, but she stopped writing fiction in those years, and publishing opportunities for women were increasingly limited to promoting their image as model workers and mothers, with the outstanding exceptions of Olga Forsh and Vera Inber. Inber travelled the country teaching in schools and factories, publishing books and sketches celebrating the improvements in workers' lives, and described later in her memoirs how she had always felt like an 'outsider', living in a state of constant fear for her cousin Trotsky and her daughter. 'When I am reduced to tears, I take refuge in laughter', she wrote.

Writers who survived the new literary policies were often extremely well paid. Lev Nikulin's works were published in huge print-runs, and were translated into many languages and awarded many prizes – popular novels, historical biographies and travel books, his autobiographical novel *Moscow Dawns*, and his two volumes of memoirs, *People and Places* and *14 Months In Afghanistan*, with their memories of Larisa. Nadezhda Mandelstam described visiting him in his large comfortable flat in Moscow, and reported him saying, 'None of us are Dostoyevsky, we need to make money!'

He joined the Communist Party only in 1940, in his fifties, and is described by his editor as 'a conformist, but never a propagandist or Stalin apologist'. The same was said of Rozhdestvensky, who never joined the Party, and had a successful career in Leningrad as a journalist, poet and translator, writing songs and opera librettos, teaching in schools and factories.

Alexei Tolstoy, the 'red Count', attended all Stalin's show trials in the 1930s and publicly approved the executions, and worked on his heroic unfinished three-part novel *Peter the Great*. He also returned to his tender and moving *Road to Calvary*, about the lives of two sisters in the Revolution, which he had started writing in his years in exile after October. The poet Andrei Bely's Messianic spirit finally gave out in 1934, after eleven years of intense literary activity, and he died prematurely at the age of fifty-four. Shklovsky survived the Stalin years as a hugely prolific and influential author of biographies, works of literary criticism and numerous screenplays (one written with Nikulin). 'There are only two things I've never written, poetry and denunciations', he said.

In 1934, Osip Mandelstam was arrested and exiled for circulating his 'Stalin Epigram':

> He forges decrees like horseshoes, decrees, decrees, decrees.
> This one gets it in the balls, that one in the forehead, another right between the eyes.
> When he gets one he glows, like a burly Georgian munching raspberries.

Pasternak and Anna Akhmatova chose like Mandelstam not to emigrate, and lived in Russia until their deaths in the 1960s, surviving the purges in a strange secret duel with Stalin. Pasternak's name was reportedly crossed off his list of writers to be arrested with the words 'Leave the holy fool alone', and he worked throughout the 1930s on his brilliant and beautiful translations of Shakespeare's plays and sonnets. Akhmatova's son with Gumilyov, Lev, spent most of the years from 1938 to 1956 in a series of camps, and her second husband died in the *gulag*. But Stalin was said to have been persuaded to spare her by his daughter Svetlana, who loved her poetry.

In the summer of 1933, Larisa's pall-bearer Ivan Smirnov, hero of Svyazhsk, was arrested and sentenced to five years in a camp. Three years later, he was a defendant in the First Moscow Show Trial, the 'Trial of the Sixteen', accused with Zinoviev, Kamenev and thirteen others of being members of a Trotsky-led terror group allied to the Gestapo. Zinoviev and Kamenev confessed under torture, on condition that their families were spared, and all sixteen were shot 'like mad dogs'.

Lunacharsky managed to stay out of the Party struggles, and survived as Commissar of Education until four years before his death in 1933, at the age of fifty-eight. Gorky was a more complicated case, but the circumstances of his death were suspicious.

In 1922 he had settled in Italy, and his international reputation allowed him to speak out against the arrests, and he saved many from death. In 1932, he accepted Stalin's invitation to return permanently to Russia, and he was welcomed back as a hero, and was appointed Chair of the Writers' Union, and lived in unheard-of luxury. Within a year, he was under virtual house arrest. In the summer of 1936, he was said to be planning to denounce Stalin's crimes to the world, when he was sent on holiday to the Crimea, where he was encouraged to stand around bonfires that aggravated his tubercular condition. He was then called back at short notice to a cold Moscow, where he caught pneumonia and died two weeks later.

Radek was one of seventeen defendants at the Second Moscow Trial in 1937, charged with high treason and sabotage. Broken by torture, he confessed to having been part of the 'anti-Soviet Trotskyist centre', and that 'there is another organisation, of semi-Trotskyites, quarter-Trotskyites and eighth-Trotskyites, who support us too'. In a desperate attempt to save his daughter and wife, he paid tribute to 'our great Stalin', and approved the executions of Zinoviev and Kamenev, and his death sentence was commuted to ten years in jail, where he was murdered soon afterwards.

Over two thousand intellectuals, artists and writers were arrested in 1937. Alexander Voronsky was arrested and shot, the poet Nikolai Klyuev died in a Siberian camp, and Babel stopped writing. 'I have invented a new school, the school of silence', he said. He died in a camp in 1939.

Boris Pilnyak had defended Radek and supported his wife when he was in jail, and he was arrested on a variety of charges – working for Japanese intelligence agencies on a trip to Japan, commenting critically on Soviet life in his book *OK America!*, and supplying the French writer André Gide with information for his highly damaging book about his 1936 visit to the Soviet Union, *Return from the USSR*. He is thought to have been shot in jail in 1941.

Lev Reisner, hero of the Red Navy, awarded the Order of Lenin for his campaigns in the Arctic, was arrested in 1937. Many believed he was being punished for Larisa's friendship with Trotsky, but Igor was never arrested. Although not a Party member, he was able to use his Party contacts to save many of his friends, students and colleagues from the purges, and he wrote frequently to Radek in jail. But he was unable to save his brother, who was executed by firing-squad, at the age of thirty-five.

Seifullina campaigned with Igor to save him, and she too used her Party connections to take up the cases of many arrested writers. She became a good friend to their families, and Akhmatova wrote warmly of the support she gave her when her son and husband were arrested.

1938 saw a fresh series of purges of writers and intellectuals, members of the army, and old Bolsheviks. Raskolnikov was in Sofia as Ambassador to Bulgaria when he saw his play *Robespierre* and his memoirs *Kronstadt and Petersburg in 1917* on a list of banned Soviet works, with the words 'destroy all books, pamphlets and portraits'. He was recalled to Moscow a week later, and was sacked before he reached the border. Knowing what happened to disgraced diplomats who returned home, he jumped trains with his wife in Belgrade, and applied for asylum in France. They settled in Nice, where he worked on a new book of memoirs about the Revolution, and described being followed everywhere by Stalin's agents.

In June 1939, he was denounced by the Supreme Court of the USSR as a traitor and an enemy of the state for abandoning his post, and was stripped of his Soviet citizenship. He responded with a violent ten-page 'Open Letter' to Stalin: 'On the eve of war you have beheaded the Red Amy and Navy, the pride and joy of our country, the mainstay of our might ... You are indifferent to your people – workers, intellectuals, Jews, those fleeing fascist persecution ... You have annihilated the conquests of October, and built a new "Stalinist-Leninist party" on Lenin's corpse, and you have turned me into an enemy of the Revolution ...'

He died on 23 September, a month after the letter was sent. There were two official reports of his death – that he died in delirium in a Nice mental hospital, and that he jumped to his death from his hotel balcony. Many believed he had been poisoned by Stalin's agents, who then threw his body from the window to make it look like suicide.

His brother Alexander worked throughout the 1930s for the Commissariat of Foreign Affairs, first as Cultural Attaché at the Soviet Embassy in Prague, then in Leningrad, promoting international relations as the first Soviet chess ambassador, organising and competing in world tournaments with his clever beautiful wife, the dancer, singer and chess-master Taisya Alexandrovna. She and others reported that he lived in constant fear of his life after Raskolnikov left Russia.

The charges had become even more fantastic at the Third Moscow Trial, in March 1938, at which Bukharin was the main defendant, accused with twenty others from the 'Bloc of Rightists and Trotskyists' of plotting with Trotsky and the Gestapo to kill Lenin and Stalin and restore capitalism in Russia. In the dock with them were three Kremlin doctors, charged with carrying out Gorky's 'medical murder', 'on the orders of the Judas Trotsky'. One was sentenced to twenty-five years' hard labour in a camp. Nineteen of the other defendants were sentenced to death by firing-squad, as 'stinking piles of human garbage'. Bukharin, the last to be shot, was forced to witness his comrades' executions. The Chief Prosecutor at all three trials was Zinoviev's protegé Yakov Agranov, prosecutor in the trial of Gumilyov, who was himself executed a year later.

The key missing defendant at all three trials, Trotsky, had been deported from Russia in 1929, with his wife and their elder son, Lev, and he would survive in exile for the next eleven years, moving from country to country, keeping a step ahead of Stalin's hitmen, publishing some of his greatest works – his three-volume *History of the Russian Revolution*, and dozens of pamphlets, essays and articles on the fight against fascism in Germany, Spain and France. He was finally assassinated in 1940, by one of Stalin's agents in Mexico.

His younger son Sergei, who took no interest in politics, had stayed in Moscow to work as an engineer. In 1935, he was sentenced to five years in Siberia, for plotting to poison the workers at his factory, and he was executed two years later. Lev had settled in Paris, mobilising support for his father, and he died in 1938, of a suspiciously botched appendix operation.

Osip Mandelstam was re-arrested in 1938, and died that winter in a transit camp on the journey to Siberia. A year later, Seifullina's husband Valerian Pravdukhin was arrested and executed as a 'terrorist'. Her play 'Natasha', about a young woman collective farm worker, had been in rehearsals at Moscow's Meyerhold Theatre, but it was never performed. The theatre was closed that year, and Meyerhold was arrested and shot, after confessing under torture that he was a Trotskyist agent working with Japanese intelligence. (He had recently invited a Japanese Kabuki group to the theatre).

Although Stalin never overcame his old-fashioned resistance to having women shot, thousands disappeared into the icy wastes of Siberia as non-people or wives of enemies of the state. Miraculously, Seifullina was not arrested, and worked in Moscow for the next sixteen years, teaching in schools and factories, and giving talks on radio.

Writers' treatment often seemed to be a matter of chance. Demyan Bedny's friendship with Stalin soured in 1932, reportedly after he complained to a secretary that the leader had left grubby fingerprints on some books from his precious library, and he found himself evicted from the Kremlin Palace into what he called a 'rats' barn' in the suburbs. In 1936, his new libretto for Borodin's comic opera *Heroes*, satirising Russia's great mythical leaders, was condemned by the Politbureau as 'anti-historical and alien to Soviet art', and was banned from the repertoire. Two years later, despite publishing poems celebrating the trials of Zinoviev and others, he was expelled from the Party, and stripped of his membership of the Writers' Union.

Even more inexplicable was the fate of Larisa's comrade the journalist Mikhail Koltsov, a member of the Party inner circle, Foreign Editor of *Pravda*, awarded the Order of Lenin for his journalism in Russia and his frontline reports from the Spanish Civil War. In 1936, he was Stalin's envoy in the Siege of Madrid, where he met the writer Ernest Hemingway, who would make him the model for the *Pravda* journalist Karkov in his Civil War novel *For Whom the Bell Tolls* – described by the hero as 'the most intelligent man he knew, with more brains and inner dignity and outer insolence than anyone had ever met in his life'.

A great admirer of his journalism abroad was the English communist Claude Cockburn, foreign editor of the party paper the *Daily Worker*, who was also in Madrid then reporting on the War, and Koltsov appointed him *Pravda's* chief London correspondent. Cockburn wrote of 'Koltsov's powerful enthusiasm for life, as interested in Elizabethan poetry as in a good circus, his talent for savaging sacred cows, and his wildly indiscreet love life. He had the most expressive face I have ever seen. What it principally expressed was a gleeful amusement – the lively hope that you and everyone else, however depressing the circumstances, would do your best to make things livelier still. He lived dangerously, and had no illusions about the dangers'.

But Cockburn was deeply shocked when he learnt of his arrest in December 1938 as a 'public enemy'. He was shot two years later, at the age of forty-one, and Cockburn reported that many in Russia were convinced he was still alive, and had fled abroad.[4]

In 1934, while working as a journalist in Germany, Koltsov had adopted a little boy called Hubert, the son of a poor miner, who had been feted with banquets and parties when he brought him back to Moscow with him. After his arrest, Hubert was placed in an orphanage, and in the first days of the Nazi invasion, he was sent east with other Germans living in Russia, and was never heard of again.

Koltsov's younger brother, the artist Boris Efimov, had campaigned tirelessly for his release in the two years he was in jail, and was fired from his job at *Izvestiya*. Efimov had also been a close friend of Trotsky's, who had written

---

4 Cockburn, *In Time of Trouble*, 1957, pp. 245–9.

the introduction to his 1921 book *Political Caricatures*, and he had visited him and his family in Moscow until the day he was deported from Russia, and had accompanied them to the station. Yet despite this, he went on to have a spectacularly successful eighty-year career as a cartoonist. During the Nazi occupation, his caricatures of Hitler were blown up into giant posters and displayed on buildings – a crab with a Hitler moustache crushed by a Soviet tank, a Hitler-faced rat with a Red bayonet rammed down its throat. After the war, he became internationally famous as the official Soviet artist at the Nuremberg Trials, and he was drawing until the day he died, in 2008, aged 109, nine years after voting for Putin in the 1999 presidential elections

In Larisa's writings from Germany, she had warned of President Hindenberg's drive to rearm for a new war. It was Hindenburg's brutal military regimes in large parts of occupied Eastern Europe in the First World War that inspired the psychopathology of *Lebensraum*, used in Hitler's programme to exterminate forty-five million Slavs, and it was Hindenberg who appointed Hitler Chancellor in January 1933.

'Our forces are invincible. The enemy will discover this soon', Stalin said in July 1941, two weeks after the tanks of the *Wehrmacht* rolled into Russia. Vera Inber joined the Party in Leningrad in the first days of the invasion, and lived through the horrors of the thirty-month Nazi Blockade, in which over two million died of starvation and disease, mainly women and children, and she came close to dying herself. She became a familiar voice on Leningrad Radio, recording people's sacrifices and daily acts of heroism, and at nights she would carry her typewriter down to the bomb-shelter under her building to write her *Leningrad Diary*, her testament to the city's survival in the face of unspeakable suffering.

Anna Akhmatova joined the three million who were evacuated east in the first week of the Blockade, and spent most of the war in Tashkent in Uzbekistan. Gumilyov's widow Anna Engelhardt and her twenty-eight-year-old daughter Lena, who had both been working in Leningrad as actresses, were trapped there and starved to death with her parents. Rozhdestvensky led an engineering detachment outside the city fighting to break the Blockade, and fought as a sapper on the Northern Front for the rest of the war, publishing articles, songs and poems in *Pravda* and *Izvestiya*, which he read at the battlefields.

Raskolnikov's brother Alexander led a trench-building brigade in Leningrad in the first weeks of the invasion, and was killed on 3 September, five days before the start of the Blockade. According to official reports, he was mortally wounded on a barge that came under enemy bombing. His wife and others close to him were in no doubt that he was killed by the regime. He was said to have died carrying the precious briefcase his comrade and fellow exile Lenin had given him in Switzerland.

As the Panzer units advanced on Moscow in the first months of the invasion, millions stayed to fight in the battles to defend the capital. Four million were evacuated east, along with ninety-two factories, down to the last worker and doorman, its main theatres and the University, which reopened in Ashkhabad in Turkestan. Igor Reisner resumed his teaching work there, and his wife Maria Pevzner worked in a children's psychiatric clinic. Film studios were evacuated to Alma Ata in Kazakhstan, where Victor Shklovsky headed a unit of Moscow writers drafted in to write screenplays for patriotic films. Lydia Seifullina toured the Western Front as a journalist, and gave patriotic talks on Moscow Radio. Alexei Tolstoy headed the government commission investigating the Nazis' use of mobile gas-vans in their extermination programme, and died three months before the end of the war, ten months before the commission presented its evidence to the Nuremberg Trials.

Nikulin was evacuated from Moscow in 1941, with five thousand of the capital's writers and members of its main theatres, ballets and orchestras, to Chelyabinsk in the Urals, 'Tankograd', the forge of Soviet victory. Two hundred factories with their workers and families were evacuated there from all over the country, and fifty new factories were built, in the most desperate conditions, with production often starting even before the roofs were on, men, women and teenagers working twelve-hour shifts to produce tanks and artillery for the Red Army. Workers needed more than Stalin's speeches to keep their spirits alive, and the war years saw an extraordinary flourishing of culture in Chelyabinsk. Nikulin worked with local writers, musicians, actors and filmmakers, putting on plays, concerts and film shows in clubs and factories, and he joined the management board of Moscow's Maly Theatre, working with the cast and directors on its repertoire – works by Shakespeare and Schiller, Chekhov and Ostrovsky, and vast patriotic pageants staged in parks, factories, hospitals and military units. The Maly also played a major role in the city's new musical life. In the summer of 1942, Nikulin and his team invited the composer Shostakovich to give talks to workers in the factories about his Seventh Symphony, the 'Leningrad', which had its third performance in Chelyabinsk in October, under the great conductor Evgeny Mravinsky.

Eight hundred thousand women fought with the Red Army, as tank-crew members, pilots, machine-gunners, dispatch riders and intelligence agents, and two hundred thousand were decorated for their war services, as were three hundred writers, including Alexei Tolstoy and Demyan Bedny, who read his poems at hundreds of battlefields, and worked his way back into Stalin's favour to become one of the most popular poets of the war. His poem 'The Barbarians Defeated' was published on the front page of *Pravda* on Soviet Victory Day, 9 May 1945, two weeks before his death of a heart-attack.

Nikulin returned to his writing career after the war, with another series of successful novels. His *True Sons of Russia*, published in 1952, about the Russian army in the Napoleonic wars, was awarded the State Prize for Literature, and he was given access to secret government intelligence files for his last novel, *The Deadly Swell*, about Soviet and Western espionage after the Revolution, later turned into a successful film with his screenplay. He died in Moscow in 1967, at the age of seventy-six. Rozhdestvensky worked in Leningrad as a journalist, poet and translator, and died ten years later, in his eighties. Lydia Seifullina died in Moscow in 1954, at the age of fifty-five, and was mourned by those whose lives she had touched with her warmth and kindness. The novelist Alexander Fadeev remembered her as 'a person of crystal purity and integrity, and a wonderful comrade and teacher, who supported me and many others in our first steps as writers'.

Igor joined the Party at the end of the war, and returned with his old passion to his interrupted academic research. In 1947 he published his magisterial two-volume *Development of Feudalism and the State in Afghanistan*, and in 1954 he was appointed Director of the India Institute at the Academy of Sciences. He was teaching and writing until his death four years later at the age of sixty, of a heart-attack.

Shklovsky outlived them all, and died in 1984, at the age of ninety-one, ascribing his extraordinary output and longevity partly to the distancing 'defamiliarisation' literary technique he had formulated in the months after the Revolution.

After Stalin's death in 1953, the new Party Secretary, Nikita Khrushchev, began the process of dismantling his personality cult, destroying monuments to him, returning cities to their old names, releasing thousands of his victims from the camps. In 1954, Koltsov was one of the first of the old Bolsheviks to be posthumously rehabilitated by the Supreme Court of the USSR, 'for lack of evidence of a crime'. In 1957, Raskolnikov's name appeared on a list of twenty old Bolsheviks to be pardoned, and in 1963 he was declared 'fully rehabilitated'. In an essay that year in the journal *Questions of History* on the heroes of the Revolution, he was praised as 'a fearless fighter for the Bolshevik Party, and a true Leninist to the end of his days', whose 'Open Letter' 'unmasked Stalin's arbitrariness, and the discredit he cast on Soviet socialism'. The Writers' Union set up a commission to publish his 'literary heritage', and his widow and twenty-three-year-old daughter, born after his death, travelled from France to hand over his manuscripts.

Two years later, the policy changed, and he became a posthumous non-person again. With the ramping up of the Cold War after the fall of Khrushchev, there was renewed hostility to those who had defected to the West, and he was called an 'active Trotskyist' and 'fascist White Guard filth' – 'de-rehabilitated', as his translator Brian Pearce nicely puts it.

Censorship remained firmly in place, but was relaxed, and with the freeing up of intellectual life, Vera Inber became one of the leading writers of the post-Stalin 'Thaw', who worked to restore the cultural values that had been destroyed, writing screenplays and works for the stage, publishing literary translations, essays on psychoanalysis, and three volumes of memoirs, in which she wrote of the everyday pleasures of home people clung to in times of danger – 'home is the illusion of certainty, and illusions help us survive the minefields of the mind, the places we daren't think about, our absent families and friends'.

Akhmatova's works had finally been republished in 1940, after her fifteen-year silence, her 'vegetable years'. Her tragic *Requiem* cycle about the Terror, which she had kept in her head in the years Stalin was alive, afraid to put on paper, was published in Germany a month after his death.

The policy of tolerating Pasternak ended in 1957, with the publication of his novel *Doctor Zhivago*, his story of the camps and the purges and the power of poetry to keep people alive. Banned from publication in Russia, the manuscript was circulated in *samizdat*, then smuggled out of the country to be published in Italy. The first novel from Soviet Russia with a mass readership abroad, *Doctor Zhivago* became a *cause celebre* of the Cold War. The Soviet press called Pasternak 'worse than a pig, fouling the spot where he eats'. In the West, the novel was awarded the Nobel Prize for Literature, and was turned into an Oscar-winning film, with Julie Christie in the starring role of Lara. 'When I wrote *Doctor Zhivago*, I named my heroine Lara in memory of Larisa Mikhailovna Reisner', Pasternak told the poet Varlam Shalamov.

The process of rehabilitating her memory began in 1958, with the publication of the first edition of her *Selected Works*. In 1964, a marble headstone with her portrait was built over her grave at the Vagankovo Cemetery, and a selection of her letters were published in the literary journal *Novy Mir*. These and other letters and more of her articles appeared in the second 1965 edition of her *Selected Works*, and in 1969 her friends published their book *Larisa Reisner Remembered by her Contemporaries*.

Gumilyov's poetry was widely circulated in *samizdat*, and his correspondence with her was published in 1980 in Paris. Hundreds of police files were opened in the 1980s under *glasnost*, and in 1986 the charges leading to his arrest and execution were declared fabricated. He was rehabilitated six years later.

Raskolnikov's 'Open Letter' to Stalin became a key *samizdat* text, and in 1987 the Party Central Committee announced that he had been rehabilitated again –

praising him for 'finding the spiritual strength to suffer the pain and danger to expose the truth'. Radek was rehabilitated in 1988, with Bukharin, Zinoviev and Kamenev, Smirnov and Rosengoltz, and dozens of others Larisa had fought with in the Civil War. The charges against Trotsky's younger son Sergei were also dropped that year. Trotsky himself has still to be rehabilitated.

Gorky's 'unknown third' was not as Larisa had hoped it would be. Sixty-five years after her death, the hammer and sickle flag flew over the Kremlin for the last time, and Boris Yeltsin occupied Moscow's White House as President of the new Russian Federation. In 1998, the bones of Tsar Nicholas and his family were dug up and reburied in St Petersburg's Peter and Paul Cathedral, and in 2000, a year after Putin was elected President, the Romanovs were canonised by the Moscow Patriarchate of the Orthodox Church as 'Passion Bearers' – those who approach death in a resigned Christ-like manner.

The centenary of the Revolution was marked officially in the new Russia as quietly as possible, so as not to remind people that a world without capitalism is possible. In the West, the usual stories of Bolshevik thuggery and repression are now being spun in this deadly new cold war with Russia into hatred and fear of Putin as the new Stalin. However often Putin denounces Lenin and Stalin equally as monsters, Russia has never been forgiven for showing that a poor backward people could defeat the most powerful armies in the world to build socialism.

A century after October, with fascism on the rise, the breakup of the EU, and Nato's endless illegal imperialist wars creating sixty-five million refugees – one in 113 people on earth – the contradictions of capitalism are exploding across the globe in historic levels of mass class unrest, against the corporate greed that is destroying our planet, the assaults on our schools, hospitals and trade unions, the poor, the old and the sick, the media lies and mass surveillance, the silencing and torturing of those who expose the truth of imperialism's crimes.

For the ninety-nine percent, socialism is beginning to seem the only alternative to the cruelties and injustices of capitalism. 'Bolshiness is back', the *Economist* warned in 2017. 'The similarities with the world that produced the Revolution in Russia are too close for comfort'.

Larisa's writings cover less than a decade, but they evoke an entire epoch. She wrote of the Revolution's heaven-storming challenge to the capitalist world, its mistakes and failures, its humanity, creativity and optimism. In her lifetime she saw the Bolsheviks grow into a mass movement, speaking to millions of people, living in extraordinary times and achieving miracles, and her headlong life and early death are their story.

'Life has been good to me', she wrote to Seifullina a week before she died. 'Broken and worthless, I fell into the rapids of the Revolution, and being under no illusions, seeing all the mistakes and all that was bad in the social deluge, I saw the brotherly courage and the supreme justice in this inexorable move forward for the better, for human happiness'.

Appendix: Figures

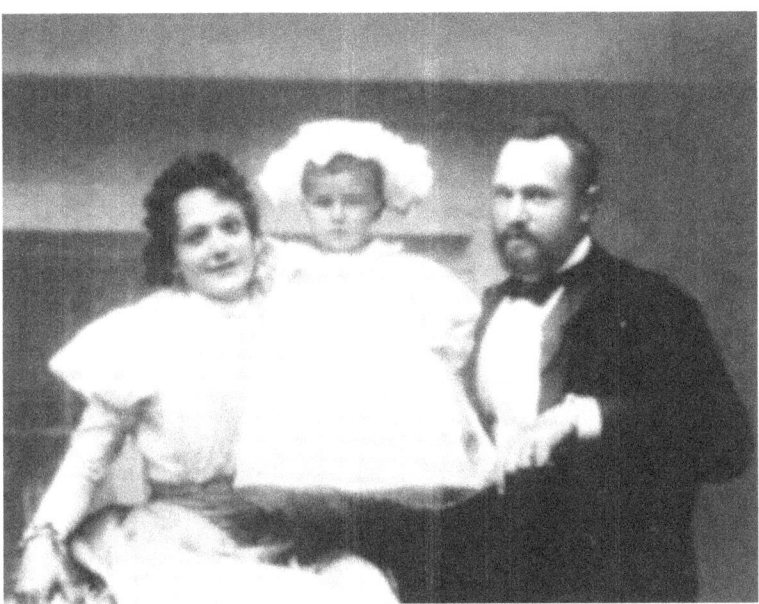

FIGURE 1   Aged six months with her parents in Lublin, 1895

FIGURE 2   With Igor and their father in Berlin, 1902

FIGURE 3
With Igor in Siberia, 1902

FIGURE 4
In Berlin, 1903

FIGURE 5
St Petersburg schoolgirl, 1910

FIGURE 6
Leonid Andreev (1871–1919)

FIGURE 7
Boris Pasternak (1890–1960)

FIGURE 8
Alexander Blok (1880–1921)

APPENDIX: FIGURES 369

FIGURE 9
Nikolai Gumilyov (1886–1921)

FIGURE 10
Anna Akhmatova (1889–1966)

FIGURE 11
Fyodor Raskolnikov

FIGURE 12
Cavalry commander, 1919

APPENDIX: FIGURES 371

FIGURE 13
Naval commissar, 1920. Watercolour portrait by Sergei Chekhonin, in Moscow's Tretyakov Gallery

FIGURE 14   Afghanistan, 1922

FIGURE 15
Karl Radek and his daughter Sonya

FIGURE 16
Igor Reisner in the 1930s

Bibliography

(*including a representative but limited number of Larisa Reisner's works*)

Alakhverdov, Georgy, et al. (eds.) 1960, *Kratkaya istoriya grazhdanskoi voiny v SSSR* (A Short History of the Civil War in the USSR), Moscow.
Ambernadi, G., et al. (eds.) 1970, *Oktyabrskie stranitsy* (Pages of October), Moscow.
Andreeva, Vera 1974, *Dom na chernoi rechke* (The House on the Black River), Moscow.
Attwood, Lynne 2012, *Gender and Housing in Soviet Russia. Private Life in a Public Sphere*, Manchester: Manchester University Press.
Balabanova, Angelica 1938, *My Life as a Rebel*, New York: Harper.
Beketova, Maria 1990, *Aleksandr Blok. Biograficheskii ocherk* (Alexander Blok. A Biographical Sketch), Moscow.
Blok, Alexander 1962, *Complete Collected Works*, vol. 6, Moscow.
Bowlt, John 2008, *Moscow and St Petersburg in Russia's Silver Age*, London: Thames & Hudson.
Bowlt, John and Olga Matich 1996, *Laboratory of Dreams. The Russian Avant-garde and Cultural Experiment*, California: Stanford University Press.
Boyarchikov, A.I. 2003, *Vospominaniya* (Memoirs), Moscow.
Bradley, John 1968, *The Allied Intervention in Russia*, New York: Basic Books.
Bruce Lockhart, Robert 1932, *Memoirs of a Secret Agent*, London: Putnam.
Caute, David 1988, *The Fellow Travellers: Intellectual Friends of Communism*, Yale University Press.
Chomsky, Noam 2014, 'The Politics of Red Lines. Putin's Takeover of Crimea Scares US Leaders Because it Challenges American Global Dominance,' *These Times*.
Christie, Stewart, and Taylor, Richard (eds. and trans.) 1988, *The Film Factory. Russian and Soviet Cinema in Documents*, Cambridge: Cambridge University Press.
Clinton, Hillary 2014, *Hard Choices*, New York: Simon and Schuster.
Chukovskaya, Lydia 1994, *The Akhmatova Journals*, London: Harvill.
Churchill, Winston 2003, *The Aftermath*, London: Penguin.
Churchill, Winston 1976, *The Collected Essays of Sir Winston Churchill*, Vol. 2, pp. 81–82, London: Library of Imperial History.
Clark, Katerina 1996, *Petersburg. Crucible of Cultural Revolution*, Cambridge, MA: Harvard University Press.
Cockburn, Claud 1957, *In Time of Trouble*, London: Rupert Hart Davis.
Cody, Gabrielle 2001, *Re: Direction. A Theoretical and Practical Guide*, London: Routledge.
Cohen, Stephen 2018, *War With Russia. From Putin and Ukraine to Trump and Russiagate*, New York: Simon & Schuster.

Deutscher Isaac, *The Non-Jewish Jew and Other Essays*, London: Verso.

Dokumenty vneshnei politiki sssr (Documents of USSR Foreign Policy), vols. I & v, Moscow, 1959.

Dukes, Paul 2015, *A History of the Urals: Russia's Crucible From Early Empire to the Post-Soviet Era*, London: Bloomsbury.

Ehrenburg, Ilya 1962, *The First Years of the Revolution, 198–21*, trans. A. Bostock and Y. Kapp, London: Macgibbon Kee.

Fleishman, L. et al. (eds.) 2003, *Russkii Berlin* (Russian Berlin), Moscow.

Gerasimov, Yury, et al. (eds.) 1965 and 1967, *Zapiski otdela rukopisei Leninskoi Biblioteki* (Notes of the Manuscript Department of the Lenin Library), vols. 27 & 29, Moscow.

Golubeva, Olga, et al. (eds.) 1972, *Russkie sovetskie pisateli prozaiki* (Russian Soviet Prose Writers), vol. 7, Leningrad.

A.V. Gorshenin 2004, *Vivian Azarevich Itin*, Moscow.

Gumilyov, Nikolai 1980, *Neizdannoe i nesobrannoe* (Unpublished and Uncollected Works), YMCA Press, Paris.

Haupt, Georges, and Marie, Jean-Jacques, (eds. & trans. David Bellos) 1974, *Makers of the Russian Revolution*, London: Allen Unwin.

Ilinsky, Igor 1926, 'Granyonyi talant' (A Cut-glass Talent), *Pechat i revolyutsiya* (Press and Revolution), no. 3.

Inber, Vera 1966, *Complete Works*, vol. 4, Moscow.

Inber, Vera 1927, 'Larisa Reisner', *Krasnaya Nov* (Red Virgin Soil), no. 2.

Joffe, Nadezhda 1995, *Back in Time. My Life, My Fate, My Epoch*, Oak Park Press, Maryland.

Kapur, Harish 1966, *Soviet Russia and Asia, 1917–27*, London: Michael Joseph.

Kassow, Sam 1989, *Students, Professors and the State in Tsarist Russia*, Berkeley, CA: University of California Press.

Kelly, Catriona 1994, *A History of Russian Women's Writing, 1820–1992*, Oxford: Clarendon Press.

Kollontai, Alexandra 1974, *Iz moei zhizni i raboty* (From My Life and Work), Moscow.

Kollontai, Alexandra 1999, *Love of Worker Bees*, translated Cathy Porter, London: Virago.

Konstantinov, Alexander 1964, *F.F. Ilin-Raskolnikov*, Leningrad.

Konyushenko, M.D. (ed.) 1969, *Pravda stavshaya legendoi* (Truth Becomes Legend), Moscow.

Kramov, Isaac 1962, *Literaturnye portrety* (Literary Portraits), Moscow.

Lansbury, Violet 1940, *An Englishwoman in the USSR*, Putnam, London.

Larina, Anna 1993, *This I Cannot Forget. The Memoirs of Bukharin's Widow*, London: Hutchinson.

Lenin, V.I. 1957, *Complete Collected Works*, 4th edn., vol. 36, Moscow.

'V.I. Lenin i pervyi sezd rabotnits' (V.I. Lenin and the First Congress of Women Work-

ers), in *O Vladimire Iliche Lenine. Vospominianiya 1920–1922* (Memories of Vladimir Ilich Lenin, 1920–22), Moscow, 1963, p. 97.
Lerner, Warren 1970, *Karl Radek. The Last Internationalist*, Stanford University Press, 1970.
Lerner, Warren 1966, 'The Unperson in Communist Historiography', *South Atlantic Quarterly*, no. 4.
Levine-Meyer, Rosa 1977, *Inside German Communism*, trans. D. Zane Mairowitz, London: Pluto.
Libedinsky, Yury 1958, *Sovremenniki* (Contemporaries), Moscow.
Lisovsky, D. 1957, *Oktyabr na yuzhnem Urale. Borba za istanovlenie sovetskoi vlasti 1917–1918* (October in the Southern Urals. The Battle for Soviet Power), Chelyabinsk.
Luknitskaya, Vera 1990, *Nikolai Gumilyov. Zhizn poeta po materialam domashnego arkhiva semi* (The Life of the Poet from Family Archives), Leningrad.
MacKay, John 2018, *Dziga Vertov: Life and Work*, Academic Studies Press, Boston.
Maguire, Robert 1968, *Red Virgin Soil. Soviet Literature in the 1920s*, Princeton, NJ: Princeton University Press.
Mandelstam, Nadezhda 1971, *Hope Against Hope*, London: Harvill.
Mandelstam, Nadezhda 1974, *Hope Abandoned*, London: Penguin.
Matich, Olga 2005, *Erotic Utopia. The Decadent Imagination in Russia's Fin de Siecle*, University of Wisconsin Press.
McElvanney, Katherine 2018, *Women Journalists in the Russian Revolution and Civil War: Case Studies of Ariadna Tyrkova-Williams and Larisa Reisner 1917–1926*, Ph.D thesis, Queen Mary University London.
Alexander Morozov 2006, *A. Ilin Zhenevsky. Revolyutioner, istorik, shakhmatist, literator* (A. Ilin the Genevan. Revolutionary, Historian, Chess-player, Author), St Petersburg.
Neuberg, A. 1977, *Armed Insurrection*, trans. Quintin Hoare, New Left Books, London.
Nikulin, Lev 1966, *Gody nashei zhizni* (Years Of Our Life), Moscow.
Nikulin, Lev 1923, *14 mesyatsev v Afganistane* (14 Months in Afghanistan), Moscow.
Nikulin, Lev 1962, *Lyudi i stranstviya* (People and Travels), Moscow.
Nove, Alec 1976, *An Economic History of the USSR*, London: Penguin.
Pasternak, Boris 1965, *Stikhotvoreniya i poemy* (Verses and Poems), Moscow.
'Pisma Larisy Reisner' (Letters of Larisa Reisner) 1963, *Novy Mir* (New World), no. 10.
Przhiborovskaya, Galina 2008, *Larisa Reisner*, Moscow.
Poretsky, Elisabeth 1969, *Our Own People*, Oxford: Oxford University Press.
Porter, Cathy 2013, *Alexandra Kollontai. A Biography*, London: Merlin Press.
Radek, Karl 1934, *Portrety i pamflety* (Portraits and Pamphlets), Moscow.
Radek Karl 1927–9, 'Larisa Reisner', in 'Deyateli SSSR i Oktyabrskoi Revolyutsii' (Activists of the USSR and the October Revolution), in *Encyclopaedia of the Granat Russian Bibliographical Institute*, 7th edn., Moscow.

Raskolnikov, Fyodor 1982a, *Kronstad i Petrograd v godu 1917* (Kronstadt and Petrograd in 1917), Leningrad, 1925. Trans. Brian Pearce, London: New Park Publications.

Raskolnikov, Fyodor 1982b, *Rasskazy michmana Ilina* (Tales of Sub-Lieutenant Ilin), Moscow, 1922. Trans. Brian Pearce, London: New Park Publications.

Raskolnikov, Fyodor 1989, *O vrememi i o sebe. Vospominaniya, pisma, dokumenty* (My Life and Times. Memoirs, Letters and Documents), Leningrad.

Reeder, Roberta 1995, *Anna Akhmatova, Poet and Prophet*, London: Allison & Busby.

Reisner, Igor 1929, *Afghanistan*, Moscow.

Reisner, Larisa 1928, *Sobranie sochinenii* (Collected Works), Moscow/Leningrad.

Reisner, Larisa 1965, *Izbrannoe* (Selected Works), ed. A. Naumova, Moscow.

Reisner, Larisa 1913, 'Zhenskie tipy Shekspira: Ofelia i Kleopatra' (Shakespeare's Female Characters Ophelia and Cleopatra), in *Nauka i zhizn* (Science And Life), nos. 25 & 34, Riga.

Reisner, Larisa 1920, 'Putevye zametki' (Traveller's Notes), *Izvestiya*, 12 November.

Reisner, Larisa 1920, '25 oktyabrya v Rige' (25 October in Riga), *Izvestiya*, 14 November.

Reisner, Larisa 1920, 'Kak otvalivaetsya pushistyi khvost' (How the Bushy Tail Falls Off), *Izvestiya*, 14 November, 1920. (Original manuscript from Andrew Rothstein).

Reisner, Larisa 1920, 'Heroic Sailors of the Russian Revolution', trans. A. Rothstein, *Communist Review*, no. 1, May.

Reisner, Larisa 1925, *Afghanistan*, State Publishing House, Moscow/Leningrad.

Reisner, Larisa 1977, *Hamburg At the Barricades and Other Writings on Weimar Germany*, trans. & ed. Richard Chappell, London: Pluto.

Reisner, Larisa 1925, *Ugol zhelezo i zhivye lyudi* (Coal Iron and Living People), Moscow/Leningrad.

Reisner, Larisa 1926, 'Protiv literaturnogo banditizma' (Against Literary Banditry), *Zhurnalist*, 1926, no. 1.

Reisner, Larisa 1983, *Rudin*, Leningrad.

Reisner, Mikhail 1925, *Sudebnyi protses Karla Libknekhta protiv russkogo tsarya* (Karl Liebknecht's Case Against the Russian Tsar), Ryazan.

Reisner, Mikhail 1906, *Russkii absolyutism i evropeiskaya reaktsiya* (Russian Absolutism and European Reaction), St Petersburg.

Reisner, Mikhail 1908, *Teorii L.N. Petrazhitskogo marksisma i sotsialnoi ideologii* (L.N. Petrazhitsky's Theories on Marxism and Social Ideology), Moscow.

Reisner, Mikhail 1909, *L. Andreev i ego sotsialnaya ideologiya* (L. Andreev and his Social Ideology), Moscow.

Reisner, Mikhail 1912, *Gosudarstvo. Posobie k lektsiyam po obshchemu ucheniyu o zakone* (The State. A Textbook of Lectures in the General Study of Law), St Petersburg.

Reisner, Mikhail 1921, *Bog i birzha. 6 revolyutsionnykh pes* (God and the Stock Exchange. 6 Revolutionary Plays), Moscow.

Rhodes James, Robert 1973, *Churchill. A Study in Failure, 1900–39*, Harmondsworth Press, London.

Roberts, Glyn 1938, *The Most Powerful Man in the World. The Life of Sir Henry Deterding*, New York: Covici Friede.
Robertson, Jack 2021, *The Hammer and the Anvil*, London: Redwords.
Ross, E. Saul 1973, 'Fedor Raskolnikov, A Secondary Bolshevik', *Russian Review*, April 1973, 32, 2: 131–42.
Rothstein, Andrew 1979, *When Britain Invaded Russia. The Consul Who Rebelled* Journeyman Press, London.
Rothstein, Andrew 2014, *Soldiers' Strikes of 1919*, London: Macmillan.
Ryklin, Georgy 1968, *Esli pamyat ne izmenyaet* (If Memory Doesn't Deceive Me), Moscow.
Sakwa, Richard 2015, *Frontline Ukraine. Crisis in the Borderlands*, London: Taurus.
Savchenko, Vladimir 2002, *Otstupnik. Drama Fyodora Raskolnikova* (Renegade. The Drama of Fyodor Raskolnikov), Moscow.
Sergei Schultz 1997, *Dom iskusstv* (The House of the Arts), St Petersburg.
Scott, John 1942, *Behind the Urals. An American Worker in Russia's City of Steel*, London: Secker & Warburg.
Seifullina, Lidia 1969, *Complete Collected Works*, vol. 4, Moscow.
Seifullina, Lidia 1969, *Prostye rasskazy* (Simple Stories), Moscow.
Serge, Victor 1963, *Memoirs of a Revolutionary, 1901–1941*, trans. Peter Sedgwick, Oxford: Oxford University Press.
Serge, Victor 1972, *Year One of the Revolution*, trans. & ed. Peter Sedgwick, Allen Lane, London.
Service, Robert 2009, *Trotsky. A Biography*, London: Macmillan.
Sevruk, V. 1973, *The Young in the Revolution*, Moscow: Progress Publishers.
Shalamov, Varlam 2001, *Vospominaniya* (Memoirs), Moscow, 2001, p. 156.
Sheng, Yueh 1971, *The Sun Yat-sen University in Moscow and the Chinese Revolution. A Personal Account*, University of Kansas Press.
Shkapskaya, Maria 1927, *Sama po sebe* (For Myself), Leningrad.
Shklovsky, Victor 1970, 'Bessmyslneishaya smert' (A Senseless Death), in *Gamburgskie shchety* (Hamburg Debts), Leningrad, 1928, pp. 60–1.
Shklovsky Victor 1970, *Sentimental Journey*, trans. Richard Sheldon, Cornell University Press.
Shubinsky, Valery 2004, *Nikolai Gumilyov. Zhizn poeta* (Nikolai Gumilyov. Life of the Poet), St Petersburg.
Scheijen, Sjen 2010, *Diaghilev. A Life*, Profile Books, London.
Smirnov, Nikolai 1926, 'Pamyati Larisy Reisner' (Memories of Larisa Reisner), *Novy Mir*, 23.
Smirnov, Nikolai 1961, *Lidia Seifullina v vospominaniyakh sovremennikov* (Lydia Seifullina Remembered by her Contemporaries), Moscow.
Solovei, Eleonora 1985, *Larisa Reisner. Ocherk zhizni i tvorchestva* (Larisa Reisner. A Sketch of her Life and Work), Moscow.

Solovei, Elonora 1985, 'Rudin', in the journal *Neva*, 3.
Sosnovsky, Lev 1927, 'V pamyati Larisa Reisner' (In Memory of Larisa Reisner), in *Lyudi nashego vremeni* (People Of Our Time), Moscow.
Stites, Richard 1978, *The Women's Liberation Movement in Russia*, Princeton, NJ: Princeton University Press.
Stites, Richard 1992, *Russian Popular Culture*, Cambridge: Cambridge University Press.
Subtelny, Orest 1994, *Ukraine. A History*, Toronto: University of Toronto Press.
Sukhanov, Nikolai 1955, *The Russian Revolution, 1917*, trans. J. Carmichael, Oxford University Press.
Tomashevsky, Yury (ed.) 1969, *Larisa Reisner v vospominaniyakh sovremennikov* (Larisa Reisner Remembered By her Contemporaries), Moscow.
Trotsky, Lev 1975, *My Life*, Penguin, London.
Trotsky, Lev 1977, 'H.G. Wells', *Portraits*, New York: Pathfinder Press.
Trotsky, Lev 2005, *Literature and Revolution*, trans. Rose Strunsky, Chicago: Haymarket Books.
Troyat, Henri 1991, *Gorky*, trans. Lowell Blair, London: Allison and Busby.
Ullman, Richard 1961, *Intervention and the War*, Princeton, NJ: Princeton University Press.
Vasileva, Irina 1983, *V. Rozhdestvensky. Ocherk zhizni i tvorchestva* (V. Rozhdestvensky. His Life and Work), Leningrad.
Vasileva, Larissa 1994, *Kremlin Wives*, trans. Cathy Porter, London: Weidenfeld & Nicholson.
Vestnik kommunisticheskoi akademii 1928 (Herald of the Communist Academy; containing a biography of Mikhail Andreevich Reisner), Moscow.
Volkov, Fyodor 1986, *Secrets from Whitehall and Downing Street*, trans. D. Hagen and K. Judelson, Moscow.
Volkov, Solomon 1995, *St Petersburg. A Cultural History*, trans. Antonina Bouis, Simon & Schuster, New York.
Voronsky, Alexander 1926, *Literaturnye Zapisi* (Literary Memoirs), Moscow.
Vucinich, Alexander 1970, *Science in Russian Culture*, Stanford University Press.
Wells, H.G. 1920, *Russia in the Shadows*, London: Hodder & Stoughton.
Yakubovsky, G. 1925, 'Sochineniya L. Seifullinoi i ee kritiki' (L. Seifullina's Works and her Critics), *Novy Mir*, 1925, 10.
Zeide, Alla 1992, 'Larisa Reisner. Myth as Justification for Life', *Russian Review*, January.
Zhitomirskaya, Sofia 1975, 'Muzyka revolyutsii: po stranitsam rukopisei Larisy Reisner' (The Music of the Revolution: From the Pages of Larisa Reisner's Manuscripts), *Literaturnaya gazeta* (Literary Gazette), 21 May.

Index

Abortions, abortion rights   181, 217, 331, 348
Abyssinia   49, 50, 59, 60, 67, 75, 163, 330
Acmeist poets   34–35, 41, 43, 49, 51, 53–54, 64, 66, 71, 83, 162, 165, 213, 274
'Aelita Queen of Mars,' film   239
Afghanistan
   The 'Great Game'   155, 188
   Soviet Afghan relations   155, 187 ff.
   Soviet Afghan Friendship Treaty 1921   190
   LR in Afghanistan 1921–1923. *Afghanistan* 199–231, 327
Agitki   131, 164
Agit-trains   100, 131–132, 182–183, 192
Agranov, Yakov   211–212, 217, 356
Akhmatova, Anna   3, 34–35, 47–53, 55–56, 59, 66, 68, 70, 77–79, 81, 163, 166–167, 210, 315, 238, 328, 342–343, 353, 358, 361, 369
Allied intervention against Revolution. Civil War   100 ff.
   LR's life at the front, 1918–1920. 'Letters from the Front,' *The Front*   109, 119, 122, 129–130, 132–133, 137 ff., 162, 222, 242, 273–275
All-Russian Exhibition of Agriculture and Light Industry   243
Altvater, Admiral Vasily   143–144, 147–148, 150
Amanullah, Emir of Afghanistan   155, 187 ff.
Amritsar Massacre   189
Andreev, Leonid   14, 16, 26–28, 31, 34–36, 38, 43, 45–46, 56, 65, 92, 329
Andreev, Vadim   14–16, 27, 44–45, 56, 90
Anthroposophy and Theosophy   26
Arkhangelsk   85, 116, 119, 144, 148, 179, 100, 208
Armenian genocide   153
Azerbaijan   2, 81, 108, 116, 149, 156–157, 169, 232, 348
Azev, Evno   32
Azin, Vladimir   128, 130, 134

Babel, Isaac   75, 82, 237, 241, 272, 275, 309, 328, 334, 341, 354
Baku   116, 126, 149, 156–157, 165, 169, 238

Ballets Russes   43, 47, 49, 175
Balmont, Konstantin   14, 24
Baltic Fleet   57, 108, 138, 161, 182, 192, 252
Bandera, Stepan   300, 301
Baratov, Arshak   231–232
basmachi   192, 223
Battleship *Aurora*   89
Battleship *Potemkin*   22, 325
Bebel, August   20
Bedny, Demian   24, 237, 311–312, 356–357, 359, 360
Behrens, Admiral Evgeny   150, 152
Bekhterev, Vladimir   27, 37–38, 48, 57, 325, 346–347
'Beloved comrades'   166
Bely, Andrei   26, 31, 40, 92, 105, 213, 236, 257, 353
Besprizorniki (homeless children and orphans)   47, 133, 142, 151, 271, 303–304, 305, 308, 319, 357
Bezymensky, Alexander   245–246, 351
Black Hundreds   9, 22, 105–106, 170, 303
Blok, Alexander   15, 24, 26, 27, 30–31, 34, 40–41, 49, 63, 64, 92, 105, 165, 210
'Bloody Sunday,' 1905 revolution   22–24
'Days of Freedom'   24, 28
Bloomsbury set   81
Britain
   Soviet British relations   97 ff., 144, 148–149, 169, 187 ff., 218–219, 229–231
   Hands Off Russia! campaign   145, 179
   British Labour Party   147, 179, 273, 324
   Communist Party of Britain   179
   British Arctic convoys WW2   199
Bryusov, Valery   14, 64
Buchan, John, Richard Hannay   116
Buddhism   34, 187, 153, 193, 198
Bukhara   90, 188, 191–193, 205, 223–224, 230, 232, 311
Bukharin, Nikolai   20, 181, 242–243, 255, 257, 259, 304, 309, 356, 362
Bulgakov, Mikhail   94, 309, 340
Burtsev, Vladimir   27, 32, 63, 70, 73, 214

Capitalism, development in Russia   9–10, 288
Caspian Sea   2, 108, 116, 152, 158
Catherine the Great   8, 11, 89, 94, 276, 352
Censorship
    In tsarist Russia   8, 60, 62, 63, 69, 73, 75
    In Soviet Russia   237–238, 244, 349, 361
Chapaev, Vasily   241, 245
Chaplin, Charlie   239
Cheka   91, 106, 133, 147, 162, 211–212, 220, 281, 285
Chekhov, Anton   30, 164, 307, 359
Chess in Russia   84–85, 175, 355, 376
Chiang Kai-shek   322–323, 331, 349
Chicherin, Georgy   155, 187, 190, 202, 219, 224, 230–231, 304
Childbirth in Russia   27, 103, 216–217, 264, 344
China
    Soviet Chinese relations. Trotsky Stalin clash in Comintern   321–323
    Chinese Revolution 1911   321
    Communist Party of China   321
Chronicle   75, 77–79, 82, 242
Chukovskaya, Lydia   53, 77–79, 167, 374
Churchill, Winston   99, 116, 144, 174, 218, 374, 377
Cinema in Russia
    First Russian films   30–31
    Early Soviet cinema   131–132, 226, 239–240, 352
    Newsreels of LR in Afghanistan   239
Circuses   30, 131, 164
Clinton, Hillary   298
Cockburn, Claud   357
Comedians Inn Cabaret   70, 77
Comintern (Communist International)   147, 169, 252, 322
Commissariat of Education (LR's work after October)   2, 90, 92, 94, 131, 168, 354
Commissariats of Health and Social Welfare   90, 103, 216
Commissariat of Justice   93, 147, 195, 220
Commissariat of Naval Affairs. LR appointed commissar 1918   2, 102, 105
Communist Manifesto   10
Computer Sciences Corporation Wiesbaden   317

Constituent Assembly, Constituent Assembly Committees   97, 100, 106, 111, 128, 138, 177–178
Curzon, George, Marquis of Kedleston   144, 157, 169, 170, 180, 187, 188, 218
'Curzon Ultimatum'   229–231
Czech legions in Allied Intervention   99–100, 106, 109, 114, 116–117, 127, 128, 278

d'Annunzio, Gabriele   51–52, 60, 62, 204, 213, 227
Decembrist uprising   64, 276, 325 ff.
    LR's Decembrist writings   331–337, 351
Declaration of the Rights of Working and Exploited People, Soviet Constitution   93, 147, 181, 348
Denikin, General Anton   91, 107, 143, 147, 149, 154, 157, 158, 161, 230, 291, 303
Deutscher, Isaac   146, 330
Diaghilev, Sergei   49, 175–176, 378
Diplomatic couriers   199–200, 202, 214, 224, 226, 232, 235, 263
Dobbs, Sir Henry   190, 200
Donetsk Cossack Revolutionary Committee, 1918   291
Donetsk People's Republic, May 2014 to present   298–300
Dostoyevsky, Fyodor   53, 83, 317, 353
Duma   23, 24, 26, 68, 73, 74, 80, 312
Dybenko, Pavel   86, 88, 89
Dzerzhinsky, Felix   162, 220
'Dziga Vertov' (David Kaufman)   38, 48, 132, 192, 346, 376

Efimov, Boris   357
Eisenstein, Sergei   132, 237, 239, 327, 352
    'Glumov's Diary'   239
    'Battleship *Potemkin*'   325, 346
    'Strike'   327
    'Black Majesty'   352
Engelhardt, Anna   59, 66, 68, 78–79, 163, 213, 358
Engels, Friedrich   28, 57, 73, 223, 345
Esenin, Sergei   49, 61, 75, 82, 237, 238, 257, 334, 335, 342
'The Extraordinary Adventures of Mr West in the Land of the Bolsheviks'   239

INDEX 381

Fadeev, Alexander   240, 360
Family policy in Soviet Russia. Marriage, divorce, women's rights, the new sexual morality   86, 103–104, 141, 151, 155, 233, 283, 303, 304, 333, 344, 347
Famines in Russia
   1898   9–10, 16
   1921   200–201
   1933   294–295, 301
Fascism
   Italy   226, 250, 259
   Germany   146, 198, 219, 249, 250, 260, 264, 249, 317, 346, 349–250
   Ukraine   295, 297–301
Fedin, Konstantin   241
Fellow travellers   243, 268, 270, 328
Fifth House of Soviets   99, 235
Finland   13, 16, 21, 24, 27, 37, 39, 88, 92, 97–98, 116, 168
   Winter War with Soviet Union, 1939–1940   27–28
Foch, Marshal Ferdinand   149
Forsh, Olga   212, 272, 352
France
   Soviet French relations   144, 148–149, 218–219
French Revolution   61, 64, 102, 122, 164, 349, 352
Freud, Sigmund   26, 53, 75, 257, 325, 347, 361
   Marxism and psychoanalysis   325
Furmanov, Dmitry   241, 245, 308
Futurists   35, 42–43, 53, 54, 58, 64–65, 81, 132, 162, 237, 239, 241, 242–3, 350

Genoa Conference   218–219, 230–231
Germany
   Soviet German relations   89, 97, 219, 249 ff., 317 ff.
   Brest-Litovsk Treaty   99–100, 116, 144, 148, 219, 254
   German Communist Party   146, 160, 254
   1918 German revolution   146, 254
   Treaty of Rapallo   219, 231, 249, 317
   Radek Zinoviev clash in Comintern   249
   LR in exile in Germany as a child   19–26
   Comintern agent and journalist 1923.
   Hamburg at the Barricades, Berlin, October 1923   3, 250-ff, 262–265
   In Germany 1925. *In Hindenburg's Country*   3, 317–318, 321, 338–339

Gladkov, Fyodor, *Cement*   241, 350
Goebbels, Josef   295
Goering, Marshal Hermann   259
Gorky, Maxim   24, 27, 75–76, 82–83, 92, 94, 96, 163–164, 172–173, 175, 201, 236, 238, 240, 242, 268, 277–278, 349, 351–352, 356
Gorodetsky, Sergei   61, 66, 165, 172, 213
Grosz, George   262
Gumilyov, Nikolai
   His life and poetry and women, LR's love affair with him   34, 47, 50, 51, 59, 60, 61, 66–67, 69–71, 73–74, 75, 76, 78, 81, 163, 164, 165–167
   Arrest and execution   211–214, 236
   Rehabilitated   361

Habibullah, Emir of Afghanistan   188, 189, 191, 199
'Hamburg at the Barricades,' film   346
Harar   67
Hashish   205, 206
Himmler, Heinrich   259, 296
Hindenburg, Field Marshal von   3, 317–318, 358
Hitler, Adolf   3, 9, 148, 259, 264, 288, 295, 296, 314, 358
Homosexuality in tsarist and Soviet Russia   48–49, 103, 347–348
Housing in Russia. Soviet housing policy   94, 99, 121, 136, 148, 163, 167, 235, 280, 281, 286, 294, 323, 331, 333, 334
   Communes, communal housing   90, 304, 342, 344
Humphrys, Sir Francis   218, 224, 228, 229–230

Ilin, Alexander (Raskolnikov's brother)   83–85, 90, 131, 166, 175, 326, 355, 358, 359
Ilinsky, Igor   39–40, 69, 76, 275, 327, 338, 343
Inber, Vera   3, 43, 62, 265, 274, 305, 311, 316, 338, 341–342, 352, 358, 361
India   144, 157–159, 187–189, 191, 195, 198, 200–202, 204–206, 209, 223, 226–227, 229–230, 345–356, 348, 360
Influenza pandemic 1918   145
International Women's Day   42, 80, 185
Israeli government   300, 301

Japan
  Russo-Japanese War   21 ff.
  Japanese army in Allied intervention   116, 128, 177
Jews in tsarist and Soviet Russia   4, 8–11, 12, 18, 22–23, 37–39, 46, 63, 93, 76, 116, 121, 144, 155, 282, 300, 303, 313–315, 349
  Jewish *Bund*   13, 93
  Party Jewish Sections   142, 348
  Anti-Semitism of White armies and in Allied propaganda   116, 140, 303, 313, 330
  Holocaust in Nazi-occupied Ukraine, Belarus, Lithuania, Poland   295–296, 314–315
Joffe, Nadezhda   177
Jones, Gareth   295, 301
'July Days'   88, 254
Jung, Carl   25

Kalinin, Mikhail   182, 307
Kamenev, Alexander ('Lyutik')   118, 120, 304
Kamenev, Lev   229, 266, 304
Karsavin, Platon   168
Karsavina, Tamara   47, 168, 175
Kerensky, Alexander   87–88, 90–91, 95–96, 127
Khrushchev, Nikita   360
Kirillov, Mikhail (LR's secretary)   105, 149, 150, 181, 192, 217
Kolbasev, Evgeny   221, 221n
Kolchak, Admiral Alexander   91, 106, 132, 143, 147, 149, 154, 156, 161, 241, 277–278, 280, 286, 288, 291, 302
Kollontai, Alexandra   5, 9, 22, 75, 81, 86, 88, 90, 99, 103–104, 141–142, 181, 216, 217, 221–222, 233, 235, 304, 333, 342
Kolosov, Mark   244–245, 343, 351
Koltsov, Mikhail   39–40, 82, 92, 131, 240
  Arrest and death   357
  Rehabilitated   360
Komsomol (Communist Youth League)   118, 237, 242, 244, 302, 304, 307, 313, 324, 333, 351
Koonen, Alisa   269, 350–351
Kornilov, General Lavr   88, 91
Krasnov, General Pyotr   91, 116, 142, 147

Kronstadt Naval Base   23, 80, 82–83, 85–89, 91, 107, 115, 118, 129, 137, 140, 144, 147, 155–156, 161–162, 164, 166, 181, 182
  Kronstadt uprising 1921   184–185, 187, 213, 273, 349, 350
Krupp steel factories   286, 318–319
Krupskaya, Nadezhda   65, 242, 267, 323
Kuchek-Khan   159
Kuleshov, Lev (the 'Kuleshov effect')   132, 239
Kuomintang   321–324, 349
Kuzmin, Mikhail   49, 175

Lansbury, George   147, 324, 344
Lansbury, Violet   344–345
Lena Goldfields Massacre   35, 212
Lenin, Vladimir Ilich   23–24, 82–83, 85–86, 88–93, 99–100, 127, 131, 140–142, 157–158, 169, 173–174, 181, 188–189, 238, 242, 255–256, 267, 270–271, 289, 306–307, 321, 331, 338, 355–357, 359
Lenin Enrolment to the Party   280, 282–283, 286, 293
Leuchtenberg, Duke Andrei   29, 91, 214
Libedinsky, Yury   245, 265, 317
Liebknecht, Karl   20, 21, 22, 26, 56, 68, 73
  Murdered   145–146
Literacy in Russia, *Likbez* (Commission to Liquidate Illiteracy)   131, 270
Lloyd George, David   99, 144, 148, 156, 178
Lockhart, Robert Bruce   255
Lunacharsky, Anatoly   75, 82, 88, 90, 92–93, 94, 105, 163–164, 168, 242–243, 257, 268
Luxemburg, Rosa   11, 13, 20, 56, 68, 103
  Murdered   145–146

MacDonald, Ramsay   174, 267
Makarov, Alyosha (LR's foster son)   303–316, 331, 344
Malevich, Kazimir   43
Mandelstam, Nadezhda   102, 166, 191, 232, 353
Mandelstam, Osip   5, 27, 34, 39, 40, 45, 61, 66, 70, 79, 102, 163, 166, 175, 233, 237, 346, 353, 356
Mann, Thomas   257, 264
Mao Tse-tung   331, 349
Markin, Nikolai   83, 88, 108, 119, 122, 123–124, 128, 130, 135–136, 137, 155

INDEX

Marinetti, Filippo   53
Marx, Karl. Marxism in Russia, Marx on revolution in Russia   10, 13, 19, 23, 25, 28, 51, 55, 57, 73, 84, 93, 152, 204, 223, 322, 325, 330, 331, 346, 348, 351
  'Seeking Marxists'   25–26, 75
Mayakovsky, Vladimir   43, 53, 54, 55, 58, 64, 71, 75, 82, 91–92, 105, 131, 230, 237–238, 243, 257, 306–307, 350
May Day   14, 35, 42
McCain, Senator John   297, 298
Merezhkovsky, Dmitry   58, 93
Meyerhold, Vsevolod   42, 01, 92, 164, 176, 217, 220, 243, 324, 327, 356
Miss Mary   199, 201, 224–225, 226
Moscow Show Trials, 1936, 1937, 1938   355, 356
'Mr Jones,' film   295, 301
Muslims in tsarist and Soviet Russia   8, 58, 100, 188–190, 193, 209, 348–349
Mussolini, Benito   226, 228, 250, 259
'Mystical anarchists'   26

Nabokov, Vladimir   257
Naletny, Semyon, film director   192, 199–200, 209, 224–226, 236, 239
Nesterovych, Olga   183–184, 333–334
New Economic Policy (NEP)   185, 211, 233, 281, 312
New Life   82–83, 92, 94–95
New Soviet journalism   240, 309
New Soviet fiction
  Socialist realism   240–241, 334, 349
  'Red detective' novels   238–239
  'Industrial' fiction   241, 350
  Historical novels   351–353
New Soviet theatre   43, 131, 136, 164, 269
  Blue Blouse Drama Collective   164
  'On the Volga,' agitprop drama about LR's life at the front   165
Nietszche, Friedrich   51, 83
Nikulin, Lev   31, 46–47, 64, 69, 70–71, 76, 104–106, 116, 161–162, 164, 167–168, 194–196, 198–201, 203, 216, 231–232, 238, 339, 353, 359–360
Novy Mir   328, 361, 376, 378–379
Nuremburg Trials   318, 358–359

Obama, President Barak   297
On Guardists and *Young Guardists*   244, 245–246, 351

Palme-Dutt, Clemens   345
Pasha, General Enver   192, 223
Pasternak, Boris   1–2, 39, 141, 236, 257, 268–269, 308, 311, 329, 342, 353, 361
Pavlov, Professor Ivan   17, 37
Persia
  Soviet Persian relations   158, 159, 169, 231, 339
  Anglo Persian Agreement   152, 157
  Persian campaign   161, 229
Peter the Great   28, 68, 90, 94, 277, 329, 337, 351
Petlyura, Symon   149, 291, 300, 303
Pilnyak, Boris   243, 268, 308, 328, 341, 354
Plekhanov, Georgy   55
von Plehve, Vyacheslav   21, 32
Poland
  Soviet Polish relations   147
  Pilsudski, General Jozef   149, 174, 177
  Treaty of Riga   177, 211
Political commissars   142–143, 150, 161, 245, 350
Populists   11
Poretsky, Elisabeth   257, 376
Poroshenko, Petro, Ukrainian President   298, 300, 301
Proletkult   75, 105, 237, 239, 242–243, 244, 245, 268, 328, 275, 311, 327, 351
Provisional Government   80–82, 87, 89–90, 92, 95, 107, 321
Psychoanalytical Society   325, 347
Psychoneurology Institute. LR's student years   37–40, 57, 62, 68, 155, 325, 346, 351
Pugachev, Emelian   107, 276, 288, 331, 338
Pushkin, Alexander   30, 34, 46, 52–53, 64, 68, 92, 210, 223, 238, 326, 351
Putin, Vladimir   121, 290, 296, 298, 300, 301, 358, 362

Rabfaks   244, 245, 273, 280
Radek, Karl
  Life as a revolutionary and relationship with LR   6, 37, 233, 248, 249–252, 256,

Life as a revolutionary and relationship with LR (*cont.*)   260–261, 267–269, 275, 278, 304, 320–323, 330–333
  Arrest and death   354
  Rehabilitated   362
Rand, Ayn   168n
RAPP (Russian Association of Proletarian Writers)   349–351
Raskolnikov, Fyodor
  His revolutionary work and relationship with LR   83–91, 101–102, 107–108, 118 ff., 144 ff., 154, 200, 215 ff., 222–223, 225, 235–236, 268, 269, 349
  'Enemy of the State' and death   355
  Rehabilitated   360–361
Rasputin, Grigory   41, 58, 66, 74, 85, 105, 167
Ras Tafari, Emperor Haile Selassi   50, 67
Rathenau, Walter, German Foreign Minister   219
Red Army   107–108, 110, 117–118, 120, 125–127, 138, 140, 142, 161, 170, 172, 174, 223, 277–230, 282–283, 350
Red Clydeside   145
Red Guards   80, 82, 87, 88–91, 94, 100, 105, 118, 138, 152, 293, 303
Red Navy   2, 105, 108, 142, 144, 158, 162, 304, 355
Red Paper   170, 251, 318
Red Terror   106, 127, 177
Red Virgin Soil   43, 192, 268
Reed, John   169, 274
Reisner, Ekaterina (LR's mother)
  Early life, marriage, family life in exile and Russia, and after 1917   11–12, 15, 17, 29, 35, 44, 101, 119–120, 320–321
  After LR's death   344, 348–349
Reisner, Igor (LR's brother)   17, 18–19, 28–30, 34, 43–44, 140, 155, 187, 190, 192, 198–201, 219–220, 223, 261, 317–318, 323–324
  After LR's death   344–345, 346, 348, 349, 355, 360
Reisner, Lev (LR's adopted brother)   57, 98, 138, 304, 344, 353, 355, 356
Reisner, Mikhail (LR's father)
  Work, politics and writings before the Revolution   12 ff., 24, 25, 32–34
  After October 1917   93–94, 101, 140, 147–148, 220, 325, 344
  Revolution March 1917   80–89

Revolution October 1917   89 ff.
Requiem (LR's autobiographical novel, later titled *Rudin*)   19, 20, 21, 33
Rimbaud, Arthur   67
Robeson, Paul   352
Roshal, Semyon   37, 39, 57, 68, 82, 83, 86, 88, 155–156, 161
ROSTA   131–132
Rothstein, Andrew   5, 178–180, 204–205, 269, 309, 342
Rozhdestvensky, Vsevolod   39, 49–41, 45, 47, 58–61, 63, 120, 175, 340, 358, 360
Rudin (journal)   61–64, 69, 70, 73, 75, 95, 105, 213–214, 242, 342
Russian Orthodox Church   8, 9, 12–13, 16, 39, 45, 52, 71, 76, 84, 93, 103, 107, 151, 211, 299, 336, 362
Russian Social Democratic Workers' Party   13, 18

Sappho   48
Savinkov, Boris   127
Scryabin, Alexander   48, 70
Seifullina, Lydia   270–273, 275, 303–305, 328–329, 342, 344, 350, 352, 355–356, 362
  The Lawbreakers   271, 304
  Virineya   271–272, 308, 329
Serafimovich, Alexander   241
Serapion Brothers   243, 268
Serge, Victor   51–52, 117–118, 121, 147, 163, 182, 185–186, 211, 213, 250, 253, 255, 257
Shaginyan, Marietta   59, 163, 238, 243
  'Jim Dollar,' *Mess Mend*   238–239
Shakespeare, William   30, 35, 38, 35, 54, 57, 68, 145, 353, 359
Shalamov, Varlam   236, 247, 342, 361
Shaw, George Bernard   174
Sheng, Yueh   330–331
Sheremeteva, Ekaterina (LR's cousin)   15, 34, 57, 101, 216
Shklovsky, Victor   58, 76, 82, 90, 107, 109, 140–141, 161, 163, 210, 236–237, 243, 272, 338, 353, 360
Shostakovich, Dmitry
  movie pianist   239
  Seventh Symphony, the 'Leningrad'   359
Silver Age of Russian literature   34
Smirnov, Ivan   122, 354

INDEX

Smirnov, Nikolai   272, 309
Socialist Revolutionaries   18, 21–22, 24, 27, 32, 127
Sosnovsky, Lev   3, 118, 166, 244, 265, 343
Soviet industrialisation and collectivisation,
    Five Year Plans   182, 185, 277, 283, 294, 295, 345, 347, 348
    LR in Urals and Ukraine. *Coal Iron and Living People*   3, 5, 278, 280, 294, 302, 306, 310–311, 347, 348
Sowing Committees   182–183, 184
Spanish Civil War   127, 357
Spartacist League   68, 97, 146
Stakhanovites   292
Stalin, Joseph   142–143, 174, 220, 256, 267, 277, 289, 295, 304, 311–312, 322–323, 331, 346–350, 353–356, 358–359, 361–362
    Personality cult   292, 360
    Gulag   276, 354
    Destalinisation, the 'Thaw'   360
Steiner, Rudolf   26
Stolypin, Pyotr   33
Stray Dog Cafe   47–50
Sukhomlinov, General Vladimir, Minister of War   35, 41, 55, 62, 68
Sun Yat-sen   321, 323, 330–331
Sun Yat-sen University for the Toilers of China   322–323, 330, 349
Suritz, Yakov   190, 198–199, 200, 201, 278, 327
Sverdlov, Yakov   278
Svyatlovsky, Vladimir   57, 60, 73, 214
Symbolist poets   34–35, 105

Tairov Theatre   269, 341, 350
Tarzi, Mahmud, Aghan Foreign Minister   190
Tarzi, Soraya, Queen of Afghanistan   191, 201–202, 204, 216
TASS   309
Tolstoi, Alexei   237, 239, 353, 359
Tolstoi, Lev   9, 13, 14, 26–27
Toussaint Louverture, Haiti   352
Trade union debate in Party 1921   181
Trans-Caspian Railway   188, 191, 192
Trans-Siberian Railway   17, 276, 278, 324
Triolet, Elsa   257
Trotsky, Lev   1, 4–5, 13, 23–24, 88–90, 98, 100, 117–118, 120–122, 125–127, 136, 143–144, 169–170, 174, 222–223, 243, 255–256, 267–269, 278, 311–312, 322–323, 330–333, 355–357, 362
'Trotsky,' Russian TV series   121–122
Trump, Donald   296, 300
Tsar Alexander II   8, 12, 24
Tsarevich Alexei   120
Tsaritsyn   2, 108, 116, 126, 149, 151–152, 154, 156, 161, 256, 311
    Trotsky Stalin clash   142–143, 256, 311
Tsar Nicholas II   9, 12, 16, 30, 42, 46, 58, 95, 326, 362
Tukhachevsky, Mikhail   128, 156, 174
Tumpovskaya, Margarita   52, 59, 66, 68, 76, 78
Turkey   8, 153, 169, 188, 190, 214, 230
Tyahnybok, Oleh   297–298

Ukraine
    Civil War, 1918–1920   104
    Nazi occupation, 1941–1944   295–296
    'Euromaidan,' 2014   297–298
    War with Russia, 2014 to present   296–301
Ulya Hazrat, Queen of Afghanistan   188, 191, 204, 205, 226
Union of Soviet Writers   350, 351, 354, 357, 360
University of Tomsk   16–19

Vanderlip, Washington B. Junior   208–210
Versailles Treaty   141, 148–149, 169, 178, 219, 249, 319, 321
V.I. Lenin Hydroelectric Power Station (Dneprostroi)   303
Vishnevsky, Vsevolod   119, 136, 350–351
    Vishnevsky's play about LR 'An Optimistic Tragedy'   136, 350–351, 358
Volga Naval Flotilla   108, 127–128, 139, 192, 199
Voronsky, Alexander   242, 271, 327, 334, 350, 354
Voroshilov, Kliment   143, 151, 256, 304

Wells, H.G.   173–175
White Terror   106, 132–133, 147, 291
Wilde, Oscar   48, 269
WikiLeaks Panama Papers   301

Wild Rose 28
Wilhelm, Kaiser of Imperial Germany 20, 55, 141, 317
Women in Civil War 104, 142
Workers' Opposition 181, 185, 220–221
Workers' soviets 142, 235, 277, 303
   St Petersburg/Petrograd Soviet 24, 82, 87–88, 109, 163, 166, 185, 256, 311
World Socialist Website 325n
World War One 55–141
World War Two. Nazi occupation of Soviet Union 27, 289, 295–296, 358–360
Wrangel, Baron Pyotr 143, 149, 291

Yatsenyuk, Arsenyi 297, 298
Yudenich, General Nikolai 149, 154, 156, 241

Zalkind, Aaron 347
Zelenskyi, Volodymir 301
Zhenotdel (Party Women's Department) 155, 181, 183, 221, 241, 308–309, 333, 347
Zinoviev, Grigory 13, 169, 171, 211, 229, 250, 255–256, 259, 266, 267, 312, 356, 357, 362
Zola, Emile 35, 310

www.ingramcontent.com/pod-product-compliance
Lightning Source LLC
Chambersburg PA
CBHW071228070526
44583CB00017B/2086